SOURCES OF PROTESTANT THEOLOGY

CONTEMPORARY THEOLOGY SERIES
GENERAL EDITORS: J. FRANK DEVINE, S.J.
RICHARD W. ROUSSEAU, S.J.

SOURCES OF PROTESTANT THEOLOGY is one of the volumes in the ecclesial theology section of this series.

AUTHOR:

Dr. William A. Scott was formerly chairman of theology at Le Moyne College. He is a contributor to such publications as *Theological Studies* and *Commonweal,* and is the author of such books as *Historical Protestantism* and *The Role of Theology in the University*. Dr. Scott is presently chairman of theology at Lewis-St. Francis College.

GENERAL EDITORS:

J. FRANK DEVINE has for a number of years taught courses in biblical literature and ecumenism at Boston College and at the Pope John XXIII National Seminary.

RICHARD W. ROUSSEAU was a member of the Department of Religious Studies at Boston College and Fairfield University. He is at present assistant director of the Faith and Order Department of the National Council of Churches.

SOURCES OF
PROTESTANT THEOLOGY

EDITED BY WILLIAM A. SCOTT
Lewis-St. Francis College

THE BRUCE PUBLISHING COMPANY / NEW YORK
COLLIER-MACMILLAN LIMITED / LONDON

©Copyright, The Bruce Publishing Company, 1971

Library of Congress Catalog Card Number: 70-143783

THE BRUCE PUBLISHING COMPANY, NEW YORK
COLLIER-MACMILLAN CANADA, LTD., TORONTO, ONTARIO

Made in the United States of America

To My Former Students at Le Moyne College

ACKNOWLEDGMENTS

The editors and publishers of *Sources of Protestant Theology* are grateful to the following for permission to reprint excerpts from their publications:

A. & C. Black Ltd., London, and Stanford University Press, Stanford, Calif., for excerpts from Lessing's *Theological Writings* in their series *A Library of Modern Religious Thought,* edited and translated by Henry Chadwick (1965).

Henry Steele Commager, for excerpts from *Theodore Parker: An Anthology,* published by Beacon Press, Boston, Mass. (1960).

The Centennial Review and John B. Cobb, for excerpts from "From Crisis Theology to the Post-Modern World" by John B. Cobb, in Vol. VIII, No. 2 (Spring 1964).

Delacorte Press, New York, for excerpts from *The New Christianity,* edited with an introduction by William R. Miller (1967).

John Knox Press, Richmond, Va., and Wm. Collins Sons & Co. Ltd., London, for excerpts from *The Humanity of God* by Karl Barth, translated by John Newton Thomas, copyright C. D. Deans, 1960.

The Lancaster Theological Seminary, Lancaster, Pa., for excerpts from *Theology and Life* (Summer 1963).

"Contemporary Christianity," reprinted with permission of The Macmillan Company from *Letters and Papers From Prison* by Dietrich Bonhoeffer. Copyright by The Macmillan Company, 1953. © SCM Press Ltd., London, 1967.

Mennonite Publishing House, Scottdale, Pa., for excerpts from *The Doctrines of the Mennonites* by J. C. Wenger. Copyright by Mennonite Publishing House, Scottdale, Pa. Used by permission.

James Nisbet & Co. Ltd., Hertfordshire, England, for excerpts from Reinhold Niebuhr's *The Nature and Destiny of Man,* Vol. 1, *Human Nature,* (1941).

"The Nature of Justification," from *Melanchthon: On Christian Doctrine. Loci Communes 1555,* by Clyde L. Manschreck. Copyright © 1965 by Oxford University Press, Inc. Reprinted by permission.

Philosophical Library, New York, and Lutterworth Press, London, for excerpts from *The Reformation Writings of Martin Luther,* Vol. II, *The Spirit of the Protestant Reformation,* edited and translated by Bertram Lee Wolf (1956).

"The Christian Message and the Modern World View," reprinted by permission of Charles Scribner's Sons from *Jesus Christ and Mythology,* pages 35–44, by Rudolf Bultmann. Copyright © 1958 Rudolf Bultmann; and S.C.M. Press Ltd., London.

"The Christian View of the Nature of Man: Image of God, Creature, Sinner," reprinted by permission of Charles Scribner's Sons from Volume I, *The Nature and Destiny of Man,* pages 150–186, by Reinhold Niebuhr. Copyright 1941 Charles Scribner's Sons.

"Symbolic Theology," reprinted with the permission of Charles Scribner's Sons from *Principles of Christian Theology,* pages 161–170, by John Macquarrie. Copyright © 1966 John Macquarrie.

"You Are Accepted," reprinted with the permission of Charles Scribner's Sons from *The Shaking of the Foundations,* pages 153–163, by Paul Tillich. Copyright 1948 Charles Scribner's Sons.

Frederick Ungar Publishing Company, New York, for excerpts from "Christianity Not Mysterious" by John Toland in *Deism and Natural Religion,* edited with an introduction by E. G. Waring (1967); from "Christianity As Old As the Creation" by Matthew Tindal, quoted from the same book; and from *John Calvin: On God and Man,* selections from *Institutes of the Christian Religion,* edited by F. W. Strothman (1964).

From *The New Reformation?* by John A. T. Robinson. Published in the U.S.A. 1965, by the Westminster Press, Philadelphia, Pa. © S.C.M. Press Ltd., London, 1965. Used by permission.

CONTENTS

THE NINETEENTH CENTURY

Editors' Introduction
CONTEMPORARY THEOLOGY SERIES

This series begins with the presupposition that theology is necessary. It is necessary if Christian intelligence is to search for meaning in its dialogue with God, man, and the world. Since Christian intelligence is not the exclusive possession of the theological specialist, the search must be carried out in all those areas of life, secular as well as religious, including the college situation, where meaning is to be found.

This search is a peaceful one, for in some mysterious way it has already achieved its goal: the vision of faith and the fullness of love. Still it remains a relentless and universal search. Its inner certainty must radiate out not only to the edges of the mind but also into the farthest recesses of the world. We could call it "lay" theology, but this word seems too pale a description for such an exciting enterprise of the Christian life.

In view of this the editors of this series are convinced that new questions had to be asked, new structures created, and new books written. These books would be neither catechetical nor apologetic. They would be purely and simply theological. The primary audience would be believers, but all thinking men would find them useful. In scope they would be broad enough to insure perspective. They would be scholarly enough to be intellectually relevant. They would avoid pedantry. In short, they would try to present such a rich and deep understanding of revelation that today's college students would be able to respond with a Christian faith and life that are culturally mature and scientifically precise. Finally the authors of these books would be, for the most part, teachers in colleges and universities, where much of the contemporary theological dialogue is now going on.

The series falls into four parts: biblical, historical, ecclesial, and ethical.

The divisions were not predetermined by the editors; they follow the shape of the most vigorous theological work now being done.

The books in the biblical section are intended to go beyond the traditional treatment of Bible history and the now familiar perspectives of salvation history. They concentrate on various books of the Bible, and their method has been especially designed for college work. Tentatively it might be called "exegetical theology." Every verse is not considered after the fashion of a commentary, narratives are not developed as biographies, nor is there any attempt to create complete theological syntheses. Rather the individual books are studied in chronological sequence; key passages are treated in detail and the rest are summarized. At the same time some attention is paid to the growing theological synthesis.

Since systematic theology is already represented by individual works and sets of textbooks, the books in our historical section study dogmatic questions from a developmental point of view. In this way the editors hope to make the college students more aware of the great wealth of theological thinking that recent historico-theological studies have uncovered. This method, which is more inductive than deductive, should happily coincide with the thought processes of the college students. The three basic poles for synthesis are: God, Christ, and man. In each area the historical development will be studied and a significant number of basic source texts presented. The problems raised in these studies will range all the way from Augustinian pessimism to Teilhardian optimism.

The textbooks for the third part of the series will deal ecumenically with issues of great contemporary religious importance. This part is called the ecclesial theology section to indicate that these concerns are those of the Christian community as a whole, the *ecclesia,* as well as those of the peoples comprising the other great religious traditions of the world. Thus the self-identity of the Christian Church is studied first. This includes its rapidly developing worship life, the history of the Christian Church in America, and contemporary Protestant thought. The scope then broadens to include studies in the sources and ideals of Judaism and the great religious traditions of the East.

The fourth and final section of the series is devoted to Christian moral response. The editors subscribe to the position that it is proper to examine ethical questions in a revelational as well as a philosophical context. The insights of both biblical and systematic theology can be valuable here. These studies will address themselves to those ethical problems that are most urgent in the present day.

Finally the editors would like to express their thanks to all those whose interest, advice, and cooperation have made this series possible. They are especially grateful to the individual authors who so graciously added to their heavy burden of academic responsibility by undertaking these books. We can only express the hope that their share in the shaping and influencing of many minds will be far more meaningful to them than any meager thanks of ours.

The Editors,

J. Frank Devine, S. J.
Boston College

Richard W. Rousseau, S. J.
National Council of Churches

AUTHOR'S INTRODUCTION

This sourcebook is designed as an introduction to Protestantism from its beginnings in the sixteenth century to its expressions in the twentieth century. Two basic principles have determined its composition. First, I have tried, when feasible, to include the major figures of Protestant thought and to allow the great names of that religious movement to speak at some length on subjects central to their thought. It is hoped that a picture of the essential lineaments of Protestantism will emerge from their writings. Second, I have tried to choose selections that explain how Protestant Christianity has influenced and has been influenced by the course of history in the West. In each century this religious tradition has been confronted with different religious needs and diverse cultural situations that have called for varying responses from Christianity. These responses have helped Protestantism to fashion its own self-consciousness and its particular manner of presenting the Christian message to men.

The book is divided into five sections, one for each of the five centuries from the sixteenth to the twentieth. Each section is preceded by a general discussion of the major themes of religious thought in that century as well as an explanation of the ways in which the chosen selections deal with those themes. There follow ten extended selections drawn from either significant Protestant thinkers or authoritative credal statements of that century.

Out of the interplay of great mind and historical event emerges an awareness of the essential strength of Protestantism: its ability and willingness to confront each age, and its constantly and creatively rethought presentation of Christianity's answer to man's situation. At present there are signs that that strength is again at work reformulating Christianity's message for a radically new age. It is the final conviction of this volume that the story of the past and of the present offers the surest hope that the future can be faced optimistically.

In general the selections presented have been left in their original form. The only exception to that principle has been the modernization of spelling wherever the original seemed to distract from the sense of the passage.

William A. Scott

SOURCES OF PROTESTANT THEOLOGY

THE SIXTEENTH CENTURY
Introduction

The formative period of the Protestant Reformation was roughly the second quarter of the sixteenth century. It was during those years that the main lines of Protestantism's interpretation of the Christian faith were worked out. By the middle of the century most of the early charismatic leadership was gone. To the second generation of Protestants fell the task of preserving and explaining the patrimony of the fathers of the Reformation. Thus a history of Protestantism in the sixteenth century falls naturally into two parts, the founding years and the period of consolidation. The selections that follow fall into these two divisions.

THE BEGINNING OF REFORM

The religious situation in Western Christendom had been moving towards crisis for several hundred years when the sixteenth century opened. The forces in the late medieval church that were crying for reform finally found their focus in Martin Luther, the first of the great Reformers. Luther's vision of the gospel, forged in the crucible of a dozen years of agonized struggle with the problem of salvation, crystallized itself in three basic insights: (1) God alone gives a man salvation (*sola gratia*). (2) That gift is conditioned on man's coming to believe that God saves him not through his own works but solely because of the merits of Christ (*sola fides*). (3) One finds this message of salvation only in God's Word, the Scripture (*sola Scriptura*).

Luther's *Preface to Paul's Epistle to the Romans* is one of his earliest, clearest, and most moving expositions of these three principles which stand at the heart of any real understanding of the nature of Protestant Christianity.

Twenty-six years Luther's junior, John Calvin is the second of the great Reformers. His greatest contribution to Protestantism is his understanding of who God is. Humans, for Calvin, can only know the plan of salvation and find their place in that plan when they have learned the nature of God and of His revelation to men. God is the absolutely sovereign, totally other, completely mysterious Lord of all creation. All that happens in creation happens because He wills it so. His willing is but the explication of the divine plan that created reality exists only to show forth the wonder and the goodness of its creator. Once a man sees this he will recognize that his own place in the scheme of things is to be found in humble adoration of the divine will and wholehearted submission to that will. Such an attitude will bring one the supreme gift that God gives His own, the conviction of election to glory. Armed with such a conviction the Christian believer is thereby freed from further self-concern and ready for a lifelong dedication to making God's glory manifest in all areas of life. All these themes: the divine sovereignty, God's will for man's final salvation or loss, the proper human response to that will, are treated in the selection on predestination, drawn from the third book of Calvin's *Institutes of the Christian Religion.*

Classical Protestantism was dedicated to the reformation of the Christian church. But there were those in the early period of the Reformation who saw the situation within Christendom as calling for a far more drastic response than mere reformation of the church. In the early 1520s small groups began to spring up in Switzerland who took Luther's principle of "Scripture alone" with a seriousness and a literalness far beyond any intent of his. For them reformation was not at all sufficient. What was needed was a restitution of the church to the model depicted in the New Testament. Christianity could exist in its authentic form only in small groups of committed believers. Total separation from the world and its sinfulness, communal life and the sharing of all possessions in common, unshakable opposition to the state and its use of force to impose its will, uncomplaining acceptance of whatever penalties such a stance might bring —these were the characteristics of the Radical Reformation (popularly called Anabaptism because of its practice of rebaptizing converts to the movement).

As the movement spread it fragmented into three forms. The first form was that of the quiet, peaceful groups that asked from the civil government and the great state churches, Protestant and Catholic, only that they be allowed to live their separated existence in peace. The spirit and mode of Christian belief characteristic of this form of Anabaptism is well caught in the *Schleitheim Confession,* written by Michael Sattler and a group of Swiss Mennonites in 1527.

But the radical reform met unbending resistance and ruthless persecution from church and state alike. In consequence, leadership in some segments of the movement passed into the hands of visionaries and fanatics. Anabaptism then became apocalyptic. God's kingdom was at hand; rather than waiting quietly for the Lord to usher in the days of His final kingdom it became the sacred obligation of His followers to hasten His coming by taking up the sword against His enemies. Thomas Müntzer is an example of this type of Anabaptism. Only a year before his violent death during the peasants' uprising (1524), he preached a sermon, *The Sermon Before the Princes,* wherein he epitomizes the spirit of apocalyptic and violent Anabaptism, urging the princes to be ruthless in their extermination of all who stood in the way of the restoration of Christianity to its pristine state.

In addition to the call to violence, the sermon is also of interest for its doctrine of revelation. All that God has to reveal to His people is not contained in Scripture. He continues to reveal Himself and His will to chosen souls in every age, through His Spirit indwelling the soul of the believer. Revelation, therefore, is an ongoing and never-completed process. Here is one of the earliest expressions of what will become a fundamental principle of such later forms of Protestant Christianity as Quakerism and the various spiritualist and holiness sects. Within ten years after Müntzer's death, violent Anabaptism had run its course. Since then the Radical Reformation has survived in the peaceful, separated form it took among such groups as the Hutterites and Mennonites.

At the far left of the spectrum of sixteenth-century Protestantism the radical reform took one final form: the spiritualists. Where classical Protestantism wanted reform, and Anabaptism sought the restoration of the primitive church, the spiritualists tended towards complete dissolution of any external structure of church life or belief. Spiritualism is perhaps most strongly rooted in the medieval mystical tradition. Religion and belief are a matter of the heart and of the individual. The believing Christian must strive for a personal and deeply experienced relationship with God and with Christ.

The selection from John Denck's *Whether God Is the Cause of Evil* is an example of the spiritualist tradition. Running through the selection are the typical spiritualist themes: the inner Word of God in the soul, and the imitation of Christ leading the Christian to divinization and a life of total self-disregard.

During the same period that classical and radical Protestantism were establishing themselves in Western Europe, the movement of reform also crossed the water into England. As implemented there, the reform was embodied in the national church of England. Anglicanism was in doctrine a thoroughly Protestant church. It subscribed to the Christian vision of Luther and Calvin; that vision was written into its official credal formulation, the *Thirty-Nine Articles.* The Church of England, however, was different from the continental Reformation in two important respects: its liturgical life, expressed in *The Book of Common Prayer,* retained much of the medieval Catholic liturgy modified to bring it into accord with a Protestant doctrinal position. The second major difference in Anglicanism was in the structure of its church government. Where Lutheranism, Calvinism, and the Reformed tradition tended to center church life in the local church and its pastor, the Church of England decided upon a church governed by bishops. Richard Hooker in his *Laws of Ecclesiastical Polity* provided the doctrinal justification for this episcopal church. The selection presented here summarizes his chief argument in defense of episcopacy. Scripture, he held, provided no absolute evidence for the necessity of any single form of church polity. Early in her history, therefore, the church herself made a decision in favor of a church taught and governed by bishops. This choice had been the dominant form of church life in Christendom for over fifteen hundred years. Hooker's argument is that Scripture alone is normative for matters of Christian belief. Only what is contained in Scripture is to be believed by the Christian. But there is another factor at work in determining Christian life and polity, and that is tradition. What has always been in the Christian church is, for Hooker, a convincing argument in defense of an episcopal church.

The Reformers were unanimous in their rejection of the seven sacraments of the medieval church. Relying on the testimony of Scripture alone, they concluded that only two sacraments, baptism and the Lord's Supper, were scripturally warranted. Although they were in agreement on the number of the Christian sacraments, early and permanent disagreement developed in their manner of interpreting the meaning of these sacraments.

On the subject of baptism the major difference in understanding focused on the role that personal faith played in the reception of this sacrament. Lutheranism, the Reformed churches, and Anglicanism continued the traditional practice of baptizing children. Faith was held to be present in the person of the sponsors who stood warranty that the child would be raised within the community of faith. Anabaptism, on the other hand, insisted that personal faith in the recipient was an absolute essential prior to baptism, and so the radical reformers practiced only the baptism of believers (cf. the *Schleitheim Confession*).

On the subject of the Eucharist, the Reformers were at one in rejecting the Roman sacrifice of the mass. Christ's sacrifice on the cross, they argued, was all-sufficient. To speak of any other sacrifice than that was, in their eyes, a blasphemy. Such unanimity was not, however, reached regarding the nature of Christ's presence in the Eucharist. Luther believed in and taught the real, physical presence of Christ's body and blood: these were received when the believer received communion. Zwingli's position, which came to be the other dominant view within Protestantism, is explained in the excerpt from his *Account of Faith* which he submitted to the Emperor Charles V in 1530. For Zwingli, Christ's presence was, and could only be, because of his bodily ascension into heaven, a spiritual presence in the sacrament. "This is my body, this is my blood" are to be understood as meaning that this bread and this wine *signify* his body and blood. The Eucharist is a memorial service, an opportunity for the rekindling of the faith of the believer in the benefits that the Lord "bestowed on us in His Son."

THE PERIOD OF CONSOLIDATION

With the passing of the early giants of the Reformation, leadership passed into the hands of lesser men. An era of organizing and systematizing the initial insights set in. The latter half of the sixteenth century marked the beginning of Protestant Scholasticism, the trend towards reducing the brilliance and originality, the passion and fire of the early Reformers to rational and systematic treatises.

Philip Melanchthon, Luther's earliest and ablest associate, put the master's vision into the ordered treatment of his *Loci Communes* (1555). The excerpt included here is drawn from the section of that work on the nature of justification. Luther's insistence on the absolute gratuity of God's grace is retained, but the language has been tempered; it is more sober, more carefully nuanced; the breathtaking quality of Luther's first discovery of the greatness of God's love has been considerably toned down. The vision is strained through the net of scholastic terminology.

Heinrich Bullinger represents the further development of the Reformed tradition, begun by Calvin and Zwingli. Bullinger replaced Zwingli as pastor in Zurich. In the course of his long tenure there, he became the acknowledged leader and spokesman of the Reform in German-speaking Switzerland. As a theologian, Bullinger, along with Melanchthon, is a good example of the second-generation Reformers. His work is consistently a careful and irenic attempt to state the Reformation understanding of the gospel in clear and temperate prose. The selection included here is drawn from his *Decades,* a collection of sermons delivered during the decades of his pastorate in Zurich. It is a typical expression of early Protestantism's view of the nature of the church.

While the continental reform moved towards consolidation, events in England took a different turn. After the turbulent years under Henry VIII, Edward VI, and Mary, England and her queen, Elizabeth, wanted nothing so much as peace and order. It was to serve this end that Elizabeth and her bishops settled upon the final form of the church in England. It was to be a Protestant church, under an episcopacy, with a liturgical life modelled on medieval Christianity's ritual and ceremony. To this church every Englishman was required by law to belong. Aside from this required membership and regular attendance, broad tolerance was granted in religious opinion and practice so long as the peace of the realm was not disturbed. Elizabeth hoped by such a policy to make religion an instrument of order in England.

There were, however, those who had spent the years of Mary's reign in exile in Switzerland. They had learned their Protestantism in the school of Calvin, and for them Elizabeth's church was an abomination in the sight of the Almighty. It retained far too much of the practice of the Roman church, and much in its belief and polity had no warrant in Scripture. To purify the church in England of these deformities became their sacred duty. Thus was Puritanism born in England. While Elizabeth was alive it was held in check. Once she was gone it waxed in strength, and for one short period in the seventeenth century (1640–60) Puritanism ruled in England.

Under Elizabeth dissent was limited for the most part to pamphleteering, to outraged outbursts against the corrupt state of the church in England. One of the earliest of these pamphlets (1582) was Robert Browne's *Reformation without Tarrying for Any*. The passage from that work illustrates the principle of dissent at work within early Protestantism. Browne rails against the pastors of England and their unwillingness to risk reform in the church for fear of incurring the wrath of the government (the magistrates). It is on literature such as this that the nonconformist, or dissenting, tradition within English Christianity is built. This principle will be seen at work again in the English church movements of the seventeenth and eighteenth centuries.

MARTIN LUTHER (1483–1546)

The Nature of Salvation

This epistle is in truth the most important document in the New Testament, the gospel in its purest expression. Not only is it well worth a Christian's while to know it word for word by heart, but also to meditate on it day by day. It is the soul's daily bread, and can never be read too often or studied too much. The more you probe into it the more precious it becomes, and the better its flavor. God helping me, I shall try my best to make this Preface serve as an introduction which will enable everyone to understand it in the best possible way. Hitherto, this epistle has been smothered with comments and all sorts of irrelevancies; yet, in essence, it is a brilliant light, almost enough to illumine the whole Bible.

The first thing needed is to master the terminology. We must learn what St. Paul means by such words as law, sin, grace, faith, righteousness, flesh, spirit, and the like; otherwise we shall read and only waste our time. You must not understand the term LAW in its everyday sense as something which explains what acts are permitted or forbidden. This holds for ordinary laws, and you keep them by doing what they enjoin, although you may have no heart in it. But God judges according to your inmost convictions; His law must be fulfilled in your very heart, and cannot be obeyed if you merely perform certain acts. Its penalties do indeed apply to certain acts done apart from our inmost convictions, such as hypocrisy and lying. Psalm 117 declares that all men are liars, because no one keeps God's law from his heart; nor can he do so, for to be averse to goodness and prone to evil are traits found in all men. If we do not choose goodness freely, we do not keep God's law from the heart. Then sin enters in, and divine wrath is incurred even though, to outward appearance, we are doing many virtuous works and living an honorable life.

In Chapter 2, St. Paul therefore asserts that the Jews are all sinners. He says that only those who keep the law are righteous in God's eyes, his point being that no one keeps the law by "works." Rather, Paul says to the Jews, "You teach us not to commit adultery, but you commit adultery yourselves, since you do the very things which you condemn." It is as if he were to say, To outward appearance, you observe the law scrupulously, condemning those who do not observe it, and being quick to teach one and all. You see the splinter in the other man's eye, but you are unaware of the timber in your own. Granted that, in appearance and conduct, you observe the law, owing to your fear of punishment or hope of reward, yet you do nothing from free choice and out of love for the law, but unwillingly and under compulsion; were there no law, you would rather do something else. The logical conclusion is that, in the depths of your heart, you hate the law. What is the use of teaching others not to steal if you are a thief at heart yourself and, if you dared, would be one in fact? Of course, the outer conduct of this kind is not continued for long by humbugs of this kind. It follows that, if you teach others but not your own selves, you do not know what you teach and have not rightly understood the nature of the law. Nay, the law increases your guilt, as Paul says in Chapter 5. A man only hates the law the more, the more it demands what he cannot perform.

That is why, in Chapter 7, Paul calls the law spiritual; spiritual because, if the law were corporeal, our works would meet its demands. Since it is spiritual, however, no one keeps it, unless everything you do springs from your inmost heart. Such a heart is given us only by God's spirit, and this spirit makes us equal to the demands of the law. Thus we gain a genuine desire for the law, and then everything is done with willing hearts, and not in fear or under compulsion. Therefore, because that law is spiritual when it is loved by hearts that are spiritual, and demands that sort of mind, if that spirit is not in our hearts, sin remains; a grudge abides together with hostility to the law, although the law itself is right and good and holy.

Therefore, familiarize yourself with the idea that it is one thing to do what the law enjoins and quite another to fulfill the law. All that a man does or ever can do of his own free will and strength is to perform the works required by the law. Nevertheless, all such works are vain and useless as long as we dislike the law and feel it a constraint. That is Paul's meaning in Chapter 3 when he says, "Through the works of the law shall no man be justified before God." It is obvious—is it not?—that the sophisticators wrangling in the schools are misleading when they teach us to prepare ourselves for grace by our works. How can anyone use works to prepare himself to be good when he never does a good work without a certain reluctance or unwillingness in his heart? How is it possible for God to take pleasure in works that spring from reluctant and hostile hearts?

To fulfill the law, we must meet its requirements gladly and lovingly; live virtuous and upright lives without the constraint of the law, and as if

THE NATURE OF SALVATION 9

neither the law nor its penalties existed. But this joy, this unconstrained love, is put into our hearts by the Holy Spirit, as St. Paul says in Chapter 5. But the Holy Spirit is given only in, with, and through faith in Jesus Christ, as Paul said in his opening paragraph. Similarly, faith itself comes only through the word of God, the gospel. This gospel proclaims Christ as the Son of God; that He was man; that He died and rose again for our sakes, as Paul says in Chapters 3, 4, and 10.

We reach the conclusion that faith alone justifies us and fulfills the law; and this because faith brings us the spirit gained by the merits of Christ. The spirit, in turn, gives us the happiness and freedom at which the law aims, and this shows that good works really proceed from faith. That is Paul's meaning in Chapter 3 when, after having condemned the works of the law, he sounds as if he had meant to abrogate the law by faith; but says that, on the contrary, we confirm the law through faith, i.e. we fulfill it by faith.

The word SIN in the Bible means something more than the external works done by our bodily action. It means all the circumstances that act together and excite or incite us to do what is done; in particular, the impulses operating in the depths of our hearts. This, again, means that the single term, "doing," includes the case where a man gives way completely and falls into sin. Even where nothing is done outwardly, a man may still fall into complete destruction of body and soul. In particular, the Bible penetrates into our hearts and looks at the root and the very source of all sin, i.e., unbelief in the depth of our heart. Just as faith alone gives us the spirit and the desire for doing works that are plainly good, so unbelief is the sole cause of sin; it exalts the flesh, and gives the desire to do works that are plainly wrong, as happened in the case of Adam and Eve in the garden of Eden, Genesis 3.

Christ therefore singled out unbelief and called it sin. In John 16, He says, The spirit will convict the world of sin because they do not believe in me. Similarly, before good or evil works are performed, and before they appear as good or evil fruits, either faith or unbelief must be already in our hearts. Here are the roots, the sap and the chief energy of all sin. This is what the Bible calls the head of the serpent and of the old dragon, which Christ, the seed of the woman, must crush, as was promised to Adam.

The words GRACE and GIFT differ inasmuch as the true meaning of grace is the kindness of favor which God bears toward us of His own choice, and through which He is willing to give us Christ, and to pour the Holy Spirit and His blessings upon us. Paul makes this clear in Chapter 5 when he speaks of the grace and favor of Christ, and the like. Nevertheless, both the gifts and the spirit must be received by us daily, although even then they will be incomplete, for the old desires and sins still linger in us and strive against the spirit, as Paul says in Romans 7 and Galatians 5. Again, Genesis 3 speaks of the enmity between the woman's children and the serpent's brood. Yet grace is sufficient to enable us to be accounted entirely and completely righteous in God's sight, because His grace does not come in portions and pieces, separately, like so many gifts; rather, it takes us up completely into its embrace for the sake of Christ our mediator and intercessor, and in order that the gifts may take root in us.

This point of view will help you to understand Chapter 7, where Paul depicts himself as still a sinner; and yet, in Chapter 8, [he] declares that no charge is held against those who are "in Christ," because of the spirit and the (still incomplete) gifts. Insofar as our flesh is not yet killed, we are still sinners. Nevertheless insofar as we believe in Christ, and begin to receive the spirit, God shows us favor and goodwill. He does this to the extent that He pays no regard to our remaining sins and does not judge them; rather He deals with us according to the faith which we have in Christ until sin is killed.

FAITH is not something dreamed, a human illusion, although this is what many people understand by the term. Whenever they see that it is not followed either by an improvement in morals or by good works, while much is still being said about faith, they fall into the error of declaring that faith is not enough, that we must do "works" if we are to become upright and attain salvation. The reason is that, when they hear the gospel, they miss the point; in their hearts, and out of their own resources, they conjure up an idea which they call "belief," which they treat as genuine faith. All the same, it is but a human fabrication, an idea without a corresponding experience in the depths of the heart. It is therefore ineffective and not followed by a better kind of life.

Faith, however, is something that God effects in us. It changes us and we are reborn from God (John 1). Faith puts the old Adam to death and makes us quite different men in heart, in mind and in all our powers; and it is accompanied by the Holy Spirit. O, when it comes to faith, what a living, creative, active, powerful thing it is. It cannot do other than good at all times. It never waits to ask whether there is some good work to do. Rather, before the question is raised, it has done the deed and keeps on doing it. A man not active in this way is a man without faith. He is groping about for faith and searching for good works, but knows neither what faith is nor what good works are. Nevertheless, he keeps on talking nonsense about faith and good works.

Faith is a living and unshakeable confidence, a belief in the grace of God so assured that a man would die a thousand deaths for its sake. This kind of confidence in God's grace, this sort of knowledge of it, makes us joyful, high-spirited and eager in our relations with God and with all mankind. That is what the Holy Spirit effects through faith. Hence the man of faith, without being driven, willingly and gladly seeks to do good to everyone, serve everyone, suffer all kinds of hardships, for the sake of the love and glory of the God who has shown him such grace. It is impossible, indeed, to separate works from faith, just as it is impossible to separate heat and light from fire. Beware, therefore, of wrong conceptions of your own, and of those who talk nonsense while thinking they are pronouncing shrewd judgments on faith and works whereas they are showing themselves the greatest of fools. Offer up your prayers to God, and ask Him to create faith in you; otherwise you will always lack faith, no matter how you try to deceive yourself, or what your efforts and ability.

RIGHTEOUSNESS means precisely the kind of faith we have in mind, and should properly be called "divine righteousness," the righteousness which holds good in God's sight, because it is God's gift and shapes a man's nature to do his duty to all. By his faith, he is set free from sin, and he finds delight in God's commandments. In this way, he pays God the honor that is due to Him, and renders Him what he owes. He serves his fellows willingly according to his ability, so discharging his obligations to all men. Righteousness of this kind cannot be brought about in the ordinary course of nature, by our own free will or by our own powers. No one can give faith to himself, nor free himself from unbelief; how, then, can anyone do away with even his smallest sins? It follows that what is done in the absence of faith on the one hand, or in consequence of unbelief on the other, is naught but falsity, self-deception and sin (Romans 14), no matter how well it is gilded over.

FLESH and SPIRIT must not be understood as if flesh had only to do with moral impurity and spirit only with the state of our hearts. Rather, flesh, according to St. Paul, as also according to Christ in John 3, means everything that is born from the flesh, i.e. the entire self, body and soul, including our reason and all our senses. This is because everything in us leans to the flesh. It is therefore appropriate to call a man "carnal" when, not having yet received grace, he gibbers and jabbers cheerfully about the high things of the spirit in the very way which Galatians 5 depicts as the works of the flesh, and calls hypocrisy and hatred works of the flesh. Moreover, Romans 8 says that the law is weakened by the flesh. This is not said simply of moral impurity, but of all sins. In particular, it is said of lack of faith, which is a kind of wickedness more spiritual in character than anything else.

On the other hand, the term spiritual is often applied to one who is busied with the most outward of works, as when Christ washed His disciples' feet, and when Peter went sailing his boat and fishing. Hence the term "flesh" applies to a person who, in thought and in fact, lives and labors in the service of the body and the temporal life. The term "spirit" applies to a person who, in thought and fact, lives and labors in the service of the spirit and of the life to come. Unless you give these terms this connotation, you will never comprehend Paul's epistle to the Romans, nor any other book of Holy Scripture. Beware then of all teachers who use these terms differently, no matter who they may be, whether Jerome, Augustine, Ambrose, Origen, or their like; or even persons more eminent then they. . . .

JOHN CALVIN (1509–1564)

Predestination

The discussion of predestination, a subject rather intricate in itself, is made very perplexing and therefore dangerous by human curiosity, which cannot be restrained by any barriers from wandering into forbidden labyrinths and from soaring beyond its sphere as if determined to leave none of the Divine secrets unscrutinized or unexplored. As we see multitudes everywhere guilty of this arrogance and presumption, and among them some who are not censurable in other respects, it is proper to admonish them that they are duty-bound not to go too far in this inquiry.

First, then, let them remember that, when they inquire into predestination, they penetrate to the inmost recesses of Divine wisdom, where the careless and confident intruder will obtain no satisfaction of his curiosity, but will enter a labyrinth from which he will find no exit. For it is unreasonable that man should scrutinize with impunity those things which the Lord has determined to be hidden in Himself; it is unreasonable that man should investigate to all eternity that sublimity of wisdom which God, in order to incite our admiration of His glory, would have us adore but not comprehend. Those secrets of His will which were to be revealed to us He tells us in His word; and these were all, as He foresaw, that would concern us or be to our advantage.

Others, desirous of remedying this evil, would like all mention of predestination to be buried, as it were. They teach men to avoid every question concerning predestination as they would teach them to avoid a precipice. Though their moderation, in judging that mysteries ought to be handled with such great restraint, is to be commended, yet since they go too far they have little influence on the mind of man, which refuses to submit to unreasonable restrictions.

To determine therefore the legitimate area for the inquiring mind, we must recur to the word of the Lord, which affords a safe rule for our understanding. For the Scriptures are the school of the Holy Spirit, in which neither anything necessary and useful to know is omitted nor anything detrimental to know is taught. Whatever, therefore, is declared in the Scriptures concerning predestination we must be careful not to withhold from believers, lest we appear either to defraud them of the favor of their God or to reprove and censure the Holy Spirit for publishing what it would by all means be useful to suppress.

Predestination, by which God grants to some the hope of life and condemns others to eternal death, will hardly be denied absolutely by anyone desirous of the credit of piety. But it is involved in many quibbles, especially by those who make foreknowledge the cause of it.

We maintain that both foreknowledge and predestination pertain to God; but that it is preposterous to represent predestination as depending on foreknowledge.

When we attribute foreknowledge to God, we mean that all things have always been and will perpetually remain before His eyes, so that to His knowledge nothing is future or past, but all things are present, and present in such a manner that He does not merely conceive of them from ideas formed in His mind, in the way that things remembered by us appear present to our minds, but beholds and sees them as if they were actually placed before Him. And this foreknowledge extends to the whole world and to all creatures.

Predestination we call that eternal decree of God by which He has determined in Himself what is to become of every human individual. For men are not all created with the same destiny, but eternal life is foreordained for some and eternal damnation for others. Every man, therefore, being created for one or the other of these ends, is, we say, predestined either to life or to death.

It is a notion commonly entertained that God, foreseeing what would be the respective merits of every individual, makes a correspondent distinction between different persons, so that He adopts as His children such as He foreknows will be deserving of His grace, and determines to the damnation of death others whose dispositions, as He foresees, will be inclined to wickedness and impiety.

Nor is this widely held notion merely a common opinion, for it has great advocates in all ages, which I candidly confess, so that no one may cherish the hope of injuring our cause by opposing us with their names. For the truth of God on this point is too certain to be shaken, and too clear to be overthrown by the authority of men.

"He hath chosen us," says Paul, "before the foundation of the world, according to the good pleasure of His will, that we should be holy and without blame before Him." The clause stating us to have been "chosen that we might be holy" fully refutes the error which makes foreknowledge the cause of election; for Paul declares, on the contrary, that all the virtue displayed by men is the effect of election. If any inquiry be made after a superior cause, Paul replies that God thus "predestined" and that it was "according to the good pleasure of His will." This negates any cause for election which men imagine to exist in themselves, for Paul represents all the benefits conferred by God for the spiritual life as flowing from the fact that God elected whom He would.

The clause "that we should be holy" removes every difficulty. For if you say "Because He foresaw they would be holy, therefore He chose them," you invert the order of Paul. We may safely infer, then, that if He chose us so that we should be holy, His foresight of our future holiness was not the cause of His choice.

But, it will be said, Ambrose, Origen, and Jerome believed that God dispenses His grace among men according to His foreknowledge of the good use which every individual will make of it.

Augustine also was once of the same opinion. But when he had made greater progress in scriptural knowledge, he not only retracted but powerfully combated this opinion. After having discarded all merits antecedent to election, Augustine says, "Here undoubtedly falls to the ground the vain reasoning of those who argue that predestination depends on the foreknowledge of God rather than on His grace and who affirm that we were elected before the foundation of the world because God foreknew that we would be good, not that He himself would make us good. This is not the language of Him who says, 'Ye have not chosen me, but I have chosen you.' "

When the human mind hears these things, its petulance breaks through all restraint, and it displays as serious and as violent an agitation as if alarmed by the sound of a martial trumpet. Many, indeed, as if they wished to save God from odium, admit election in such a way as to deny that anyone is reprobated. But this is puerile and absurd, because election itself could not exist without reprobation. God is said to set apart those whom He adopts for salvation. To say that others may obtain by chance, or acquire by their own efforts, that which election alone confers on a few, would be worse than absurd. Whom God passes by, therefore, He reprobates, and that for no other reason than His determination to exclude them from that inheritance which He predestines for His children.

Foolish mortals enter into many contentions with God, as though they could bring Him into court to defend Himself against their accusations. If such a thought ever enters the minds of pious men, they will be sufficiently enabled to break its force by one consideration: how exceedingly presumptuous it is to even inquire into the causes of the Divine will, which is, in fact, and is justly entitled to be, the cause of everything that exists. For if God's will had any cause, then there would have to be something antecedent to which that will were linked, which it is impious to suppose. For the will of God is the highest rule of justice, so that what He wills must be considered just for the very reason that He wills it. When it is inquired, therefore, why the Lord did this or that, the answer must be "Because He willed it." But if you go further and ask why He so willed, you are in search of something greater and higher than the will of God, which can never be found.

If anyone should put to us the question why God has from the beginning predestined some men to death who, not yet being brought into existence, could not yet deserve the sentence of death, we will reply by asking them, in return, what they suppose God owes to a man, if He chooses to judge that man on the basis of his own nature. As we are all corrupted by sin, we must necessarily be odious to God, and that not from tyrannical cruelty, but from most equitable justice. If all whom the Lord predestines to death are in their natural condition liable to the sentence of death, what injustice do they complain of? Let all the sons of Adam come forward, let them all contend and dispute with their Creator, because, by His eternal providence, they were previous to their birth condemned to endless misery. What murmur will they be able to raise against this vindication when God, on the other hand, shall call them to an appraisal of themselves? If they have all been taken from a corrupt mass, it is no wonder that they are subject to condemnation.

All things being at God's disposal, and the decision of salvation or death residing in Him, He orders all things by His counsel and decree in such a manner that some men are born destined from the womb for certain death, so that His name may be glorified in their destruction. If anyone pleads that no necessity was imposed on these men by the foreknowledge of God, but that they were created by Him in the state of reprobation in consequence of His foresight of their future depravity, it will amount to nothing. God foresees future events only in consequence of His decree that they shall happen. It is useless, therefore, to quarrel about foreknowledge, since it is evident that all things come to pass rather by ordination and decree.

They say it is nowhere declared in express terms that God decreed that Adam should perish by his defection; as though the same God whom the Scriptures represent as doing whatever He pleases, created the noblest of His creatures without any determinate end. They maintain that Adam was possessed of free choice, so that he might be the author of his own fate, and that God decreed nothing more than to treat him according to his deserts. If so weak a scheme as this be accepted, what will become of God's omnipotence, by which He governs all things according to His secret counsel, independently of every other person or thing?

But whether they wish it or dread it, predestination exhibits itself in Adam's posterity. For the loss of salvation by the whole race through the guilt of one parent was an event which did not happen from natural causes. The Scriptures proclaim that all men were, in the person of their father, sentenced to eternal death. Since this sentence is not attributable to nature, it evidently must have proceeded from the unfathomable decree of God.

It is an awful decree, I confess, but no one can deny that God foreknew the future final fate of man before He created him, and that He foreknew this fate because it was appointed by His own decree.

The first man fell because the Lord had determined it was expedient. The reason for this determination is unknown to us. Yet it is certain that God determined thus only because He foresaw it would tend to the just illustration of the glory of His name. We should feel no reluctance to submit our understanding to the infinite wisdom of God and acquiesce in its many mysteries. To be ignorant of things which it is neither possible nor lawful to know is to be learned; an eagerness to know such things is a species of madness.

MICHAEL SATTLER (1490?–1527)

An Anabaptist Confession of Faith

May joy, peace and mercy from our Father through the atonement of the blood of Christ Jesus, together with the gifts of the Spirit—Who is sent from the Father to all believers for their strength and comfort and for their perseverance in all tribulation until the end, Amen—be to all those who love God, who are the children of light, and who are scattered everywhere as it has been ordained of God our Father, where they are with one mind assembled together in one God and Father of us all: Grace and peace of heart be with you all, Amen.

Beloved brethren and sisters in the Lord: First and supremely we are always concerned for your consolation and the assurance of your conscience (which was previously misled) so that you may not always remain foreigners to us and by right almost completely excluded, but that you may turn again to the true implanted members of Christ, who have been armed through patience and knowledge of themselves, and have therefore again been united with us in the strength of a godly Christian spirit and zeal for God.

It is also apparent with what cunning the devil has turned us aside, so that he might destroy and bring to an end the work of God which in mercy and grace has been partly begun in us. But Christ, the true Shepherd of our souls, Who has begun this in us, will certainly direct the same and teach [us] to His honor and our salvation, Amen.

Dear brethren and sisters: we who have been assembled in the Lord at Schleitheim on the Border make known in points and articles to all who love God that as concerns us we are of one mind to abide in the Lord as God's obedient children, [His] sons and daughters, we who have been and shall be separated from the world in everything, [and] completely at peace. To God alone be praise and glory without the contradiction of any brethren. In this we have perceived the oneness of the Spirit of our Father and of our common Christ with us. For the Lord is the Lord of peace and not of quarreling, as Paul points out. That you may understand in what articles this has been formulated you should observe and note [the following].

A very great offense has been introduced by certain false brethren among us, so that some have turned aside from the faith, in the way they intend to practice and observe the freedom of the Spirit and of Christ. But such have missed the truth and to their condemnation are given over to the lasciviousness and self-indulgence of the flesh. They think faith and love may do and permit everything, and nothing will harm them nor condemn them, since they are believers.

Observe, you who are God's members in Christ Jesus, that faith in the Heavenly Father through Jesus Christ does not take such form. It does not produce and result in such things as these false brethren and sisters do and teach. Guard yourselves and be warned of such people, for they do not serve our Father, but their father, the devil.

But you are not that way. For they that are Christ's have crucified the flesh with its passions and lusts. You understand me well and [know] the brethren whom we mean. Separate yourselves from them for they are perverted. Petition the Lord that they may have the knowledge which leads to repentance, and [pray] for us that we may have constancy to persevere in the way in which we have espoused, for the honor of God and of Christ, His Son, Amen.

The articles which we discussed and on which we were of one mind are these: 1. Baptism; 2. The Ban [Excommunication]; 3. Breaking of Bread; 4. Separation from the Abomination; 5. Pastors in the Church; 6. The Sword; and 7. The Oath.

First. Observe concerning baptism: Baptism shall be given to all those who have learned repentance and amendment of life and who believe truly that their sins are taken away by Christ; and to all those who walk in the resurrection of Jesus Christ and wish to be buried with Him in death, so that they may be resurrected with Him; and to all those who with this significance request it [baptism] of us and demand it for themselves. This excludes all infant baptism, the highest and chief abomination of the pope. In this you have the foundation and testimony of the apostles. Matt. 28, Mark 16, Acts 2, 8, 16, 19. This we wish to hold simply, yet firmly and with assurance.

Second. We are agreed as follows on the ban: The ban shall be employed with all those who have given themselves to the Lord, to walk in His commandments, and with all those who are baptized into the one body of Christ and who are called brethren or sisters, and yet who slip sometimes and fall into error and sin, being inadvertently overtaken. The same shall be admonished twice in secret and the third time openly disciplined or banned according to the command of Christ. Matt. 18. But this shall be done according to the regulation of the Spirit (Matt. 5) before the breaking of bread, so that we may break and eat one bread, with one mind and in one love, and may drink of one cup.

Third. In the breaking of bread we are of one mind and are agreed [as follows]: All those who wish to break one bread in remembrance of the broken body of Christ, and all who wish to drink of one drink as a remembrance of the shed blood of Christ, shall be united beforehand by baptism in one body of Christ which is the church of God and whose Head is Christ. For as Paul points out we cannot at the same time be partakers of the Lord's table and the table of devils; we cannot at the same time drink the cup of the Lord and the cup of the devil. That is, all those who have fellowship with the dead works of darkness have no part in the light. Therefore all who follow the devil and the world have no part with those who are called unto God out of the world. All who live in evil have no part in the good.

Therefore it is and must be [thus]: Whoever has not been called by one God to one faith, to one baptism, to one Spirit, to one body, with all the children of God's church, cannot be made [into] one bread with them, as indeed must be done if one is truly to break bread according to the command of Christ.

Fourth. We are agreed [as follows] on separation: A separation shall be made from the evil and from the wickedness which the devil planted in the world, in this manner: simply that we shall not have fellowship with them [the wicked] and not run with them in the multitude of their abominations. This is the way it is: Since all who do not walk in the obedience of faith, and have not united themselves with God so that they wish to do His will, are a great abomination before God, it is not possible for anything to grow or issue from them except abominable things. For truly all creatures are in but two classes, good and bad, believing and unbelieving, darkness and light, the world and those who [have come] out of the world, God's temple and idols, Christ and Belial; and none can have part with the other.

To us then the command of the Lord is clear when He calls upon us to be separate from the evil and thus He will be our God and we shall be His sons and daughters.

He further admonishes us to withdraw from Babylon and the earthly Egypt that we may not be partakers of the pain and suffering which the Lord will bring upon them.

From all this we should learn that everything which is not united with our God and Christ cannot be other than an abomination which we should shun and flee from. By this is meant all popish and antipopish works and church services, meetings and church attendance, drinking houses, civic affairs, the commitments [made in] unbelief and other things of that kind, which are highly regarded by the world and yet are carried on in flat contradiction to the command of God, in accordance with all the unrighteousness which is in the world. From all these things we shall be separated and have no part with them for they are nothing but an abomination, and they are the cause of our being hated before our Christ Jesus, Who has set us free from the slavery of the flesh and fitted us for the service of God through the Spirit Whom He has given us.

Therefore there will also unquestionably fall from us the unchristian, devilish weapons of force—such as sword, armor and the like, and all use [either] for friends or against one's enemies—by virtue of the word of Christ, "Resist not [him that is] evil."

Fifth. We are agreed as follows on pastors in the Church of God: The pastor in the Church of God shall, as Paul has prescribed, be one who out-and-out has a good report of those who are outside the faith. This office shall be to read, to admonish and teach, to warn, to discipline, to ban in the church, to lead out in prayer for the advancement of all the brethren and sisters, to lift up the bread when it is to be broken, and in all things to see to the care of the body of Christ, in order that it may be built up and developed, and the mouth of the slanderer be stopped.

This one moreover shall be supported [by] the church which has chosen him, wherein he may be in need, so that he who serves the gospel may live of the gospel as the Lord has ordained. But if a pastor should do something requiring discipline, he shall not be dealt with except [on the testimony of] two or three witnesses. And when they sin they shall be disciplined before all in order that the others may fear.

But should it happen that through the cross this pastor should be banished or led to the Lord [through martyrdom] another shall be ordained in his place in the same hour so that God's little flock and people may not be destroyed.

Sixth. We are agreed as follows concerning the sword: The sword is ordained of God outside the perfection of Christ. It punishes and puts to death the wicked, and guards and protects the good. In the law the sword was ordained for the punishment of the wicked and for their death, and the same [sword] is [now] ordained to be used by the worldly magistrates.

In the perfection of Christ, however, only the ban is used for a warning and for the excommunication of the one who has sinned, without putting the flesh to death—simply the warning and the command to sin no more.

Now it will be asked by many who do not recognize [this as] the will of Christ for us, whether a Christian may or should employ the sword against the wicked for the defense and protection of the good, or for the sake of love.

Our reply is unanimously as follows: Christ teaches and commands us to learn of Him, for He is meek and lowly in heart and so shall we find rest to our souls. Also Christ says to the heathenish woman who was taken in for adultery, not that [she should be stoned] according to the law of His Father (and yet He says, "As the Father has commanded me, thus I do"), but in mercy and forgiveness and warning, to sin no more. Such [an attitude] we also ought to take completely according to the rule of the ban.

Secondly, it will be asked concerning the sword, whether a Christian shall pass sentence in worldly dispute and strife such as unbelievers have with one another. This is our united answer: Christ did not wish to decide or pass judgment between brother and brother in the case of the inheritance, but refused to do so. Therefore we should do likewise.

Thirdly, it will be asked concerning the sword, [whether] one [shall] be a magistrate if one should be chosen as such. The answer is as follows: They wished to make Christ king, but He fled and did not view it as the arrangement of His Father. Thus shall we do as He did, and follow Him, and so shall we not walk in darkness. For He Himself says, "He who wishes to come after me, let him deny himself and take up his cross and follow me." Also, He Himself forbids the [employment of] the force of the sword saying that the worldly princes lord it over them, etc., but not so shall it be with you. Further, Paul says, Whom God did foreknow He also did predestinate to be conformed to the image of His Son, etc. Also Peter says, Christ has suffered (not ruled) and left us an example, that [we] should follow His steps.

Finally it will be observed that it is not appropriate for a Christian to serve as a magistrate because of these points: The government magistracy is according to the flesh, but the Christians' is according to the Spirit. Their houses and dwelling remain in this world, but the Christians' are in heaven; their citizenship is in this world, but the Christians' citizenship is in heaven; the weapons of their conflict and war are carnal and against the flesh only, but the Christians' weapons are spiritual, against the fortifications of the devil. The worldlings are armed with steel and iron, but the Christians are armed with the armor of God, with truth, righteousness, peace, faith, salvation and the Word of God. In brief, as is the mind of Christ toward us, so shall the mind of the members of the body of Christ be through Him in all things, that there may be no schism in the body through which it would be destroyed. For every kingdom divided against itself will be destroyed. Now since Christ is as it is written of Him, His members must also be the same, that His body may remain complete and united to its own advancement and upbuilding.

Seventh. We are agreed as follows concerning the oath: The oath is a confirmation among those who are quarreling or making promises. In the law it is commanded to be performed in God's Name, but only in truth, not falsely. Christ, who teaches the perfection of the law, prohibits all swearing to His [followers], whether true or false—neither by heaven, nor by the earth, nor by Jerusalem, nor by our head— . . . for the reason which He shortly thereafter gives: For you are not able to make one hair white or black. So you see it is for this reason that all swearing is forbidden: we cannot fulfill that which we promise when we swear, for we cannot change [even] the very least thing on us.

Now there are some who do not give credence to the simple command of God, but object with this question: Well now, did not God swear to Abraham by Himself (since He was God) when He promised him that He would be with him and that He would be his God if he would keep His commandments? Why then should I not also swear when I promise to someone? Answer: Hear what the Scripture says: God, since He wished more abundantly to show unto the heirs the immutability of His counsel, inserted an oath, that by two immutable things (in which it is impossible for God to lie) we might have a strong consolation. Observe the meaning of this Scripture: What God forbids you to do, He has power to do, for everything is possible for Him. God swore an oath to Abraham, says the Scripture, so that He might show that His counsel is immutable. That is, no one can withstand nor thwart His will; therefore He can keep His oath. But we can do nothing, as is said about by Christ, to keep or perform [our oaths]; therefore we shall not swear at all [*nichts schweren*].

Then others further say as follows: It is not forbidden of God to swear in the New Testament, when it is actually commanded in the Old, but it is forbidden only to swear by heaven, earth, Jerusalem and our head. Answer: Hear the Scripture: He who swears by heaven swears by God's throne and by Him who sitteth thereon. Observe: it is forbidden to swear by heaven, which is only the throne of God. How much more is it forbidden [to swear] by God Himself! Ye fools and blind, which is greater, the throne or Him that sitteth thereon?

Further some say: Because evil is now [in the world, and] because man needs God for [the establishment of] the truth, so did the apostles Peter and Paul also swear. Answer: Peter and Paul only testify of that which God promised to Abraham with the oath. They themselves promised nothing, as the example indicates clearly. Testifying and swearing are two different things. For when a person swears he is in the first place promising future things, as Christ was promised to Abraham Whom we a long time afterwards received. But when a person bears testimony he is testifying about the present, whether it is good or evil, as Simeon spoke to Mary about Christ and testified: Behold this [child] is set for the fall and rising of many in Israel, and for a sign which shall be spoken against.

Christ also taught us along the same line when He said, "Let your communication be Yea, yea; Nay, nay; for whatsoever is more than these cometh of evil." He says, Your speech or word shall be yea and nay. [However] when one does not wish to understand, he remains closed to the meaning. Christ is simply Yea and Nay, and all those who seek Him simply will understand His Word. Amen.

THOMAS MÜNTZER (1488–1525)

Apocalyptic Anabaptism

Firstly. . . . It is known that poor, ailing, disintegrating Christendom can be neither counseled nor aided unless the diligent, untroubled servants of God daily work through the Scriptures, singing, reading, and preaching. But therewith the head of many a pampered priest will continuously have to suffer great blows or [he will] miss out in his handiwork. But how ought one otherwise to deal with him at a time when Christendom is being so wretchedly devastated by ravenous wolves, as it is written in Isaiah (ch. 5:1–23) and in Ps. 80 (vs. 9–14) concerning the vineyard of God? And St. Paul teaches how one should exercise oneself in singing divine praises (Eph. 5:19). For just as in the times of the beloved prophets Isaiah, Jeremiah, Ezekiel, and the others, the whole congregation of the elect of God had become so utterly implicated in the way of idolatry that even God could not help them but had to let them be led away captive and punish them in the midst of the heathen to the point where they once again recognized his holy name, as it stands written (Isa. 29:17–24; Jer. 15:11; Ezek. 36:8–12; Ps. 89:31–38) so, no less is it true in the time of our fathers and our time, that poor Christendom is even more deeply obdurate and the more so for having the unspeakable semblance of the divine name with which the devil and his servants adorn themselves (Luke 21:5; II Tim. 3:5; II Cor. 11:13–15).

Yea, so nicely that the real friends of God are thereby misled; and even with the diligence of the most intense application, they are scarcely able to detect their error, as Matthew (ch. 24:24) clearly shows. This is what the simulated sanctity and the flattering absolution of the godless enemies of God accomplish. For they say the Christian church cannot err, even though, in order to protect against error, it should be continuously edified by the Word of God and held free of error. Surely [the true church] should also acknowledge sin through ignorance (Lev. 4:13f.; Hos. 4:6; Mal. 2:1–7; Isa. 1:10–17). But that is indeed true. Christ the Son of God and his apostles and indeed, before him, his holy prophets began a real pure Christianity, having sown pure wheat in the field, that is, [they] planted the precious Word of God in the hearts of the elect as Matthew (ch. 12:24–30), Mark (ch. 4:26–29), and Luke (ch. 8:5–15) have written, and Ezekiel (ch. 36:29). But the lazy, neglectful ministers of this same church have not wished to accomplish this and maintain it by dint of diligent watchfulness; but rather they have sought their own [ends], not what was Jesus Christ's (Phil. 2:4, 21). For this reason they have allowed the harmfulness of the godless vigorously to take over, that is, the weeds (Ps. 80:9–14). For the cornerstone, here (Dan. 2:34f., 44f.) indicated, was still small. Of this Isaiah (ch. 28:16) [also] speaks. To be sure, it has not yet come to fill the whole world, but it will soon fill it and make it full, very full. Therefore the prepared cornerstone was in the beginning of the new Christianity rejected by the builders, that is, the rulers (Ps. 118:22f. and Luke 20:17b). Thus I say the church since its beginning has become in all places dilapidated, up to the present time of the "divided" world (Luke 21:10; Dan. 2:35; I Esdras 4:45). For Hegesippus [and Eusebius] in [*Ecclesiastical History*] IV, 22, concerning the [early] Christian church, declares that the Christian congregation did not remain a virgin any longer than up to the time of the death of the disciples of the apostles and soon thereafter became an adulteress, as had indeed already been prophesied by the beloved apostles (II Peter 2:12–15). And in the Acts of the Apostles (ch. 20:28–31a) Saint Paul said to the shepherds of the sheep in clear, translucent words: Take heed therefore unto yourselves, and to all the flock, over which the Holy Ghost hath made you overseers, to feed the church of God, which he hath purchased with his own blood. For I know this, that after my departing shall ravenous wolves enter in among you, not sparing the flock. Also of your own selves shall men arise, speaking perverse things, to draw away disciples after them. Therefore watch. . . .

The same is to be found in the general letter of the apostle Jude (vs. 4–19). Revelation (ch. 16:13) points to the same. Therefore our Lord Christ warns us to be on guard against false prophets (Matt. 7:15). Now it is as clear as day that nothing is esteemed so bad and unimportant— before God be it said in sorrow—as the Spirit of Christ, and yet none may be saved unless the selfsame Holy Spirit have previously assured one of salvation, as it is written (Rom. 8:9; Luke 12:8; John 6:63; 17:2f.). But how do we miserable little worms expect to come to this, as long as we hold the prestige of the godless in such respect that Christ, the gentle Son of God, unfortunately appears in contrast to the great titles and names of this world like a hempen hobgoblin to scare the birds or a painted doll of a man? And yet he is the very Stone, which will be thrown from the mountain into the sea (Ps. 46:2ff.), away from the splendorous luxury of this world. He is the Rock which was made without human hands and cut out of the great mountain, his name is Jesus Christ (I Cor. 10:4), who was born precisely when that greatest of all bondage [slavery] prevailed (Luke 1:52; 2:1–3) in the time of Octavian, when the whole world was in motion and was taxed. Then it was that one powerless in the Spirit, a miserable dung sack, wanted to have the whole world, which was of no use to him, however, except for splendor and arrogance. Indeed he let himself imagine that he alone was great. O how very small was that cornerstone Jesus Christ then in the eyes of men! He was assigned to the cow stall like an outcast of men (Ps. 22:6). Accordingly the scribes refused him (Ps. 118;22; Matt. 21:44–46; Mark 12:10–12; Luke 20:17–19), as they are still accustomed to do today. Verily in fact they have been reenacting the Passion with him, ever since the pupils of the apostles died. They have taken the Spirit of Christ for laughingstock and do indeed as it is written in Ps. 69 (11f.). They have quite openly stolen him like the thieves and murderers (John 10:1). They have robbed Christ's sheep of the true voice and have made the true crucified Christ into an utterly fantastic idol. How has this happened? Answer: They have rejected the pure handiwork of God and set in his place a pretty little golden statue of deity, before which the poor peasants slobber, as Hosea has clearly said (ch. 4:8–10) and [again] Jeremiah in Lamentations (ch. 4:5): They that did eat fine spiced food have now received in its place dirt and filth. O woe to the abomination of desolation of which Christ himself says (Matt. 24:15) that he will be so wretchedly mocked with the devilish holding of Mass, with superstitious preaching, ceremonies, and manner of life! And yet all the time there is nothing there but a mere wooden statue of deity—yea, a superstitious wooden priest, and a gross, boorish, coarse people who are unable to conceive of God in the slightest. Is that not a great pity, a sin, and a scandal? Yes, I maintain, the beasts of the belly (Phil. 3:19) and the swine (of which it is written in Matt. 7:6, II Peter 2:22) have completely trampled the precious Stone Jesus Christ with their feet as far as they could. For he has become for the whole world like a rag to wipe off one's boots. . . .

Secondly. We must examine further and well that abomination which despises this Stone. If we are, however, to recognize the rightfulness of him, we must be daily conscious of the [fresh] revelation of God. Oh, that it is become quite precious and rare in this wicked world, for the wily expedients of the captiously clever would overwhelm us every moment, and hold us much more strongly from the pure Handiwork of God (Prov. 4:16–19; Ps. 37:12–15, 32f.). Such a person one must stave off in the fear of the Lord. If only the same [the fear] would be assured in us, then surely holy Christendom could come easily again to the spirit of wisdom and revelation of divine will. This is all comprehended in Scripture (Ps. 145:18f., Ps. 111:5,10; Prov. 1:17). But the fear of God must be pure without any fear of men or creatures (Ps. 19:10; Isa. 66:2; Luke 12:4f.). O how highly necessary fear is for us! For as little as one can happily serve two masters (Matt. 6:24), so little can one happily reverence both God and his creatures. Nor can God have mercy upon us (as the Mother of Christ Our Lord says [Luke 1:50]), unless we fear him with our whole heart. Therefore God says (Mal. 1:6): If I be your Father, where is my honor? If I be your Lord, where then is my fear? Thus, ye amiable princes, it is necessary that we apply utmost diligence in these parlous days (I Tim. ch. 4), as all the dear fathers have delineated in the Bible from the beginning of the world, in order to cope with this insidious evil. For the age is dangerous and the days are wicked (II Tim. 3:1; Eph. 5:15f.). Why? Simply because the noble power of God is so wretchedly disgraced and dishonored that the poor common people are misled by the ungodly divines all with such rigmarole, as the prophet Micah (ch. 3:5–37) says of it: This is now the character of almost all divines, with mighty few exceptions. They teach and say that God no longer reveals his divine mysteries to his beloved friends by means of valid visions or his audible Word, etc. Thus they stick with their inexperienced way (cf. Ecclesiasticus 34:9) and make into the butt of sarcasm those persons who go around in possession of revelation, as the godless did to Jeremiah (ch. 20:7f.). . . .

Thirdly. You ought to know the view that God is so utterly well disposed toward his elect that if even in very minor matters he could warn them (Deut. 1:42–44; 32:29; Matt. 23:37), he would surely do it if they could but receive the same in the immensity of unbelief. For our text in Daniel agrees here with Saint Paul in I Corinthians (ch. 2:9f.) which is taken from the holy Isaiah (ch. 64:4), saying that: Eye hath not seen, nor ear heard, neither have entered into the heart of man, the things which God hath prepared for them that love him. But God hath revealed them unto us by his Spirit: for the Spirit searcheth all things, yea, the deep things of God. Therefore in short it is one's earnest conviction that we must know—and not merely be up in the air in our belief—whether what is given us be from God or from the devil or from nature. For if our natural understanding of the same [—what comes from God and what not—] ought to be captured for the service of faith (II Cor. 10:5), it must arrive at the final degree in [its capacity for] judgment as is shown in Romans (ch. 1:18–23) and Baruch (ch. 3:12–37). Of these judgments one is incapable of proving any in good conscience without God's revelation. For man will clearly discover that he cannot run with his head through heaven but rather that he must first become wholly and utterly a fool. . . .

Fourthly. You ought to know that the elect person who wishes to know which vision or dream is from God, nature, or the devil must with his mind and heart and also his natural understanding take leave of all temporal consolation of the flesh; and it must happen to him as to beloved Joseph in Egypt (Gen., ch. 39) and with Daniel here in this very chapter. For no sensual person will accept it [the Word] (Luke 7:25), since the thistles and thorns—these are the pleasures of this world, as the Lord says (Mark 4:18f.)—stifle the whole working of the Word, which God speaks in the soul. Therefore when God has already spoken his holy Word in the soul, man cannot hear it, if he is unpracticed (Ps. 49:20), for he does not turn in upon himself or look inwardly upon himself and the deeps of his soul. Man will not crucify his life with its vices and desires, as Paul the holy apostle teaches (Gal. 5:24). Therefore the field of the Word of God remains full of thistles and thorns and full of big bushes, all of which must be gotten out of the way for this work of God, in order that a person not be found neglectful or slothful (Prov. 24:3f.). Accordingly, if a man has regard for the fruitfulness of the field and the rich growth at the end, then will such a person become aware for the first time that he is the dwelling place of God and the Holy Spirit for the duration of his days, yea, that he has been created truly for the one purpose that he might search out the testimonies of God in his own life. . . .

It is true, and [I] know it to be true, that the Spirit of God is revealing to many elect, pious persons a decisive, inevitable, imminent reformation [accompanied] by great anguish, and it must be carried out to completion. Defend oneself against it as one may, the prophecy of Daniel remains unweakened, even if no one believes it, as also Paul says to the Romans (ch. 3:3). This passage of Daniel is thus as clear as the sun, and the process of ending the fifth monarchy of the world is in full swing.

The first [kingdom] is set forth by the golden knop. That was the kingdom of Babylon. The second [was represented] by the silver breast and arms. That was the kingdom of the Medes and Persians. The third was the kingdom of the Greeks, which, resounding with its science, was symbolized by the [sounding] brass. The fourth [was] the Roman Empire, which was won by the sword and a kingdom of coercion. But the fifth [symbolized by the iron and clay feet] is that which we have before our eyes, which is also of iron and would like to coerce. . . .

Therefore, you much beloved and esteemed princes, learn your judgments directly from the mouth of God and do not let yourselves be misled by your hypocritical parsons nor be restrained by false consideration and indulgence. For the Stone [made] without hands, cut from the mountain [which will crush the fifth kingdom, Dan. 2:34], has become great. The poor laity [of the towns] and the peasants see it much more clearly than you. Yea, God be praised, it has become so great [that] already, if other lords or neighbors should wish to persecute you for the gospel's sake, they would be driven back by their own people! . . .

If you could only as clearly recognize the harm being [done] to Christendom and rightly consider it, you would acquire just the same zeal as Jehu the king (II Kings, chs. 9 and 10); and the same as that which the whole book of Revelation proclaims. And I know for a certainty that you would thereupon hold yourselves back only with great effort from [letting] the sword exert its power. For the pitiable corruption of holy Christendom has become so great that at the present time no tongue can tell it all. Therefore a new Daniel must arise and interpret for you your vision and this [prophet], as Moses teaches (Deut. 20:2), must go in front of the army. He must reconcile the anger of the princes and the enraged people. For if you will rightly experience the corruption of Christendom and the deception of the false clerics and the vicious reprobates, you will become so enraged at them that no one can think it through. Without doubt it will vex you and go right to your heart that you have been so kindly after they, with the very sweetest words, misled you into the most shameful conceptions (Prov. 6:1ff.) against all established truth. For they have made fools of you so that everyone swears by the saints that the princes are in respect to their office a pagan people. They are said to be able to maintain nothing other than a civil unity. O beloved, yea, the great Stone there is about to fall and strike these schemes of [mere] reason and dash them to the ground, for he says (Matt. 10:34): I am not come to send peace but a sword. What should be done, however, with the same? Nothing different from [what is done with] the wicked who hinder the gospel: Get them out of the way and eliminate them, unless you want to be ministers of the devil rather than of God, as Paul calls you (Rom. 13:4). You need not doubt it. God will strike to pieces all your adversaries who undertake to persecute you, for his hand is by no means shortened, as Isaiah (ch. 59:1) says. . . .

Now if you want to be true governors, you must begin government at the roots, and, as Christ commanded, drive his enemies from the elect. For you are the means to this end. Beloved, don't give us any old jokes about how the power of God should do it without your application of the sword. Otherwise may it rust away for you in its scabbard! May God grant it, whatever any divine may say to you! Christ says it sufficiently (Matt. 7:19; John 15:2,6): Every tree that bringeth not forth good fruit is rooted out and cast into the fire. If you do away with the mask of the world, you will soon recognize it with a righteous judgment (John 7:24). Perform a righteous judgment at God's command! You have help enough for the purpose (Wisdom of Solomon, ch. 6), for Christ is your Master (Matt. 23:8). Therefore let not the evildoers live longer who make us turn away from God (Deut. 13:5). For the godless person has no right to live when he is in the way of the pious. In Ex. 22:18 God says: Thou shalt not suffer evildoers to live. Saint Paul also means this where he says of the sword of rulers that it is bestowed upon them for the retribution of the wicked as protection for the pious (Rom. 13:4). God is your protection and will teach you to fight against his foes (Ps. 18:34). He will make your hands skilled in fighting and will also sustain you. But you will have to suffer for that reason a great cross and temptation in order that the fear of God may be declared unto you. That cannot happen without suffering, but it costs you no more than the danger of having risked all for God's sake and the useless prattle of your adversaries. For though even pious David was drawn from his castle by Absalom, he finally came again into ascendancy when Absalom got hung up and was stabbed. Therefore, you cherished fathers of Saxony, you must hazard all for the sake of the gospel. . . .

The sword is necessary to wipe out the godless (Rom. 13:4). That this might now take place, however, in an orderly and proper fashion, our cherished fathers, the princes, should do it, who with us confess Christ. If, however, they do not do it, the sword will be taken from them (Dan. 7:26f.). For they confess him all right with words and deny him with the deed (Titus 1:16). They [the princes], accordingly, should proffer peace to the enemies (Deut. 2:26–30). If the latter wish to be spiritual [in the outmoded sense] and do not give testimony of the knowledge of God (cf. I Peter 3:9,12), they should be gotten out of the way (I Cor. 5:13). But I pray for them with the devout David where they are not against God's revelation. Where, however, they pursue the opposition, may they be slain without any mercy as Hezekiah (II Kings 18:22), Josiah (ch. 23:5), Cyrus (cf. II Chron. 36:22f.), Daniel (ch. 6:27), Elijah (I Kings 18:40) destroyed the priests of Baal; otherwise the Christian church cannot come back again to its origin. The weeds must be plucked out of the vineyard of God in the time of harvest. Then the beautiful red wheat will acquire substantial rootage and come up properly (Matt. 13:24–30). The angels (v. 39), however, who sharpen their sickles for this purpose are the serious servants of God who execute the wrath of the divine wisdom (Mal. 3:1–6). . . .

. . . the godless rulers should be killed, especially the priests and monks who revile the gospel as heresy for us and wish to be considered at the same time as the best Christians. When hypocritical, spurious goodness becomes engaged and embittered beyond the average, it then wishes to defend the godless and says Christ killed no one, etc. And since the friends of God thus quite ineffectually command the wind, the prophecy of Paul (II Tim. 3:5) is fulfilled. In the last days the lovers of pleasures will indeed have the form of godliness, but they will denounce its power. Nothing on earth has a better form and mask than spurious goodness. For this reason all corners are full of nothing but hypocrites, among whom not a one is so bold as to be able to say the real truth. Therefore in order that the truth may be rightly brought to the light, you rulers—it makes no difference whether you want to or not—must conduct yourselves according to the conclusion of this chapter (ch. 2:48f.), namely, that Nebuchadnezzar made the holy Daniel an officer in order that he might execute good, righteous decisions, as the Holy Spirit says (Ps. 58:10f.). For the godless have no right to live except as the elect wish to grant it to them, as it is written in Ex. 23:29–33. Rejoice, you true friends of God, that for the enemies of the cross their heart has fallen into their breeches. They must do right even though they have never dreamed it. If we now fear God, why do we want to enrage ourselves before slack, defenseless people (Num. 14:8f.; Josh. 11:6)? Be but daring! He who wishes to have rule himself, to him all power on earth and heaven is given (Matt. 28:18). May he preserve you, most beloved, forever. Amen.

JOHN DENCK (1500?–1527)

Spiritualist Anabaptism

The Word which is in the heart one should not deny, but rather [one should] listen diligently and earnestly to what God would declare in us. At the same time [one should] not arbitrarily throw out all external testimony, but rather hear and test all and make, in fear of the Spirit, comparisons. Thus the understanding could, day to day, become ever more pure the longer we wait, until we would hear God in uttermost forthrightness speak with us, and we would become certain of his will: which is to leave off all of selffulness and to yield oneself to the freedom which is God. For man imitates God, takes on the traits of the divine generation, as one who is the son of God and coheir with Christ. Therefore such a one also lives, according to his measure, just as Christ lived. Yea, he himself does not live alone but Christ in him. He does not consider it robbery that he is in some sense equal to God (Phil. 2:6), but rather, even though he is a lord of all creatures, he submits himself to all creatures most humbly, not in order that they serve him, but rather that he, according to his measure, might serve them, fulfilling the will of his Father.

You may say: In a sense, then, do you not make all Christians the equal of Christ? That sounds exactly as though they would have no need of Christ. Answer: All Christians are in some sense like Christ, for, as he offered himself up to the Father, so they are ready to offer themselves. Not, I say, that they are so perfect, as Christ was, but rather that they seek exactly the perfection which Christ never lost. In like manner the earthly and elementary fires are also equal and one with warming, drying, burning, and lighting; and yet the elementary is in an ineffable way more subtle than the earthly fire. Thus Christ calls himself a light of the world and calls also his disciples, that is, all Christians, a light of the world. Again, he is come to kindle a fire (Luke 12:49) which also Jeremiah (ch. 5:14) lighted, as the Holy Spirit says to him: Behold! I will make my words in thy mouth fire, and this people wood, and it shall devour them. And of the same there is much. In sum, all Christians, that is, they who have received the Holy

Spirit, are in God, like unto Christ and equal to him, in such a way that what refers to the one refers also to the other. As Christ does, so do they also. And thus they have Christ as a Lord and Master, for the reason that he is the most perfect mirror of his Father (Wisdom of Solomon 7:26), than which he could not be more perfect unless he had not become man [at all]. And if he could have become more perfect even by a shade and did not, he would not have been the true Saviour; we would have had to seek another. Far be that! That he was, in fact, the most perfect he proved in that he, on his own, offered up his life, without complaint, without acclaim, through the power of the Father and received it back. And in all this he never wavered a moment but rather finished all for the best in due season, neither too early nor too late. This none has ever done. And in so far as anyone has done this he has merely taken from Him, that is, righteousness out of grace. But he received it from none except from the Father, that is, grace out of righteousness.

That we need him, however, and would not want to be without him may be demonstrated and perceived from the following. Since God does not wish to have forced anyone and [wishes] to have everyone in his service of one's own free will and [since] we have nevertheless, without his fault, completely rejected him in such a way that we, as far as in us lay, were utterly without God and lay in darkness and could not even stand up any more (for we had withdrawn ourselves from God and all good and all capacities which we had from God)—accordingly, it did not behoove God merely to set us up again without means—the more so for the reason that we did not ever want to have him, and [that] he does not wish to hold up anybody against the person's will. Still the good pleasure of his will remained unabated such as he has determined it from all eternity, namely, that he desires the salvation of all men. Accordingly, he sets forth a means, which had been prepared from eternity, [and] in which men would be saved just as they had been created therein; that is, his Word. In this Word is hidden alike the mercy and the righteousness of God. And the operation which was impossible has become through the omnipotence of God again possible also through the Word. For man could not accept grace without grace, so also God could not impart his righteousness to unrighteousness without this means. Now, however, this means is so near to all persons (however much they have wanted to reject God) that they can easily receive it in [simply] returning to God. Not that they themselves are able to do anything, but rather because the Word is always in them trying to unite them with the Father, and they will not have it. And nevertheless, as said, God wishes to have forced no one; the fault is theirs who do not wish to do what they very well could by means of the Word. And they are liars and God remains nonetheless sincere and true, as Paul says to the Romans (ch. 3:4) and as has been asserted above.

You may say: Maybe there is a voice in me, but I do not hear it, because I am deaf by reason of sin. Maybe a light does shine in me, but I do not see it, because I am blind. Answer: This is a false excuse, as are they all [which are designed to] put themselves in a good light and to blame and condemn God. For the Word of God surely addresses everyone clearly: the dumb, the deaf, the blind; yea, unreasoning animals, indeed, leaf and grass, stone and wood, heaven and earth, and all that is therein, in order that they might hear and do his will. Only man, who does not wish to be nothing and yet is even more than nothing, strives against him. O what a perverse way! Has then God promised eternal life to the unreasoning animals and not much more to human beings? But only continue to do what you do so long as nothing else appeals to you. If you knew, however, what was still to come over you, you would be eager enough! For sometimes you would give yourselves up gladly to suffer all if he would only, with a single little word, comfort you.

You may say: If, then, the Word is thus in all people, what need had it of the humanity of Jesus of Nazareth? Could not the Word, in some other way, carry out the will of the Father? Answer: The Word was in human beings for this purpose that it might divinize them, as happens to all the elect. And the Scripture (John 10:34) calls them therefore also gods, and they are not therefore many gods or idols who point away and turn one away from the one God, but they [who are] many are all one in the one true God. Nevertheless whoever honors them apart from God makes them, without their fault, into idols, which they were not and never would be. The Word, however, had to become man in Jesus for this reason, that people both in spirit and in the flesh, from within and without, behind and before, and in all places might have testimony. Both [would thus have testimony], the elect for their furtherance and salvation, the others for the reason that they then could not say: God leaves a person free to lay hold of whatever he will to the end that he actually sin and die, which would [,accordingly,] be God's secret pleasure, however much he might give the appearance of its not pleasing him. Thus argue the perverse even in this day, and this argument is so common that many elect also agree with them, though not yet with the same satisfaction as the perverse. May this lie, however, be understood as punished and stigmatized [precisely] by the *humanity* of Jesus, since God has created all persons equal to himself, but none has so remained except one, who is Jesus, who has so loved all the others, that he offered up to the Father his life for their death, which he must surely have learned from the Father, since he was completely equal to the Father and heeded him in all things. Thus God has always had this love from eternity which Jesus displayed under Pilate. He had always loved his Son like the apple of his eye. Yet he found heart-deep satisfaction in his death, which he would have preferred to suffer himself had such a thing not been against order and had men been able to perceive the spiritual, for he is a Spirit, which no fleshly eyes or ears can see or hear.

You may say: Yes, he died indeed out of love but not for all; rather, only for a few. Answer: Since love in him was perfect and [since] love hates or is envious of none, but includes everyone, even though we were all his enemies, surely he would not wish to exclude anyone. And if he had excluded anyone, then love would have been squint-eyed and a respecter of persons. And that, [love] is not! Why should it, however, be strange that we should reject the Son as before we rejected the Father? Should it therefore be not true that he died for all, just because all are not saved? Should it therefore be not true that the Father created all men good just because they have not remained good? Far from it! Indeed, Christ was so extremely resigned that, although he loves all men without measure, if it had pleased the Father, he would also have willed to suffer even in vain. Therefore this sacrifice was accordingly pleasing to the Father. If there had been even a thousand times as many worlds, it would nevertheless have satisfied him for the guilt of all. That Scripture does say (Matt. 20:28; Mark 10:45) that he died for *many,* and yet again (I John 2:2) for *all* is not contradictory but rather written to this end that not all have received the light, although it has illumined all (John 1:9) and though many deny the Lord, who has nevertheless ransomed them all, as Scripture abundantly testifies.

You may say: These your arguments sound just as though God did not himself know the moment of a man's conversion and [as though] the foreknowledge and providence of God were uncertain. Answer: God has indeed known from the beginning how he would relate himself to creatures and the creatures to him, namely, how he would always offer the best and they would always desire the worst, and he would also give it to them occasionally, but nevertheless always for the best. And although he did not wish the death and destruction of the sinner (and knew nevertheless that his will would be effected) since it did not become him to draw by force into his service, he continued to use death in such a way that it [became] the eternal praise of his holiness as we [have misused] his grace to our disgrace and ridicule. Therefore he, marvelous to relate, found satisfaction in the death, not for its own sake but rather for the sake of the trophy, namely, that the uncreated death should be swallowed up in the created death. This is the great secret, which the great and the wise of this world do not perceive, while the angels marvel thereat and praise the Lord, who reigns in eternity and forever. Amen.

He who ordains evil and [yet] can compensate with greater gain than [the loss he cannot] prevent is not to be blamed for the evil. As an example: If there were a child with a propensity to steal and the father put a penny before him in order to find out whether he would steal it and thereupon to punish him and to get rid of the naughtiness, would the father now be guilty of this sin for the reason that he had deposited the penny, even though he had previously often forbidden and enjoined the child not to steal? No one could say this. In like manner, the Father in heaven warned his child Israel from its youth up by means of the law not to steal, that is, to take possession of the creaturely instead of himself, and nevertheless he laid before him so much thereof that he surely had occasion to steal something. Now the boy did not leave it, and the father regarded him for a little while in order that he would have reason to punish the child with success, which before the sin he would not have found suitable. Also it would not have been for the boy's improvement. If he, however, wishes now to discipline him, the boy remonstrates with the father and says: "Why did you put the money in my way, if you didn't want me to steal it? Didn't you very well know? Didn't you have some satisfaction in it, otherwise why didn't you prevent it?" Say now, all you who hear and behold this. Is it now fair that the child should speak this way? Is not this very talk even more punishable than the thieving which took place? Truly, if the boy will not leave off his complaint, the father will lead him to the judges at the gate to deal with him according to the law of Moses (Deut. 21:18–21) as with a disobedient child, to the end that he be covered with stones, if he will not take switches for his improvement.

Therefore, although the Lord of all things knew reason enough to indicate why it would have pleased him to disregard our sin, nevertheless it is not seemly for us to question it, but rather, if he wishes to punish us, to attend to it that we hold still for him without any retort, since we know we are guilty. For all the arguments that children improvise after they have sinned, they do only to excuse themselves, and thus only the more so do they accuse themselves. It does not help us, dearest brothers, our questioning and disputing about [God's] foreknowledge, whether it be before or after our sin. It serves no other purpose than to excuse ourselves, which is the worst of all poisons. Yea, Adam our father also sought a similar idle alibi; but it would not help him, even though he was not so impious that he would have ascribed the fault to God, as we do so completely; although also here again, the excuses of Adam and of all people are of such sort that they do not leave God unjustified. People make out as though they feared they could do something against God's foreknowledge, or God would err and [they] make him into a liar, when they, studious of his command and law, think themselves that all is carried out when they with ardent mouth above a cold heart say: We are poor sinners. They would like thus in their mind to leave to God all honor even though in the eyes of all pagans he has nothing from us but shame and outrage. How gross this rogue is to look at, however subtle and facile he is! For if someone burdens himself to do something against God, why does he not take heed of His commandments which He has given for the purpose that they be obeyed, rather than of foreknowledge about which absolutely nothing has been ordered or revealed? If he does not will sin and nevertheless knows that it takes place, we should not in this case bother ourselves about him. He will not become disparate in himself, as do we. His foreknowledge, which is unknown to us, will surely, without our prying spirit, accord with his will, which even the perverse know in part. But the [theologically] clever thus have to become fools who yearn to know God's mystery and [yet] despise the commonly recognized intention of his commandments.

You may say: We do not need [the doctrine of] foreknowledge, as you say, except as a comfort for all the elect that they might know that their help and salvation lie in the hand of God and that there is no power so mighty which will or could wrest it from him. Answer: This comfort you can give to none and also none can take it from you. For whoever has yielded himself to the chastisement of the Father [and who] has in a measure tasted the sweetness of the bitter cross, to him the Father has revealed himself through his Spirit in defiance before that person's enemies, but [he is] not the less to fear God because of it nor to despise anyone. For whom God has received in faith, he can and wills to reject again in case the person does not remain in faith, since he did not even spare the angels for the reason that they were so certain of the matter that they thereby developed satisfaction in themselves and forgot God. Therefore also the elect instrument of God, Paul, says not in vain (I Cor. 10:12): Let him that thinketh he standeth take heed lest he fall. If God gave his Spirit to King Saul and took it away again and it is nevertheless true that he never rues his gifts, what blame should there be in him if he should wish to take back from us the talent which he had given us, so that we have nothing—that is [from those of us for] whom grace also means nothing—and yet remain [in our sight] sincere and just? Is it not mishandling providence to wish to be certain of the reward of the Lord, however we may serve him? In brief we'd be saying: God has provided for the salvation of his own regardless of their works. Thus we would be saying further: Regardless also of faith. Therewith Christ would be completely thrust from the middle. For if works are in this manner, without distinction, to be rejected, why then does Paul say so earnestly (I Cor. 6:9f.): No fornicator, no adulterer, no miser, no drunkard, no idolater will inherit the Kingdom of God. And Christ says (Matt. 10:39) that whoever does not lose himself is not worthy of him. And we [who] wish to be so highly worthy of him with our own loquacious faith have not left off in the slightest from creaturely things for his sake, to say nothing of ourselves, which we therefore suppose to be impossible also for God to do. Therefore, the whole of nominal Christendom is full of adulterers, misers, drunkards, and more of the same.

Clearly, all who truly fear God must renounce the world. And in the measure that they have to use the world out of necessity, they ought always to be prepared for struggle and ready for adversity as sojourners upon the earth. Whoever lives in security and happiness in the world should take care lest he be overtaken with her, and the ignominy of his fornication become publicly exposed and rebuked. For the Lord cometh, He will come at night, when none will take note of him, like a thief, to take off what he commended to us as shepherds, to serve him therewith, and which like thieves we have appropriated for ourselves in order to rule. Then it will help no one to cry: Lord, I have preached the gospel! Lord, I have heard it [preached]. For he will answer (Matt. 25:12): I do not know you. Or, do we suppose he will not with full right make use of this answer? Or ought he only to get rid of pagans in this fashion? How so, when the same will have as good a case before him as we? O dear brethren! He will not need a long reckoning with us: The words which he declared from the beginning and which we have heard will convict us. He always says (Luke 11:28): Blessed is he who heareth the Word of God and keepeth it; (Matt. 7:26): Whoever heareth it and doeth it not is like unto a fool; (John 10:3): He is a sheep of Christ who hears his voice and obeys. For they who hear the law of God and do not fulfill it in practice are not righteous before God. If now someone wishes to come before God without the righteousness which holds before God, he kicks out of the way the Means, which is what the whole world does. Woe, woe, and again woe to the perverse, who know the will of their Lord and do it not, and yet want to be regarded as justified. How much more unbearable it will be for them than for them for whom it has been in part hidden! Is it not disgrace upon disgrace that we should want to learn to know Christ and yet none the less retain our old godless nature? And we excuse ourselves accordingly with the saying of Paul (I Cor. 7:20) which has it that every single one should abide in his calling wherein he was called. [And we take it] in the sense that if the Lord called someone in adultery, he should remain therein! Why then did not Matthew remain in the customs house? Verily, the fishermen, according to our view, did wrong in leaving their work! This is the way it works out for us when we sort out Scripture in fragments and mend the old garment with new patches. What Paul (I Cor., ch. 7) spoke of the married and single, we would like to apply also to our profligate handiwork, bargaining, usury, and offices. Not so, but rather—to be brief—whoever is not ready with Zacchaeus (Luke 19:8) to make fourfold restitution, if anyone should have aught against him, is not worthy of Christ and will not hear the voice of the Bridegroom. Yea, if he hears it in his mind, it becomes plain poison for him and damnation. We should bring empty hearts to Christ which should be ready to renounce themselves—all that we have—if we could but be receptive to his mystery. For really we are bringing only crowded hearts and presume to accomplish only *our* purpose with Christ, however it may be. In this manner laborers seek for good days with Christ, the poor for wealth, and the servants for rule. Likewise the idle wish to enrich themselves, and the masters do not wish to give themselves over to lose anything but rather through him to retain everything. Nevertheless they all ought to lose themselves in him if they hearken otherwise to his voice and don't want to be children of the world.

You may say: We come therefore and seek Christ in order to find and learn all this in his presence, but you have it [that] one ought already to have this [attitude]. How does this all fit together? Answer: The Word of God is already with you before you seek it; gives to you before you ask; opens up for you before you knock. No one comes of himself to Christ except the Father draw him, which he truly does of course according to his goodness. Whoever on his own initiative, however, undrawn, wishes to come on his own, presumes to give God something which he has not received from him. He wishes to be deserving from God in order that he need not thank him for his grace. Abraham (John 8:56) rejoiced in the day of Christ before he had seen it. Cornelius (Acts 10:2) was a spiritual and God-fearing man long before he acknowledged Christ. Paul (Phil. 3:6) had a righteous and godly zeal for the law before the revelation of Christ. The disciples of Christ (Matt. 19:27) left at once house and home, wife and child for Christ's sake and did not yet know who he was. All the elect seek and rejoice and do not themselves know for what and why, all of which is without disadvantage to the gospel of Christ. For such a work has not gone forth from human beings but rather from God, from whom comes all, that in truth may be called something, as also the gospel testifies. Therefore, no one can vaunt himself before God for his works or his faith, for whoever glorifies within himself has in himself sufficient satisfaction and is one of the rich whom God sends empty away. The poisoned selfulness of the flesh which man has taken on himself against God and without God ought and must be mortified. Where this has begun in a person and he ascribes it to himself, such a one steals from God his honor and slurps up the poison and the devil's milk and, more than that, all on his own wishes to be something over against God—which he is not. But whoever does not want to endure this work of mortification but prefers to practice the works of darkness will not be able to excuse himself before any creature and much less before God. For whoever wishes to excuse himself before God ascribes to God what He has not done and never at all will do, and God must be to him what He had not been before. For if God were in truth that which such a one accuses him of being, he could and would not punish anybody (since he is righteous and punishes none without guilt), unless all creatures were repentant, which is not ever the case, but rather one must first come at it through some Means. But this Means is Christ, whom none may truly know unless he follow after him with his life. And no one can follow after him except in so far as one previously knows him. Whoever does not know him has him not and cannot without him come to the Father. But whoever knows him and does not testify thereto by his manner of life, God will judge along with others who are perverse, regardless of the fact that the person had been previously called and received in the fellowship of the gospel. With this he cannot comfort himself otherwise than in repudiating himself.

You may say: Now do I rightly take it from you that the foreknowledge of God is variable? Answer: God is and remains sincere in all things and his decree will not be reversed. But to whom has he revealed it that one may rely upon it and not fail? The Truth and the Word of God is in itself constant. We, however, are inconstant and vacillate therein. Blessed is the man in whom the Word is true as it is true in God and remains true in eternity for all eternity. Therefore, those whose hearts God hardens so that they cannot believe, he has not rejected in the sense that he does not want to have them but rather that he might beforehand show them their unbelief, all to the end that they might recognize the pity of it and bewail it and be comforted. Just so, a father goes about it with a naughty child. He may punish or disown it as vehemently as he wants; if the child should come back and pray for mercy, he would receive it back. . . . This even men who are wicked do. Will not God wish the same and be able to accomplish it, he whose wealth and bounty none can sufficiently imagine or declare? O blessed is the man who recognizes the mercy of God in fear and pain and contrariwise, is fearful in grace. . . .

Of this truth I speak freely in the Lord who makes [us] dead and quick. Whoever wishes to offer himself in the depths of his soul and in truth to the Lord, that is, whoever wishes to leave off his own will and to seek the will of God and has respect for the work of God, him the merciful Father will receive with great joy and take back regardless of how he has conducted himself hitherto, however despicably he has used up his inheritance, yea, regardless of whatever the Father himself might have decided against him. O that the whole world would come in this manner! The Lord would surely be wonderfully ready to favor them. He bids all people be called and proffers his mercy to everyone in cordial earnestness and yearning in order to fulfill all that he has promised in truth. Is it not therefore malicious when our divines say that he bids someone be invited to the Supper but that it is not his will that this person come? The good Spirit of God has surely not bidden them to say this and the like—he who does sincerely all that he does. Surely he does not say, Come hither, and intend or wish secretly that this person remain where he is. Surely he does not give someone grace and secretly wish to withdraw it again. Surely he does not work up repentance in us for our sins and secretly adjudge us guilty of hell. For he is ever constant and sincere in all his gifts. And when he has considered us to be inconstant (which comes from our guilt alone and the sin in us and is not in him), he is nevertheless ever anew ready to entertain [the possibility] that he perchance has changed, indeed that we ourselves have changed. But you can sing and say to us, call and shout at us, whatever you want, the world does not wish to hear. And even those children of the world who do hear would like to be observed in this respect and thus conceal their wickedness. They say yes to the command of the Father but do not carry it out. O these are extremely bad children! Therefore also the Lord has already, not unfairly, blinded some and will blind, harden, and punish them still more, simply for the reason that they do not accept the Lord in truth, that is, they wish to come to the Father without the Son, wish to rule with God and not to be ruled with Christ. They wish to find their souls and not lose them, to do God's will and not leave off their own. They speak of spiritual freedom and remain in fleshly thralldom and imprisonment. But I testify and [I] beseech you, by the Advent of Christ our Lord, all [of you] who in the foregoing manner behold, or otherwise perceive the truth *of God,* that you will to accept it in the truth *of Christ*—that is, according to the manner, way, and form which Christ taught and himself demonstrated, that is, by denying and losing himself—in order that you may stand before his Judgment Seat blameless and confident; otherwise the Truth is and will be for you the greatest lie, because of your perverse manner. And if you do not return while the Lord gives you opportunity and time, then you will have part with him who from the beginning bore forth the lie out of his own substance (John 8:44). This inheritance is the gnawing worm that none can kill and the eternal fire that none can quench (Mark 9:44).

He for whom these words go to the heart ought and will have satisfaction in the fact that we get covered over with scorn and shame because of sin, and [yet he] does not alienate himself [from us], even when we are persecuted by all creatures. For one may still and indeed ought to beseech

God, merciful and sincere, that he take the shame from us in his good time and according to his very best will, not for our sakes, but rather in order that his name might be praised among all pagans and nations, all of which he promised us through his servants, the holy prophets and his Son Jesus the Anointed, whom he has for this reason established as King over all kings and Lord over all lords (Rev. 19:16). Before him the whole world is afraid and yet it does not believe but will in truth soon experience [him] on the Day to which all the saints look forward in joy. Amen.

RICHARD HOOKER (1553–1600)

The Scriptural Form of Church Polity

But we must note, that he which affirmeth speech to be necessary amongst all men throughout the world, doth not thereby import that all men must necessarily speak one kind of language; even so the necessity of Polity and Regiment in all Churches may be held without holding any one certain Form to be necessary in them all. Nor is it possible that any Form of Polity, much less of Polity Ecclesiastical, should be good, unless God himself be author of it. "Those things that are not of God [saith Tertullian], they can have no other than God's adversary for their author." Be it whatsoever in the Church of God, if it be not of God, we hate it. Of God it must be; either as those things sometime were, which God supernaturally revealed, and so delivered them unto Moses for government of the commonwealth of Israel; or else as those things which men find out by help of that light which God hath given them unto that end. . . . But forasmuch as no Form of Church-Polity is thought by them to be lawful, or to be of God, unless God be so the author of it that it be also set down in Scripture; they should tell us plainly, whether their meaning be that it must be there set down in whole or in part. For if wholly, let them shew what one Form of Polity ever was so. Their own to be so taken out of Scripture they will not affirm; neither deny they that in part, even this which they so much oppugn is also from thence taken. Again, they should tell us, whether only that be taken out of Scripture which is actually and particularly there set down; or else that also which the general principles and rules of Scripture potentially contain. The one way they cannot as much as pretend, that all the parts of their own Discipline are in Scripture; and the other way their mouths are stopped when they would plead against all other Forms besides their own; seeing the general principles are such as do not particularly prescribe any one, but sundry may equally be consonant unto the general axioms of the Scripture. But to give them some larger scope, and not to close them up in these straits: let their allegations be considered, wherewith they earnestly bend themselves against all which

THE SCRIPTURAL FORM OF CHURCH POLITY   45

deny it necessary that any one complete Form of Church-Polity should be in Scripture. First, therefore, whereas it hath been told them that matters of Faith, and, in general, matters necessary unto Salvation, are of a different nature from Ceremonies, Order, and the kind of Church-government; that the one are necessary to be expressly contained in the Word of God, or else manifestly collected out of the same, the other not so; that it is necessary not to receive the one, unless there be something in Scripture for them; the other free, if nothing against them may thence be alleged. Although there do not appear any just or reasonable cause to reject or dislike of this; nevertheless, as it is not easy to speak to the contentation of minds exulcerated in themselves, but that somewhat there will be always which displeaseth; so herein for two things we are reported. The first is, misdistinguishing, because matters of Discipline and Church-government are [as they say] matters necessary to Salvation and of Faith, whereas we put a difference between the one and the other. Our second fault is, injurious dealing with the Scripture of God, as if it contained only the principal points of Religion, some rude and unfashioned matter of building the Church, but had left out that which belongeth unto the form and fashion of it; as if there were in the Scripture no more than only to cover the Church's nakedness, and not chains, bracelets, rings, jewels, to adorn her; sufficient to quench her thirst, to kill her hunger, but not to minister a more liberal and [as it were] a more delicious and dainty diet. In which case our apology shall not need to be very long.

The mixture of those things by speech which by Nature are divided, is the mother of all error. To take away therefore that error, which confusion breedeth, distinction is requisite. Rightly to distinguish, is by conceit of mind to sever things different in Nature, and to discern wherein they differ. So that if we imagine a difference where there is none, because we distinguish where we should not, it may not be denied that we misdistinguish. The only trial whether we do so, yea or no, dependeth upon comparison between our conceit and the nature of things conceived. Touching matters belonging unto the Church of Christ, this we conceive, that they are not of one suit. Some things are *merely* of Faith, which things it doth suffice that we know and believe; some things not only to be known but done, because they concern the actions of men. Articles about the Trinity are matters of mere Faith, and must be believed. Precepts concerning the works of charity are matters of action; which to know unless they be practised, is not enough. This being so clear to all men's understanding, I somewhat marvel that they especially should think it absurd to oppose Church-government, a plain matter of action, unto matters of Faith, who know that themselves divide the Gospel into Doctrine and Discipline. For if matters of Discipline be rightly by them distinguished from matters of Doctrine, why not matters of Government by us as reasonably set against matters of Faith? Do not they under Doctrine comprehend the same which we intend by matters of Faith? Do not they under Discipline comprise the Regiment of the Church? When they blame that in us which themselves follow, they give men great cause to doubt that some other thing than judgment doth guide their speech. What the Church of God standeth bound to know or do, the same in part Nature teacheth. And because Nature can teach them but only in part, neither so fully as is requisite for man's Salvation, nor so easily as to make the way plain and expedite enough that many may come to the knowledge of it, and so be saved; therefore in Scripture hath God both collected the most necessary things that the school of Nature teacheth unto that end, and revealeth also whatsoever we neither could with safety be ignorant of, nor at all be instructed in but by supernatural Revelation from him. So that Scripture containing all things that are in this kind any way needful for the Church, and the principal of the other sort, this is the next thing wherewith we are charged as with an error: We teach that whatsoever is unto salvation termed *necessary* by way of excellency; whatsoever it standeth all men upon to know or to do that they may be saved; whatsoever there is whereof it may truly be said, This not to believe, is eternal death and damnation; or, This every soul that will live, must duly observe; of which sort the Articles of Christian Faith, and the Sacraments of the Church of Christ, are; all such things if Scripture did not comprehend, the Church of God should not be able to measure out the length and the breadth of that way wherein for ever she is to walk; Heretics and Schismatics never ceasing, some to abridge, some to enlarge, all to pervert and obscure, the same. But as for those things that are accessory hereunto, those things that so belong to the way of Salvation as to alter them, is no otherwise to change that way, than a path is changed by altering only the uppermost face thereof; which be it laid with gravel, or set with grass, or paved with stone, remaineth still the same path; in such things, because discretion may teach the Church what is convenient, we hold not the Church further tied herein unto Scripture, than that against Scripture nothing be admitted in the Church, lest that path which ought always to be kept even, do thereby come to be overgrown with brambles and thorns. If this be unsound, wherein doth the point of unsoundness lie? It is not that we make some things *necessary,* some things *accessory* and appendent only: for our Lord and Saviour himself doth make that difference, by terming judgment, and mercy, and fidelity, with other things of like nature, "the greater and weightier matters of the Law." Is it then that we account Ceremonies (wherein we no not comprise Sacraments, or any other the like substantial duties in the exercise of Religion, but only of such external Rites as are usually annexed unto Church actions), is it an oversight that we reckon these things and matters of Government in the number of things accessory, not things necessary in such sort as hath been declared? Let them which therefore think us blameable consider well their own words. Do they not plainly compare the one unto garments, which cover the body of the Church: the other unto rings, bracelets, and jewels, that only adorn it? The one to that food which the Church doth live by, the other to that which maketh her diet liberal, dainty, and more delicious? Is dainty fare a thing necessary to the sustenance; or to the clothing of the body, rich attire? If not, how can they urge the necessity of that which themselves resemble by things not necessary? or by what construction shall any man living be able to make those comparisons true, holding that distinction untrue, which putteth a difference between things of external Regiment in the Church and things necessary unto Salvation. . . .

Of the Episcopal Form of Government

A thousand five hundred years and upward the Church of Christ hath now continued under the sacred Regiment of Bishops. Neither for so long hath Christianity been ever planted in any Kingdom throughout the world but with this kind of Government alone; which to have been ordained of God, I am for mine own part even as resolutely persuaded, as that any other kind of Government in the world whatsoever is of God. In this Realm of England, before Normans, yea before Saxons, there being Christians, the chief Pastors of their souls were Bishops. This Order from about the first establishment of Christian Religion, which was publicly begun through the virtuous disposition of King Lucie not fully two hundred years after Christ, continued till the coming in of the Saxons; by whom Paganism being everywhere else replanted, only one part of the Island, whereinto the ancient natural inhabitants, the Britons, were driven, retained constantly the Faith of Christ, together with the same form of spiritual regiment, which their fathers had before received. Wherefore in the Histories of the Church we find very ancient mention made of our own Bishops. At the Council of Ariminum, about the year three hundred and fifty-nine, Britain had three of her Bishops present. At the arrival of Augustine, the Monk, whom Gregory sent hither to reclaim the Saxons from Gentility about six hundred years after Christ, the Britons he found observers still of the selfsame Government by Bishops over the rest of the Clergy; under this form Christianity took root again, where it had been exiled. Under the selfsame form it remained till the days of the Norman Conqueror. By him and his successors thereunto sworn, it hath from that time till now, by the space of above five hundred years more, been upheld. O nation utterly without knowledge, without sense! We are not through error of mind deceived, but some wicked thing hath for undoubtedly be-witched us, if we forsake that Government, the use whereof universal ex-perience hath for so many years approved, and betake ourselves unto a Regiment neither appointed of God himself, as they who favour it pretend, nor till yesterday ever heard of among men. . . .

Great things are hoped for at the hands of these new Presidents, whom Reformation would bring in: notwithstanding the time may come, when Bishops, whose Regiment doth now seem a yoke so heavy to bear, will be longed for again, even by them that are the readiest to have it taken off their necks. But in the hands of divine Providence we leave the ordering of all such events, and come now to the Question itself which is raised con-cerning Bishops. For the better understanding whereof, we must before-hand set down what is meant, when in this question we name a Bishop.

For whatsoever we bring from Antiquity, by way of defence, in this cause of Bishops, it is cast off as impertinent matter; all is wiped away with an odd kind of shifting answer, That the Bishops which now are, be not like unto them which were. We therefore beseech all indifferent judges to weigh sincerely with themselves how the case doth stand. If it should be at this day a controversy whether Kingly Regiment were lawful or no, per-adventure in defence thereof, the long continuance which it hath had sith-ence the first beginning might be alleged; mention perhaps might be made what Kings there were of old, even in Abraham's time, what Sovereign Princes both before and after. Suppose that herein some man, purposely bending his wit against Sovereignty, should think to elude all such allega-tions by making ample discovery through a number of particularities, wherein the Kings that are, do differ from those that have been, and should therefore in the end conclude, that such ancient examples are no convenient proofs of that Royalty which is now in use. Surely for decision of truth in this case there were no remedy, but only to shew the nature of Sovereignty; to sever it from accidental properties; make it clear that an-cient and present Regality are one and the same in substance, how great odds soever otherwise may seem to be between them. In like manner, whereas a question of late hath grown, Whether Ecclesiastical Regiment by Bishops be lawful in the Church of Christ or no? in which question, they that hold the negative, being pressed with that general received Order, ac-cording whereunto the most renowned Lights of the Christian world have governed the same in every age as Bishops; seeing their manner is to reply, that such Bishops as those ancient were, ours are not, there is no remedy but to shew, That to be a Bishop is now the selfsame thing which it hath been; that one definition agreeth fully and truly as well to those elder, as to these latter, Bishops. Sundry Dissimilitudes we grant there are, which notwithstanding are not such that they cause any equivocation in the

Name, whereby we should think a Bishop in those times to have had a clean other definition than doth rightly agree unto Bishops as they are now. Many things there are in the state of Bishops, which the times have changed; many a Parsonage at this day is larger than some ancient Bishoprics were; many an ancient Bishop poorer than at this day sundry under them in degree. The simple hereupon, lacking judgment and knowledge to discern between the nature of things which changeth not, and these outward variable accidents, are made to believe that a Bishop heretofore and now are things in their very nature so distinct that they cannot be judged the same. Yet to men that have any part of skill, what more evident and plain in Bishops, than that augmentation or diminution in their precincts, allowances, privileges, and such like, do make a difference indeed, but no essential difference between one Bishop and another? As for those things in regard whereof we use properly to term them Bishops, those things whereby they essentially differ from other Pastors, those things which the natural definition of a Bishop must contain; what one of them is there more or less appliable unto Bishops now than of old? The name Bishop hath been borrowed from the Grecians, with whom it signifieth one which hath principal charge to guide and oversee others. The same word in Ecclesiastical Writing being applied unto Church-governors, at the first unto all and not unto the chiefest only, grew in short time peculiar and proper to signify such Episcopal authority alone, as the chiefest Governors exercised over the rest: for with all names this is usual, that inasmuch as they are not given till the things whereunto they are given have been sometime first observed; therefore generally, things are ancienter than the Names whereby they are called. . . .

But to let go the Name and come to the very nature of that thing which is thereby signified. In all kinds of Regiment, whether Ecclesiastical or Civil, as there are sundry operations public, so likewise great inequality there is in the same operations, some being of principal respect, and therefore not fit to be dealt in by everyone to whom public actions and those of good importance, are notwithstanding well and fitly enough committed. From hence have grown those different degrees of Magistrates or public persons, even Ecclesiastical as well as Civil. Amongst Ecclesiastical persons, therefore, Bishops being chief ones, a Bishop's Function must be defined by that wherein his Chiefty consisteth. A Bishop is a Minister of God, unto whom, with permanent continuance, there is given, not only power of administering the Word and Sacrament which power other Presbyters have; but also a farther power to ordain Ecclesiastical persons, and a power of chiefty in government over Presbyters as well as Laymen, a power to be by way of jurisdiction a Pastor even to Pastor themselves. So that his Office, as he is a Presbyter or Pastor, consisteth in those things which are common unto him with other Pastors, as in ministering the Word and Sacraments; but those things incident unto his Office, which do properly make him a Bishop, cannot be common unto him with other Pastors. Now even as Pastors, so likewise Bishops, being principal Pastors, are either at large or else with restraint: at large, when the subject of their Regiment is indefinite, and not tied to any certain place; Bishops with restraint, are those whose Regiment over the Church is contained within some definite, local compass, beyond which compass their jurisdiction reacheth not. Such therefore we always mean, when we speak of that Regiment by Bishops which we hold a thing most lawful, divine, and holy, in the Church of Christ. . . .

This we boldly therefore set down as a most infallible truth, That the Church of Christ is at this day lawfully, and so hath been sithence the first beginning, governed by Bishops having permanent Superiority and ruling Power over other Ministers of the Word and Sacraments.

ULRICH ZWINGLI (1484–1531)

On the Nature of the Sacraments

I believe, indeed I know, that all the sacraments are so far from conferring grace that they do not even convey or dispense it. In this matter, most
powerful Emperor, I may seem to thee perhaps too bold. But my opinion
is firm. For as grace comes from or is given by the Divine Spirit (when I
speak of grace I use the Latin term for pardon, i.e. indulgence or spontaneous favor), so this gift pertains to the Spirit alone. Moreover, a channel
or vehicle is not necessary to the Spirit, for He Himself is the virtue and
energy whereby all things are borne, and has no need of being borne; neither do we read in the Holy Scriptures that visible things, as are the sacraments, carry certainly with them the Spirit, but if visible things have ever
been borne with the Spirit, it has been the Spirit, not the visible things,
that have done the bearing.

Thus when the rush of the mighty wind took place (Acts 2:2) at the
same time the tongues were conveyed by the power of the wind; the wind
was not conveyed by the power of the tongues. Thus the wind brought the
quails and carried away the locusts (Num. 11:31ff.; Ex. 10:44ff.); but no
quails nor locusts were ever so fleet as to bring the wind. Likewise when a
wind, strong enough to remove mountains, passed Elijah (I Kings 19:11)
the Lord was not borne by the wind, etc. Briefly, the Spirit breathes wherever it wishes, i.e. just as the wind bloweth where it listeth, and thou hear-
est the sound thereof, and canst not tell whence it cometh and whither it
goeth, so is everyone that is born of the Spirit (John 3:8), i.e. invisibly and
imperceptibly illumined and drawn.

Thus the Truth [Christ] spake. Therefore, the Spirit of grace is conveyed not by this immersion, not by this drinking, not by that anointing.
For if it were thus, it would be known how, where, whence and whither
the Spirit is borne. If the presence and efficacy of grace are bound to the
sacraments, they work whithersoever they are carried; and where they are
not used, everything becomes feeble. Nor can theologians plead that the
proper disposition of the subject is demanded as a prerequisite [for the

right use of the sacraments]. For example, the grace of baptism or of the Eucharist [so they say] is conferred upon him who is first prepared for it. For he who according to their opinion receives grace through the sacraments, either prepares himself for it or is prepared by the Spirit. If he prepares himself, we can do something of ourselves and prevenient grace is nothing. If he is prepared by the Spirit for the reception of grace, I ask whether this be done through the sacraments as a channel or independent of the sacraments? If the sacraments mediate, man is prepared by the sacrament for the sacrament, and thus there will be a process *ad infinitum;* for a sacrament will be required as a preparation for a sacrament. But if we be prepared without the sacrament for the reception of sacramental grace, the Spirit is present in His goodness before the sacrament, and hence grace has been shown and is present before the sacrament is administered.

From this it follows (as I willingly and gladly admit in regard to the subject of the sacraments) that the sacraments are given as a public testimony of that grace which is previously present to every individual. Thus baptism is administered in the presence of the Church to one who before receiving it either confessed the religion of Christ or has the word of promise, whereby he is shown to belong to the Church. Hence it is that when we baptize an adult we ask him whether he believes. And only when he answers "yes," then he receives baptism. Faith therefore, has been present before he receives baptism, and is not given by baptism. But when an infant is offered, the question is asked whether its parents offer it for baptism. When they have answered through witnesses that they wish it baptized, then the infant is baptized. Here the promise of God precedes, that He regards our infants, no less than those of the Hebrews, as belonging to the Church. For when members of the Church offer it, the infant is baptized under the law that, since it has been born of Christians, it is regarded by the divine promise among the members of the Church. By baptism, therefore, the Church publicly receives one who has previously been received through grace. Hence baptism does not convey grace but the Church certifies that grace has been given to him to whom it is administered.

I believe, therefore, O Emperor, that a sacrament is a sign of a sacred thing, i.e. of grace that has been given. I believe that it is a visible figure or form of the invisible grace, provided and bestowed by God's bounty; i.e. a visible example which presents an analogy to something done by the Spirit. I believe that it is a public testimony. Thus when we are baptized the body is washed with the purest element; by this it is signified that by the grace of divine goodness we have been gathered into the assembly of the Church and of God's people, wherein we should live upright and pure. Thus Paul explains the mystery in Romans VI. The recipient of baptism testifies, therefore, that he belongs to the Church of God, which worships its Lord in soundness of faith and purity of life. For this reason the sacraments which are sacred ceremonies (for the Word is added to the element and it becomes a sacrament) should be religiously cherished, i.e., highly valued and treated with honor. For though they are unable to bestow grace, they nevertheless associate visibly with the Church us who have previously been received into it invisibly; and this should be regarded with the highest veneration, since with their administration the words of the divine promise are declared and pronounced.

For if we think otherwise of the sacraments, namely that their external use cleanses internally, it would be but a return to Judaism, which believed that, by various anointings, oblations, offerings, sacrifices and feasts, sins could be atoned and grace could be purchased and secured. Nevertheless, the prophets, especially Isaiah and Jeremiah, always most steadfastly urged in their teaching that the promises and benefits of God are given by God's free goodness, and not with respect to merits or external ceremonies.

On the Meaning of the Eucharist

I believe that in the holy Eucharist, i.e., in the supper of thanksgiving, the true body of Christ is present by the contemplation of faith. This means that they who thank the Lord for the benefits bestowed on us in His Son acknowledge that He assumed true flesh, in it truly suffered, truly washed away our sins by His blood; and thus everything done by Christ becomes as it were present to them by the contemplation of faith. But that the body of Christ in essence and really, i.e., the natural body itself, is either present in the supper or masticated with our mouth and teeth, as the Papists or some who look back to the fleshpots of Egypt assert, we not only deny, but constantly maintain to be an error, contrary to the Word of God. This, with the divine assistance, I will in a few words, make as clear as the sun to your majesty, O Emperor. First, by citing the divine oracles; secondly, by attacking the opponents with arguments derived therefrom, as with military engines; lastly, by showing that the ancient theologians held our opinion. Meanwhile, thou Creator, thou Spirit, be present, enlighten the minds of thy people, and fill with grace and light the hearts that thou hast created!

Christ Himself, the mouth and wisdom of God saith: "The poor ye have always with you; but me ye have not always" (John 12:8). Here the presence of the body alone is denied, for according to His divinity, He is always present, because He is always everywhere, according to His other word: "Lo, I am with you always, even unto the end of the world" (Matt. 28:20), viz. according to divinity, power and goodness. Augustine agrees with us. Neither is there any foundation for the assertion of the opponents that the humanity of Christ is wherever the divinity is, otherwise the person is divided; for this would destroy Christ's true humanity. Only the deity can be everywhere. That humanity is in one place, but divinity everywhere, divides the person just as little as the Son's assumption of humanity divides the unity of the divine essence. Indeed, it would be easier to effect a separation in the unity of essence if one person of the divine being would assume the form of a creature but the others not at all, than to separate the person if the humanity be at one place but the divinity everywhere; since we see even in creation that bodies are confined to one place, but their power and influence extend very far. An example is the sun, whose body is in one place, while his power pervades all things. The human mind also surmounts the stars and penetrates the underworld, but the body is nevertheless in one place.

Christ says also: "Again I leave the world and go to the Father" (John 16:28). Here the word "to leave" is used, just as "to have" before, so that the opponents cannot say: "We do not have Him visibly." For when He speaks of the visible withdrawal of His body, He says: "A little while and ye shall not see me," etc. (John 16:16). Neither would we maintain anything but a delusion if we were to contend that His natural body were present but invisible. For why should He evade sight, when He nevertheless would be here, who so often manifested himself to the disciples after the resurrection? "But it is expedient for you," He says, "that I go away" (John 16:7). But if He were here, it would be expedient that we should see Him. For as often as the disciples thought about seeing Him, He manifested Himself openly, so that neither sense nor thought might suffer in aught. "Handle me," He says; and "Be not afraid, it is I," and "Mary, touch me not," etc. (Luke 24:39; John 6:20; 20:17).

When in departing He commended His disciples to His Father, He said: "I am no more in the world" (John 17:11). Here we have a substantive verb ["I *am* no more in the world"], no less than in the words: "This *is* my body"; so that the opponents cannot say that there is a trope here, since they deny that substantives admit of the trope. But the case has no need of such arguments, for there follows: "But these are in the world." This antithesis clearly teaches that He was not, according to His human nature, in the world at a time when His disciples were.

And that we may know when He took His departure—not, as they invent rather than explain, when He made Himself invisible—Luke says: "While he blessed them he was parted from them, and carried up into heaven" (Luke 24:51). He does not say: "He vanished," or "rendered himself invisible." About this Mark says: "After the Lord had spoken to them he was received up into heaven, and sat at the right hand of God" (Mark

16:19). He does not say: "He remained here, but rendered his body invisible." Again Luke says in Acts: "When he had said these things, as they were looking, he was taken up; and a cloud received him out of their sight" (Acts 1:9). A cloud covered Him, of which there would have been no need if He had only removed His appearance but otherwise had continued to be present. Nor would there have been any need of removal and elevation. Again: "This same Jesus, who was taken up from you into heaven, shall so come in like manner as ye beheld him going into heaven" (Acts 1:11). What is clearer than this? "From you," He says, "he was taken up": therefore, He was not with them visibly or invisibly, according to His human nature. When, then, we shall see Him return as He departed, we shall know that He is present. Otherwise He sits, according to His human nature, at the right hand of His Father until He will return to judge the quick and the dead.

But since there are some who deprive the body of Christ of restriction to a place and say that He is not in a place, let them see how clearly, and with closed eyes, they oppose the truth. He was in the manger, on the cross, at Jerusalem when His parents were on their journey home; in the sepulchre and out of the sepulchre; for the angel says: "He is risen, he is not here: behold the place where they laid him" (Mark 16:6). And that they may not be able to say that His body is everywhere, let them hear: "When the doors were shut, Jesus came and stood in their midst" (John 20:19). What need had He of coming if His Body was everywhere, but invisible? It would have been enough to come, but merely as one who was present to manifest Himself. But let such sophistical trifles be gone, which rob us of the truth both of Christ's humanity and of the Holy Scriptures.

These testimonies deny the presence of Christ's body anywhere but in heaven, scripturally speaking, i.e., as far as scripture tells us about the nature and properties of the body assumed by Christ. And however far the contradictions, which are involved in our propositions regarding the power of God, drive us, we ought not to wrest it to such a point that we believe that God acts contrary to His Word. That would be a sign of impotence, not of power. Moreover, that the natural body of Christ is not eaten with our mouth, He Himself showed us when He said to the Jews, disputing about the corporeal eating of His flesh: "The flesh profiteth nothing" (John 6:63), namely, eaten naturally, but eaten spiritually it profits much, for it gives life.

"That which is born of the flesh is flesh; and that which is born of the Spirit is spirit" (John 3:6). If, therefore, the natural body of Christ is eaten with our mouth, what else than flesh can come out of flesh, eaten naturally? And lest anyone think lightly of this argument, let him hear the second part: "That which is born of the Spirit is spirit." Therefore, that which is spirit is born of the Spirit. If then the flesh is salutary to the soul, it should be eaten spiritually, not carnally. This applies also to the sacraments, that spirit is born of Spirit, and not of any corporeal matter, as we have already indicated.

Paul announces that if he once knew Christ according to the flesh, henceforth, he would know Him no more after the flesh (II Cor. 5:16).

In view of these passages we are compelled to confess that the words: "This is my body," should not be understood naturally, but figuratively, just as the words: "This is Jehovah's passover" (Ex. 12:11). For the lamb that was eaten every year with the celebration of the festival was not the passing over of the Lord, but it signified that such a passing over had formerly taken place. Besides there is the temporal succession, in that the Lord's Supper followed the eating of the lamb; which reminds us that Christ used words similar to those employed at the passover, for succession leads to imitation. Moreover, the arrangement of the words is the same. The time affords an additional argument, since in the same evening meal the passover was discontinued and the new act of thanksgiving was instituted. . . . Now follow the proofs:

As the body cannot be nourished by a spiritual substance, so the soul cannot be nourished by a corporeal substance. But if the natural body of Christ is eaten, I ask whether it feeds the body or the soul? Not the body, hence the soul. If the soul, then the soul eats flesh, and it would not be true that spirit is only born of Spirit.

In the second place, I ask: What does the body of Christ, eaten naturally, bring about? If it be the forgiveness of sins, as one party claims, then the disciples obtained forgiveness of sins in the Lord's Supper, and therefore, Christ died in vain. If that which is eaten imparts the virtue of Christ's passion, as the same party claims, then the virtue of the passion and redemption was dispensed before it had taken place. If the body is fed for the resurrection, as another [Luther] very ignorantly asserts, much more would the sacrament heal our body and deliver it from sickness. But Irenaeus wants to be understood differently, when he says that our body is nourished by Christ's body for the resurrection. For he desires to show that the hope of our resurrection is strengthened by Christ's resurrection. Behold, what an appropriate figure of speech!

Thirdly—If the natural body of Christ was given to the disciples in the Supper, it necessarily follows that they ate it as it then was. But it was then capable of suffering; hence they ate a vulnerable body, for it was not yet glorified. For if they say: They ate the same body, yet not as it was capable of suffering, but the same as it was after the resurrection, I reply: Either He had two bodies, one not yet glorified and another glorified, or one and the same body was at the same time capable of suffering and incapable. And so, since He dreaded death so much He was doubtless unwilling to suffer, but wanted to make use of that bodily endowment, by virtue of which He was free from pain. Therefore He did not truly suffer, but only by appearance; in this way Marcion is again brought back by these blindfolded gladiators. Six hundred arguments could be adduced, O Emperor, but we shall be content with these.

Moreover, that the ancients agree with us on the last part of this article I shall now establish by two witnesses, both of the first rank, viz.:

By Ambrose, who in the [Commentary on the] First Epistle to the Corinthians says concerning the words: "Ye do show forth the Lord's death," etc.: "Mindful that by the Lord's death we have been freed, we signify in our eating and drinking the flesh and the blood which were offered for us," etc. Now Ambrose is speaking of the food and drink of the Supper, and asserts that we signify those things which were offered for us.

By Augustine also, who in his thirtieth discourse on John affirms that the body of Christ which rose from the dead must be in one place. Here the printed copies have "can be" instead of "must be," but incorrectly, for in the Master of the "Sentences" [Peter Lombard] and the Canonical Decrees [of Gratian], in which this opinion of Augustine is quoted, the reading is "must." By this we plainly see that whatever the ancients said so excellently concerning the Supper, they thought not of the natural but of the spiritual eating of Christ's body. For since they knew that the body of Christ must be in one place, and that it is at the right hand of God, they did not withdraw it thence to submit it for mastication to the foul teeth of men.

Augustine likewise teaches in the twelfth chapter "Against Adimantus" that the three expressions: "The blood is the life," and "This is my body" and "The rock was Christ," were spoken symbolically, i.e., as he himself says, in a figure and figuratively. And among many other things he at length comes to these words: "I can interpret that command as given for a sign. For the Lord did not hesitate to say: 'This is my body,' when He was giving a sign of His body." Thus far Augustine. Lo, a key for us whereby we can unlock all the declarations of the ancients concerning the Eucharist! That which is only a sign of the body, he says, is called the body.

Let them who wish go now and condemn us for heresy, only let them know that by the same process they are condemning the opinions of the theologians, contrary to the decrees of the Pontiffs. For from these facts it becomes very evident that the ancients always spoke figuratively when they attributed so much to the eating of the body of Christ in the Supper; meaning, not that sacramental eating could cleanse the soul but faith in God through Jesus Christ, which is spiritual eating, whereof this external eating is but symbol and shadow. And as bread sustains the body and wine enlivens and exhilarates, thus it strengthens the soul and assures it of God's mercy that He has given us His Son; thus it renews the mind by the confidence that, by His blood, the sins with which it was being consumed were destroyed. With these passages we shall now rest content, although any one could compile whole volumes in expounding and confirming the fact that the ancients are of our opinion.

PHILIP MELANCHTHON (1496–1560)

The Nature of Justification

In a worldly sense it is obvious that justification means conformity to the law. . . . To speak of complete, perfect justification of the law before God, such as that which angels have and men who are saved will have in eternity, is to speak of justification as conformity with God, which is as much as to say, with God's law; for God is thus as he gives himself to be known in the law.

This perfect justification in eternity means God himself is in the saved. As St. Paul says, "God will be all in all" (cf. I Cor. 15:28; 12:6; Col. 3:11), that is, God himself is in the saved and makes them like himself, so that they are entirely pure, without sin. . . .

Although in this mortal life believers have a spark, the gospel nevertheless preaches to us the justification of *Christ,* of the *Mediator* between God and us, and says that the Mediator's entire obedience, from his Incarnation until the Resurrection, is the true justification which is pleasing to God, and is the merit for us. God forgives us our sins, and accepts us, in that he imputes righteousness to us for the sake of the Son, although we are still weak and sinful. We must, however, accept this imputed righteousness with faith.

So now in this moral life, that by which we are pleasing to God is the righteousness of *Christ,* which is imputed to us. We receive forgiveness of sins, and are pleasing to God for the sake of the Christ, namely on account of his obedience, as St. Paul says, Romans 5:19, "By one man's [namely *Christ's*] obedience many will be made righteous."

Thus we are clothed with a strange righteousness. Although our nature itself is still not uniform with God, nevertheless, as the Mediator Christ in his complete obedience is uniform with God and covers our sins with his righteousness, so we are justified, have forgiveness of sins, and are pleasing to God, for *Christ's* sake, whose righteousness is accepted on our behalf. And this we must accept *with faith.* . . .

In all this Christ effects life in us and gives us the Holy Spirit, and eternal righteousness is begun in us, as written in John's letter: "He who has the Son has life" (I Jn. 5:12). To have the Son is to receive him in faith; God gives us, for the sake of his Son, forgiveness of sins, and accepts us. The Son speaks this comfort to us and gives us his Holy Spirit, who kindles love and joy to God in our hearts, as written in the same letter, "By this we know that we abide in him and he in us, because he has given us of his own Spirit" (I Jn. 4:13).

Now the Holy Spirit is a living divine motion in us, producing in us that which is akin to God, of which Jeremiah speaks in the thirty-first chapter, "I will put my law within them, and I will write it upon their hearts" (v. 33). God is as he reveals himself in the law: wise, true, good, just, pure, and chaste; one who punishes sin. And when he says he wants to give us his law in our hearts, this signifies that the Son of God reveals to us the wisdom of the eternal Father through the gospel, that we may recognize the Father. He also gives us the Holy Spirit, who produces in us joy to God, cleanness of heart and other virtues, as the law teaches. Thus there is a spark of new obedience in those who are converted to God; but the faith that *for the sake of the Lord Christ* we have forgiveness of sins, and are pleasing to God, must always precede, and this faith must be grounded on the *obedience of the Lord Christ,* God and Man. When this comfort is in the heart, then we are the dwelling place of God and obedience is begun. . . .

This definition is also in the words of Paul. By *are justified* he means this comfort in the midst of true anguish, forgiveness of sins received through faith, and being pleasing to God for the sake of the Lord Christ. But the renewal that follows, which God effects in us, he calls *sanctification,* and these two words are clear and distinct.

These words and the doctrine itself are further clarified in the following counter arguments. . . .

The first argument: Since the devils also believe [have faith], how then can belief be that whereby a man is justified?

Answer: The devils believe only the history, they do not believe that the Son of God has come to them for good. Yes, they know that he will punish them in eternity, and for this reason they rage against God and against the Son of God. In hate, they blaspheme God among themselves, and they drive poor wretched men to idolatry, murder, immorality, and other vices.

However, we should firmly believe that the Son of God is sent to us for good, as expressed in the symbol, "who for the sake of men and for our salvation came down from heaven." . . . The devils in their knowledge do not believe that forgiveness of sins is given to them; they see nothing but wrath and punishment; and, therefore, furious hate follows. . . .

The second argument: Since it is quite impossible to be justified by knowledge only, and as faith is a matter of knowledge and thought, and not some power of will and heart, how then is a man to be justified through faith?

Answer: The faith of which St. Paul speaks when he says, "Since we are justified through faith, we have peace with God," is not only knowledge and thought but something in the will and heart, a burning reliance on the Son of God, an earnest, ardent desire and will to accept the precious treasure, forgiveness of sins and grace. It cries out to God, Dear Father! As St. Paul says in Romans 8:15, "God has placed the Spirit of his Son in your hearts, which cries, 'Abba, dear Father!' "

As far as heaven and hell are from one another, so far are we to separate this *true faith* from the *knowledge* that the devil and godless men possess. What true faith is, and how it shines in men, is learned only when, in the midst of great anguish, we are again quickened, and drawn out of the vengeance of hell. . . . Thus this faith is not simply a knowledge and thought that men by themselves produce: it is a light and joy which the Son of God produces through the gospel and the Holy Spirit. . . .

The third argument: Why say that we have forgiveness of sins and are justified *only* through faith? Surely many virtues must accompany faith, repentance and sorrow for sins, belief, good resolution, and hope.

Answer: The exclusive *sola* or *gratis* must be fully maintained, as will be explained later more adequately. It shuts out *all our merit;* it teaches that we receive forgiveness of sins and are justified *for the sake of Christ alone,* that is, we are pleasing to God, and the heart must receive this with faith. This great grace is given through the knowledge of Christ, as Isaiah says. This knowledge is the faith about which we speak. Here an order is established by God that makes a distinction between God's children and others. The children of God are those who thus recognize Christ and accept him with faith. There must be an *application* of the grace of Christ; and this *application* occurs through faith, and faith results from preaching, contemplation of the gospel, and the sacraments.

And it is true, as indicated in the explanation of the second argument, that where true faith is, there at the same time are many virtues. However, they are not meritorious; they are not *causae justificationis;* they are not reasons why God accepts us. They result from faith; as indicated above, we receive grace and gift. As the sun has both light and the power to warm, and the two cannot be separated, so wherever there is true faith, a recognition of God's mercy, there also is love, invocation of God, and hope, and a will which willingly subjects itself to God, and is obedient. These accompany faith as light and heat accompany a fire. Nevertheless, there is no merit in these virtues. Merit lies only in the faith by which we receive forgiveness of our sins, and is received *for the sake of the Christ.* This we receive in the word and through the word; the Lord Christ is active through the gospel.

Why must we firmly maintain *Exclusivam: fide sola* or *gratis?*

Answer: For five reasons. The first, so that Christ may be given his special honor, for *his* obedience *alone* is merit for us. On his account God is willing to forgive us our sins, receive us graciously, and make us heirs of eternal blessedness; and *our* wretched deeds, sufferings, and works *do not* merit this exalted grace.

The second reason is that God in his great mercy wants the grace which he has offered to men in his promise to stand certain, firm, and immovable, for the promise is called an eternal testament. This comfort is certain if it is grounded *only on the Son of God* and *not* on our merit. For this reason we say, *Only* through faith may the heart be assured that God is gracious, for the sake of Christ. If this depended on our merit, it would not only be uncertain, but the promise would be empty, for in this wretched life we always have much sin, ignorance, and transgression. Paul says, "Therefore, *out of faith, without merit on our part,* the promise remains firm."

The third reason is that there is no other means whereby we acknowledge and accept the Lord Christ and his grace except by *faith alone.* God's unchangeable counsel is that there be a clear distinction between the children of God and other men, that the Son of God be rightly known by the children of God; this knowledge is faith. Faith hears the preaching of the gospel, in which Christ and his grace are conveyed to us, and faith accepts. When we recognize God's mercy, the heart is revived and drawn out of hell. And therefore it is crude to say, *Fides apprehensiva et quietativa.*

The fourth reason: so that the distinction between law and the gospel may be clear. The law says that when we are as the law commands, then we are justified. But no man, with the exception of our Lord and Savior Christ, is as the law teaches. But when we *believe in the Son of God,* we have forgiveness of sins, and we are pleasing to God *for the sake of Christ,* freely, without any merit on our part, although our sinful nature is very unlike the law.

The fifth reason: so that we may be able to call on God. Without this Mediator, the Son of God, we could not approach God. If invocation depended on our merit, then the heart would flee from God. Therefore, the Lord says, we are to invoke in *his* name, that is, *in the faith* that he is the Mediator and High Priest who bears our prayer before God and that we are heard *for the sake of his merit.*

The fourth argument. Why do you say, "Not out of works"? Is faith itself not also a work?

Answer: When one says, "Through faith we have forgiveness and are justified," this, according to Paul, means *for the sake of the Lord Christ and through him* we have forgiveness of sins and are justified, or pleasing to God, but not on account of our works or virtues. Nevertheless, we must accept Christ, through faith, for God wants this Savior, his Son, to be known; and he wants to gather to himself an eternal Church through knowledge of the gospel, through which the Son of God himself works and gives comfort and life. He wants a distinction to be made between the heathen and us; therefore he must enlighten us with knowledge of the Lord and true faith. No distinction would be possible between us and the heathen if God saved men without knowledge of Christ and without faith! This we should consider diligently, and also know that we have forgiveness of sins, and are pleasing to God, for the sake of Christ the *Mediator,* who presents his obedience for us, and is our Intercessor, not on account of the worthiness of our virtues.

The fifth argument. Righteousness is uniformity with, or fulfillment of, the entire law, and to this belongs not only faith, but love and all the other virtues, so why say, *sola fide,* "by faith *alone"?*

Answer: It is legal language to say that righteousness is uniformity with the divine law or with God, or that it is the fulfillment of the entire law, or as Osiander childishly says, Righteousness is that which makes us do right. All this is legal language. The blessed are justified, that is, one with the law in that God himself is in them and enlightens them, and gives to them his light, so that they are one with him, without any sin, for as Paul says, "God will be all in all."

In this weak life we do not have perfect righteousness. Therefore, the gospel preaches to us about forgiveness of sins, and says how a poor sinner may come to God, obtain forgiveness, and become pleasing to him. The gospel calls this an imputed righteousness, for the sake of Christ. *Christ's obedience,* accordingly, is the oneness with God which is received on our behalf, and with which we are clothed so that the wrath of God is not poured over us, and does not destroy our wretched nature.

Clearly, in this mortal life we cannot approach God and invoke him unless we first receive forgiveness of sins and are justified, or pleasing to God, on account of *Christ,* whose righteousness is accepted for us, and who clothes us. This occurs *only through faith,* when the heart in true anguish trusts on the Mediator *Jesus Christ,* God and Man; all the prophets, Christ himself, and the apostles teach this about invocation. . . .

The sixth argument: Solomon says, "Man does not know whether he pleases God or not" (cf. Prov. 21:2; II Chron. 6:36). Then why say that we must believe that we have forgiveness of sins and are justified, that is, are pleasing to God?

Answer: The monks have ushered into the Church a frightful blindness; they stubbornly fight for an error, for they say that man shall always doubt whether he is pleasing to God. They falsely interpret the passage in Solomon, and yet recently, just six years ago, they established their devilish error in the Council of Trent. Over against this it is very necessary to know and to uphold the true doctrine of faith. Such blind error should be clearly and openly rebuked.

We boldly say that all men who are not converted to God and who persist in their sins against conscience certainly do not know that they are not in God's grace, and if they are not converted, they will surely fall into eternal punishment. . . .

Truly, all men ought to obey God and hear the Son Jesus Christ, for the divine voice states, "To this [my Son] shall you listen" (Mt. 17:5; Mk. 9:7; Lk. 9:35). He punishes sin; to those who truly tremble before God's wrath and do not persist in sins against the conscience, to those who desire to have comfort and salvation, he will give forgiveness of sins and grace. Terrified consciences are obliged to believe that God gives to them for the sake of Christ, without merit of their own, forgiveness of sins, and that God receives them into grace through faith. They are not to remain mired in doubt. Doubt in the terrified heart is a deep, terrible anger against God, which blocks invocation, as the experience of true anguish shows. Christians are to understand this struggle in the heart.

Romans 4 indicates that we should not remain mired in doubt, "Because the promise rests *on faith, without merit.*" There Paul teaches that one must receive the promise with faith, that for him who does not receive it with faith, but remains in doubt, the promise is vain. . . .

Romans 5:1: "Therefore, since we are justified by faith, we have peace with God." Doubt is a deep anger against God, and finally plunges men into despair and hellish anger and fury. And when man remains in doubt, there is no true invocation, for St. Paul asks, "How can they pray if they do not believe" (Rom. 10:14)?

When we repeat the Creed, saying, "I believe in the forgiveness of sins" we should understand that this means not only that the sins of others, of Peter or Paul, are forgiven, but that *our own* sins are forgiven. The passages about faith serve to strengthen this belief.

But the weak heart says, "Ah, I find much impurity in myself; how then can I be pleasing to God?" Answer: The faith in the men who are converted to God is not grounded on their own purity, but on the Son of God. They should hold to the promise written in Psalm 130:5, "I wait for the Lord, and in his word I hope." And the passage in Augustine is true, for he shows in his book on meditation that the entire certainty of trust depends on the noble blood of Christ. . . .

The seventh argument: In I Corinthians 13:2 St. Paul says, "If I have all faith, but have not love, I am nothing." Also I John 3:14, "He who does not love remains in death." These and many similar passages are cited against the *Exclusivam: sola fide,* "by faith *alone.*"

Answer: These and similar passages say that love and a new obedience must be in us; that is true. However, love and new obedience do not merit forgiveness or cause a person to be pleasing to God. A person has forgiveness and is pleasing to God *for the sake of the Mediator alone,* whom one appropriates only by *faith,* and Christ gives His Holy Spirit, who is the flame of true love and joy in God. This single true answer explains many passages.

The eighth argument: In I Corinthians 13, St. Paul says that love is the greatest virtue. Now if it is greater than faith, then it appears to follow that one is more justified for the sake of love than for the sake of faith.

Answer: The reason we have forgiveness of sins and are justified before God, that is, pleasing to God, is *Christ alone.* He is many hundred thousands of times greater than all virtues, all angels, and all men, and this Lord Christ we must recognize and accept with faith.

Which virtues among themselves are greater or smaller is a teaching of the law, and has nothing to do with the comfort of faith. We should remember that all our works and virtues begun in this wretched life are very weak. All of them belong in the category of which Job declares, "I know truly that no man is justified before God" (cf. 9:2–3, 28); however, the Son of God is our Mediator and Reconciler, and places before the eternal Father *his* obedience. *For this Reconciler's sake* we are justified by grace, that is, we have forgiveness of sins and are pleasing to God. . . .

HEINRICH BULLINGER (1504–1575)

Of the Holy Catholic Church

The order and course of things so leading us, next after God, the workman and author of all things, we come to speak of his most excellent work, that is, the Church. For so great is the goodness of our good God and most loving Father, that he does not desire to live happily and blessedly alone, but rather to bestow and pour upon us men, his beloved creatures, all kinds of blessedness; and that we should enjoy his goods in every possible way. And to that end he chooses to himself men who live in this world, that he may sometime translate them to himself: in whom also (even while they live here) he may dwell, whom he may enrich with all his goods, in whom he may reign; and that they should be called by his name, that is a people, a house, a kingdom, an inheritance, a flock, a congregation or Church, of the living God. Of which Church (being aided by your prayers) I will speak such things as the Lord of the Church shall grant unto me to utter.

The word *Ecclesia,* which signifies a church or congregation, is a Greek word, used and received among the Latins, signifying, as I said, a congregation, communion, or assembly [in German *ein Gemeind*], or a people called together to hear matters of the common good; for that is how St. Luke is found to use the word in the nineteenth chapter of the Acts. But it was translated to a holy use, and began to be called a congregation, assembly, or company of the faithful, calling upon the name of the Lord. St. Paul says that he persecuted the congregation or Church of God, and in another place he says: "I received authority from the high priests to bind all those that call upon the name of Christ." Those whom in the first passage he terms the Church in the second he describes as those that call upon the name of Christ. Elsewhere the word *Ecclesia,* the church or congregation, is indicative of a calling forth together; for in the Greek tongue *ekkaleo* means to call forth. For God calls forth from all parts of the wide world, and from all the congregation of men, all believers and their seed, that they may be his peculiar people, and he again may be their God; that is to say, that they may be the Church of the living God. . . .

The Church is the whole company and multitude of the faithful, as it is partly in heaven and partly remains still upon earth; and as it agrees plainly in unity of faith or true doctrine, and in the lawful partaking of the sacraments: for it is not divided, but united and joined together as it were in one house and fellowship.

This Church is usually called catholic, that is to say, universal. For it sends out its branches into all places of the wide world, in all times and all ages; and it comprehends generally all the faithful the whole world over. For the Church of God is not tied to any one region, nation or kindred; to condition, age, sex, or kind: all the faithful generally and each one in particular, wherever they may be, are citizens and members of this Church. St. Paul the apostle says: "There is neither Jew nor Greek, neither bondman nor free, neither man nor woman: for ye be all one in Christ Jesus."

The Church is distinguished into the two parts, the Church triumphant and the Church militant. The Church triumphant is the great company of holy spirits in heaven, triumphing because of the victory which has now been won against the world, and sin and the devil, and enjoying the vision of God, in which there consists the fulness of all kinds of joy and pleasure, and concerning which they set forth God's glory and praise his goodness for ever. . . .

The Church militant is a congregation of men upon earth, professing the name and religion of Christ, and still fighting in the world against the devil, sin, the flesh and the world, in the camp and tents and under the banner of our Lord Christ. This Church again must be taken in two ways. For either it must be taken strictly, in which case it comprises only those who are not only called but are in actual fact the Church, the faithful and elect of God, lively members, knit unto Christ not merely with outward bands or marks but in spirit and faith, and often by the latter without the former, of which we shall speak later. This inward and invisible Church of God may well be termed the elect bride of Christ, known only to God, who alone knows who are his. It is this Church especially which we confess when we say as we are instructed in the Apostles' Creed: "I believe in the holy Catholic Church, the Communion of Saints." . . .

Or the Church in the wider sense comprises not only those who are truly faithful and holy, but also those who although they have no true or unfeigned faith and are not clean and holy in the conversation of their lives do acknowledge and profess true religion together with true believers and holy men of God, approving and accepting virtues and reproving evil, and not as yet separating themselves from the unity of this holy Church militant. . . .

But as we began to say, the catholic Church of God has continued with us from age to age from the very first, and at this very time it is dispersed throughout the whole world, both visibly and invisibly; and the Lord's people and God's house shall remain upon the earth to the world's end. For there has never yet been any world, neither shall there be any age, in which God has not sanctified or will not sanctify some men to himself, in whom he may dwell, and that they shall be his flock and holy house; . . .

But as Christ has always had his Church here upon earth, and still has, and shall have for ever, so too the devil, as long as the world continues, shall never be without his people in whom he may reign. This church of the devil had its first beginning with Cain, and shall continue to the last wicked person, comprising all those evil peoples that have been in the meantime and shall be between the beginning and the end. But even while they live here upon earth, these have society and communion with those who are tormented in hell. For just as all the good are one body under the one head Christ, so all the wicked are one incorporate body under one head Satan. . . .

Now since we have said that the Church militant upon earth is marked by God with certain tokens and marks by which it may be known in this world, it follows that we must now speak of those outward marks of the Church of God. And there are two particular and principal marks, the sincere preaching of the Word of God, and the lawful partaking of the sacraments of Christ. There are some who add to these the study of godliness and unity, patience in affliction, and the calling on the name God by Christ, but we include these in the two already mentioned. St. Paul writing to the Ephesians says: "Christ gave himself for the congregation, that he might sanctify it, and cleanse it in the fountain of water through the word." In this testimony of the apostles you have the marks of the Church, that is, the Word and the sacrament by which Christ makes to himself a Church. For with his grace he calls, with the blood of Christ he purifies: and he proclaims this by his Word to be received with faith, and seals it with sacraments, in order that the faithful should have no doubts concerning their salvation obtained through Christ. . . .

Having treated of the marks of the Church, we must now add that it is as a common rule that these marks declare and note the members of the Church. For there are certain special members who although they lack these marks are not excluded from the society and communion of the true Church of Christ. For it is most certain that there are many in the world who do not hear the ordinary preaching of God's Word, or come into the company of those that call upon God, or receive the sacraments: not because they despise them, or find pleasure in being absent from sermons and the preaching of God's Word, but because through necessity, such as imprisonment or sickness or the constraint of other evils, they cannot attain to that which they earnestly desire; and yet for all that they are true and lively members of Christ and of the catholic Church. . . .

Therefore the Word and sacraments are by common decree the marks of the Church, but they do not separate or mark off from the communion and society of the faithful those believers who by some necessity are shut out from the visible company of the faithful. . . .

Apart from these outward marks of the Church which true believers have in common with hypocrites, there are certain inward marks which belong especially to the godly alone: or if you prefer, call them rather bonds or peculiar gifts. It is these which make the outward marks to be fruitful and make men worthy and acceptable in the sight of God if for some necessary cause the outward marks are absent. For without them no man can please God. Therefore in them we have the true mark of God's children. They are the fellowship of God's Spirit, a sincere faith, and twofold charity, for by these the faithful, as true and lively members of Christ, are united and knit together, first to their head Christ, and then to all members of the body ecclesiastical. And the consideration of this point belongs chiefly to the knowledge of the true Church of God, which although it tolerates rotten members is not defiled by them through their outward conjunction, for by continual study it labours by all means to keep itself undefiled to God. And first of all the evangelical and apostolic doctrine teaches us that Christ is joined to us by his Spirit, and that we are tied to him in mind or spirit by faith, that he may live in us and we in him. . . .

Therefore Christ our Lord is joined unto us in spirit, and we are tied to him in mind and faith, as the body to the head. Therefore those who lack this knot and bond, that is, who have not the Spirit of Christ, nor true faith in Christ, are not the true and lively members of Christ, the Lord himself in the Gospel again witnessing and saying: "If a man abide not in me, he is cast forth as a branch, and withereth; and men gather them, and cast them into the fire, and they burn." In imitation of these words of our Saviour the apostle (as we have just quoted) says: "He that hath not the Spirit of Chirist is none of his." But those who are not destitute of the Spirit of Christ are inflamed with the love of God. Nor do we separate love from faith, for the same St. John teaches us the second time and says: "God is love; and he that dwelleth in love dwelleth in God, and God in him." For the Lord says in the Gospel: "If a man love me, he will keep my word; and my Father will love him, and we will come unto him, and will dwell with him."

But although, strictly, faith joins us to our head Christ, yet it also knits us to all Christ's members upon earth. For since there is amongst them only one faith, and therefore the same Spirit, there can only be the same mouth, the same mind and the same sentence, even though faith be understood not only as a confidence in the mercy of God through Christ, but also as an outward confession of faith. For as we all confess one faith and one and the same head, with one spirit and mouth we also profess together that we are all members of one and the same body. Nor is there anything in the world that more unappeasably dissevereth the minds of men than the diversity of faith or religion; and therefore there is nothing that can more closely join us together than unity of faith.

We now come to speak of love, which, I said, joins together the members of the body ecclesiastical mutually among themselves. The Lord says in the Gospel: "A new commandment give I unto you, that ye love one another; as I have loved you, that ye also love one another. By this shall all men know that ye are my disciples, if ye have love one to another." There is therefore no doubt that after faith the only mark of the Church is love, a bond which most firmly knits together all the members. It grows from the communion of Christ and unity of the Spirit. For since Christ, the king, the head and high bishop of the catholic Church, enduing us all with one and the same Spirit, has made us all his members, the sons of God, brethren and fellow-heirs, whom without doubt he tenderly loves, the faithful man can only with fervent love embrace the members and fellow-heirs of their kind, their head and their high bishop. For John the apostle says: "Every one that loveth him that begat, doth love him also that is born of him. If any man say, I love God, and hateth his brother, he is a liar: for how can he that loveth not his brother whom he hath seen, love God whom he hath not seen?" Paul, in order most properly to express for us and as it were to set before our eyes this unity and agreement of the members, uses a parable taken from the members of a man's body, saying: "For as we have many members in one body, and all members have not one office; so we being many are one body in Christ, and every one one another's members." . . . From all this it appears that the marks of the true and lively Church of Christ are the communion of the Spirit of Christ, sincere faith, and Christian charity, without which no man is a partaker of this spiritual body. And by these things you may easily judge whether you are in the fellowship of the Church or not.

Moreover, from what we have already discussed concerning the marks of Christ's Church we gather what is the source of the Church and how it is planted, propagated and preserved. Its source is heavenly, for St. Paul speaking of the Church says: "Jerusalem which is above is free, which is the mother of us all." Therefore he calls the Church heavenly, not because it dwells completely in heaven, but because although it is on earth it has a heavenly beginning. For the children of God are not born of flesh and blood, but from heaven, by the renewing of the Holy Spirit, who through the preaching of God's Word plants faith in our hearts, by which faith we are made the true members of Christ and his Church. . . .

Therefore, since faith comes by hearing, and hearing by the Word of God, and that distinctly, the Church cannot possibly spring up or be built up by the decrees and doctrines of men. Hence we affirm that only the Word of God is apt for the building up of the Church of God. The doctrines of men set up the churches of men, but Christ's Word builds up the Christian Church. For the doctrines of men proceed from flesh and blood. But Peter, confessing Christ with a true faith, and therefore grounded upon Christ who is the foundation of the Church, heard these words from Christ himself: "Flesh and blood hath not revealed these things unto thee, but my Father which is in heaven." And therefore Paul says: "When it pleased God that I should preach his Son among the Gentiles, I conferred not of the matter with flesh and blood," etc. And obviously excluding all doctrines of men from the setting up and establishing of faith and the Church, and commending only the Word of God, he says to the Corinthians: "My word and preaching stood not in the enticing speech of man's wisdom, but in plain evidence of the Spirit, and of power; that your faith should not be in the wisdom of men, but in the power of God." . . .

It seems to me that in this context we may not inappropriately handle or briefly expound the famous question, Whether the Church of God may err? In order that it may be better understood I will briefly discuss the parts of this question. I have taught that the catholic Church of God comprises, first the blessed spirits in heaven, then all faithful Christians here on earth: to whom I said that the wicked or hypocrites belong in that they feign faith for a time. Now, therefore, if we understand by the Church the blessed spirits in heaven the Church can never err. But if we understand the wicked or hypocrites joined and mingled with the good, and the wicked alone, they do not do anything else but err, but as they are joined unto the good and faithful and follow them, they either err or do not err. For the Church of the good and the faithful on earth both errs and does not err. This we will declare when we have weighed the diversities of errors and gathered them all together in a bundle. There are some errors in doctrine and faith, and some in life and conduct, and what they both are, everyone knows. Let us see then whether the Church of the faithful on earth does err or not, and if so, in what point and to what extent. As concerning the manners and life of the Church, it cannot wholly and clearly acquit itself of errors, that is to say, of sin. For always, as long as it is living here on earth, it prays heartily: "And forgive us our trespasses, as we do forgive them that trespass against us." And God for his mercy's sake always purges in his saints all dregs and infirmities as long as they live in this world, the elect being continually renewed and defiled. I am not unaware of your difficulty, faithful reader. If the Church, you say, is not holy and pure, how does the apostle call it holy, without spot and wrinkle? I answer, If you will not acknowledge any Church upon earth but that which is completely without blemish, then you will not be able to acknowledge any. For there never will remain any such Church upon earth, where the most righteous God, as Scripture testifies, hath shut up all things under sin, that he might take mercy on all men. Therefore St. Paul calls the Church pure, without spot or wrinkle, on account of the benefit and sanctification of Christ. It is not that while it is in the flesh it is without spot in itself, but that those spots which might otherwise cleave to it, by the innocency of Christ are not imputed to those who embrace Christ by faith, and finally that in the world to come the same Church shall be without spot or wrinkle. For when it has put off the flesh and cast off all miseries, it will at length be in the position where it has no lack of anything. Moreover the Church is said to be without spot because of the continual study with which it labours and travails by all means to have as few spots as it possibly can. And by that means, and above all by the benefit of imputation, the Church does not err but is most pure and as it were without sin.

Moreover, as touching doctrine and faith, the Church of Christ does not err. For it hears only the voice of the shepherd but does not know the voice of strangers: for it follows the one shepherd, Christ, who says: "I am the light of the world: he that followeth me shall not walk in darkness, but shall have the light of life." Paul also says to Timothy: "These things hitherto have I written unto thee, that thou mayest know how thou oughtest to behave thyself in the house of God, which is the Church of the living God, the pillar and ground of truth." But the Church is the pillar and ground of truth because being established upon the foundation of the prophets and apostles, Christ himself, which is the everlasting truth of God and the Church's only strength, by the fellowship which it has with him it is granted to be with him the pillar and foundation of the truth. For the truth of God is in the Church, it is spread abroad by the ministry of the Church, and being assaulted and warred against by its enemies it abides fast and is not overcome, in so far as being made one body with Christ, the Church perseveres in the fellowship of Christ, without whom it can do nothing. Again, the same Church does err in doctrine and faith whenever it turns from Christ and goes after men and the counsels and decrees of the flesh; for it forsakes the thing which has hitherto prevented it from erring, which is the Word of God and Christ. I do not think that any man will deny that the great congregation of the people of Israel in the desert was an excellent Church of God, with which the Lord made a covenant and bound himself to it by sacraments and ordinances. And yet we all know how shamefully it erred when it neglected God's Word, and because Aaron the high-priest of religion did not constantly and earnestly resist, it both made a golden calf and worshipped it as a god. For this reason it shall surely be necessary more diligently to examine and mark the whole number of the Church, for when many in the Church err, it does not follow that none at all is free from error. For as in the church of Israel the Lord reserved to himself a remnant, I mean Moses, Joshua and undoubtedly many more, both in that congregation and elsewhere, so there is no doubt that although many do err in the Church, the Lord by his mercy preserves to himself a certain number who both understand aright and by whose faith and diligence errors are destroyed and the wandering flock of the Lord are brought back again into the holy fold.

Therefore the Church is said to err when a part of it has lost the Word of God and errs. And it does not err wholly or altogether, for certain remnants [by the grace of God] are reserved, by whom the truth can flourish again and be spread abroad again in every place. . . .

Having considered these things, we shall not have any great difficulty in knowing the duties of the holy Church of God. For (as I have just said) it executes the power which it has received of God most carefully and faithfully, in order that it may serve God, and be holy, and please him. And to reckon up the sum of its duties in particular: first, it worships, calls upon and serves one God in Trinity, and does not take anything in hand without having first consulted the Word of this true God. For it orders all its doings according to the rule of God's Word: it judges by the Word of God: and by the same Word it frames all its buildings, and when they are built maintains them, and when they have fallen down repairs or restores them. It fervently assists and loves the assemblies and congregations of saints upon earth. In these assemblies it listens diligently to the preaching of the Word of God, it partakes devoutly of the sacraments and with great joy and delight of heavenly things. It prays to God by the intercession of our only mediator Christ with a strong faith, fervently, continually and most attentively. It praises the goodness and majesty of God for ever, and with great joy it gives thanks for all his heavenly benefits. It highly esteems all the institutions of Christ, not neglecting any of them. But above all it acknowledges that it receives all the things which belong to its life, salvation, righteousness or felicity, from the only Son of God, our Lord Jesus Christ, as the one who alone chose it, and then by his Spirit and blood sanctified it and made it a Church, that is, a chosen people, who is its only king, redeemer, high priest and defender, and without whom there is no salvation. Therefore it rests alone in God by our Lord Jesus Christ; him alone it desires and loves; and for his sake it rejoices to lose all the things that belong to this world, and indeed to pour out its blood and its life. And therefore it cleaves inseparably to Christ by faith, nor does it hate anything more bitterly than apostasy from Christ and desperation, for without Christ nothing at all in life seems to be pleasant. With Satan it has an unappeasable enmity as with a deadly enemy. Against heresies and errors it strives both constantly and wisely. The simplicity of the Christian faith and the sincerity of the doctrine of the apostles it keeps most diligently. As far as possible it keeps itself unspotted from the world and the flesh, and from all carnal and spiritual infection. And therefore it flees from and in every way detests all unlawful congregations and profane religions, and all wicked men, and willingly and openly confesses Christ both in word and deed, even at the risk of its life. It is exercised with afflictions, but never overcome. It keeps unity and concord carefully. It loves all its members most tenderly. It does good to all men, as much as power and ability allow. It hurts no man. It forgives willingly. It bears with the weak as a brother until they are advanced to perfection. It is not puffed up with pride, but by humility is kept in obedience and moderation and all the duties of godliness. But I ask who can recite all the specific duties of the Church even in a long discourse, much less in this short recital? And who would not desire to be a member of so divine and heavenly a congregation?

And now, lifting up our minds to heaven, let us give thanks to the Lord our God, who through his beloved Son has purified us and gathered us together, to be a chosen people to himself, and to be heirs of all his heavenly treasures. To him therefore be all praise and glory, world without end. Amen.

ROBERT BROWNE (1550–1633)

On Reformation of the Church

Seeing in this book we show the state of Christians, and have labored also in good conscience to live as Christians, it is marvelled and often talked of among many, why we should be so reviled and troubled of many, and also leave our country. Forsooth [say the enemies] there is some hidden thing in them more than plainly appeareth: for they bear evil will to their Princess Queen Elizabeth and to their country, yea they forsake the church of God and condemn the same, and are condemned of all, and they also discredit and bring into contempt the preachers of the Gospel. To answer them, we say that they are the men which trouble Israel, and seek evil to the Prince, and not we. And that they forsake and condemn the Church and not we. . . .

But for the magistrates, how far by their authority or without it, the Church must be builded and reformation made, and whether any open wickedness must be tolerated in the Church because of them, let this be our answer. For chiefly in this point they have wrought us great trouble, and dismayed many weaklings from embracing the truth. We say therefore, and often have taught, concerning our sovereign Queen Elizabeth, that neither the Pope nor other Popeling, is to have any authority either over her or over the Church of God, and that the Pope of Rome is Antichrist, whose kingdom ought utterly to be taken away. Again we say, that her authority is civil and that power she hath as highest under God within her Dominions, and that over all persons and causes. By that she may put to death all that deserve it by Law, either of the Church or commonwealth, and none may resist her or the magistrates under her by force or wicked speeches, when they execute the laws. Seeing we grant and hold thus much, how do they charge us evil willers to the Queen? Surely, for that we hold all those preachers and teachers accursed, which will not do the duties of pastors and teachers till the magistrates do force them thereto. They say, the time is not yet come to build the Lord's house (Hag.1), they must tarry for the magistrates and for parliaments to do it. They want the civil sword, forsooth, and the magistrates to hinder the Lord's building and kingdom and keep away his government. Are they not ashamed thus to slander the magistrates? They have run their own swords upon the wall and broken them and now would they snatch unto them the magistrates' sword? Indeed can the Lord's spiritual government be no way executed but by the civil sword, or is this the judgment that is written (Psalm 149), such honour shall be to all his Saints? Is this to bind the kings in chains, and the nobles with fetters of iron, by the high acts of God in their mouths, and a two edged sword in their hands?

Those bands and chains which is the spiritual power of the Church, they have broken from themselves and yet would they have magistrates bound with them, to begin discipline. They would make the magistrates more than gods and yet also worse than beasts. For they teach that a lawful pastor must give over his charge at their discharging, and when they withhold the church government, it ought for to cease, though the church go to ruin thereby. Behold now, doth not the Lord's kingdom give place unto theirs? And do they not pull down the head Christ Jesus (Col. 1:18), to set up the hand of the magistrate? Yea and more than this, for they first proclaim the names and titles of wicked bishops and popish officers, and the Lord's name after: Seeing also the bishops must discharge the lawful preachers and stop their mouths, though the Lord God have given them a charge for to speak, and not to keep silence. The Lord hath exalted Christ Jesus (Phil. 2) and given him a name above every name, that all things should bow and serve unto him, and yet have they exalted the power of wicked bishops above him. Behold a great and most wholesome river, and yet their puddle water is preferred before it. Except the magistrates will go into the tempest and rain and be weatherbeaten with the hail of God's wrath, they must keep under the roof of Christ's government. They must be under a pastoral charge; they must obey to the scepter of Christ, if they be Christians. How then should the pastor, which hath the oversight of the magistrate, if he be of his flock, be so overseen of the magistrate as to leave his flock, when the magistrate shall unjustly and wrongfully discharge him. Yet these preachers and teachers will not only do so, but even holding their charge and keeping with it, will not guide and reform it aright because the magistrates do forbid them forsooth. But they slander the magistrates and because they dare not charge them as forbidding them their duties, they have gotten this shift, that they do but tarry for the magistrate's authority, and then they will guide and reform as they ought. Behold, is not all this one thing, seeing they lift up the throne of the magistrates, to thrust out the kingdom of Christ? For his government or discipline is wanting [say they] but we keep it not away. And who then? . . .

Now then if the magistrates be enemies unto the Lord's kingdom, why are not these men better warriors to uphold the same? For they give up the weapons of their warfare into the enemies' hands, and they say, they cannot do with all. By their weapons I mean those whereof Paul doth speak (II Cor. 10) that they are not carnal, but mighty through God, to cast down holds, and so forth: These weapons have they given from them, for they have not the keys of the kingdom of heaven to bind and loose (Matt. 18, John 20) and to retain or pronounce remitted the sins of men, seeing they grant much open wickedness uncurable among them, and also avouch that it must needs be suffered. Yea they have given up these keys to the magistrates, or to the spiritual courts, and therefore have no right to call themselves the Church of God, or lawful pastors thereof. . . . Yea we must press unto his kingdom not tarrying for any, as it is written in Luke (Luke 16), and again in Matthew (Matt. 11), the kingdom of God suffereth violence, and the violent take it unto them by force.

For will any man else give over his calling, or abridge the full execution thereof when the magistrates forbid them, will they cease the teaching or due guiding of their households and charge for their dischargings, and should the laborers in God's spiritual husbandry give over and cease? For it is God's husbandry (I Cor. 3) and not theirs, the Church is his building and not their. They are but members thereof if they be Christians, and are not any way to stay the building, neither is it to tarry or wait upon them. But these wicked preachers eat up and spoil the Lord's harvest themselves, and then set open the gap as though the Magistrates brake in like wild boars, and spoiled the harvest. They say, "Behold we have a Christian prince, and a mother in Israel," but can they be Christians, when they make them to refuse or withstand the government of Christ in his Church, or will not be subject unto it? If they therefore refuse and withstand, how should they be tarried for? If they be with them, there is no tarrying: and if they be against them, they are no Christians, and therefore also there can be no tarrying. For the worthy may not tarry for the unworthy. . . .

He that will be saved must not tarry for this man or that: and he that puts his hand to the plow, and then looks back, is not fit for the kingdom of God (Luke 9). Therefore woe unto you, ye blind guides, which cast away all by tarrying for the magistrates. The Lord will remember this iniquity and visit this sin upon you. Ye will not have the kingdom of God, to go forward by his spirit, but by an army and strength forsooth (Zech. 4): ye will not have it as leaven hidden in three pecks of meal, till it leaven all (Matt. 13), but at once ye will have all aloft, by civil power and authority: you are offended at the baseness and small beginning, and because of the troubles in beginning reformation, you will do nothing. Therefore shall Christ be that rock of offense unto you, and ye shall stumble and fall, and shall be broken, and shall be snared, and shall be taken. You will be delivered from the yoke of Antichrist, to the which you do willingly give your necks by bow and by swords, and by battle, by horses and by horsemen (Hos. 2), that is, by civil power and pomp of magistrates: by their proclamations and parliaments: and the kingdom of God must come with observation (Luke 17), that men may say, Lo, the parliament or lo the bishops' decrees: but the kingdom of God should be within you. The inward obedience to the outward preaching and government of the Church, with newness of life, that is the Lord's kingdom. This ye despise, therefore shall ye desire to see the kingdom of God, and shall not see it, and to enjoy one day of the Son of man, and ye shall not enjoy it. For ye set aloft man's authority above God's, and the preacher must hang on his sleeve for the discharge of his calling. . . .

Whatsoever doth most edify, that must we choose, and avoid the contrary; and whatsoever is most expedient, that must be done, and so we must apply ourselves all unto all, that notwithstanding we hold our liberty. For if either magistrate or other would take that from us, we must not give place by yielding unto them, no, not for an hour (Gal. 2), and this liberty is the free use of our callings and gifts, as we see most agreeing to the word of God, and expedient for his glory. Therefore, the magistrate's commandment must not be a rule unto me of this and that duty, but as I see it agree with the word of God. So then it is an abuse of my gift and calling if I cease to preach, yea and woe unto me, if I preach not, for necessity is laid upon me, and if I do it unwillingly, yet the dispensation is committed unto me (I Cor. 9). And this dispensation did not the magistrate give me, but God by consent and ratifying of the Church, and therefore as the magistrate gave it not, so can he not take it away. Indeed, if God take it away for my wickedness and evil desert, he may remove me from the Church, and withhold me from preaching; but if God do it not, and his word doth approve me as most meet for that calling, I am to preach still, except I be shut up in prison, or otherwise with violence withheld from my charge. For the magistrate so using me cannot be a Christian, but forsaketh the Church; and how then should my office in the Church depend on him which is none of the Church. And the welfare of the Church must be more regarded and sought, than the welfare of whole kingdoms and countries. . . .

Yea the Church hath more authority concerning Church government than magistrates (Isa. 45), They shall follow thee, and shall go in chains; they shall fall down before thee, and make supplication unto thee. For who knoweth not, that though magistrates are to keep their civil power above all persons, yet they come under the censure of the Church, if they be Christians, and are openly to humble themselves in unfeigned repentance, when they have openly and grievously trespassed. They are indeed to keep their royal dignity, yet keeping that they are to abase themselves unto God before the face of the Church. For all powers shall serve and obey Christ, saith the Prophet (Isa. 60): and that kingdom and nation which will not also serve his Church (for so is the text) shall perish and the nation shall be utterly destroyed. . . .

Go to therefore, and the outward power and civil forcings, let us leave to the magistrates: to rule the commonwealth in all outward justice belongeth to them: but let the church rule in spiritual wise, and not in worldly manner: by a lively law preached, and not by a civil law written; by holiness in inward and outward obedience, and not in straightness of the outward only. But these handsome prelates would have the mace and the scepter in their hands, and then having safety and assurance by a law on their sides, they would make a goodly reformation. . . .

THE SEVENTEENTH CENTURY
Introduction

Three currents carry the development of Protestant thought through the seventeenth century. The first of these, dominant in the first half of the century, was the struggle within orthdox Protestantism to determine the correct interpretation of Scripture. The second is the story of the progress made by the Radical Reformation during the course of the century both in terms of a growing clarification of its own identity and in terms of the widening influence that its fundamental position on the nature of Christianity began to have on the larger Protestant community. The third, the commanding one during the second half of the century, was the rise of rationalism and the various reactions it generated within Protestantism.

Of the selections chosen for this century, the first four illustrate the orthodox development; the next three are examples of growth and influence within the left wing of the Reformation; the last three express the rising challenge of rationalism and the initial response to it.

ORTHODOX PROTESTANTISM—
THE INTERPRETATION OF SCRIPTURE

The original Reformers had made the principle of Scripture alone normative for Protestantism. Article 6 of the *Thirty-Nine Articles,* for example, phrases the principle in these words:

Holy Scripture containeth all things necessary to salvation: so that whatsoever is not read therein, nor may be proved thereby, is not to be required of any man, that it should be believed as an article of Faith, or be thought requisite or necessary to salvation.

Left undecided, however, was the issue of how the meaning of Scripture was to be determined. By the beginning of the seventeenth century this had become a major problem. Put simply, the question was: Who determines the meaning of the Word of God? Two seventeenth-century developments made clear the orthodox answer that the church was responsible for the interpretation of the Bible.

1. *The Nature of Predestination.*—The place of the first dispute about Scripture's meaning was the Reformed Church in Holland where, at the beginning of the century, questions arose about the scriptural doctrine of predestination. Calvin and the Reformed tradition after him had found in their reading of the Word of God that God's part in determining the salvation or loss of man was absolute. From eternity, and quite independently of any consideration of the worth of man's activity, the divine will predestined some to glory and others to damnation. In the determination of their eternal destiny men had no part.

Jacob Arminius, a professor at the University of Leyden, challenged this interpretation on the same grounds on which it was asserted, the evidence of Scripture. He did not believe that the testimony supported the Calvinist interpretation. His own view, derived from his reading of the scriptural evidence on the question, was that what men did in the course of their lives affected their salvation or damnation. It was in the light of their activity that the divine decision was made. Perhaps the strongest argument he offered in support of his position was the universal efficacy of Christ's redemptive death. That Christ had died for all men was a fundamental assertion of the New Testament. If this were true, then it must be correspondingly true that all men could profit from that redemption. It was hard to reconcile such a conclusion with absolutely antecedent predestination. Whether or not men accepted the salvation offered through Christ seemed crucial. Thus man's decision for or against belief in the saving efficacy of Christ's death did make a difference in the determination of his final destiny.

Orthodox Calvinism refused, however, to accept the view of Arminius. A synod representing the major Reformed Churches of Europe met at Dort in Holland in 1618–19. It issued a series of doctrinal statements reaffirming that the divine decree of predestination preceded and was unaffected by any human activity and that, in consequence, Christ had died only for the elect. The decrees of Dort meant that one interpretation of the meaning of Scripture would remain normative for the majority of the Calvinist tradition. The followers of Arminius had the choice of accepting this interpretation or of breaking with the mother church. The first fundamental difference in understanding God's relation with men as that relationship is described in the Word of God had entered Reformed Protestantism.

The first two selections in this section illustrate the two points of view. The first is an excerpt from Arminius' *Declaration of Sentiments,* the presentation and defense of his position delivered before the States of Holland, the governing body of that country, on October 30, 1608. The second is drawn from the *Canons of the Synod of Dort,* issued in 1619 and signed by representatives of most of the Reformed Churches of Europe.

2. *The Nature of The Church.*—The central issue in the century's second quarrel over the meaning of Scripture was the nature of the church. The precise question was: What does the New Testament say Christ's church should be? The locale of this dispute was the church in England from 1600 to 1660, where Anglican and Puritan struggled for supremacy.

The Puritan party was descended from those Englishmen who had learned their Protestantism in Calvin's Geneva and in the Reformed cantons of Switzerland during the Marian exile. In their eyes the English church as established by Elizabeth was in need of substantial purification in its doctrine, liturgy, and polity. Only radical reform could bring that church into line with the church as depicted in the New Testament.

Puritanism's sole norm for what was allowable in the church was that it be explicitly mentioned in Scripture. Judged by this rule much in the liturgical practice of England's church demanded removal; episcopal government, since scripturally unfounded, must yield to presbyterianism or congregationalism, the only forms of church polity clearly operative in the New Testament church. Finally, the statements of belief of the Church of England must be purified of Roman deformities and superstitions and cast in the austere language of Calvinism which most nearly reflected the New Testament vision of the Christian faith.

The defenders of the Church of England as established by Elizabeth, on the other hand, contended that Christian history provided conclusive evidence that both reason and tradition had also had significant part in determining how the church worshipped her God, expressed her belief, and lived her life. They agreed that the church could teach nothing contrary to Scripture, but they also insisted that Scripture left much unsaid regarding the church's life and practice, thereby implicitly leaving to the church of every age broad discretion for determining the details of Christian life and worship suitable to each time.

The dispute was, in brief, between Scripture alone or Scripture plus reason and tradition as normative for the interpretation of Scripture. In the end the quarrel was not decided at the level of theological debate but in the arena of political power. The religious party in power determined which theological position would be operative within the church. This meant that the Anglican position prevailed as long as the crown was strong. When Parliament and Cromwell came to power Puritanism was adopted. By 1660 Puritan power had waned, and the restoration of the monarchy brought with it the return of Anglicanism. Thus, within English Protestantism, Scripture, reason, and tradition prevailed as the norms for understanding and living Christianity. Puritanism, with its insistence on Scripture alone as normative, became the first in a line of dissenting churches in England.

Two selections are included to illustrate this quarrel. The first is drawn from the *Conference between William Laud and Mr. Fisher* (1639). Laud was Archbishop of Canterbury at the time and leader of the Anglican party. The selection makes clear that though he viewed Scripture as supreme in determining Christian belief, yet he saw that both the tradition of the church and reason had a part to play in the life of the church. The other selection is excerpted from the *Westminster Confession of Faith* (1647). This is a statement of the belief of the church in England during the time of the Puritan ascendancy. It was composed by a group of Puritan divines under order from Parliament to write a confession of faith to replace the *Thirty-Nine Articles*. The text reflects the Calvinist view of the nature of the Christian church and faith.

THE RADICAL REFORMATION— GROWTH IN SELF-CONSCIOUSNESS AND INFLUENCE

The course of the Radical Reformation during the seventeenth century ran along two lines. First, the original groups of the movement, now generally freed of the fanatical persecution that had harried them throughout the previous century, continued to lead their separated and strongly communal existence. Within such groups it remained important to preserve their self-understanding in the face of their minority status within Western Christendom. And so, much attention was given to deepening and exploring the implications of original Anabaptist positions. One example is chosen to illustrate this process, the *Dordrecht Confession* drawn up in 1632 by a group of Dutch Mennonites. A comparison with the *Schleitheim Confession* of 1527 indicates that the conventicles of left-wing Protestantism had grown to realize during this hundred years how important for their survival was a carefully structured view of the church and her mode of life and government. Hence there is stress put on the care to be exercised in the choice of church leadership as well as explicit delineation of the duties attaching to various offices in the church; recognition of the need for excommunication if the community was to be kept free from internal decay is also evident.

While Anabaptism continued to explore and strengthen its self-identity, a second line of development effected by the Radical Reformation also runs quite evidently through the century. This is the gradual spread of Anabaptist tenets throughout the general body of Protestantism. The clearest example of this is the diffusion of the notion of religious tolerance.

In the sixteenth century there were few voices raised in favor of religious toleration. For the Christianity of that century, Roman and Protestant alike, toleration of heterodoxy in belief was unthinkable. Error had no rights and was dangerous to the common good; hence it was to be ruthlessly stamped out. Such is a fair summary of the sixteenth century's reaction to Anabaptism's plea for freedom of conscience.

However, a century of wars in the cause of religion and of bloodletting in the name of Christianity brought a growing number of thoughtful Christians to see the wisdom of some form of religious liberty as essential to peace if not implicit in the very nature of Christianity. Political events probably had as much to do with this type of thinking as real intellectual conviction of its rightness. But whatever the reason, writing in support of tolerance became more and more commonplace in seventeenth-century literature. The selection included here is drawn from Jeremy Taylor's *On the Liberty of Prophesying*. In this tract Taylor argues for freedom of conscience at least in the limited sense that Christians should not be "hasty in calling every disliked opinion by the name of heresy." He urges charity and a spirit of forebearance as attitudes basic to true Christian living.

There was another expansion of Anabaptist thought at work in the seventeenth century. This was their approach to the understanding of Scripture, which was for the radical reformers God's Word, intended for every man. The Christian was to read his Bible, confident that the Spirit of God who dwelt in him would lead him to an understanding of that Word as it applied to his own life. Each believer carried within him his own source and safeguard of biblical interpretation in the person of the Holy Spirit.

With the coming of Protestant scholasticism and its trend towards carefully formulated, rationally impeccable treatises on the meaning of Scripture and the nature of Christianity, a counter-development was bound to spring up. One form which it took was Pietism with its insistence that God wanted to speak His Word to the heart of man, not to his head. Another approach is typified by the teaching of George Fox, founder of the Quakers. For Fox, each man is granted by God an "inner light" which, if heeded, will lead men to that knowledge of truth which will save them. In his thought the indwelling Spirit has become the light that illumines all men. Knowledge of Scripture is not necessary to salvation. What a man must do to be saved is to follow his inner light. A selection describing the nature and operation of this inner light is included, drawn from Robert

Barclay's *Apology for the True Christian Divinity*. Barclay is generally regarded as the clearest expositor of Quakerism.

RATIONALISM AND REACTION

Beginning with the second half of the century the influence that was to shape its form and set its direction for the next three hundred years began to assert itself in Protestant thought. This was the influence of rationalism. The age of faith was drawing to a close. The dominance of revelation in providing man with his knowledge of God started its long process of yielding to human reason as the ultimate norm for determining religious truth and error.

At its inception rationalism's progress can be charted along two main lines. The first of these is observable in the gradually growing reliance on human reason in theological discourse. Where formerly Scripture as the Word of God had held pride of place as the major source of human knowledge about God, now the tendency set in to show how thoroughly reasonable it was to accept the tenets of the Christian faith. The selection from John Locke's *On the Reasonableness of Christianity* makes clear that reason now takes over center stage, and revelation is acceptable only in terms of its reasonableness. Human reason begins to move towards the replacement of divine revelation.

The second main line of rationalism's development was determined by the opening up of the new field of the history of religions. A comparative study of the world's great religions made it clear that all through his history man had shown himself to be religious, interested in ultimate truth and concerned about the morality of his action.

Setting aside accidental differences between the various religions of man's history, it became clear that the religious patrimony of mankind could be expressed in a few quite simple propositions: God exists and should be worshipped by man. There was a moral order of right and wrong. Man is held to observance of this order; he will be rewarded or punished in an afterlife in accordance with his human conduct.

Christianity shares this common religious heritage with all the other great religions. It differs from them principally in the sublimity of its embodiment of these generally shared beliefs. The selection from Lord Herbert of Cherbury's *De Veritate* (1624) is included as illustrative of this development. Herbert's book was an extended investigation and explanation of mankind's universal religious beliefs.

As rationalism's presentation of the nature of God and of religious truth in general developed, it became more and more clear that its God and its religion was of the mind, not of the heart. Theological writing spoke much of God as Celestial Architect and little of God as Father. Preaching took on the tone of rational discourse about the deity and the reasonableness of believing in Him and eschewed touching on Christ's love for men and man's need of repentance and faith. Popular devotion, especially in its more "enthusiastic" modes, was looked down on as being too much emotion and too little reason. In consequence, the appeal of Christianity to the whole man, heart as well as mind, emotion as well as reason, tended to dry up into a shallow stream of rationality that did little to nourish the religious life of the ordinary Christian. Reaction was inevitable and was not slow in coming.

The initial stages of the reaction were centered in Germany in the movement known as Pietism. This movement set aside reason and argument as the main focus of Christian faith, not because such elements were thought unimportant but rather because this approach to Christianity did not feed the piety of the ordinary Christian, nor help him much to lead a good life. Pietism concentrated, rather, on engaging man's heart in his religion, on feeding his emotions rather than his reason. Its written expressions make quite clear its emphasis on simple piety and warm devotion to the person of Christ. A passage from Philip Spener's *The Spiritual Priesthood* is included as a sample of the pietistic approach to Christianity. He is the first in a line which will stretch out over the next century and a half, finding its continuing expression in the revivalist meetings of eighteenth-century America and in John Wesley's religion of the heart.

JACOB ARMINIUS (1560–1609)

The Nature of Predestination

I have hitherto been stating those opinions concerning the article of Predestination which are inculcated in our churches and in the University of Leyden, and of which I disapprove. I have at the same time produced my own reasons, why I form such an unfavorable judgment concerning them; and I will now declare my own opinions on this subject, which are of such a description as, according to my views, appear most conformable to the word of God.

I. The FIRST absolute decree of God concerning the salvation of sinful man, is that by which he decreed to appoint his Son, Jesus Christ, for a Mediator, Redeemer, Savior, Priest and King, who might destroy sin by his own death, might by his obedience obtain the salvation which had been lost, and might communicate it by his own virtue.

II. The SECOND precise and absolute decree of God, is that in which he decreed to receive into favor those who repent and believe, and, in Christ, for HIS sake and through HIM, to effect the salvation of such penitents and believers as persevered to the end; but to leave in sin, and under wrath, all impenitent persons and unbelievers, and to damn them as aliens from Christ.

III. The THIRD divine decree is that by which God decreed to administer in a sufficient and efficacious manner the MEANS which were necessary for repentance and faith; and to have such administration instituted (1) according to the Divine Wisdom, by which God knows what is proper and becoming both to his mercy and his severity, and (2) according to Divine Justice, by which he is prepared to adopt whatever his wisdom may prescribe and put it in execution.

IV. To these succeeds the FOURTH decree, by which God decreed to save and damn certain particular persons. This decree has its foundation in the foreknowledge of God, by which he knew from all eternity, those individuals who would, through his preventing grace, believe, and, through his subsequent grace would persevere, according to the before described administration of those means which are suitable and proper for conversion and faith; and, by which foreknowledge, he likewise knew those who would not believe and persevere.

PREDESTINATION, when thus explained, is

1. The foundation of Christianity, and of salvation and its certainty.

2. It is the sum and the matter of the gospel; nay it is the gospel itself, and on that account necessary to be believed in order to salvation, as far as the two first articles are concerned.

3. It has had no need of being examined or determined by any Council, either general or particular, since it is contained in the Scriptures clearly and expressly in so many words; and no contradiction has ever yet been offered to it by any orthodox divine.

4. It has constantly been acknowledged and taught by all Christian teachers who held correct and orthodox sentiments.

5. It agrees with that *Harmony of All Confessions,* which has been published by the Protestant churches.

6. It likewise agrees most excellently with the Dutch Confession and Catechism. . . .

7. It is also in excellent accordance with the nature of God—with his wisdom, goodness, and righteousness; because it contains the principal matter of all of them, and is the clearest demonstration of the Divine wisdom, goodness, and righteousness (or justice).

8. It is agreeable in every point with the nature of man—in what form soever that nature may be contemplated, whether in the primitive state of creation, in that of the fall, or in that of restoration.

9. It is in complete concert with the act of creation, by affirming that the creation itself is a real communication of good, both from the intention of God, and with regard to the very end or event; that it had its origin in the goodness of God; that whatever has a reference to its continuance and preservation, proceeds from divine love; and that this act of creation is a perfect and appropriate work of God, in which he is at complaisance with himself, and by which he obtained all things necessary for an unsinning state.

10. It agrees with the nature of life eternal, and with the honorable titles by which that life is designated in Scripture.

11. It also agrees with the nature of death eternal, and with the names by which that death is distinguished in Scripture.

12. It states sin to be a real disobedience, and the meritorious cause of condemnation; and on this account, it is in the most perfect agreement with the fall and with sin.

13. In every particular, it harmonizes with the nature of grace, by as-

cribing to it all those things which agree with it, (or adapted to it,) and by reconciling it most completely to the righteousness of God and to the nature and liberty of the human will.

14. It conduces most conspicuously to declare the glory of God, his justice and his mercy. It also represents God as the cause of all good and of our salvation, and man as the cause of sin and of his own damnation.

15. It contributes to the honor of Jesus Christ, by placing him for the foundation of predestination and the meritorious as well as communicative cause of salvation.

16. It greatly promotes the salvation of men: It is also the power, and the very means which lead to salvation—by exciting and creating within the mind of man sorrow on account of sin, a solicitude about his conversion, faith in Jesus Christ, a studious desire to perform good works, and zeal in prayer—and by causing men to work out their salvation with fear and trembling. It likewise prevents despair, as far as such prevention is necessary.

17. It confirms and establishes that order according to which the gospel ought to be preached, (1) by requiring repentance and faith—(2) and then by promising remission of sins, the grace of the Spirit, and life eternal.

18. It strengthens the ministry of the gospel, and renders it profitable with respect to preaching, the administration of the sacraments and public prayers.

19. It is the foundation of the Christian religion; because in it, the two-fold love of God may be united together—God's love of righteousness (or justice), and his love of men, may, with the greatest consistency, be reconciled to each other.

20. Lastly, This doctrine of Predestination has always been approved by the great majority of professing Christians, and even now, in these days, it enjoys the same extensive patronage. It cannot afford any person just cause for expressing his aversion to it; nor can it give any pretext for contention in the Christian Church.

It is therefore much to be desired, that men would proceed no further in this matter, and would not attempt to investigate the unsearchable judgments of God—at least that they would not proceed beyond the point at which those judgments have been clearly revealed in the scriptures. . . .

There are certain other articles of the Christian Religion, which possess a close affinity to the doctrine of Predestination, and which are in a great measure dependent on it: Of this description are the Providence of God, the Free-will of Man, the Perseverance of Saints, and the Certainty of Salvation. On these topics, if not disagreeable to your mightinesses, I will in a brief manner relate my opinion.

The Providence of God

I consider Divine Providence to be "that solicitous, continued, and universally present inspection and oversight of God, according to which he exercises a general care over the whole world, but evinces a particular concern for all his (intelligent) creatures without any exception, with the design of preserving and governing them in their own essence, qualities, actions, and passions, in a manner that is at once worthy of himself and suitable to them, to the praise of his name and the salvation of believers." In this definition of Divine Providence, I by no means deprive it of any particle of those properties which agree with it or belong to it; but I declare that it preserves, regulates, governs and directs all things, and that nothing in the world happens fortuitously or by chance. Besides this, I place in subjection to Divine Providence both the free-will and even the actions of a rational creature, so that nothing can be done without the will of God, not even any of those things which are done in opposition to it; only we must observe a distinction between good actions and evil ones, by saying, that "God both wills and performs good acts," but that "He only freely permits those which are evil." Still farther than this, I very readily grant, that even all actions whatever, concerning evil, that can possibly be devised or invented, may be attributed to Divine Providence—employing solely one caution, "not to conclude from this concession that God is the cause of sin."

The Free-Will of Man

This is my opinion concerning the Free-will of man: In his primitive condition as he came out of the hands of his Creator, man was endowed with such a portion of knowledge, holiness and power, as enabled him to understand, esteem, consider, will, and to perform the true good, according to the commandment delivered to him. Yet none of these acts could he do, except through the assistance of Divine Grace. But in his lapsed and sinful state, man is not capable, of and by himself, either to think, to will, or to do that which is really good; but it is necessary for him to be regenerated and renewed in his intellect, affections or will, and in all his powers, by God in Christ through the Holy Spirit, that he may be qualified rightly to understand, esteem, consider, will, and perform whatever is truly good. When he is made a partaker of this regeneration or renovation, I consider that, since he is delivered from sin, he is capable of thinking, willing and doing that which is good, but yet not without the continued aids of Divine Grace.

The Grace of God

In reference to Divine Grace, I believe, (1) It is a gratuitous affection by which God is kindly affected towards a miserable sinner, and according to which he, in the first place, gives his Son, "that whosoever believeth in him might have eternal life," and, afterwards, he justifies him in Christ Jesus and for his sake, and adopts him into the right of sons, unto salvation. (2) It is an infusion (both into the human understanding and into the will and affections,) of all those gifts of the Holy Spirit which appertain to the regeneration and renewing of man—such as faith, hope, charity, etc.; for, without these gracious gifts, man is not sufficient to think, will, or do anything that is good. (3) It is that perpetual assistance and continued aid of the Holy Spirit, according to which He acts upon and excites to good the man who has been already renewed, by infusing into him salutary cogitations, and by inspiring him with good desires, that he may thus actually will whatever is good; and according to which God may then will and work together with man, that man may perform whatever he wills.

In this manner, I ascribe to grace the commencement, the continuance and the consummation of all good, and to such an extent do I carry its influence, that a man, though already regenerate, can neither conceive, will, nor do any good at all, nor resist any evil temptation, without this preventing and exciting, this following and co-operating grace. From this statement it will clearly appear, that I by no means do injustice to grace, by attributing, as it is reported of me, too much to man's free-will. For the whole controversy reduces itself to the solution of this question, "Is the grace of God a certain irresistible force?" That is, the controversy does not relate to those actions or operations which may be ascribed to grace, (for I acknowledge and inculcate as many of these actions or operations as any man ever did,) but it relates solely to the mode of operation, whether it be irresistible or not. With respect to which, I believe, according to the scriptures, that many persons resist the Holy Spirit and reject the grace that is offered.

The Perseverance of the Saints

My sentiments respecting the perseverance of the Saints are, that those persons who have been grafted into Christ by true faith, and have thus been made partakers of his life-giving Spirit, possess sufficient powers (or strength) to fight against Satan, sin, the world and their own flesh, and to gain the victory over these enemies—yet not without the assistance of the grace of the same Holy Spirit. Jesus Christ also by his Spirit assists them in all their temptations, and affords them the ready aid of his hand; and, provided they stand prepared for the battle, implore his help, and be not wanting to themselves, Christ preserves them from falling. So that it is not possible for them, by any of the cunning craftiness or power of Satan, to be either seduced or dragged out of the hands of Christ. But I think it is useful and will be quite necessary in our first convention, (or Synod) to institute a diligent enquiry from the Scriptures, whether it is not possible for some individuals through negligence to desert the commencement of their existence in Christ, to cleave again to the present evil world, to decline from the sound doctrine which was once delivered to them, to lose a good conscience, and to cause Divine grace to be ineffectual.

Though I here openly and ingenuously affirm, I never taught that a true believer can either totally or finally fall away from the faith, and perish; yet I will not conceal, that there are passages of Scripture which seem to me to wear this aspect; and those answers to them which I have been permitted to see, are not of such a kind as to approve themselves on all points to my understanding. On the other hand, certain passages are produced for the contrary doctrine (of unconditional perseverance) which are worthy of much consideration.

The Assurance of Salvation

With regard to the certainty (or assurance) of salvation, my opinion is, that it is possible for him who believes in Jesus Christ to be certain and persuaded, and, if his heart condemn him not, he is now in reality assured, that he is a Son of God, and stands in the grace of Jesus Christ. Such a certainty is wrought in the mind, as well by the action of the Holy Spirit inwardly actuating the believer and by the fruits of faith, as from his own conscience, and the testimony of God's Spirit witnessing together with his conscience. I also believe, that it is possible for such a person, with an assured confidence in the grace of God and his mercy in Christ, to depart out of this life, and to appear before the throne of grace, without any anxious fear or terrific dread: and yet this person should constantly pray, "O Lord, enter not into judgment with thy servant!"

But, since "God is greater than our hearts, and knoweth all things," and since a man judges not his own self—yea, though a man know nothing by himself, yet is he not thereby justified, but he who judgeth him is the Lord, (I John iii.19; I Cor. iv.3) I dare not (on this account) place this assurance (or certainty) on an equality with that by which we know there is a God, and that Christ is the Savior of the world. Yet it will be proper to make the extent of the boundaries of this assurance, a subject of enquiry in our convention.

The Perfection of Believers in This Life

Besides those doctrines on which I have treated, there is now much discussion among us respecting the perfection of believers, or regenerate persons, in this life; and it is reported, that I entertain sentiments on this subject, which are very improper, and nearly allied to those of the Pelagians, viz. "That it is possible for the regenerate in this life perfectly to keep God's precepts." To this I reply, though these might have been my sentiments, yet I ought not on this account to be considered a Pelagian, either partly or entirely, provided I had only added that "they could do this by the Grace of Christ, and by no means without it." But while I never asserted, that a believer could perfectly keep the precepts of Christ in this life, I never denied it, but always left it as a matter which has still to be decided. For I have contented myself with those sentiments which St. Augustine has expressed on this subject, whose words I have frequently quoted in the University, and have usually subjoined, that I had no addition to make to them.

Augustine says, "Four questions may claim our attention on this topic. The first is, was there ever yet a man without sin, one who from the beginning of life to its termination never committed sin? The second, has there ever been, is there now, or can there possibly be, an individual who does not sin, that is, who has attained to such a state of perfection in this life as not to commit sin, but perfectly to fulfill the law of God? The third, is it possible for a man in this life to exist without sin? The fourth, if it be possible for a man to be without sin, why has such an individual never yet been found?" St. Augustine says, "that such a person as is described in the first question never yet lived, or will hereafter be brought into existence, with the exception of Jesus Christ." He does not think, that any man has attained to such perfection in this life as is portrayed in the second question. With regard to the third, he thinks it possible for a man to be without sin, by means of the grace of Christ and free-will. In answer to the fourth, "man does not do what it is possible for him by the grace of Christ to perform, either because that which is good escapes his observation, or because in it he places no part of his delight." From this quotation it is apparent that St. Augustine, one of the most strenuous adversaries of the Pelagian doctrine, retained this sentiment, that "it is possible for a man to live in this world without sin."

Besides this, the same Christian Father says, "Let Pelagius confess, that it is possible for man to be without sin, in no other way than by the grace of Christ, and we will be at peace with each other." The opinion of Pelagius appeared to St. Augustine to be this—"that man could fulfill the law of God by his own proper strength and ability; but with still greater facility by means of the grace of Christ." I have already most abundantly stated the great distance at which I stand from such a sentiment; in addition to which I now declare, that I account this sentiment of Pelagius to be heretical, and diametrically opposed to these words of Christ, "Without me ye can do nothing" (John xv.5). It is likewise very destructive, and inflicts a most grievous wound on the glory of Christ.

I cannot see that anything is contained in all I have hitherto produced respecting my sentiments, on account of which any person ought to be "afraid of appearing in the presence of God," and from which it might be feared that any mischievous consequences can possibly arise. . . .

CANONS OF THE SYNOD OF DORT (1619)

Predestination

Art. I. As all men have sinned in Adam, lie under the curse, and are obnoxious to eternal death, God would have done no injustice by leaving them all to perish, and delivering them over to condemnation on account of sin, according to the words of the Apostle (Rom. iii.19), "that every mouth may be stopped, and all the world may become guilty before God;" (ver. 23) "for all have sinned and come short of the glory of God;" and (vi.23), "for the wages of sin is death."

Art. II. But "in this the love of God was manifested, that he sent his only-begotten Son into the world," "that whosoever believeth on him should not perish, but have everlasting life" (I John iv.9; John iii.16).

Art. III. And that men may be brought to believe, God mercifully sends the messengers of these most joyful tidings to whom he will, and at what time he pleaseth; by whose ministry men are called to repentance and faith in Christ crucified. "How then shall they call on him in whom they have not believed? And how shall they believe in him of whom they have not heard? And how shall they hear without a preacher? And how shall they preach, except they be sent?" (Rom. x.14,15).

Art. IV. The wrath of God abideth upon those who believe not this gospel; but such as receive it, and embrace Jesus the Saviour by a true and living faith, are by him delivered from the wrath of God and from destruction, and have the gift of eternal life conferred upon them.

Art. V. The cause of guilt of this unbelief, as well as of all other sins, is nowise in God, but in man himself: whereas faith in Jesus Christ, and salvation through him is the free gift of God, as it is written, "By grace ye are saved through faith, and that not of yourselves; it is the gift of God" (Eph. ii.8); and, "Unto you it is given in the behalf of Christ, not only to believe on him," etc. (Phil. i.29).

Art. VI. That some receive the gift of faith from God, and others do not receive it, proceeds from God's eternal decree. "For known unto God are all his works from the beginning of the world" (Acts. xv.18; Eph.

i.11). According to which decree he graciously softens the hearts of the elect, however obstinate, and inclines them to believe; while he leaves the non-elect in his just judgement to their own wickedness and obduracy. And herein is especially displayed the profound, the merciful, and at the same time the righteous discrimination between men, equally involved in ruin; or that decree of election and reprobation, revealed in the Word of God, which, though men of perverse, impure, and unstable minds wrest it to their own destruction, yet to holy and pious souls affords unspeakable consolation.

Art. VII. Election is the unchangeable purpose of God, whereby, before the foundation of the world, he hath, out of mere grace, according to the sovereign good pleasure of his own will, chosen, from the whole human race, which had fallen through their own fault, from their primitive state of rectitude, into sin and destruction, a certain number of persons to redemption in Christ, whom he from eternity appointed the Mediator and head of the elect, and the foundation of salvation.

This elect number, though by nature neither better nor more deserving than others, but with them involved in one common misery, God hath decreed to give to Christ to be saved by him, and effectually to call and draw them to his communion, by his Word and Spirit; to bestow upon them true faith, justification, and sanctification; and having powerfully preserved them in the fellowship of his Son, finally to glorify them for the demonstration of his mercy, and for the praise of the riches of his glorious grace: as it is written, "According as he hath chosen us in him before the foundation of the world, that we should be holy and without blame before him in love; having predestinated us unto the adoption of children by Jesus Christ to himself, according to the good pleasure of his will, to the praise of the glory of his grace wherein he hath made us accepted in the Beloved" (Eph. i.5–6). And elsewhere, "Whom he did predestinate, them he also called; and whom he called, them he also justified; and whom he justified, them he also glorified" (Rom. viii.30).

Art. VIII. There are not various decrees of election, but one and the same decree respecting all those who shall be saved both under the Old and New Testament; since the Scripture declares the good pleasure, purpose, and counsel of the divine will to be one, according to which he hath chosen us from eternity, both to grace and to glory, to salvation and the way of salvation, which he hath ordained that we should walk therein.

Art. IX. This election was not founded upon foreseen faith, and the obedience of faith, holiness, or any other good quality or disposition in man, as the prerequisite, cause, or condition on which it depended; but men are chosen to faith and to the obedience of faith, holiness, etc. Therefore election is the fountain of every saving good; from which proceed faith, holiness, and the other gifts of salvation, and finally eternal life it-self, as its fruits and effects, according to that of the Apostle. "He hath chosen us [not because we were, but] that we should be holy and without blame before him in love" (Eph. 1.4).

Art. X. The good pleasure of God is the sole cause of this gracious election; which doth not consist herein that God, foreseeing all possible qualities of human actions, elected certain of these as a condition of salva-tion, but that he was pleased out of the common mass of sinners to adopt certain persons as a peculiar people to himself, as it is written, "For the children being not yet born, neither having done any good or evil," etc., "it was said [namely, to Rebecca] the elder shall serve the younger; as it is written, Jacob have I loved, but Esau have I hated" (Rom. ix.11–13); and, "As many as were ordained to eternal life believed" (Acts xiii.48).

Art. XI. And as God himself is most wise, unchangeable, omniscient, and omnipotent, so the election made by him can neither be interrupted nor changed, recalled nor annulled; neither can the elect be cast away, nor their number diminished.

Art. XII. The elect, in due time, though in various degrees and in dif-ferent measures, attain the assurance of this their eternal and unchangeable election, not by inquisitively prying into the secret and deep things of God, but by observing in themselves, with a spiritual joy and holy pleasure, the infallible fruits of election pointed out in the Word of God; such as a true faith in Christ, filial fear, a godly sorrow for sin, a hungering and thirsting after righteousness, etc.

Art. XIII. The sense and certainty of this election afford to the children of God additional matter for daily humiliation before him, for adoring the depth of his mercies, and rendering grateful returns of ardent love to him who first manifested so great love towards them. The consideration of this doctrine of election is so far from encouraging remissness in the obser-vance of the divine commands or from sinking men into carnal security, that these, in the just judgment of God, are the usual effects of rash pre-sumption or of idle and wanton trifling with the grace of election, in those who refuse to walk in the ways of the elect.

Art. XIV. As the doctrine of divine election by the most wise counsel of God was declared by the Prophets, by Christ himself, and by the Apos-tles, and is clearly revealed in the Scriptures both of the Old and New Tes-tament, so it is still to be published in due time and place in the Church of God, for which it was peculiarly designed, provided it be done with rever-ence, in the spirit of discretion and piety, for the glory of God's most holy name, and for enlivening and comforting his people, without vainly at-tempting to investigate the secret ways of the Most High.

Art. XV. What peculiarly tends to illustrate and recommend to us the eternal and unmerited grace of election is the express testimony of sacred Scripture, that not all, but some only, are elected, while others are passed by in the eternal decree; whom God, out of his sovereign, most just, irreprehensible and unchangeable good pleasure, hath decreed to leave in the common misery into which they have willfully plunged themselves, and not to bestow upon them saving faith and the grace of conversion; but permitting them in his just judgment to follow their own way; at last, for the declaration of his justice, to condemn and punish them forever, not only on account of their unbelief, but also for all their other sins. And this is the decree of reprobation which by no means makes God the author of sin (the very thought of which is blasphemy), but declares him to be an awful, irreprehensible, and righteous judge and avenger.

Art. XVI. Those who do not yet experience a lively faith in Christ, an assured confidence of soul, peace of conscience, an earnest endeavor after filial obedience, and glorying in God through Christ, efficaciously wrought in them, and do nevertheless persist in the use of the means which God hath appointed for working these graces in us, ought not to be alarmed at the mention of reprobation, nor to rank themselves among the reprobate, but diligently to persevere in the use of means, and with ardent desires devoutly and humbly to wait for a season of richer grace. Much less cause have they to be terrified by the doctrine of reprobation, who, though they seriously desire to be turned to God, to please him only, and to be delivered from the body of death, can not yet reach that measure of holiness and faith to which they aspire; since a merciful God has promised that he will not quench the smoking flax, nor break the bruised reed. But this doctrine is justly terrible to those who, regardless of God and of the Saviour Jesus Christ, have wholly given themselves up to the cares of the world and the pleasures of the flesh, so long as they are not seriously converted to God.

Art. XVII. Since we are to judge of the will of God from his Word, which testifies that the children of believers are holy, not by nature, but in virtue of the covenant of grace, in which they together with the parents are comprehended, godly parents have no reason to doubt of the election and salvation of their children whom it pleaseth God to call out of this life in their infancy.

Art. XVIII. To those who murmur at the free grace of election, and just severity of reprobation, we answer with the Apostle: "Nay but, O man, who art thou that repliest against God?" (Rom. ix.20); and quote the language of our Saviour: "Is it not lawful for me to do what I will with mine own?" (Matt. xx.15). And therefore with holy adoration of these mysteries, we exclaim, in the words of the Apostle: "O the depth of the riches both of the wisdom and knowledge of God! how unsearchable are his judgments, and his ways past finding out! For who hath known the mind of the Lord, or who hath been his counselor? or who hath first given to him, and it shall be recompensed unto him again. For of him, and through him, and to him are all things: to whom be glory forever. Amen." (Rom. xi.33–36)

Of the Death of Christ, and the Redemption of Men Thereby

Art. I. God is not only supremely merciful, but also supremely just. And his justice requires (as he hath revealed himself in his Word) that our sins committed against his infinite majesty should be punished, not only with temporal, but with eternal punishments, both in body and soul; which we can not escape, unless satisfaction be made to the justice of God.

Art. II. Since, therefore, we are unable to make that satisfaction in our own persons, or to deliver ourselves from the wrath of God, he hath been pleased of his infinite mercy to give his only-begotten Son for our surety, who was made sin, and became a curse for us and in our stead, that he might make satisfaction to divine justice on our behalf.

Art. III. The death of the Son of God is the only and most perfect sacrifice and satisfaction for sin; is of infinite worth and value, abundantly sufficient to expiate the sins of the whole world.

Art. IV. This death derives its infinite value and dignity from these considerations; because the person who submitted to it was not only really man and perfectly holy, but also the only-begotten Son of God, of the same eternal and infinite essence with the Father and Holy Spirit, which qualifications were necessary to constitute him a Saviour for us; and because it was attended with a sense of the wrath and curse of God due to us for sin.

Art. V. Moreover the promise of the gospel is, that whosoever believeth in Christ crucified shall not perish, but have everlasting life. This promise, together with the command to repent and believe, ought to be declared and published to all nations, and to all persons promiscuously and without distinction, to whom God out of his good pleasure sends the gospel.

Art. VI. And, whereas many who are called by the gospel do not repent nor believe in Christ, but perish in unbelief; this is not owing to any defect or insufficiency in the sacrifice offered by Christ upon the cross, but is wholly to be imputed to themselves.

Art. VII. But as many as truly believe, and are delivered and saved from sin and destruction through the death of Christ, are indebted for this benefit solely to the grace of God given them in Christ from everlasting, and not to any merit of their own.

Art. VIII. For this was the sovereign counsel and most gracious will and purpose of God the Father, that the quickening and saving efficacy of the most precious death of his Son should extend to all the elect, for bestowing upon them alone the gift of justifying faith, thereby to bring them infallibly to salvation: that is, it was the will of God, that Christ by the blood of the cross, whereby he confirmed the new covenant, should effectually redeem out of every people, tribe, nation and language, all those, and those only, who were from eternity chosen to salvation, and given to him by the Father; that he should confer upon them faith, which, together with all the other saving gifts of the Holy Spirit, he purchased for them by his death; should purge them from all sin, both original and actual, whether committed before or after believing; and having faithfully preserved them even to the end, should at last bring them free from every spot and blemish to the enjoyment of glory in his own presence forever.

Art. IX. This purpose proceeding from everlasting love towards the elect, has, from the beginning of the world to this day, been powerfully accomplished, and will, henceforward, still continue to be accomplished, notwithstanding all the ineffectual opposition of the gates of hell; so that the elect in due time may be gathered together into one, and that there never may be wanting a Church composed of believers, the foundation of which is laid in the blood of Christ, which may steadfastly love and faithfully serve him as their Saviour, who, as a bridegroom for his bride, laid down his life for them upon the cross; and which may celebrate his praises here and through all eternity. . . . .

WILLIAM LAUD (1573–1645)

On Scripture and Reason

To gather up whatsoever may seem scattered in this long discourse to prove that Scripture is the Word of God, I shall now, in the last place, put all together, that so the whole state of the question may the better appear.

First, then, I shall desire the reader to consider, that every rational science requires some principles quite without its own limits, which are not proved in that science, but presupposed. Thus rhetoric presupposes grammar; and music, arithmetic. Therefore it is most reasonable, that Theology should be allowed to have some principles also, which she proves not, but presupposes. And the chiefest of these is, That the Scriptures are of Divine authority.

Secondly, That there is a great deal of difference in the manner of confirming the principles of Divinity, and those of any other art or science whatsoever.

For the principles of all other sciences do finally resolve, either into the conclusions of some higher science, or into those principles which are *per se nota*, "known by their own light," and are the grounds and principles of all science. And this is it, which properly makes them sciences, because they proceed with such strength of demonstration as forces reason to yield unto them. But the principles of Divinity resolve not into the grounds of natural reason,—for then there would be no room for faith, but all would be either knowledge or vision,—but, into the maxims of Divine knowledge supernatural. And of this we have just so much light, and no more, than God hath revealed unto us in the Scripture.

Thirdly, That though the evidence of these supernatural truths which Divinity teaches, appears not so manifest as that of the natural, yet they are in themselves much more sure and infallible than they. For they proceed immediately from God, that Heavenly Wisdom, which being the fountain of ours, must needs infinitely precede ours, both in nature and excellence. "He that teacheth man knowledge, shall not He know?" And therefore, though we reach not the order of their deductions, nor can in this life come to the vision of them, yet we yield as full and firm assent, not only to the articles, but to all the things rightly deduced from them, as we do to the most evident principles of natural reason. This assent is called faith; and "faith being of things not seen," would quite lose its honour, nay itself, if it met with sufficient grounds in natural reason whereon to stay itself. For faith is a mixed act of the will and the understanding; and the will inclines the understanding to yield full approbation to that whereof it sees not full proof. Not but that there is most full proof of them, but because the main grounds which prove them are concealed from our view and folded up in the unrevealed counsel of God, God in Christ resolving to bring mankind to their last happiness by faith, and not by knowledge, that so the weakest among men may have their way to blessedness open. And certain it is, that many weak men believe themselves into heaven, and many over-knowing Christians lose their way thither, while they will believe no more than they can clearly know. In which pride and vanity of theirs they are left, and have these things *hid from them.*

Fourthly, That the credit of the Scripture, the book in which the principles of faith are written, as of other writing also, depends not upon the subservient inducing cause that leads us to the first knowledge of the author, which leader here is the Church, but upon the author himself, and the opinion we have of his sufficiency, which here is the Holy Spirit of God, whose penmen the Prophets and Apostles were. And therefore the mysteries of Divinity contained in this book, as the Incarnation of our Saviour, the Resurrection of the Dead, and the like, cannot finally be resolved into the sole testimony of the Church, who is but a subservient cause to lead to the knowledge of the author, but into the wisdom and sufficiency of the author, Who, being omnipotent and omniscient, must needs be infallible.

Fifthly, That the assurance we have of the penmen of the Scriptures, the Holy Prophets and Apostles, is as great as any can be had of any human authors of like antiquity. For it is morally as evident to any pagan, that St. Matthew and St. Paul writ the Gospel and Epistles, which bear their names, as that Cicero or Seneca wrote theirs. But that the Apostles were divinely inspired whilst they writ them, and that they are the very Word of God expressed by them, this hath ever been a matter of faith in the Church, and was so even while the Apostles themselves lived, and was never a matter of evidence and knowledge, at least as knowledge is opposed to faith. Nor could it at any time then be more demonstratively proved than now. I say, not *scientifice,* not demonstratively. For, were the Apostles living, and should they tell us that they spake and writ the very oracles of God, yet this were but their own testimony of themselves, and so not alone able to enforce belief on others. And for their miracles, though they were very great inducements of belief, yet were neither they evident and convincing proofs, alone and of themselves, both because there may be counterfeit miracles, and because true ones are neither infallible nor inseparable marks of truth in doctrine.

Not infallible, for they may be marks of false doctrine in the highest degree; not proper and inseparable, for all which wrote by inspiration did not confirm their doctrine by miracles. For we do not find that David, or Solomon, with some other of the prophets, did any; neither were any wrought by St. John the Baptist. So, as credible signs, they were, and are still, of as much force to us as it is possible for things on the credit of relation to be: for the witnesses are many, and such as spent their lives in making good the truth which they saw. But that the workers of them were Divinely and infallibly inspired in that which they preached and writ was still to the hearers a matter of faith, and no more evident, by the light of human reason, to men that lived in those days than to us now. For, had that been demonstrated or been clear, as prime principles are, in its own light, both they and we had apprehended all the mysteries of Divinity by knowledge, not by faith. But this is most apparent it was not. For, had the Prophets or Apostles been ordered by God to make this demonstratively or intuitively, by discourse or vision, appear as clear to their auditors as to themselves it did, that whatsoever they taught was divine and infallible truth, all men which had the true use of reason must have been forced to yield to their doctrine. Isaiah could never have been at *Domine quis? Lord, who hath believed our report?* Nor Jeremy at *Domino, factus sum, Lord I am in derision daily.* Nor could any of St. Paul's auditors have *mocked at him,* as some of them did, for *preaching the resurrection,* if they had had as full a view as St. Paul himself had in *the assurance,* which God gave of it, in and by *the resurrection of Christ.* But the way of knowledge was not that which God thought fittest for man's salvation. For man having sinned by pride, God thought fittest to humble him at the very root of the tree of knowledge, and make him deny his understanding, and submit to faith, or hazard his happiness. The credible object all the while, that is, the mysteries of religion and the Scripture which contain them, is Divine and infallible; and so are the penmen of them by revelation. But we and all our fore-fathers, the hearers and readers of them, have neither knowledge nor vision of the prime principles in or about them, but faith only. And the revelation, which was clear to them, is not so to us, nor therefore the prime tradition itself delivered by them.

Sixthly, That hence it may be gathered that the assent which we yield to this main principle of Divinity, "that the Scripture is the Word of God," is grounded upon no compelling or demonstrative ratiocination, but relies upon the strength of faith more than any other principle whatsoever. For all other necessary points of Divinity may, by undeniable discourse, be inferred out of Scripture itself, once admitted; but this concerning the authority of Scripture is not possible, but must either be proved by revelation, which is not now to be expected, or presupposed and granted as manifested in itself, like the principles of natural knowledge, which reason alone will never grant; or by tradition of the Church both prime and present, with all other rational helps, preceding or accompanying the internal light in Scripture itself, which though it give light enough for faith to believe, yet light enough it gives not to be a convincing reason and proof for knowledge. And this is it which makes the very entrance into Divinity inaccessible to those men who, standing high in the opinion of their own wisdom, will believe nothing but that which is irrefragably proved from rational principles. For as Christ requires a denial of a man's self, that he may be able to follow Him, so as great a part as any of this denial of his whole self, for so it must be, is the denial of his understanding, and the composing of the unquiet search of this grand inquisitor into the secrets of Him that made it, and the overruling the doubtfulness of it by the fervency of the will.

Seventhly, That the knowledge of the supreme cause of all, which is God, is most remote, and the most difficult thing reason can have to do with. The *quod sit,* that there is a God, blear-eyed reason can see; but the *quid sit,* what that God is, is infinitely beyond all the fathoms of reason. He is a light indeed, but such as no man's reason can come at for the brightness. If anything, therefore, be attainable in this kind it must be by revelation, and that must be from Himself: for none can reveal but he that comprehends, and none doth or can comprehend God but Himself. And when He doth reveal, yet He is no further discernible than Himself pleases. Now, since reason teaches that the soul of man is immortal and capable of felicity; and since that felicity consists in the contemplation of the highest cause, which again is God Himself; and since Christ therein confirms that dictate, that man's eternal happiness is to know God, and Him Whom He hath sent; and since nothing can put us into the way of attaining to that contemplation but some revelation of Himself and of the way to Himself; I say, since all this is so, it cannot reasonably be thought by any prudent man that the all-wise God should create man with a desire of felicity, and then leave him utterly destitute of all instrumental helps to make the attainment possible, since "God and nature do nothing but for an end," and help there can be none sufficient but by revelation. And once grant me that revelation is necessary, and then I will appeal to reason itself, and that shall prove abundantly one of these two: That either there was never any such revelation of this kind from the world's beginning to this day,—and that will put the *frustra* upon God in point of man's felicity; or, that the Scriptures which we now embrace as the Word of God is that revelation. And that is it we Christians labour to make good against all atheism, profaneness, and infidelity.

Last of all, To prove that the Book of God, which we honour as His Word, is this necessary revelation of God and His truth, which must, and is alone able to, lead us in the way to our eternal blessedness, or else the world hath none, comes in a cloud of witnesses, some for the infidel and some for the believer, some for the weak in faith and some for the strong, and some for all. For then first comes in the tradition of the Church,—the present Church, so it is no heretical or schismatical belief; then the testimony of former ages, so it is no new belief; then the consent of times, so it is no divided or partial belief; then the harmony of the prophets and them fulfilled, so it is not a "devised" but a forespoken belief; then the success of the doctrine contained in this Book, so it is not a belief stifled in the cradle, but it hath spread through the world in despite of what the world could do against it, and increased from weak and unlikely beginnings to incredible greatness; then the constancy of this truth, so it is no moon-belief, for in the midst of the world's changes, it hath preserved its creed entire through many generations; then, that there is nothing carnal in the doctrine, so it is a chaste belief. And all along it hath gained, kept, and exercised more power upon the minds of men, both learned and unlearned, in the increase of virtue and repression of vice, than any moral philosophy or legal policy that ever was. Then comes the inward light and excellency of the text itself, and so it is no dark or dazzling belief. And it is an excellent text. For see the riches of natural knowledge which are stored up there as well as supernatural. Consider how things quite above reason consent with things reasonable. Weigh it well what majesty lies there hid under humility; what depth there is with a perspicuity unimitable: what delight it works in the soul that is devoutly exercised in it: how the sublimest wits find in it enough to amaze them, while the simplest want not enough to direct them: and then we shall not wonder, if,—with the assistance of God's Spirit, Who alone works faith and belief of the Scriptures and their Divine authority, as well as other articles,—we grow up into a most infallible assurance; such an assurance as hath made many lay down their lives for this truth: such as that, *though an angel from Heaven should preach unto us another Gospel,* we would not believe him or it. No, though we should see as great and as many miracles done over again to dissuade us from it as were at first to win the world to it. To which firmness of assent, by the operation of God's Spirit, the will confers as much or more strength than the understanding clearness, the whole assent being an act of faith and not of knowledge. And therefore the question should not have been asked of me, by F [isher] "How I knew?" but "Upon what motives I did believe Scripture to be the Word of God?" And I would have him take heed lest hunting too close after a way of knowledge, he lose the way of faith, and teach other men to lose it too.

So then the way lies thus, as far as it appears to me, The credit of Scripture to be Divine resolves finally into that faith which we have touching God Himself, and in the same order. For as that, so this, hath three main grounds, to which all other are reducible. The first is, the tradition of the Church: and this leads us to a reverend persuasion of it. The second is, the light of Nature: and this shows us how necessary such a revealed learning is, and that no other way it can be had. Nay more, that all proofs brought against any point of faith, neither are nor can be demonstrations but soluble arguments. The third is, the light of the Text itself, in conversing wherewith we meet with the Spirit of God inwardly inclining our hearts, and sealing the full assurance of the sufficiency of all three unto us. And then, and not before, we are certain that the Scripture is the Word of God, both by Divine and by infallible proof. But our certainty is by faith, and so voluntary; not by knowledge of such principles as in the light of nature can enforce assent, whether we will or no. . . .

Though reason without grace cannot see the way to heaven nor believe this Book in which God hath written the way, yet grace is never placed but in a reasonable creature, and proves by the very seat which it hath taken up that the end it hath is to be spiritual eye-water, to make reason see what "by nature only it cannot," but never to blemish reason in that which it can, "comprehend." Now the use of reason is very general, and man, do what he can, is still got to search and seek for a reason why he will believe; though, after he once believes, his faith grows stronger than either his reason or his knowledge. And great reason for this, because it goes higher, and so upon a safer principle, than either of the other can in this life.

In this particular the books called the Scripture and commonly and constantly reputed to be the Word of God, and so infallible verity, cannot keep him from going to weigh it at the balance of reason, whether it be the Word of God or not. To the same weights he brings the Tradition of the Church, the inward motives in Scripture itself, all testimonies within, which seem to bear witness to it; and in all this there is no harm. The danger is when a man will use no other scale but reason, or prefer reason before any other scale. For the Word of God, and the Book containing it, refuse not to be weighed by reason. But the scale is not large enough to contain, nor the weights to measure out, the true virtue and full force of either. Reason, then, can give no supernatural ground into which a man may resolve his faith that Scripture is the Word of God infallible; yet reason can go so high, as it can prove that Christian Religion, which rests upon the authority of this Book, stands upon surer grounds of nature, reason, common equity, and justice, than anything in the world which any infidel or mere naturalist hath done, doth, or can adhere unto, against it, in that which he makes, accounts, or assumes as religion to himself.

THE WESTMINSTER CONFESSION OF FAITH (1647)

On the Nature of the Christian Faith

Of the Holy Scripture

1. Although the light of nature, and the works of creation and providence, do so far manifest the goodness, wisdom, and power of God, as to leave men inexcusable; yet are they not sufficient to give that knowledge of God, and of his will, which is necessary unto salvation; therefore it pleased the Lord, at sundry times, and in divers manners, to reveal himself, and to declare that his will unto his Church; and afterwards, for the better preserving and propagating of the truth, and for the more sure establishment and comfort of the Church against the corruption of the flesh, and the malice of Satan and of the world, to commit the same wholly unto writing; which maketh the holy Scripture to be most necessary; those former ways of God's revealing his will unto his people being now ceased. . . .

5. We may be moved and induced by the testimony of the Church to an high and reverent esteem of the holy Scripture; and the heavenliness of the matter, the efficacy of the doctrine, the majesty of the style, the consent of all the parts, the scope of the whole (which is to give all glory to God), the full discovery it makes of the only way of man's salvation, the many other incomparable excellencies, and the entire perfection thereof, are arguments whereby it doth abundantly evidence itself to be the Word of God; yet, notwithstanding, our full persuasion and assurance of the infallible truth and divine authority thereof, is from the inward work of the Holy Spirit, bearing witness by and with the Word in our hearts.

6. The whole counsel of God, concerning all things necessary for his own glory, man's salvation, faith, and life, is either expressly set down in Scripture, or by good and necessary consequence may be deduced from Scripture: unto which nothing at any time is to be added, whether by new revelations of the Spirit, or traditions of men. Nevertheless we acknowledge the inward illumination of the Spirit of God to be necessary for the saving understanding of such things as are revealed in the Word; and that

there are some circumstances concerning the worship of God, and government of the Church, common to human actions and societies, which are to be ordered by the light of nature and Christian prudence, according to the general rules of the Word, which are always to be observed.

7. All things in Scripture are not alike plain in themselves, nor alike clear unto all; yet those things which are necessary to be known, believed, and observed, for salvation, are so clearly propounded and opened in some place of the Scripture or other, that not only the learned, but the unlearned, in a due use of the ordinary means, may attain unto a sufficient understanding of them.

8. The Old Testament in Hebrew (which was the native language of the people of God of old), and the New Testament in Greek (which at the time of the writing of it was most generally known to the nations), being immediately inspired by God, and by his singular care and providence kept pure in all ages, are therefore authentical; so as in all controversies of religion the Church is finally to appeal unto them. But because these original tongues are not known to all the people of God who have right unto, and interest in the Scriptures, and are commanded, in the fear of God, to read and search them, therefore they are to be translated into the vulgar language of every nation unto which they come, that the Word of God dwelling plentifully in all, they may worship him in an acceptable manner, and, through patience and comfort of the Scriptures, may have hope.

9. The infallible rule of interpretation of Scripture is the Scripture itself; and therefore, when there is a question about the true and full sense of any Scripture (which is not manifold, but one), it must be searched and known by other places that speak more clearly.

10. The Supreme Judge, by which all controversies of religion are to be determined, and all decrees of councils, opinions of ancient writers, doctrines of men, and private spirits, are to be examined, and in whose sentence we are to rest, can be no other but the Holy Spirit speaking in the Scripture. . . .

Of the Fall of Man, of Sin, and of the Punishment thereof

1. Our first parents, being seduced by the subtilty and temptation of Satan, sinned in eating the forbidden fruit. This their sin God was pleased, according to his wise and holy counsel, to permit, having purposed to order it to his own glory.

2. By this sin they fell from their original righteousness and communion

with God, and so became dead in sin, and wholly defiled in all the faculties and parts of soul and body.

3. They being the root of all mankind, the guilt of this sin was imputed, and the same death in sin and corrupted nature conveyed to all their posterity descending from them by ordinary generation.

4. From this original corruption, whereby we are utterly indisposed, disabled, and made opposite to all good; and wholly inclined to all evil, do proceed all actual transgressions.

5. This corruption of nature, during this life, doth remain in those that are regenerated; and although it be through Christ pardoned and mortified, yet both itself and all the motions thereof are truly and properly sin.

6. Every sin, both original and actual, being a transgression of the righteous law of God, and contrary thereunto, doth in its own nature, bring guilt upon the sinner, whereby he is bound over to the wrath of God and curse of the law, and so made subject to death, with all miseries spiritual, temporal, and eternal.

Of God's Covenant with Man

1. The distance between God and the creature is so great that although reasonable creatures do owe obedience unto him as their Creator, yet they could never have any fruition of him as their blessedness and reward but by some voluntary condescension on God's part, which he hath been pleased to express by way of covenant.

2. The first covenant made with man was a covenant of works, wherein life was promised to Adam, and in him to his posterity, upon condition of perfect and personal obedience.

3. Man by his fall having made himself incapable of life by that covenant, the Lord was pleased to make a second, commonly called the covenant of grace: wherein he freely offered unto sinners life and salvation by Jesus Christ, requiring of them faith in him that they may be saved, and promising to give unto all those that are ordained unto life his Holy Spirit, to make them willing and able to believe.

4. This covenant of grace is frequently set forth in the Scripture by the name of a testament, in reference to the death of Jesus Christ the testator, and to the everlasting inheritance, with all things belonging to it, therein bequeathed.

5. This covenant was differently administered in the time of the law and in the time of the gospel: under the law it was administered by promises, prophecies, sacrifices, circumcision, the paschal lamb, and other types and ordinances delivered to the people of the Jews, all fore-signifying Christ to come, which were for that time sufficient and efficacious, through

the operation of the Spirit, to instruct and build up the elect in faith in the promised Messiah, by whom they had full remission of sins and eternal salvation; and is called the Old Testament.

6. Under the gospel, when Christ the substance was exhibited, the ordinances in which this covenant is dispensed are the preaching of the word and the administration of the sacraments of Baptism and the Lord's Supper; which, though fewer in number, and administered with more simplicity and less outward glory, yet in them it is held forth in more fullness, evidence, and spiritual efficacy, to all nations, both Jews and Gentiles; and is called the New Testament. There are not, therefore, two covenants of grace differing in substance, but one and the same under various dispensations. . . .

Of Free-will

1. God hath endowed the will of man with that natural liberty, that is neither forced nor by any absolute necessity of nature determined to good or evil.

2. Man, in his state of innocency, had freedom and power to will and to do that which is good and well-pleasing to God, but yet mutably, so that he might fall from it.

3. Man, by his fall into a state of sin, hath wholly lost all ability of will to any spiritual good accompanying salvation; so as a natural man, being altogether averse from that good, and dead in sin, is not able, by his own strength, to convert himself, or to prepare himself thereunto.

4. When God converts a sinner, and translates him into the state of grace, he freeth him from his natural bondage under sin, and by his grace alone enables him freely to will and to do that which is spiritually good; yet so as that, by reason of his remaining corruption, he doth not perfectly, nor only, will that which is good, but doth also will that which is evil.

5. The will of man is made perfectly and immutably free to good alone, in the state of glory only.

Of Effectual Calling

1. All those whom God hath predestinated unto life, and those only, he is pleased, in his appointed and accepted time, effectually to call, by his Word and Spirit, out of that state of sin and death, in which they are by nature, to grace and salvation by Jesus Christ; enlightening their minds, spiritually and savingly, to understand the things of God; taking away their heart of stone, and giving unto them an heart of flesh; renewing their wills, and by his almighty power determining them to that which is good, and ef-

fectually drawing them to Jesus Christ; yet so as they come most freely, being made willing by his grace.

2. This effectual call is of God's free and special grace alone, not from any thing at all foreseen in man; who is altogether passive therein, until, being quickened and renewed by the Holy Spirit, he is thereby enabled to answer this call, and to embrace the grace offered and conveyed in it.

3. Elect infants, dying in infancy, are regenerated and saved by Christ through the Spirit, who worketh when, and where, and how he pleaseth. So also are all other elect persons, who are incapable of being outwardly called by the ministry of the Word.

4. Others, not elected, although they may be called by the ministry of the Word, and may have some common operations of the Spirit, yet they never truly come unto Christ, and therefore can not be saved: much less can men, not professing the Christian religion, be saved in any other way whatsoever, be they never so diligent to frame their lives according to the light of nature and the law of that religion they do profess; and to assert and maintain that they may is very pernicious, and to be detested.

Of Justification

1. Those whom God effectually calleth he also freely justifieth; not by infusing righteousness into them, but by pardoning their sins, and by accounting and accepting their persons as righteous: not for any thing wrought in them, or done by them, but for Christ's sake alone; nor by imputing faith itself, the act of believing, or any other evangelical obedience to them, as their righteousness; but by imputing the obedience and satisfaction of Christ unto them, they receiving and resting on him and his righteousness by faith; which faith they have not of themselves, it is the gift of God.

2. Faith, thus receiving and resting on Christ and his righteousness, is the alone instrument of justification; yet is it not alone in the person justified, but is ever accompanied with all other saving graces, and is no dead faith, but worketh by love.

3. Christ, by his obedience and death, did fully discharge the debt of all those that are thus justified, and did make a proper, real, and full satisfaction to his Father's justice in their behalf. Yet inasmuch as he was given by the Father for them, and his obedience and satisfaction accepted in their stead, and both freely, not for any thing in them, their justification is only of free grace; that both the exact justice and rich grace of God might be glorified in the justification of sinners.

4. God did, from all eternity, decree to justify all the elect, and Christ

did, in the fullness of time, die for their sins, and rise again for their justification: nevertheless, they are not justified until the Holy Spirit doth, in due time, actually apply Christ unto them.

5. God doth continue to forgive the sins of those that are justified; and although they can never fall from the state of justification, yet they may by their sins fall under God's fatherly displeasure, and not have the light of his countenance restored unto them, until they humble themselves, confess their sins, beg pardon, and renew their faith and repentance.

6. The justification of believers under the Old Testament was, in all these respects, one and the same with the justification of believers under the New Testament. . . .

Of Saving Faith

1. The grace of faith, whereby the elect are enabled to believe to the saving of their souls, is the work of the Spirit of Christ in their hearts, and is ordinarily wrought by the ministry of the Word; by which also, and by the administration of the sacraments and prayer, it is increased and strengthened.

2. By this faith a Christian believeth to be true, whatsoever is revealed in the Word, for the authority of God himself speaking therein; and acteth differently upon that which each particular passage thereof containeth; yielding obedience to the commands, trembling at the threatenings, and embracing the promises of God for this life and that which is to come. But the principal acts of saving faith are accepting, receiving, and resting upon Christ alone for justification, sanctification, and eternal life, by virtue of the covenant of grace.

3. This faith is different in degrees, weak or strong; may be often and many ways assailed and weakened, but gets the victory; growing up in many to the attainment of a full assurance through Christ, who is both the author and finisher of our faith. . . .

Of Good Works

1. Good works are only such as God hath commanded in his holy Word, and not such as, without the warrant thereof, are devised by men out of blind zeal, or upon any pretense of good intention.

2. These good works, done in obedience to God's commandments, are the fruits and evidences of a true and lively faith; and by them believers manifest their thankfulness, strengthen their assurance, edify their brethren, adorn the profession of the gospel, stop the mouths of the adversaries, and glorify God, whose workmanship they are, created in Christ Jesus

thereunto, that, having their fruit unto holiness, they may have the end, eternal life.

3. Their ability to do good works is not at all of themselves, but wholly from the Spirit of Christ. And that they may be enabled thereunto, besides the graces they have already received, there is required an actual influence of the same Holy Spirit to work in them to will and to do of his good pleasure; yet are they not hereupon to grow negligent, as if they were not bound to perform any duty unless upon a special motion of the Spirit; but they ought to be diligent in stirring up the grace of God that is in them.

4. They who in their obedience attain to the greatest height which is possible in this life, are so far from being able to supererogate and to do more than God requires, as that they fall short of much which in duty they are bound to do.

5. We cannot, by our best works, merit pardon of sin, or eternal life at the hand of God, by reason of the great disproportion that is between them and the glory to come, and the infinite distance that is between us and God, whom by them we can neither profit nor satisfy for the debt of our former sins; but when we have done all we can, we have done but our duty, and are unprofitable servants; and because, as they are good, they proceed from his Spirit; and as they are wrought by us, they are defiled and mixed with so much weakness and imperfection that they can not endure the severity of God's judgment.

6. Yet notwithstanding, the persons of believers being accepted through Christ, their good works also are accepted in him, not as though they were in this life wholly unblamable and unreprovable in God's sight; but that he, looking upon them in his Son, is pleased to accept and reward that which is sincere, although accompanied with many weaknesses and imperfections.

7. Works done by unregenerate men, although for the matter of them they may be things which God commands, and of good use both to themselves and others; yet because they proceed not from a heart purified by faith, nor are done in a right manner, according to the Word, nor to a right end, the glory of God; they are therefore sinful, and can not please God, or make a man meet to receive grace from God. And yet their neglect of them is more sinful and displeasing unto God.

Of the Perseverance of the Saints

1. They whom God hath accepted in his Beloved, effectually called and sanctified by his Spirit, can neither totally nor finally fall away from

the state of grace; but shall certainly persevere therein to the end and be eternally saved.

2. This perseverance of the saints depends, not upon their own free-will, but upon the immutability of the decree of election, flowing from the free and unchangeable love of God the Father; upon the efficacy of the merit and intercession of Jesus Christ; the abiding of the Spirit, and of the seed of God within them; and the nature of the covenant of grace: from all which ariseth also the certainty and infallibility thereof.

3. Nevertheless they may, through the temptations of Satan and of the world, the prevalency of corruption remaining in them, and the neglect of the means of their preservation, fall into grievous sins; and for a time continue therein: whereby they incur God's displeasure, and grieve his Holy Spirit; come to be deprived of some measure of their graces and comforts; have their hearts hardened, and their consciences wounded; hurt and scandalize others, and bring temporal judgments upon themselves. . . .

Of the Church

1. The catholic or universal Church, which is invisible and consists of the whole number of the elect, that have been, are, or shall be gathered into one, under Christ the head thereof; and is the spouse, the body, the fullness of him that filleth all in all.

2. The visible Church, which is also catholic or universal under the gospel (not confined to one nation as before under the law) consists of all those, throughout the world, that profess the true religion, and of their children; and is the kingdom of the Lord Jesus Christ, the house and family of God, out of which there is no ordinary possibility of salvation.

3. Unto this catholic, visible Church Christ hath given the ministry, oracles, and ordinances of God, for the gathering and perfecting of the saints, in this life, to the end of the world: and doth by his own presence and Spirit, according to his promise, make them effectual thereunto.

4. This catholic Church hath been sometimes more, sometimes less visible. And particular churches, which are members thereof, are more or less pure, according as the doctrine of the gospel is taught and embraced, ordinances administered, and public worship performed more or less purely in them.

5. The purest churches under heaven are subject both to mixture and error; and some have so degenerated as to become no churches of Christ but synagogues of Satan. Nevertheless, there shall be always a Church on earth to worship God according to his will.

6. There is no other head of the Church but the Lord Jesus Christ: nor can the Pope of Rome, in any sense, be head thereof; but is that Antichrist, that man of sin and son of perdition, that exalteth himself in the Church against Christ, and all that is called God. . . .

THE DORDRECHT CONFESSION (1632)

Anabaptist View of Christianity

Article VI:
Of Repentance and
Amendment of Life

We believe and confess, that, as the "imagination of man's heart is evil from his youth," and consequently inclined to all righteousness, sin, and wickedness, that, therefore, the first doctrine of the precious New Testament of the Son of God is, Repentance and amendment of life. (Gen. 8:21; Mark 1:15)

Therefore those who have ears to hear, and hearts to understand, must "bring forth fruits meet for repentance," amend their lives, believe the Gospel, "depart from evil and do good," desist from wrong and cease from sinning, "put off the old man with his deeds and put on the new man," which after God is created in "righteousness and true holiness." For neither *Baptism, Supper, nor church-fellowship,* nor any other external ceremony, can, without faith, the new birth, and a change or renewal of life, help, or qualify us, that we may please God, or receive any consolation or promise of salvation from Him. (Luke 3:8; Eph. 4:22–24; Col. 3:9,10)

But on the contrary, we must go to God "with a sincere heart in full assurance of faith," and believe in Jesus Christ, as the Scriptures speak and testify of Him. Through which faith we obtain the pardon of our sins, become sanctified, justified, and children of God; yea, partakers of His mind, nature and image, as we are born again of God through His incorruptible seed from above. (Heb. 10:21, 22; John 7:38; II Pet. 1:4)

Article VII: Of Holy Baptism

Regarding baptism, we confess that all penitent believers who through faith, the new birth and renewal of the Holy Ghost, have become united with God, and whose names are recorded in heaven, must, on such Scriptural confession of their faith, and renewal of life, according to the command and doctrine of Christ, and the example and custom of the apostles, be baptized with water in the ever adorable name of the Father, and of the Son, and of the Holy Ghost, to the burying of their sins, and thus to become incorporated into the communion of the saints; whereupon they must learn to observe all things whatsoever the Son of God taught, left on record, and commanded His followers to do. (Matt. 3:15; 28:19,20; Mark 16:15,16; Acts 2:38; 8:12,38; 9:18; 10:47; 16:33; Rom. 6:3,4; Col. 2:12)

Article VIII: Of the Church of Christ

We believe in and confess a visible Church of God, consisting of those, who, as before remarked, have truly repented, and rightly believed; who are rightly baptized, united with God in heaven, and incorporated into the communion of the saints on earth. (I Cor. 12:13)

And these, we confess, are a "chosen generation, a royal priesthood, an holy nation," who have the testimony that they are the "bride" of Christ; yea, that they are children and heirs of eternal life—a "habitation of God through the Spirit," built on the foundation of the apostles and prophets, of which "Christ Himself is the chief cornerstone"—the foundation on which His church is built. (John 3:29; Matt. 16:18, Eph. 2:19-21; Tit. 3:7; I Pet. 1:18,19; 2:9)

This church of the living God, which He has purchased and redeemed through His own precious blood, and with which He will be—according to His own promise—for her comfort and protection, "always, even unto the end of the world"; yea, will dwell and walk with her, and preserve her, that no "winds" nor "floods," yea, not even the "gates of hell shall prevail against her"—may be known by her evangelical faith, doctrine, love, and godly conversation; also by her pure walk and practice, and her observance of the true ordinances of Christ, which He has strictly enjoined on His followers. (Matt. 7:25; 16:18; 28:20; II Cor. 6:16)

Article IX: Of the Election, and Offices of Teachers Deacons, and Deaconesses in the Church

Regarding the offices, and election of persons to the same in the church, we believe and confess: That, as the church cannot exist and prosper, nor continue in its structure, without offices and regulations, that therefore the Lord Jesus has Himself (as a father in his house), appointed and prescribed His offices and ordinances, and has given commandments concerning the same, as to how each one should walk therein, give heed to His own work and calling, and do it as it becomes Him to do. (Eph. 4:11,12)

For He Himself, as the faithful and great Shepherd, and Bishop of our souls, was sent into the world, not to wound, to break, or destroy the souls of men, but to heal them; to seek that which is lost, and to pull down the hedges and partition wall, so as to make out of many one; thus collecting out of Jews and heathen, yea, out of all nations, a church in His name; for which (so that no one might go astray or be lost) He laid down His own life, and thus procured for them salvation, made them free and redeemed them, to which blessing no one could help them or be of service in obtaining it. (I Pet. 2:25; Matt. 18:11; Eph. 2:13,14; John 10:9,11,15)

And that He, besides this, left His church before His departure, provided with faithful ministers, apostles, evangelists, pastors, and teachers, whom He had chosen by prayer and supplication through the Holy Spirit, so that they might govern the church, feed His flock, watch over, maintain, and care for the same: yea, do all things as He left them an example, taught them, and commanded them to do; and likewise to teach the church to observe all things whatsoever He commanded them. (Eph. 4:11,12; Luke 6:12,13; 10:1; Matt. 28:20)

Also that the apostles were afterwards, as faithful followers of Christ and leaders of the church, diligent in these matters, namely, in choosing through prayer and supplication to God, brethren who were to provide all the churches in the cities and circuits, with bishops, pastors, and leaders, and to ordain to these offices such men as took "heed unto themselves and unto the doctrine," and also unto the flock; who were sound in the faith, pious in their life and conversation, and who had—as well within the church as "without"—a good reputation and a good report; so that they might be a light and example in all godliness and good works; might worthily administer the Lord's ordinances—baptism and supper—and that they (the brethren sent by the apostles) might also, at all places, where such were to be had, appoint faithful men as elders, who were able to teach others, confirm them in the name of the Lord "with the laying on of hands," and who (the elders) were to take care of all things of which the church stood in need; so that they, as faithful servants, might well "occupy" their Lord's money, gain thereby, and thus "save themselves and those who hear them." (I Tim. 3:1; 4:14–16; Acts 1:23,24; Tit. 1:5; Luke 19:13)

That they should also take good care (particularly each one of the charge over which he had the oversight), that all the circuits should be well provided with deacons, who should have the care and oversight of the poor, and who were to receive gifts and alms, and again faithfully to distribute them among the poor saints who were in need, and this is in all honesty, as is becoming. (Acts 6:3–6)

Also that honorable old widows should be chosen as deaconesses, who, besides the deacons are to visit, comfort, and take care of the poor, the weak, afflicted, and the needy, as also to visit, comfort, and take care of widows and orphans; and further to assist in taking care of any matters in the church that properly come within their sphere; according to their ability. (I Tim. 5:9,10; Rom. 16:1,2)

And as it further regards the deacons, that they (particularly if they are fit persons, and chosen and ordained thereto by the church), may also in aid and relief of the bishops, exhort the church, (being, as already remarked, chosen thereto), and thus assist in word and doctrine; so that each one may serve the other from love, with the gift which he has received from the Lord; so that through the common service and assistance of each member, according to his ability, the body of Christ may be edified, and the Lord's vineyard and church be preserved in its growth and structure. (II Tim. 2:2)

Article X: Of the Lord's Supper

We also believe in and observe the breaking of bread, or the Lord's Supper, as the Lord Jesus instituted the same (with bread and wine) before His sufferings, and also observed and ate it with the apostles, and also commanded it to be observed to His remembrance, as also the apostles subsequently taught and observed the same in the church, and commanded it to be observed by believers in commemoration of the death and sufferings of the Lord—the breaking of His worthy body and shedding of His precious blood—for the whole human race. So is the observance of this sacrament also to remind us of the benefit of the said death and sufferings of Christ, namely, the redemption and eternal salvation which he purchased thereby, and the great love thus shown to sinful man; whereby we are earnestly exhorted also to love one another—to love our neighbor—to forgive and absolve him—even as Christ has done unto us—and also to endeavor to maintain and keep alive the union and communion which we have with God, and amongst one another; which is thus shown and represented to us by the aforesaid breaking of bread. (Matt. 26:26; Mark 14:22; Luke 22:19,20; Acts 2:42,46; I Cor. 10:16; 11:23–26)

Article XI: Of the Washing of the Saints' Feet

We also confess a washing of the feet of the saints, as the Lord Jesus did not only institute and command the same, but did also Himself wash the feet of the apostles, although He was their Lord and Master; thereby giving an example that they also should wash one another's feet, and thus do to one another as He did to them; which they also afterwards taught believers to observe, and all this is a sign of true humiliation; but yet more particularly as a sign to remind us of the true washing—the washing and purification of the soul in the blood of Christ. (John 13:4–17; I Tim. 5:9, 10)

Article XII: Of Matrimony

We also confess that there is in the church of God an "honorable" state of matrimony between two believers of the different sexes, as God first instituted the same in paradise between Adam and Eve, and as the Lord Jesus reformed it by removing all abuses which had crept into it, and restoring it to its first order. (Gen. 1:27; 2:18,21–24)

In this manner the Apostle Paul also taught and permitted matrimony in the church, leaving it to each one's own choice to enter into matrimony with any person who would unite with him in such state, provided that it was done "in the Lord," according to the primitive order; the words "in the Lord," to be understood, according to our opinion, that just as the patriarchs had to marry amongst their own kindred or generation, so there is also no other liberty allowed to believers under the New Testament dispensation, than to marry among the "chosen generation," or the spiritual kindred of Christ; that is, to such—and none others—as are already, previous to their marriage, united to the church in heart and soul, have received the same baptism, belong to the same church, are of the same faith and doctrine, and lead the same course of life, with themselves. (I Cor. 7:39; 9:5; Gen. 24:4; 28:6,7; Num. 36:6–9)

Such are then, as already remarked, united by God and the church according to the primitive order, and this is then called, "Marrying in the Lord." (I Cor. 7:39)

Article XIII: Of the Office of Civil Government

We also believe and confess, that God has instituted civil government, for the punishment of the wicked and the protection of the pious; and also further, for the purpose of governing the world, countries and cities; and also to preserve its subjects in good order and under good regulations. Wherefore we are not permitted to despise, revile, or resist the same, but are to acknowledge it as a minister of God and be subject and obedient to it, in all things that do not militate against the law, will, and commandments of God; yea, "to be ready to every good work"; also faithfully to pay it custom, tax, tribute; thus giving it what is its due; as Jesus Christ taught, did Himself, and commanded His followers to do. That we are also to pray to the Lord earnestly for the government and its welfare, and in behalf of our country, so that we may live under its protection, maintain ourselves, and "lead a quiet and peaceable life in all godliness and honesty." And further, that the Lord would recompense them (our rulers), here and in eternity, for all the benefits, liberties, and favors which we enjoy under their laudable administration. (Rom. 13:1–7; Titus 3:1,2; I Pet. 2:17; Matt. 17:27; 22:20,21; I Tim. 2:1,2)

Article XIV: Of Defense by Force

Regarding revenge, whereby we resist our enemies with the sword, we believe and confess that the Lord Jesus has forbidden His disciples and followers all revenge and resistance, and has thereby commanded them not to "return evil for evil, nor railing for railing," but to "put up the sword into the sheath," or, as the prophet foretold, "beat them into ploughshares." (Matt. 5:39,44; Rom. 12:14; I Pet. 3:9; Isa. 2:4; Micah 4:3)

From this we see, that according to the example, life and doctrine of Christ, we are not to do wrong, or cause offense or vexation to anyone; but to seek the welfare and salvation of all men; also, if necessity should require it, to flee, for the Lord's sake, from one city or country to another, and suffer the "spoiling of our goods," rather than give occasion of offense to anyone; and if we are struck on our "right cheek, rather to turn the other also," than revenge ourselves, or return the blow. (Matt. 5:39; 10:23; Rom. 12:19)

And that we are, besides this, also to pray for our enemies, comfort and feed them, when they are hungry or thirsty, and thus by well-doing convince them and overcome the evil with good. (Rom. 12:20,21)

Finally, that we are to do good in all respects, "commending ourselves to every man's conscience in the sight of God," and according to the law of Christ, do nothing to others that we would not wish them to do unto us. (II Cor. 4:2; Matt. 7:12; Luke 6:31)

Article XV: Of the Swearing of Oaths

Regarding the swearing of oaths, we believe and confess that the Lord Jesus has dissuaded His followers from and forbidden them the same; that is, that He commanded them to "swear not at all"; but that their "Yea" should be "yea," and their "Nay, nay." From which we understand that all oaths, high and low, are forbidden; and that instead of them we are to confirm all our promises and covenants, declarations and testimonies of all matters, merely with "Yea that is yea," and "Nay that is nay"; and that we are to perform and fulfill at all times, and in all things, to every one, every promise and obligation to which we thus affirm, as faithfully as if we had confirmed it by the most solemn oath. And if we thus do, we have the confidence that no one—not even government itself —will have just cause to require more of us. (Matt. 5:34–37; Jas. 5:13; II Cor. 1:17)

Article XVI: Of the Ecclesiastical Ban or Excommunication From the Church

We also believe in and acknowledge the ban, or excommunication, a separation or spiritual correction by the church, for the amendment, and not for the destruction, of offenders; so that what is pure may be separated from that which is impure. That is, if a person, after having been enlightened, and received the knowledge of the truth, and has been received into the communion of the saints, does willfully, or out of presumption, sin against God, or commit some other "sin unto death," thereby falling into such unfruitful works of darkness, that he becomes separated from God, and is debarred from His Kingdom—that such an one—when his works are become manifest, and sufficiently known to the church—cannot remain in the "congregation of the righteous"; but must, as an offensive member and open sinner, be excluded from the church, "rebuked before all," and "purged out as a leaven," and thus remain until his amendment, as an example and warning to others, and also that the church may be kept pure from such "spots" and "blemishes"; so that not for the want of this, the name of the Lord be blasphemed, the church dishonored, and a stumbling block thrown in the way of those "without," and finally, that the offender may be convinced of the error of his ways, and brought to repentance and amendment of life. (Isa. 59:2; I Cor. 5:5,6,12; I Tim. 5:20; II Cor. 13:10)

Regarding the brotherly admonition, as also the instruction of the erring, we are to "give all diligence" to watch over them, and exhort them in all meekness to the amendment of their ways (Jas. 5:19,20); and in case any should remain obstinate and unconverted, to reprove them as the case may require. In short, the church must "put away from among herself him that is wicked," whether it be in doctrine or life.

Article XVII: Of the Shunning of Those Who Are Expelled

As regards the withdrawing from, or the shunning of, those who are expelled, we believe and confess, that if any one—whether it be through a wicked life or perverse doctrine—is so far fallen as to be separated from God, and consequently rebuked by, and expelled from, the church, he must also, according to the doctrine of Christ and His apostles, be shunned and avoided by all the members of the church (particularly by those to whom his misdeeds are known), whether it be in eating or drinking, or other such like social matters. In short, that we are to have nothing to do with him; so that we may not become defiled by intercourse with him, and partakers of his sins; but that he may be made ashamed, be affected in his mind, convinced in his conscience, and thereby induced to amend his ways. (I Cor. 5:9–11; Rom. 16:17; II Thess. 3:14; Tit. 3:10,11)

That nevertheless, as well in shunning as in reproving such offender, such moderation and Christian discretion be used, that such shunning and reproof may not be conducive to his ruin, but be serviceable to his amendment. For should he be in need, hungry, thirsty, naked, sick or visited by some other affliction, we are in duty bound, according to the doctrine and practice of Christ and His apostles, to render him aid and assistance, as necessity may require; otherwise the shunning of him might be rather conducive to his ruin than to his amendment. (I Thess. 5:14)

Therefore we must not treat such offenders as enemies, but exhort them as brethren, in order thereby to bring them to a knowledge of their sins and to repentance; so that they may again become reconciled to God and the church, and be received and admitted into the same—thus exercising love towards them, as is becoming. (II Thess. 3:15)

JEREMY TAYLOR (1613–1667)

Religious Toleration

So long as Christian religion was a simple profession of the articles of belief, and a hearty prosecution of the rules of good life, the fewness of the articles and the clearness of the rule was cause of the seldom prevarication. But when divinity is swelled up to so great a body, when the several questions, which the peevishness and wantonness of sixteen ages have commenced, are concentered into one, and from all these questions something is drawn into the body of theology till it hath ascended up to the greatness of a mountain, and the sum of divinity collected by Aquinas makes a volume as great as was that of Livy, mocked at in the epigram,

"A work which shelves like mine can scarce contain—"

it is impossible for any industry to consider so many particulars, in the infinite numbers of questions as are necessary to be considered before we can with certainty determine any. And after all the considerations which we can have in a whole age, we are not sure "not to be deceived." The obscurity of some questions, the nicety of some articles, the intricacy of some revelations, the variety of human understandings, the windings of logic, the tricks of adversaries, the subtlety of sophisters, the engagement of educations, personal affections, the portentous number of writers, the infinity of authorities, the vastness of some arguments, as consisting in enumeration of many particulars, the uncertainty of others, the several degrees of probability, the difficulties of Scripture, the invalidity of probation of tradition, the opposition of all exterior arguments to each other, and their open contestation, the public violence done to authors and records, the private arts and supplantings, the falsifyings, the indefatigable industry of some men to abuse all understandings and all persuasions into their own opinions, these and thousands more, even all the difficulty of things, and all the weaknesses of man, and all the arts of the devil, have made it impossible for any man, in so great variety of matter, not to be deceived. No man pretends to it but the pope, and no man is more deceived than he is in that very particular.

From hence proceeds a danger which is consequent to this proceeding; for if we, who are so apt to be deceived and so insecure in our resolution of questions disputable, should persecute a disagreeing person, we are not sure we do not fight against God; for if his proposition be true and persecuted, then, because all truth derives from God, this proceeding is against God; and therefore this is not to be done, upon Gamaliel's ground, "lest peradventure we be found to fight against God," of which because we can have no security (at least) in this case, we have all the guilt of a doubtful or an uncertain conscience. For if there be no security in the thing, as I have largely proved, the conscience, in such cases, is as uncertain as the question is: and if it be not doubtful where it is uncertain, it is because the man is not wise, but as confident as ignorant; the first without reason, and the second without excuse. And it is very disproportionable for a man to persecute another certainly, for a proposition, that, if he were wise, he would know is not certain, at least the other person may innocently be uncertain of it. If he be killed he is certainly killed; but if he be called heretic it is not so certain that he is an heretic. It were good, therefore, that proceedings were according to evidence, and the rivers not swell over the banks, nor a certain definitive sentence of death passed upon such persuasions which cannot certainly be defined. And this argument is of so much the more force because we see that the greatest persecutions that ever have been, were against truth, even against Christianity itself; and it was a prediction of our blessed Savior that persecution should be the lot of true believers: and if we compute the experience of suffering Christendom, and the prediction that truth should suffer, with those few instances of suffering heretics, it is odds but persecution is on the wrong side, and that it is error and heresy, that is, cruel and tyrannical, especially since the truth of Jesus Christ and of his religion, is so meek, so charitable, and so merciful. And we may in this case exactly use the words of St. Paul: "But as then he that was born after the flesh, persecuted him that was born after the Spirit; even so it is now": and so ever will it be till Christ's second coming.

Whoever persecutes a disagreeing person, arms all the world against himself, and all pious people of his own persuasion, when the scales of authority return to his adversary and attest his contradictory; and then what can he urge for mercy for himself, or his party, that showeth none to others? If he says, that he is to be spared because he believes true, but the other was justly persecuted because he was in error, he is ridiculous; for he is as confidently believed to be a heretic as he believes his adversary such; and whether he be or no, being the thing in question, of this he is not to be his own judge: but he that hath authority on his side will be sure to judge against him. So that what either side can indifferently make use of, it is good that neither would, because neither side can, with reason sufficient, do it in prejudice of the other. . . .

Either the disagreeing person is in error or not, but a true believer; in either of the cases, to persecute him is extremely imprudent. For if he be a true believer, then it is a clear case that we do open violence to God, and his servants, and his truth. If he be in error, what greater folly and stupidity than to give to error the glory of martyrdom, and the advantages which are accidentally consequent to a persecution? For as it was true of the martyrs, "As often as we die, so often do we begin to live," and the increase of their trouble was the increase of their confidence and the establishment of their persuasions, so it is in all false opinions; for that an opinion is true or false, is extrinsical or accidental to the consequents and advantages it gets by being afflicted. And there is a popular pity that follows all persons in misery, and that compassion breeds likeness of affections, and that very often produces likeness of persuasion; and so much the rather, because there arises a jealousy and pregnant suspicion that they who persecute an opinion are destitute of sufficient arguments to confute it, and that the hangman is the best disputant. For if those arguments which they have for their own doctrine were a sufficient ground of confidence and persuasion, men would be more willing to use those means and arguments which are better compliances with human understanding, which more naturally do satisfy it, which are more humane and Christian than that way is which satisfies none, which destroys many, which provokes more, and which makes all men jealous. . . .

It is unnatural and unreasonable to persecute disagreeing opinions. Unnatural; for understanding, being a thing wholly spiritual, cannot be restrained, and therefore neither punished by corporal afflictions. It is *in aliena republica,* a matter of another world. You may as well cure the colic by brushing a man's clothes, or fill a man's belly with a syllogism. These things do not communicate in matter, and therefore neither in action nor passion. And since all punishments in a prudent government punish the offender to prevent a future crime, and so it proves more medicinal than vindictive, the punitive act being in order to the cure and prevention; and since no punishment of the body can cure a disease in the soul, it is disproportionable in nature, and in all civil government, to punish where the punishment can do no good. It may be an act of tyranny, but never of justice. For is an opinion ever the more true or false for being persecuted? Some men have believed it the more, as being provoked into a confidence, and vexed into a resolution; but the thing itself is not the truer: and though the hangman may confute a man with an inexplicable dilemma, yet not convince his understanding; for such premises can infer no conclusion but that of a man's life: and a wolf may as well give laws to the understanding, as he whose dictates are only propounded in violence, and writ in blood: and a dog is as capable of a law as a man, if there be no choice in his obedience, nor discourse in his choice, nor reason to satisfy his discourse. And as it is unnatural, so it is unreasonable that Sempronius should force Caius to be of his opinion, because Sempronius is consul this year, and commands the lictors. As if he that can kill a man, cannot but be infallible: and if he be not, why should I do violence to my conscience because he can do violence to my person?

Force in matters of opinion can do no good, but is very apt to do hurt; for no man can change his opinion when he will, or be satisfied in his reason that his opinion is false because discountenanced. If a man could change his opinion when he lists, he might cure many inconveniences of his life: all his fears and his sorrows would soon disband, if he would but alter his opinion, whereby he is persuaded that such an accident that afflicts him is an evil, and such an object formidable: let him but believe himself impregnable, or that he receives a benefit when he is plundered, disgraced, imprisoned, condemned, and afflicted, neither his steps need to be disturbed, nor his quietness discomposed. But if a man cannot change his opinion when he lists, nor ever does heartily or resolutely but when he cannot do otherwise, then to use force may make him an hypocrite but never to be a right believer; and so, instead of erecting a trophy to God and true religion, we build a monument for the devil. . . .

But I consider, that in the toleration of a different opinion, religion is not properly and immediately concerned, so as in any degree to be endangered. For it may be safe in diversity of persuasions, and it is also a part of Christian religion, that the liberty of men's consciences should be preserved in all things where God hath not set a limit and made a restraint; that the soul of man should be free, and acknowledge no master but Jesus Christ; that matters spiritual should not be restrained by punishments corporal; that the same meekness and charity should be preserved in the promotion of Christianity that gave it foundation and increment and firmness in its first publication; that conclusions should not be more dogmatical than the virtual resolution and efficacy of the premises; and that the persons should not more certainly be condemned than their opinions confuted; and lastly, that the infirmities of men and difficulties of things should be both put in balance, to make abatement in the definitive sentence against men's persons. But then, because toleration of opinions is not properly a question of religion, it may be a question of policy: and although a man may be a good Christian, though he believe an error not fundamental, and not directly or evidently impious, yet his opinion may accidentally disturb the public peace, through the overactiveness of the persons, and the confidence of their belief, and the opinion of its appendant necessity: and therefore toleration of differing persuasions, in these cases, is to be considered upon political grounds, and is just so to be admitted or denied as the opinions or toleration of them may consist with the public and necessary ends of government. Only this: as Christian princes must look to the interest of their government, so especially must they consider the interests of Christianity, and not call every redargution or modest discovery of an established error, by the name of disturbance of the peace. . . . Let them remember but the gentleness of Christianity, the liberty of consciences which ought to be preserved, and let them do justice to the persons, whoever they are, that are peevish, provided no man's person be overborne with prejudice. For if it be necessary for all men to subscribe to the present established religion, by the same reason at another time a man may be bound to subscribe to the contradictory, and so to all religions in the world. And they only who by their too much confidence entitle God to all their fancies, and make them to be questions of religion, and evidences for heaven, or consignations to hell, they only think this doctrine unreasonable, and they are the men that first disturb the church's peace, and then think there is no appeasing the tumult but by getting the victory. But they that consider things wisely, understand, that since salvation and damnation depend not upon impertinencies, and yet that public peace and tranquility may,—the prince is, in this case, to seek how to secure government, and the issues and intentions of that, while there is in the cases directly no insecurity to religion, unless by the accidental uncharitableness of them that dispute: which uncharitableness is much prevented when the public peace is secured, and no person is on either side engaged upon revenge, or troubled with disgrace, or vexed with punishments by any decretory sentence against him. It was the saying of a wise stateman, I mean Thuanus, "If you persecute heretics or discrepants, they unite themselves as to a common defence: if you permit them, they divide themselves upon private interest.". . .

ROBERT BARCLAY (1648–1690)

On the Inner Light of the Quakers

Proposition V

God, out of his infinite love, who delighteth not in the death of a sinner, but that all should live and be saved, hath so loved the world, that he hath given his only Son a Light, that whosoever believeth in him shall be saved, (John iii.16), who enlighteneth every man that cometh into the world, (John i.9), and maketh manifest all things that are reprovable, (Ephes. v.13), and teacheth all temperance, righteousness, and godliness; and this Light enlighteneth the hearts of all for a time, in order to salvation; and this is it which reproves the sin of all individuals, and would work out the salvation of all, if not resisted. Nor is it less universal than the seed of sin, being the purchase of his death, who tasted death for every man: for as in Adam all die, even so in Christ all shall be made alive, (I Cor. xv.22).

Proposition VI

According to which principle or hypothesis all the objections against the universality of Christ's death are easily solved; neither is it needful to recur to the ministry of angels, and those other miraculous means which they say God useth to manifest the doctrine and history of Christ's passion unto such, who, living in parts of the world where the outward preaching of the gospel is unknown, have well improved the first and common grace. For as hence it well follows that some of the old philosophers might have been saved, so also may some, who by providence are cast into those remote parts of the world where the knowledge of the history is wanting, be made partakers of the divine mystery, if they receive and resist not that grace, a manifestation whereof is given to every man to profit withal. This most certain doctrine being then received, that there is an evangelical and saving light and grace in all, the universality of the love and mercy of God towards mankind, both in the death of his beloved Son the Lord Jesus Christ, and in the manifestation of the light in the heart, is established and confirmed, against all the objections of such as deny it. Therefore Christ hath tasted death for every man; not only for all kinds of men, as some vainly talk, but for every man of all kinds; the benefit of whose offering is not only extended to such who have the distinct outward knowledge of his death and sufferings, as the same is declared in the scriptures, but even unto those who are necessarily excluded from the benefit of this knowledge by some inevitable accident; which knowledge we willingly confess to be very profitable and comfortable, but not absolutely needful unto such from whom God himself hath withheld it; yet they may be made partakers of the mystery of his death, though ignorant of the history, if they suffer his seed and light, enlightening their hearts, to take place; in which light communion with the Father and the Son is enjoyed; so as of wicked men to become holy, and lovers of that power, by whose inward and secret touches they feel themselves turned from the evil to the good, and learn to do to others as they would be done by, in which Christ himself affirms all to be included. As they have then falsely and erroneously taught, who have denied Christ to have died for all men: so neither have they sufficiently taught the truth, who, affirming him to have died for all, have added the absolute necessity of the outward knowledge thereof, in order to obtain its saving effect. Among whom the Remonstrants of Holland have been chiefly wanting, and many other asserters of universal redemption, in that they have not placed the extent of this salvation in that divine and evangelical principle of light and life wherewith Christ hath enlightened every man that cometh into the world, which is excellently and evidently held forth in these scriptures, Gen. vi.3; Deut. xxx.14; John i.7,8,9,16; Rom. x.8; Titus, ii.11. . . .

XII. First, then, By this day and time of visitation, which we say God gives unto all, during which they may be saved, we do not understand the whole time of every man's life; though to some it may be extended even to the very hour of death, as we see in the example of the thief converted upon the cross; but such a season at least as sufficiently exonerateth God of every man's condemnation, which to some may be sooner, and to others later, according as the Lord in his wisdom sees meet. So that many men may outlive this day, after which there may be no possibility of salvation to them, and God justly suffers them to be hardened, as a just punishment of their unbelief, and even raises them up as instruments of wrath, and makes them a scourge one against another. . . .

XIII. Secondly, By this seed, grace, and word of God, and light wherewith we say every one is enlightened, and hath a measure of it, which strives with him in order to save him, and which may, by the stubbornness and wickedness of man's will, be quenched, bruised, wounded, pressed down, slain and crucified, we understand not the proper essence and nature of God precisely taken, which is not divisible into parts and measures, as being a most pure, simple being, void of all composition or division, and therefore can neither be resisted, hurt, wounded, crucified, or slain by all the efforts and strength of men; but we understand a spiritual, heavenly, and invisible principle, in which God, as Father, Son and Spirit, dwells; a measure of which divine and glorious life is in all men as a seed, which of its own nature, draws, invites, and inclines to God; and this some call *Vehiculum Dei,* or the spiritual body of Christ, the flesh and blood of Christ, which came down from heaven, of which all the saints do feed, and are thereby nourished unto eternal life. And as every unrighteous action is witnessed against and reproved by this light and seed, so by such actions it is hurt, wounded, and slain, and flees from them even as the flesh of man flees from that which is of a contrary nature to it. Now because it is never separated from God nor Christ, but wherever it is, God and Christ are as wrapped up therein, therefore and in that respect as it is resisted, God is said to be resisted; and where it is borne down, God is said to be pressed as a cart under sheaves, and Christ is said to be slain and crucified. And on the contrary, as this seed is received in the heart, and suffered to bring forth its natural and proper effect, Christ comes to be formed and raised, of which the scripture makes so much mention, calling it the new man; Christ within, the hope of glory. This is that Christ within, which we are heard so much to speak and declare of; every where preaching him up, and exhorting people to believe in the light, and obey it, that they may come to know Christ in them, to deliver them from all sin. . . .

XIV. Thirdly, We understand not this seed, light, or grace to be an accident, as most men ignorantly do, but a real spiritual substance, which the soul of man is capable to feel and apprehend; from which that real, spiritual, inward birth in believers arises, called the new creature, the new man in the heart. This seems strange to carnal-minded men, because they are not acquainted with it; but we know it, and are sensible of it, by a true and certain experience. Though it be hard for man in his natural wisdom to comprehend it, until he come to feel it in himself; and if he should, holding it in the mere notion, it would avail him little; yet we are able to make it appear to be true, and that our faith concerning it is not without a solid ground: for it is in and by this inward and substantial seed in our hearts as it comes to receive nourishment, and to have a birth or geniture in us, that we come to have those spiritual senses raised by which we are made capable of tasting, smelling, seeing, and handling the things of God: for a man cannot reach unto those things by his natural spirit and senses, as is above declared.

Next, We know it to be a substance, because it subsists in the hearts of wicked men, even while they are in their wickedness, as shall be hereafter proved more at large. Now no accident can be in a subject without it give the subject its own denomination; as where whiteness is in a subject, there the subject is called white. So we distinguish betwixt holiness, as it is an accident, which denominates man so, as the seed receives a place in him, and betwixt this holy substantial seed, which many times lies in man's heart as a naked grain in the stony ground. So also as we may distinguish betwixt health and medicine; health cannot be in a body without the body be called healthful, because health is an accident; but medicine may be in a body that is most unhealthful, for that it is a substance. And as when a medicine begins to work, the body may in some respect be called healthful, and in some respect unhealthful, so we acknowledge as this divine medicine receives place in man's heart, it may denominate him in some part holy and good, though there remain yet a corrupted unmortified part, or some part of the evil humours unpurged out; for where two contrary accidents are in one subject, as health and sickness in a body, the subject receives its denomination from the accident which prevails most. So many men are called saints, good and holy men, and that truly, when this holy seed hath wrought in them in a good measure, and hath somewhat leavened them into its nature, though they may be yet liable to many infirmities and weaknesses, yea and to some iniquities: for as the seed of sin and ground of corruption, yea and the capacity of yielding thereunto, and sometimes actually falling, doth not denominate a good and holy man impious; so neither doth the seed of righteousness in evil men, and the possibility of their becoming one with it, denominate them good or holy.

Fourthly, We do not hereby intend any ways to lessen or derogate from the atonement and sacrifice of Jesus Christ; but on the contrary do magnify and exalt it. For as we believe all those things to have been certainly transacted which are recorded in the holy scriptures concerning the birth, life, miracles, sufferings, resurrection and ascension of Christ; so we do also believe that it is the duty of every one to believe it to whom it pleases God to reveal the same, and to bring to them the knowledge of it; yea we believe it were damnable unbelief not to believe it, when so declared; but to resist that holy seed, which as minded would lead and incline every one to believe it as it is offered unto them, though it revealeth not in every one the outward and explicit knowledge of it, nevertheless it always assenteth to it, *ubi declaratur,* where it is declared. Nevertheless as we firmly believe it was necessary that Christ should come, that by his death and sufferings he might offer up himself a sacrifice to God for our sins, who his own self "bare our sins in his own body on the tree"; so we believe that the remission of sins which any partake of, is only in and by virtue of that most satisfactory sacrifice, and no otherwise. For it is by the obedience of that one that the free gift is come upon all to justification. For we affirm, that as all men partake of the fruit of Adam's fall, in that by reason of that evil seed, which through him is communicated unto them, they are prone and inclined unto evil, though thousands of thousands be ignorant of Adam's fall, neither ever knew of the eating of the forbidden fruit; so also many may come to feel the influence of this holy and divine seed and light, and be turned from evil to good by it, though they knew nothing of Christ's coming in the flesh, through whose obedience and sufferings it is purchased unto them. And as we affirm it is absolutely needful that those do believe the history of Christ's outward appearance, whom it pleased God to bring to the knowledge of it; so we do freely confess, that even that outward knowledge is very comfortable to such as are subject to and led by the inward seed and light. For not only doth the sense of Christ's love and sufferings tend to humble them, but they are thereby also strengthened in their faith, and encouraged to follow that excellent pattern which he hath left us, "who suffered for us," as saith the apostle Peter, (I Pet. ii.21), "leaving us an example that we should follow his steps": and many times we are greatly edified and refreshed with the gracious sayings which proceed out of his mouth. The history then is profitable and comfortable with the mystery, and never without it; but the mystery is and may be profitable without the explicit and outward knowledge of the history.

But Fifthly, This brings us to another question, to wit, Whether Christ be in all men or no? Which sometimes hath been asked us, and arguments brought against it; because indeed it is to be found in some of our writings that Christ is in all men; and we often are heard, in our public meetings and declarations, to desire every man to know and be acquainted with Christ in them, telling them that Christ is in them; it is fit therefore, for removing of all mistakes, to say something in this place concerning this matter. We have said before how that a divine, spiritual, and supernatural light or seed is *vehiculum Dei;* how that God and Christ dwelleth in it, and is never separated from it; also how that, as it is received and closed within the heart, Christ comes to be formed and brought forth: but we are far from ever having said, that Christ is thus formed in all men, or in the wicked: for that is a great attainment, which the apostle travailed that it might be brought forth in the Galatians. Neither is Christ in all men by way of union, or indeed, to speak strictly, by way of inhabitation; because this inhabitation, as it is generally taken, imports union, or the manner of Christ's being in the saints: as it is written, "I will dwell in them, and walk in them," (II Cor. vi.16). But in regard Christ is in all men as in a seed, yea, and that he never is nor can be separate from that holy pure seed and light which is in all men; therefore may it be said in a larger sense, that he is in all, even as we observed before. The scripture saith, (Amos ii.13), God is pressed down as a cart under sheaves; and (Heb. vi.6), Christ is crucified in the ungodly; though to speak properly and strictly, neither can God be pressed down, nor Christ, as God, be crucified. In this respect then, as he is in the seed which is in all men, we have said Christ is in all men, and have preached and directed all men to Christ in them who lies crucified in them by their sins and iniquities, that they may look upon him whom they have pierced, and repent: whereby he that now lies as it were slain and buried in them, may come to be raised, and have dominion in their hearts over all. . . .

Sixthly, It will manifestly appear by what is above said, that we understand not this divine principle to be any part of man's nature, nor yet to be any relics of any good which Adam lost by his fall, in that we make it a distinct separate thing from man's soul, and all the faculties of it: yet such is the malice of our adversaries, that they cease not sometimes to calumniate us, as if we preached up a natural light, or the light of man's natural conscience. Next, there are they that lean to the doctrine of Socinus and Pelagius, who persuade themselves through mistake, and out of no ill design to injure us, as if this which we preach up were some natural power and faculty of the soul, and that we only differ in the wording of it, and not in the thing itself; whereas there can be no greater difference than is betwixt us in that matter: for we certainly know that this light of which we speak is not only distinct, but of a different nature from the soul of man, and its faculties. Indeed that man, as he is a rational creature, hath reason as a natural faculty of his soul, by which he can discern things that are rational, we deny not; for this is a property natural and essential to him, by which he can know and learn many arts and sciences, beyond what any other animal can do by the mere animal principle. Neither do we deny but by this rational principle man may apprehend in his brain, and in the notion, a knowledge of God and spiritual things; yet that not being the right organ, as in the second proposition hath more at length been signified, it cannot profit him towards salvation, but rather hindereth; and indeed the great cause of the apostasy hath been, that man hath sought to fathom the things of God in and by this natural and rational principle, and to build up a religion in it, neglecting and overlooking this principle and seed of God in the heart; so that herein, in the most universal and catholic sense, hath Anti-Christ in every man set up himself, and sitteth in the temple of God as God, and above every thing that is called God. For men being the temple of the Holy Ghost, as saith the apostle (I Cor. iii.16), when the rational principle sets up itself there above the seed of God, to reign and rule as a prince in spiritual things, while the holy seed is wounded and bruised, there is Anti-Christ in every man, or somewhat exalted above and against Christ. Nevertheless we do not hereby affirm as if man had received his reason to no purpose, or to be of no service unto him, in no wise; we look upon reason as fit to order and rule man in things natural. For as God gave two great lights to rule the outward world, the sun and moon, the greater light to rule the day, and the lesser light to rule the night; so hath he given man the light of his Son, a spiritual divine light, to rule him in things spiritual, and the light of reason to rule him in things natural. And even as the moon borrows her light from the sun, so ought men, if they would be rightly and comfortably ordered in natural things, to have their reason enlightened by this divine and pure light. Which enlightened reason, in those that obey and follow this true light, we confess may be useful to man even in spiritual things, as it is still subservient and subject to the other; even as the animal life in man, regulated and ordered by his reason, helps him in going about things that are rational. We do further rightly distinguish this from man's natural conscience; for conscience being that in man which ariseth from the natural faculties of man's soul, may be defiled and corrupted. It is said expressly of the impure (Tit. i.15), "That even their mind and conscience is defiled"; but this light can never be corrupted nor defiled; neither did it ever consent to evil or wickedness in any; for it is said expressly, that it makes all things manifest that are reprovable (Eph. v.13), and so is a faithful witness for God against every unrighteousness in man. Now conscience, to define it truly, comes from *conscire,* and is that knowledge which ariseth in man's heart from what agreeth, contradicteth, or is contrary to any thing believed by him, whereby he becomes conscious to himself that he transgresseth by doing that which he is persuaded he ought not to do. So that the mind being once blinded or defiled with a wrong belief, there ariseth a conscience from that belief, which troubles him when he goes against it. . . .

Thus then man's natural conscience is sufficiently distinguished from it; for conscience followeth the judgement, doth not inform it; but this light, as it is received, removes the blindness of the judgement and conscience. So we confess also, that conscience is an excellent thing, where it is rightly informed and enlightened; wherefore some of us have fitly compared it to the lanthorn, and the light of Christ to a candle; a lanthorn is useful, when a clear candle burns and shines in it; but otherwise of no use. To the light of Christ then in the conscience, and not to man's natural conscience, it is that we continually commend men; this, not that, is it which we preach up, and direct people to, as to a most certain guide unto life eternal.

Lastly, This light, seed, &c., appears to be no power or natural faculty of man's mind; because a man that is in his health can, when he pleases, stir up, move, and exercise the faculties of his soul; he is absolute master of them; and except there be some natural cause or impediment in the way, he can use them at his pleasure: but this light and seed of God in man he cannot move and stir up when he pleaseth; but it moves, blows, and strives with man, as the Lord seeth meet. For though there be a possibility of salvation to every man during the day of his visitation, yet cannot a man, at any time when he pleaseth, or hath some sense of his misery, stir up that light and grace, so as to procure to himself tenderness of heart; but he must wait for it: which comes upon all at certain times and seasons, wherein it works powerfully upon the soul, mightily tenders it, and breaks it; at which time, if man resist it not, but closes with it, he comes to know salvation by it. Even as the lake of Bethesda did not cure all those that washed in it, but such only as washed first after the angel had moved upon the waters; so God moves in love to mankind, in this seed in his heart, at some singular times, setting his sins in order before him, and seriously inviting him to repentance, offering to him remission of sins and salvation; which if man accept of, he may be saved. Now there is no man alive, and I am confident there shall be none to whom this paper shall come, who, if they will deal faithfully and honestly with their own hearts, will not be forced to acknowledge that they have been sensible of this in some measure, less or more; which is a thing that man cannot bring upon himself with all his pains and industry. This then, oh man and woman! is the day of God's gracious visitation to thy soul, which if thou resist not, thou shalt be happy for ever. This is the day of the Lord, which, as Christ saith, is like the lightning, which shineth from the east unto the west; and the wind or spirit, which blows upon the heart, and no man knows whither it goes, nor whence it comes. . . .

JOHN LOCKE (1632–1704)

The Reasonableness of Christianity

Though the works of nature, in every part of them, sufficiently evidence a deity; yet the world made so little use of their reason, that they saw him not, where, even by the impressions of himself, he was easy to be found. Sense and lust blinded their minds in some, and a careless inadvertency in others, and fearful apprehensions in most (who either believed there were, or could not but suspect there might be, superior unknown beings) gave them up into the hands of their priests, to fill their heads with false notions of the deity, and their worship with foolish rites, as they pleased; and what dread or craft once began, devotion soon made sacred, and religion immutable. In this state of darkness and ignorance of the true God, vice and superstition held the world; nor could any help be had or hoped for from reason, which could not be heard, and was judged to have nothing to do in the case: the priests every where, to secure their empire, having excluded reason from having anything to do in religion. And in the crowd of wrong notions, and invented rites, the world had almost lost the sight of the one only true God. The rational and thinking part of mankind, 'tis true, when they sought after him, found the one, supreme, invisible God: but if they acknowledged and worshipped him, it was only in their own minds. They kept this truth locked up in their own breasts as a secret, nor ever durst venture it amongst the people, much less the priests, those wary guardians of their own creeds and profitable inventions. Hence we see that reason, speaking never so clearly to the wise and virtuous, had ever authority enough to prevail on the multitude, and to persuade the societies of men, that there was but one God, that alone was to be owned and worshipped. The belief and worship of one God, was the national religion of the Israelites alone; and, if we will consider it, it was introduced and supported amongst that people by revelation. . . .

In this state of darkness and error, in reference to the "true God," Our Saviour found the world. But the clear revelation he brought with him, dissipated this darkness; made the one invisible true God known to the world: and that with such evidence and energy, that polytheism and idolatry hath no where been able to withstand it. But wherever the preaching of the truth he delivered, and the light of the gospel hath come, those mists have been dispelled. And, in effect, we see that since Our Saviour's time, the belief of one God has prevailed and spread itself over the face of the earth. For even to the light that the Messiah brought into the world with him, we must ascribe the owning and professing of one God, which the Mahometan religion hath derived and borrowed from it. So that, in this sense, it is certainly and manifestly true of Our Saviour, what St. John says of him, (I John iii.8), "For this purpose the Son of God was manifested, that he might destroy the works of the devil." This light the world needed, and this light it received from him: that there is but "one God," and he "eternal, invisible"; nor like to any visible objects, nor to be represented by them. . . .

Next to the knowledge of one God, maker of all things, a clear knowledge of their duty was wanting to mankind. This part of knowledge, though cultivated with some care, by some of the heathen philosophers, yet got little footing among the people. . . . But natural religion, in its full extent, was nowhere, that I know, taken care of by the force of natural reason. It should seem, by the little that has hitherto been done in it, that 'tis too hard a task for unassisted reason, to establish morality, in all its parts, upon its true foundations, with a clear and convincing light. And 'tis at least a surer and shorter way, to the apprehensions of the vulgar, and mass of mankind, that one manifestly sent from God and coming with visible authority from him, should, as a King and law-maker, tell them their duties, and require their obedience, than leave it to the long, and sometimes intricate deductions of reason, to be made out to them: such strains of reasonings the greatest part of mankind have neither leisure to weigh, nor, for want of education and use, skill to judge. We see how unsuccessful in this, the attempts of philosophers were, before Our Saviour's time. How short their several systems came of the perfection of a true and complete morality, is very visible. And if, since that, the Christian philosophers have much outdone them, yet we may observe, that the first knowledge of the truths they have added, are owing to revelation; though as soon as they are heard and considered, they are found to be agreeable to reason, and such as can by no means be contradicted. Everyone may observe a great many truths which he receives at first from others, and readily assents to, as consonant to reason, which he would have found it hard, and perhaps, beyond his strength to have discovered himself. Native and original truth, is not so easily wrought out of the mine, as we who have it delivered, ready dug and fashioned into our hands, are apt to imagine. And how often at fifty or threescore years old, are thinking men told, what they wonder how they could miss thinking of? Which yet their own contemplations did not, and possibly never would have helped them to. Experience shows that the knowledge of morality, by mere natural light (how agreeable soever it be to it), makes but a slow progress, and little advance in the world. And the reason of it is not hard to be found in men's necessities, passions, vices, and mistaken interests, which turn their thoughts another way. And the designing leaders, as well as the following herd, find it not to their purpose to employ much of their meditations this way. Or whatever else was the cause, 'tis plain in fact, that human reason unassisted, failed men in its great and proper business of morality. It never, from unquestionable principles, by clear deductions, made out an entire body of the law of Nature. And he that shall collect all the moral rules of the philosophers, and compare them with those contained in the New Testament, will find them to come short of the morality delivered by Our Saviour, and taught by his apostles; a college made up, for the most part, of ignorant, but inspired, fishermen. . . .

But such a body of Ethics, proved to be the law of nature, from principles of reason, and reaching all the duties of life, I think nobody will say the world had before Our Saviour's time. 'Tis not enough, that there were up and down scattered sayings of wise men, conformable to right reason. The law of nature, was the law of convenience too; and 'tis no wonder that those men of parts, and studious of virtue (who had occasion to think on any particular part of it), should by meditation light on the right, even from the observable convenience and beauty of it, without making out its obligation from the true principles of the law of nature, and foundations of morality. But these incoherent apophthegms of philosophers, and wise men, however excellent in themselves, and well intended by them, could never make a morality, whereof the world could be convinced; could never rise to the force of a law that mankind could with certainty depend on. Whatsoever should thus be universally useful, as a standard to which men should conform their manners, must have its authority either from reason or revelation. 'Tis not every writer of morals, or compiler of it from others, that can thereby be erected into a law-giver to mankind; and a dictator of rules, which are therefore valid, because they are to be found in his books, under the authority of this or that philosopher. He that any one will pretend to set up in this kind, and have his rules pass for authentic directions, must shew, that either he builds his doctrine upon principles of reason, self-evident in themselves, and that he deduces all the parts of it from thence, by clear and evident demonstration; or must shew his commission from heaven, that he comes with authority from God, to deliver his will and commands to the world. In the former way, nobody that I know, before Our Saviour's time, ever did, or went about to give us a morality. 'Tis

true, there is a law of nature: but who is there that ever did, or undertook
to give it us all entire, as a law; no more nor no less, than what was contained in, and had the obligation of that law? Who, ever made out all the
parts of it, put them together, and shewed the world their obligation?
Where was there any such code that mankind might have recourse to, as
their unerring rule, before Our Saviour's time? If there was not, 'tis plain,
there was need of one to give us such a morality; such a law, which might
be the sure guide of those who had a desire to go right: and if they had a
mind, need not mistake their duty; but might be certain when they had
performed, when failed in it. Such a law of morality, Jesus Christ hath
given us in the New Testament; but by the latter of these ways, by revelation. We have from him a full and sufficient rule for our direction, and
conformable to that of reason. But the truth and obligation of its precepts,
have their force, and are put past doubt to us, by the evidence of his mission. He was sent by God: His miracles shew it; and the authority of God
in his precepts cannot be questioned. Here morality has a sure standard,
that revelation vouches, and reason cannot gainsay, nor question; but both
together witness to come from God the great law-maker. And such an one
as this out of the New Testament, I think the world never had, nor can any
one say is any where else to be found. . . .

God, out of the infiniteness of his mercy, has dealt with man as a compassionate and tender Father. He gave him reason, and with it a law, that
could not be otherwise than what reason should dictate, unless we should
think, that a reasonable creature, should have an unreasonable law. But
considering the frailty of man, apt to run into corruption and misery; he
promised a deliverer, whom in his good time he sent; and then declared to
all mankind, that whoever would believe him to be the Saviour promised,
and take him now raised from the dead, and constituted the Lord and
Judge of all men, to be their King and Ruler, should be saved. This is a
plain intelligible proposition; and the all-merciful God seems herein to
have consulted the poor of this world, and the bulk of mankind: these are
articles that the labouring and illiterate man may comprehend. This is a
religion suited to vulgar capacities, and the state of mankind in this world,
destined to labour and travail. The writers and wranglers in religion fill it
with niceties, and dress it up with notions, which they make necessary and
fundamental parts of it; as if there were no way into the Church, but
through the Academy or Lycaeum. The greatest part of mankind have not
leisure for learning and logic, and super-fine distinctions of the schools.
Where the hand is used to the plough and the spade, the head is seldom elevated to sublime notions, or exercised in mysterious reasonings. 'Tis well
if men of that rank (to say nothing of the other sex) can comprehend plain
propositions, and a short reasoning about things familiar to their minds,

and nearly allied to their daily experience. Go beyond this, and you amaze the greatest part of mankind; and may as well talk Arabic to a poor day labourer, as the notions and language that the books and disputes of religion are filled with, and as soon you be understood. . . . Had God intended that none but the learned scribe, the disputer or wise of this world, should be Christians, or be saved; thus religion should have been prepared for them filled with speculations and niceties, obscure terms, and abstract notions. But men of that expectation, men furnished with such acquisitions, the apostle tells us (I Cor.i), are rather shut out from the simplicity of the gospel, to make way for those poor, ignorant, illiterate, who heard and believed the promises of a deliverer, and believed Jesus to be him; who could conceive a man dead and made alive again, and believe that he should, at the end of the world, come again, and pass sentence on all men, according to their deeds. That the poor had the gospel preached to them, Christ makes a mark, as well as business, of his mission (Matt. xi.5). And if the poor had the gospel preached to them, it was, without doubt, such a gospel as the poor could understand, plain and intelligible: and so it was, as we have seen, in the preachings of Christ and his apostles.

LORD HERBERT OF CHERBURY (1583–1648)

Common Notions of Religion

. . . Every religion which proclaims a revelation is not good, nor is every doctrine which is taught under its authority always essential or even valuable. Some doctrines due to revelation may be, some of them ought to be abandoned. On this connection the teaching of Common Notions is important; indeed, without them it is impossible to establish any standard of discrimination in revelation or even in religion. Theories based upon implicit faith, though widely held not only in our own part of the world but also in the most distant regions, are here irrelevant. Instances of such beliefs are: that human reason must be discarded, to make room for Faith; that the Church which is infallible, has the right to prescribe the method of divine worship, and in consequence must be obeyed in every detail; that no one ought to place such confidence in his private judgment as to dare to question the sacred authority of priests and preachers of God's word; that their utterances, though they may elude human grasp, contain so much truth that we should rather lay them to heart than debate them; that to God all the things of which they speak and much more are possible. Now these arguments and many other similar ones, according to differences of age and country, may be equally used to establish a false religion as to support a true one. Anything that springs from the productive, not to say seductive, seed of Faith will yield a plentiful crop. What pompous charlatan can fail to impress his ragged flock with such ideas? Is there any fantastic cult which may not be proclaimed under such auspices? How can any age escape deception, especially when the cunning authorities declare their inventions to be heaven-born, though in reality they habitually confuse and mix the truth with falsehood? If we do not advance towards truth upon a foundation of Common Notions, assigning every element its true value, how can we hope to reach any but futile conclusions? Indeed, however those who endeavour to base their beliefs upon the disordered and licentious codes of superstition may protest, their behaviour is precisely similar to people who with the purpose of blinding the eyes of the wayfarer with least trouble to themselves offer with singular courtesy to act as guides on the journey. But the actual facts are otherwise. The supreme Judge requires every individual to render an account of his actions in the light, not of another's belief, but of his own. So we must establish the fundamental principles of religion by means of universal wisdom, so that whatever has been added to it by the genuine dictates of Faith may rest on that foundation as a roof is supported on a house. Accordingly we ought not to accept any kind of religion lightly, without first enquiring into the sources of its prestige. And the Reader will find all these considerations depend upon Common Notions. Can anyone, I beg to ask, read the huge mass of books composed with such immense display of learning, without feeling scorn for these age-long impostures and fables, save in so far as they point the way to holiness? What man could yield unquestioning faith to a body which, disguised under the name of the Church, wastes its time over a multitude of rites, ceremonies, and vanities, which fights in so many parts of the world under different banners, if he were not led to perceive, by the aid of conscience, some marks of worship, piety, penance, reward and punishment? Who, finally, would attend to the living voice of the preacher if he did not refer all his deeds and words to the Sovereign Deity? It would take too long to deal with every instance. It is sufficient to make clear that we cannot establish any of them without the Common Notions. I value these so highly that I would say that the book, religion, and prophet which adheres most closely to them is the best. The system of Notions, so far at least as it concerns theology, has been clearly accepted at all times by every normal person, and does not require any further justification. And first of all, the teaching of Common Notions, or true Catholic Church, which has never erred, nor ever will err and in which alone the glory of Divine Universal Providence is displayed, asserts that

There is a Supreme God.

No general agreement exists concerning the Gods, but there is universal recognition of God. Every religion in the past has acknowledged, every religion in the future will acknowledge, some sovereign deity among the Gods. . . . Accordingly that which is everywhere accepted as the supreme manifestation of deity, by whatever name it may be called, I term God. I pass on to consider His attributes, using the same method. And in the first place I find that He is Blessed. Secondly, He is the end to which all things move. Thirdly, He is the cause of all things, at least in so far as they are good. From which follows, according to His Providence that, in the fourth place, He is the means by which all things are produced; for how could we pass from the beginning to the end but by the means provided? We need not be deterred by the type of philosophers who have refused to grant the medium any share of providence. Since circumstances seldom fall out in accordance with their wishes, they make a desperate attempt to abolish particular Providence as though the course of events were ordained by themselves and not by the Divine will. We must realize that writers of this kind are only wrangling about the means by which Divine Providence acts; they are not, I think, disputing Providence itself. Meanwhile the utmost agreement exists concerning universal Providence, or Nature. But every religion believes that the Deity can hear and answer prayers; and we are bound to assume a special Providence—to omit other sources of proof— from the universal testimony of the sense of divine assistance in times of distress. In the fifth place, He is eternal. For we are taught by a Common Notion that what is first is eternal. In the sixth place a Common Notion tells us that the Deity is good, since the cause of all good is supremely good. In the seventh place, He is just; a Common Notion, experience and history bear witness at every point that the world is ruled under His Providence with absolute justice. For as I have often observed, Common Notions, which solve the most difficult questions of philosophy and theology, teach us that all things are governed with righteousness and justice, though their causes may be hidden from us. In the eighth place, He is wise; for marks of His wisdom do not only appear in the attributes of which I have spoken, but are manifest daily in His works. . . .

I pass now to the second Common Notion of theology:

This Sovereign Deity ought to be Worshipped.

While there is no general agreement concerning the worship of Gods, sacred beings, saints, and angels, yet the Common Notion or Universal Consent tells us that adoration ought to be reserved for the one God. Hence divine religion—and no race, however savage, has existed without some expression of it—is found established among all nations, not only on account of the benefits which they received from general providence, but also in recognition of their dependence upon Grace or particular providence. Hence, too, men have been convinced, as I have observed above, that they can not only supplicate that heavenly Power but prevail upon Him, by means of the faculties implanted in every normal man. Hence, finally, what is a more important indication, this Power was consulted by the seers in order to interpret the future and they undertook no important action without referring to it. So far the peoples were surely guided by the teaching of Natural Instinct. The All Wise Cause of the universe does not suffer itself to be enclosed within its own sphere, but it bestows general Grace on all and special Grace on those whom it has chosen. Since everyone can experience this in himself, would it not be unjust to refuse the same power to God? God does not suffer us to beseech Him in vain, as the universal experience of divine assistance proves, to pass over all other arguments. Although I find that the doctrine of special providence, or Grace, was only grudgingly acknowledged by the ancients, as may be gathered from their surviving works, yet since the worship of the Divine Power was recognized in every age, and carried with it this doctrine of Grace or Special Providence, I assert that this doctrine is a Common Notion. From this source spring supplications, prayers, sacrifices, acts of thanksgiving; to this end were built shrines, sanctuaries, and finally for this purpose appeared priests, prophets, seers, pontiffs, the whole order of ministers. And even if their activity has been equally evident in human affairs as in the affairs of God, since they have often been a crafty and deceitful tribe, prone to avarice, and often ineffective, this is because they have introduced much under the pretext of Religion which has no bearing upon Religion. In this way with extraordinary skill they have confused sacred matters with profane, truth with falsehood, possibility with probability, lawful worship with licentious ceremonies and senseless superstitions; with the result, I make bold to say, that they have corrupted, defiled, and prostituted the pure name of Religion. However necessary the priests were, whenever they brought contempt upon themselves, the fear of God and the respect due to sacred things diminished in proportion. Accordingly we must give them the honour which is due them. I obtain, then, proof of this external aspect of divine worship in any type of religion from every age, country and race. It is therefore a Common Notion. . . .

The connection of Virtue with Piety, defined in this work as the right conformation of the faculties, is and always has been held to be, the most important part of religious practice.

There is no general agreement concerning rites, ceremonies, traditions, whether written or unwritten, or concerning Revelation; but there is the greatest possible consensus of opinion concerning the right conformation of the faculties. . . . If I am to make some survey of these faculties, in respect of a person's years and the degree of wisdom which it has pleased God to give him, I would say that children recognise and seek God in their own way in the form of happiness, and acknowledge Him in the spontaneous gratitude which they accord their benefactors. No trait, therefore, is so excellent as gratitude, nothing so base as ingratitude. And when gratitude is expressed by more mature persons and the Common Notions gradually reveal their objects more clearly, Religion becomes enriched and appears in a greater variety of ways, though no practice emerges which is more admirable than this gratitude. With the advantage of age, piety and holiness of life take deeper roots within the conscience, and give birth to a profound love and faith in God. . . . It may seem paradoxical that moral virtue which is so strict and severe is and always has been esteemed by men in every age and place and respected in every land, in spite of the fact that it conflicts with our physical and, I may say, agreeable feelings. But the reason for this is as follows. Since Nature unceasingly labours to deliver the soul from its physical burden, so Nature itself instills men with its secret conviction that virtue constitutes the most effective means by which our mind may be gradually separated and released from the body, and enter into its lawful realm. And though many arguments could be cited to the same purpose, I know no more convincing proof than the fact that it is only virtue that has the power to draw our soul from the delights which engulf it, and even to restore it to its native region, so that freed from the foul embrace of vice, and finally from the fear of death itself, it can apply itself to its proper function and attain inward everlasting joy.

The minds of men have always been filled with horror for their wickedness. Their vices and crimes have been obvious to them. They must be expiated by repentance.

. . . General agreement among religions, the nature of divine goodness, and above all conscience, tell us that our crimes may be washed away by true penitence, and that we can be restored to new union with God. For this inner witness condemns wickedness while at the same time it can wipe out the stain of it by genuine repentance, as the inner form of apprehension under proper conditions proves. I do not wish to consider here whether any other more appropriate means exists by which the divine justice may be appeased, since I have undertaken in this work only to rely on truths which are not open to dispute but are derived from the evidence of immediate perception and admitted by the whole world. This alone I assert, whatever may be said to the contrary, that unless wickedness can be abolished by penitence and faith in God, and unless the Divine goodness can satisfy the Divine justice (and no further appeal can be invoked), then there does not exist, nor ever has existed any universal source to which the wretched mass of men, crushed beneath the burden of sin, can turn to obtain grace and inward peace. If this were the case, God has created and condemned certain men, in fact the larger part of the human race, not only without their desire, but without their knowledge. This idea is so dreadful and consorts so ill with the providence and goodness, and even the justice of God, that it is more charitable to suppose that the whole human race has always possessed in repentance the opportunity of becoming reconciled with God. And as long as men did not cut themselves off from it their damnation would not have been due to the benevolent will of God, but to their own sins, nor could God have been charged with blame if they failed to find salvation. All the teaching of the greatest preachers concerning eternal salvation coincides on this issue, since every means of redress is useless except penitence and becomes, as they tell us, empty and futile. Accordingly they hold it to be of such importance in relation to the divine goodness that they consider that when no readier way presents itself the

entire secret of salvation may be revealed in this process. . . . To declare
that God has cut us off from the means by which we can return to Him,
provided that we play our part to the utmost of our ability, is a blasphemy
so great that those who indulge in it seek to destroy not merely human
goodness, but also the goodness of God. They must abandon these ideas,
and their ideas and utterances, at least concerning the secret judgments of
God, must be more guarded. For they cannot deny that if not from general
providence, yet from particular providence or Grace, may flow the means
by which God's favour may be won.

There is Reward or Punishment after this life.

. . . But all religion, law, philosophy and, what is more, conscience,
teach openly or implicitly that punishment or reward awaits us after this
life. . . . In this sense there is no nation, however barbarous, which has not
and will not recognise the existence of punishments and rewards. That reward and punishment exist is, then, a Common Notion, though there is the
greatest difference of opinion as to their nature, quality, extent and mode.
It is no objection that the soul perishes with the body, as some people assert. For they refer this very fact to punishment for sin, or else they mean
only that part of the soul with which they have been familiar, namely, the
physical senses; or finally they must be ignored since they talk sheer nonsense; for there is nothing in the faculties of the mind to suggest such
ideas. That the soul could be immortal if God willed it is clearly a Common Notion in that among the most distant races, seething with every type
of superstition, there exists a general conviction that purity of life and
courage of mind promote happiness. It is on this account that they are said
to honour the bones of those who have died bravely in battle. But I do not
trouble myself about such matters, since I am not concerned with superstitions and sacred rites; it is not what a large number of men assert, but
what all men of normal mind believe, that I find important. Scanning the
vast array of absurd fictions I am content to discover a tiny Common Notion. And this is of the utmost importance, since when the general mass of
men have rejected a whole range of beliefs which it has found valueless, it
proceeds to acquire new beliefs by this method, until the point is reached
where faith can be applied.

It follows from these considerations that the Dogmas which recognise a
sovereign Deity, enjoin us to worship Him, command us to lead a holy life,
lead us to repent our sins, and warn us of future recompense or punishment, proceed from God and are inscribed within us in the form of Common Notions. But those dogmas which postulate a plurality of Gods, which
do not forbid crimes and sins, which rail against penitence, and which express eternal doubts about the eternal state of the soul, cannot be
considered either Common Notions or truths. Accordingly every religion,

if we consider it comprehensively, is not good; nor can we admit that salvation is open to men in every religion. For how could anyone who believes more than is necessary, but who does less than he ought, be saved? But I am convinced that in every religion, and indeed in every individual conscience, either through Grace or Nature, sufficient means are granted to men to win God's good will; while all additional and peculiar features which are found at any period must be referred to their inventors. It is not sufficient that they should be old if they have once been new. Ideas which are superfluous or even false may be not only novel but ancient, and truths which are only seized by a few cannot be essential to all. . . . I do not deny that sacred ceremonies can form part of religion; on the contrary I find that some ceremonies are included in every religion and serve to embellish it; so far they are valuable. But when they are made by the priests the essential elements of divine worship, then religion, and we who practise it, are the victims of imposture. Rites must be kept within bounds. We can only accept them on the understanding that religion is chaste and only requires such ornaments as render a matron more venerable and respected. When she paints and dyes herself, her appearance is too suggestive of the harlot.

Such then are the Common Notions of which the true Catholic or universal church is built. . . .

PHILIP SPENER (1635–1705)

On the Spiritual Priesthood
of All Christians

What is the Spiritual Priesthood?

The right which our Saviour Jesus Christ has purchased for all men
and for which He has anointed with His Holy Spirit those who believe on
Him, in virtue of which they bring acceptable sacrifices to God, pray for
themselves and others, and should edify, each himself and his neighbors. . . .

Why is it called a Spiritual Priesthood?

Because it brings no bodily, but only spiritual sacrifices, and, in its office, has to do only with spiritual functions.

Whence is this Spiritual Priesthood derived?

From Jesus Christ, the true High Priest, according to the order of Mel-
chisedek, who, since He has no successor in His priesthood, but remains
alone to all eternity a High Priest, has also made Christians priests before
His Father, whose sacrifices have their holiness and are accepted before
God solely because of His.

How do Christians become priests?

As in the Old Testament, priests were not elected, but were born to the
office, so it is regeneration in baptism that gives us the divine right of children of God, and therefore puts us into the spiritual priesthood which is
combined with this.

Does not anointing also pertain to the Priesthood?

Yes; and just as priests of old were set apart with holy ointment, and
just as Christ was anointed with the most holy oil of gladness, the Holy
Ghost, and, on this account, is called Christ, "the Anointed One"; so out
of grace has He made those who believe on Him partakers, although in a
less degree, of the same anointing.

Are all believers, then, partakers of the anointing?

Yes. All have received and continue to possess it, as long as they persevere in the divine order.

But for what purpose was Christ anointed?

As King, High Priest, and Prophet, since it was customary in the Old Testament to anoint such persons.

For what are those who believe on Him anointed?

Likewise as Kings, Priests and Prophets, since the office of prophet is included under that of priest.

Who are such spiritual priests?

All Christians without distinction; old and young, man and woman, bond and free.

But does not the name "priest" belong only to the preachers?

No. Preachers, according to their office, are not properly priests. They are nowhere so called in the New Testament, but are "ministers of Christ," "stewards of the mysteries of God," "bishops," "elders," "ministers of the Gospel," "of the Word," etc. On the contrary, the name "priest" is a general name of all Christians, and does not belong to preachers in any other sense than to other Christians. . . .

What are the duties of the Spiritual Priesthood?

They are of various kinds. But we may distribute them into three chief functions: (1) That of sacrifice; (2) that of praying and blessing, and (3) that of the divine Word. Of these, the former has always been known as the proper office of the priesthood, while the last is also called the prophetic office.

What have spiritual priests to offer?

First of all, themselves, with all that belongs to them, so that they desire no more to serve themselves, but only Him who has purchased and redeemed them. Therefore, as the sacrifices in the Old Testament were separated from other animals, so they must separate themselves from the world and its defilements. For this reason, they were called "an elect race."

How have we to offer our bodies and their members to God?

By devoting our bodies not to sin, but only to God's glory and service; and, therefore, keeping it under discipline, and by suppressing the wicked lusts which attempt to work through our members. This lust is known in Scripture as "cutting off" our members.

How should we offer our souls to God?

To the end that, with our bodies, they be the holy temples and dwelling-places of God; that our reason be brought into captivity to the obedience of Christ; that our will submit to the divine will with true resignation and prompt compliance; that our spirit and heart in true penitence be an acceptable offering to God.

How have we, further, to offer ourselves as a sacrifice to God?

By being willing to accept every cross from His hand; by offering ourselves for Him to send upon us whatever pleases Him; and being ready, also, to surrender our life according to His will, for His glory.

Should we not also sacrifice our old Adam to God?

Just as "the devoted thing" which was killed, was consecrated and thus sacrificed to God; so, in the same sense, should we put to death and sacrifice our old Adam.

What else have we to offer?

Our hearts and tongues for prayer, praise and thanksgiving; as well as our bodily possessions, if we see that His glory is thereby promoted, and there be occasion to show mercy to those in distress, especially to the members of Christ.

Is there nothing still further for us to offer?

Yes; especially the doctrine of the Gospel, and with it our fellow-men, who are thereby converted and sanctified to God. . . .

How often and when should we offer such sacrifices?

Always; throughout our entire lives; for while we devote and consecrate ourselves, once for all, with body and soul, when we first give our hearts to His service, such resolution should not only be often repeated, but also daily, yea hourly, such sacrifices should be offered the Lord.

Beside the sacrifices, what else belonged to the office of Christ, as Priest?

As the High Priest of the Old Testament blessed and prayed for the people; and Christ, also, as a true High Priest of the New Testament has given us His blessing, and prayed and still prays for us; it is the duty of Christians to offer to God prayers not only for themselves, but for their fellow-men, and to bless them. This prayer and blessing, for Christ's sake, is not useless, but is effectual.

What is, then, the third office of priest?

As priests were occupied with God's Law, so also it is the office of spiritual priests that the Word of God should dwell richly among them. This is known otherwise as the Prophetic office.

Are all Christians, then, preachers, and have they to devote themselves to the office of ministry?

No; but in order to fulfill this office publicly, in the Church, and before and over all, a special call is necessary. Whoever, then, assumes this right above others or attempts to force himself into the ministry, thereby sins. Hence the teachers are one, and the hearers another class. . . .

But what, then, have they to do with the Word of God?

To use it for themselves, and alongside of and with others.

How have they to use it for themselves?

Not only by hearing it when preached in the church, but also by diligently reading or having it read.

Is it, then, the duty of all Christians to diligently read the Scriptures?
Yes. Since it is a letter of the Heavenly Father to all His children, no child of God is excluded, but all have the right and command to read it.

But would it not be better, if they would simply believe all that they hear from their pastor?
No; but they are to search the Scriptures, in order to test the doctrine of their pastor, so that their faith may rest not upon their regard for and confidence in a man, but upon divine truth.

Are the Scriptures, therefore, not too difficult for simple persons who are without education?
No. For even in the Old Testament, the divine Word was given, in order to make wise the simple, and that fathers might teach it diligently to their children. But the New Testament is still clearer. Accordingly Christ did not direct His teaching to the wise and prudent of this world, but to the simple. Every one also who wants to understand Jesus must put aside all worldly wisdom and become a child. Paul, therefore, and all other Apostles did not discourse in high words but in the power of God, which was hidden from the wise, but revealed to infants, in accordance with the unsearchable wisdom of God, which "by foolish preaching" has brought to naught the wise of this world. Hence the Apostles have written their epistles mostly to unlearned and simple men, who could not have understood them, from heathen arts or sciences, but who, without them, by the grace of God, could understand them to their salvation.

But is there not in the Scriptures much that is obscure, and, therefore, too high for the simple?
The Scriptures themselves are not obscure, as they are not darkness, but a light. Nevertheless there is much in them, too high not only for the simple, but also for the most learned, and which, because of our darkened eyes, appears to us as dark.

Would it not, therefore, be better if plain persons would not read them?
No. As the learned should not be hindered from searching them by the fact that they frequently fail to understand many passages, so also we should not interfere with their study by simple, godly souls who seek in them a confirmation of their faith.

Can they then, in their simplicity, learn to understand them?
Yes, of course. As, first of all, the chief points of doctrine and rules of life are so clearly taught in the Scriptures, that every simple person as well as the learned, can learn and comprehend them; where godly minds have received and applied with obedience the first truths which are offered them, and continue, with meditation and prayer, to read the Scriptures, God the Holy Ghost will open to them their meaning more and more, so that they can also learn and understand that in Scripture which is higher

and more difficult, so far as it be necessary for the strengthening of their faith, instruction in life and consolation. . . .

Whence, then, do simple, godly Christians have the ability to understand the Scriptures?

By the illumination of the Holy Spirit, at whose prompting they were first committed to writing, so that, without His light, they cannot be understood. But God has promised the Holy Spirit to all who call upon Him, and, therefore, not merely to the learned. From His anointing and illumination, therefore, they understand according to the measure of grace allotted each one, everything in Scripture which is needed for their salvation and growth in the inner man.

But what have they to do in the reading of the Scriptures, in order to be assured of their truth?

(1) That they never come to the Scriptures without earnest prayer for the gift of the Holy Spirit, and with the purpose to accept its power and efficacy, and not only to learn to know, but also to obediently apply what they learn to the glory of God.

(2) That they do not allow their reasons to be masters, but that they most carefully attend to the words of the Holy Ghost, as they are written, and compare these words with what precedes and follows; that they ponder and believe its meaning and therefore regard every word of the Holy Ghost with the closest consideration, and examine whatever is read in the light also of other passages of Scripture.

(3) That they read everything with a personal application to themselves, so far as it concerns them and is profitable for their edification.

(4) That they, first of all, take to themselves whatever they find clear therein, and base their faith upon it, and immediately order their lives according to the obligation which they recognize.

(5) That what in the beginning they find too difficult to be understood, they pass over and reserve, until gradually after much reading and prayer, if they continue faithful to the truth they have previously known, they obtain more light in regard to passages previously not understood.

(6) That they always in humility, receive and put into practice all the knowledge which God gives them, and be content with His grace.

(7) That they be ready and willing to converse concerning Scripture with godly preachers and other Christian persons, and if they be perplexed, take counsel of such advisers, and be willing, where, by God's grace they show them the true meaning of a passage, to receive it humbly and in the fear of God.

Is it necessary, then, to the salutary and living knowledge of Scripture, that we should seek to be improved thereby?

Yes, of course; for otherwise we read it not as the Word of the great God, which it, nevertheless, is. Regard for this should not only produce in us profound reverence, but also obedience. What we hear from His Word and mouth, we should do immediately and much more zealously than if a great earthly potentate had enjoined it upon us. He who does not read the Scriptures in this way, and who does not read them as the Word of God, and thus confines their power to himself, does not attain to their true spiritual knowledge.

But how can readers hinder this use of Scripture and thus do themselves injury?

(1) When, against the rules above given, they read the Scriptures without earnest prayer and without the purpose of divine obedience, but only from motives of personal ambition and to satisfy their curiosity.

(2) When they follow the judgments of their reason, and give them more weight than the words of the Holy Ghost.

(3) When they consider not what is profitable for their edification, but only what they may use for their glory or in controversy with others.

(4) When they despise the simple passages, and those easily understood, but

(5) Apply themselves only to those that are more difficult, and concerning which there has been much controversy, in order to find in them something that is out of the ordinary range of thought, and may make them more conspicuous.

(6) When they use what they learn with pride, and so as to serve their own honor.

(7) When they think that they alone are wise, selfishly resist better instruction, take pleasure in controversy, and receive nothing with modesty and discretion.

(8) But especially when they lead a carnal life, so that the Holy Spirit cannot abide in them. In such persons, the reading of the Holy Scriptures effects nothing. They receive only a natural knowledge of the letter of the Scriptures, without the inner power of the Spirit, and, by God's judgment, can, therefore, become only the more hardened and incapable.

But would it not be better to leave the more diligent investigation of the Scriptures to the preachers, and for the rest to abide by their simplicity?

All Christians are bound to simplicity, i.e., not to desire to investigate what God has not revealed, so that their reasons should not be masters in regard to matters of faith. But if by abiding by simplicity, it be meant that they who are not preachers should not endeavor always to grow in knowledge, this is contrary to God's will, shameful ignorance, indolence and ingratitude towards the riches of divine revelation; since it is our duty to endeavor not to be simple but to be wise and intelligent, and, by means of practice, to have our senses exercised to distinguish good and evil.

What then, would one do who would commend such simplicity to the people?

He would thereby directly contradict God's command and will, detract from His glory, obstruct the progress of His kingdom, and hinder all the good which can and should arise by such growth in knowledge, to the greatest danger of the souls of others, and to his own condemnation. . . .

But are Christians always to be occupied with God's Word, so as no longer to attend to their worldly business?

It is indeed their greatest joy to be occupied with their God and His Word rather than with their own necessities. But since they live in the world, and, therefore, both need labor for the support of their bodily life, and, for the general good, have been placed by God in particular callings, where they have bodily labor and business, they discharge these also, according to the power which God has given them, with conscientious diligence, avoid all idleness, and, in such service, show their fidelity towards God and their love of their fellow-men. . . .

But how have believing Christians to use the divine Word among their fellow-men?

Since the Scriptures have been given for doctrine, for reproof, for correction, for instruction in righteousness, and besides for consolation; believing Christians should use the Scriptures for all these purposes, and, therefore, should teach, convert from error, admonish, reprove and comfort, as the Scriptures repeatedly show.

Is this then for all Christians?

Yes, according to the gifts, which God has given every one; and with observance of the rule that this should not be done publicly before the entire congregation, but privately at every opportunity, and, therefore, without any hindrance of the regular, public office of the ministry.

How have Christians to teach?

By endeavoring, when they meet with uninformed people, to instruct them in simplicity of faith, and to lead them to the Scriptures. Besides, when Christians are together and read with one another the Scriptures, that, for the edification of the rest, each one modestly and in love, states what God has enabled him to see in the Scriptures and what he deems serviceable for the edification of the rest.

How can they convert the erring?

By showing them their error plainly out of God's Word, and admonishing them to receive the truth.

What have they to do in admonition?

By frequently, and at every opportunity, admonishing and encouraging each other, by God's aid, to carry into effect what they recognize as necessary; by such admonitions hearts are greatly strengthened in that which is good.

How do they exercise the office of reproving?

That when they see their brethren sin, they kindly and tenderly reprove them for it, point out the wrong and seek to persuade them to amend their course.

How in consoling?

That when they are with the afflicted, they declare to them the divine consolations and encourage them according to their ability. Also that, in case of necessity, where no regular preacher can be had, that they give the consolation of the forgiveness of sins or absolution.

Do the offices mentioned belong to all Christians?

Yes; and not merely that fathers and mothers of families, in their houses, diligently train their children and servants, but that every Christian also has the right and authority to do so with respect to his brother and sister as the above mentioned passages prove. . . .

But how have Christian priests to conduct themselves so as to avoid disorder?

By aiming from pure love in all things at their own edification and that of their neighbor, and doing nothing for their own glory, or other carnal purposes; by not undertaking what is too high for them; and, therefore, by their confidential intercourse with godly preachers, asking for their counsel, accepting their aid and affording them every possible facility for the discharge of the duties of their office; cordially giving an account for whatever they do, and following their advice; and especially, by refraining from all detraction and censures of the same and injuring no one in his office, considering that any discord which may result thence will do more damage, than their best efforts can repair. . . .

THE EIGHTEENTH CENTURY
Introduction

As the eighteenth century opened, one fundamental idea was in the ascendancy in most of Western Europe. That was the conviction that the human mind had full ability to understand man's world and full competence to bring it under his control. In terms of religious thought, this belief expressed itself in the contest between reason and revelation. Was human reason alone sufficient to arrive at all truth, including religious truth, or did that reason need God's revelation to complement its natural capabilities?

The struggle was between the defenders of the necessity of Christian revelation and those who contended, as many did, that revelation added nothing essential to what reason alone could discover. Indeed, if revelation were to demand the assent of man to propositions beyond the comprehension of his intellect, such doctrines were to be rejected as unreasonable and, therefore, unacceptable.

The outcome of the contest was ultimately inconclusive. In consequence of it, however, there did emerge, on the one hand, a heightened respect for human reason's power to pursue religious truth and, on the other hand, a realization that human emotion also had a substantial part to play in man's religious life. The either/or form in which the eighteenth century debated the relation between reason and revelation was transcended. Henceforward their relationship would be seen as one of mutual enrichment. The struggle between reason and revelation for primacy in the interpretation of Christian faith has been with Protestant thought since then. The nineteenth century will express the tension in the attempts of Christian thinkers to cast the Christian message into thought categories acceptable to the intellectual world of the time, while at the same time they sought to discover the real meaning of Scripture in terms of the new historico-critical methods of interpretation. The issue will be joined again in the twentieth century when neo-orthodoxy under Karl Barth's leadership will attempt to restore to revelation its role as chief source of man's knowledge about God, a position lost to it during the days of nineteenth-century liberal Protestant theology.

Two sets of selections are chosen here to plot the eighteenth-century course of this dispute. In each set the first passage is reason's case. The second represents the response of revelation's defenders. The selections are chosen to point up the basic problematic of the controversy: What were the respective places of reason and revelation in human religious knowledge? What does Christian revelation add to that which reason alone can discover? The dispute was between Deism with its God of reason and Christian orthodoxy with its God of faith. Deism's objective was the relegating of revelation to a role subordinate to that of reason. It could confirm and strengthen reason's conclusions. It could not, however, add anything essentially new to that knowledge. Orthodoxy's purpose was to point out where reason ended and revelation took over in bringing men to the full knowledge of religious truth.

The first excerpt is drawn from John Toland's tract, *Christianity Not Mysterious*. The alternate title clarifies the author's intent: *A Treatise Showing That There Is Nothing in the Gospel Contrary to Reason Nor Above It: and That No Christian Doctrine Can Be Properly Called a Mystery*. Toland's argument, in sum, was that the human mind can only assent to evidence. It can, therefore, assent to Christianity only in so far as the truths of that faith are evident to human reason. Those propositions in Christianity that are not evident are unacceptable. The argument's force is perhaps better put by inverting it. Christianity must be reasonable. Where it is not such, it is not Christianity. Thus, at a stroke, the Christian faith is reduced to a natural religion; it is but a single step further to dispense with it altogether since it has nothing to offer which reason itself cannot attain alone.

The classic response to Toland's type of argument was Joseph Butler's *The Analogy of Religion, Natural and Revealed,* the second selection. Butler rested his case on a study of nature. Whereas the Deists saw in nature a clear pattern of divine wisdom and purpose at work, Butler confessed himself much more struck with the mysteries and irrationalities in nature. It was for him by no means a clear mirror of truth. The presence of such perplexities in nature meant rather that man ought to be wary of what he can know with certainty. Probability is all he ought, realistically, to hope for in most matters. There is as much dark as there is light in nature, and the human mind needs to be cautious of what nature teaches it. Turning to religion and specifically to Christianity, Butler's thought runs along analogous lines. Much in revelation is also difficult and obscure, hard for the mind to grasp. But why should revelation be denied what man grants to nature, probable truth? Thus his argument runs: If man can live with probable knowledge regarding much in nature, he should be able to live with the same in religious matters too. The weight of probability lies as much in favor of accepting religious truth as it does in favor of accepting truths about nature.

It is a modest and cautious argument. Its real power lies in the devastating blow it aimed at the basic presupposition of reason's champions. The ability of natural reason to arrive at truth was not at all as certain a proposition as they had made it out to be.

A further illustration of the debate is offered in the third and fourth selections. The former of these is from Matthew Tindal's *Christianity as Old as the Creation*. The work is often called the "deist's bible" because of its comprehensive treatment of all the arguments put forward by the proponents of natural religion. The general argument can be deduced from the title. God has from the beginning given men adequate means for knowing his will. Thus the sources of religious truth have been available to man since his creation. Christianity differs from this natural religion only in the manner of its communication. The first is drawn from created nature; the other from revelation. But they are identical in the truths they teach. His conclusion is "True religion, whether internally (i.e. by reason) or externally (i.e. by revelation) revealed, must be the same."

Tindal's argument, a strong endorsement of reason's ability to reach religious truth, was answered by William Law's *The Case of Reason*. Law's approach, essentially the same as Butler's, is to question the assumption on which Tindal's argument rests, that is, the power of reason to reach truth.

It was not his purpose to disparage reason but rather to show that reason is by no means as adequate to the discovery and grasp of truth as the Deists would make it out to be. It was, in his view, presumptuous for human reason to assume it could fathom the nature of God, and even more ridiculous for it to demand that God conform Himself to acting in accordance with what man had decided was reasonable. Man ought to acknowledge the fallibility and weakness of his reason and accept the aid given it in its pursuit of truth by divine revelation.

By the middle of the century the controversy had fairly well run its course, with neither side the clear victor and no real advance achieved in determining the relation between reason and revelation. What did emerge as the debate waned was a realization that overattention to the role of reason in matters of Christian faith had tended to rob the believer of much that Christianity had to give him. Reaction set in. Greater attention began to be given to other aspects of religion, particularly the role and value of emotion in inducing Christian faith, as well as in conferring its benefits.

This development grew out of various situations in different sectors of Western Christianity, and it followed different pathways in England, Germany, and America, but its essential thrust was everywhere the same: an appeal to the heart and the emotions rather than the mind. Four selections are included to illustrate this chapter of religious history as it unfolded in England, Germany, and America.

In England John Wesley's project of "spreading scriptural holiness throughout the land" is the prime instance of the movement. From personal experience Wesley became aware of two realities, the power of individual conversion to set the course of a man's life and the failure of the church in England to provide for this conversion. The whole of his long life was given to creating circumstances in which as many Englishmen as he could reach might experience such a conversion. Once such an experience had been induced, he was equally concerned with providing the means which would empower men to live out their conversion in the whole of life. Wesley's initial weapon in his crusade was the sermon, aimed at effecting personal conversion. One such sermon is included here. The particular point of this sermon, *On Free Grace,* is the rejection of Calvinist predestination and the insistence on man's role in the working out of his salvation. The sermon makes clear Wesley's strong conviction that what a man does indeed makes a difference.

A second example of the evangelical movement in England is also included. The passage from William Wilberforce's *Practical View of the Prevailing Religious Systems* is a frank call to serious and holy living. What a man does is more important than his intellectual grasp of the Christian mysteries. Wilberforce himself was a typical example of the evangelical movement in England. His life was a dedication to personal holiness as well as a commitment to social reforms for the alleviation of the poverty and misery now being produced among the poor of England by the nascent industrial revolution.

In America the call to a life of Christian holiness was embodied in the "Great Awakening," the flame of religious revival that swept the colonies during the first half of the century. From its beginnings, life in the colonies had been a struggle for survival. All other concerns, including the practice of religion, took second place to this prime concern. Absorption in the immediate necessities of life coupled with the scarcity of ministers and the difficulty of communication between widely scattered settlements had produced a situation of general neglect in matters religious. The problem was dramatically met when George Whitefield, one of Wesley's original associates, and also one of the great preachers of his age, arrived from England. Whitefield launched an evangelical crusade aimed at the conversion of the colonies. His emotional preaching, aimed at a deep personal experience of conversion, was taken up by the preachers of the already established churches. The technique produced the first great religious revival in America. The movement is here represented by a sermon of Jonathan Edwards, *Sinners in the Hands of an Angry God,* preached at Enfield in 1741. The sermon is cast in the typical mode of revivalism. It is directed first at producing fear of God because of one's sins; from there it passes to the fervent appeal for faith in Christ who alone can save the sinner.

In Germany the reaction against rationalism was not new in the eighteenth century. The place of Philip Spener, the father of German Pietism, was taken by Auguste Francke and the movement continued to gain strength throughout the century. A passage from Francke's *Three Practical Discourses* is cited. Its theme, as is characteristic of pietist writings, is a warmly personal and moving appeal to the Christian to yield himself to the love of God and let that love transform his life. It is a manifestation of concern not for dogma and reason but for living faith that expresses itself in charity to the neighbor.

As the century drew to its close, thinkers began to appear whose eyes were turned more to the future than to the past and whose writings were prophetic of what would be the main intellectual preoccupations of the nineteenth century. Two such thinkers are chosen as the final selections for the eighteenth century, Gotthold Lessing and Immanuel Kant, neither of whom was primarily a religious thinker. The first was interested principally in literature and literary criticism. The second was a philosopher. Seeds of the future of religious thought are discernible in both. Lessing is the forerunner of the line of nineteenth-century thinkers dedicated to the cultivation of an historical consciousness and its use as a tool in interpreting the meaning of Christianity.

Lessing is Germany's most representative thinker during the age of Enlightenment. Though primarily a man of literature, he did produce, towards the end of his life, a piece entitled *The Education of the Human Race.* A passage from it is included as illustrative of two ideas that were conspicuously absent from the thought of the age of rationalism: the notion of history and the correlative idea of development. Rationalism had tended to develop its thought in a historical vacuum. Little attention was paid to the past; tradition exercised little influence. It was as though human reason existed in a tight little universe of its own making wherein it had only its own resources to puzzle out the meaning of the universe and of human existence. Problems were rationally, not historically, focused. Lessing begins to break out of this world. He looked back to see the long, arduous pathway mankind had trod on his way to his present understanding of his world. And Lessing at least glimpsed the truth that each age builds on, while surpassing, the knowledge of a preceding age. He recognized, hesitantly and imperfectly, that human thought always occurs in and is conditioned by its historical ambiance. The notion will be thoroughly explored by thinkers after him.

Immanuel Kant was the molder of the philosophical patterns that would dominate much of nineteenth-century thought. With his sharp distinction between the world of the real and the world of the mind, the phenomena and the noumena of reality, he prefigured the intense interest that the next century would have in the subjective world of religious experience. He heralded the dramatic about-face that would occur in nineteenth-century Protestant thought. From theology, a study of religion that begins with God and His Word, that thought would move towards anthropology, a study of religion that begins with man.

For Kant the world of things as they really are is inaccessible to human thought. All that man can know of reality is the face it turns to him; that face is a shell that conceals, rather than reveals, reality's true nature. In terms of religious thought this meant that man could not know God by reason since God does not have a face nor is there any sensibly perceptible manifestation of his presence in the world.

Kant's purpose, in his analysis of human reason, was not, however, to destroy the possibility of man's belief in God. "I have found it necessary to deny knowledge," he said, "in order to leave room for faith." As the foundation for faith he turned to man's interior life and discovered there two universal human convictions that point beyond themselves: a sense of immortality and the conviction of a moral law. These are fundamental values for all men. It is on them that acknowledgement of God's existence rests. Immortality speaks of One who will fulfill man's present mortality. "Thou shalt and thou shalt not" are instinctively recognized by man as part of the pattern of his life, and they speak of One who will reward and punish beyond this life. Thus not nature but human consciousness lies at the heart of man's belief in God. An excerpt from Kant's *Critical Examination of Practical Reason* is given as illustrative of what he calls the postulates of practical reason. By this term he means that man, by analyzing his strong inherent thrust towards moral living, comes to a conviction of moral law, of immortality and, in consequence, to a necessary belief in God.

Further exploration of these twin Kantian ideas—the human subject's self-knowledge and his conviction of the presence of value in his life—will be major concerns of two of the nineteenth century's greatest and most influential thinkers: Friedrich Schleiermacher and Albert Ritschl.

JOHN TOLAND (1670–1722)

On Natural and Revealed Religion

There is nothing that men make a greater noise about than the "mysteries of the Christian religion." The divines gravely tell us "we must adore what we cannot comprehend." Some of them say "the mysteries of the Gospel" are to be understood only in the sense of the "ancient fathers." But that is so multifarious and inconsistent with itself as to make it impossible for anybody to believe so many contradictions at once. They themselves did caution their readers from leaning upon their authority without the evidence of reason. They were as injudicious, violent, and factious as other men; they were for the greatest part very credulous and superstitious in religion; in a word, they were of the same nature and make with ourselves.

Some give a decisive voice in the unravelling of "mysteries," and the interpretation of Scripture, to a General Council, and others to one man whom they hold to be the head of the church universal upon earth, and the infallible judge of all controversies. But we do not think such Councils possible, nor (if they were) to be of more weight than the fathers, for they consist of such. As for the "one judge of all controversies," we suppose none but such as are strongly prepossessed by interest or education can in good earnest digest those chimerical supreme headships and monsters of infallibility. We read nowhere in the Bible of such delegate judges appointed by Christ to supply his office, and reason manifestly proclaims them frontless usurpers.

They come nearest the thing who affirm that we are to keep to what the Scriptures determine about these matters; there is nothing more true if rightly understood. But ordinarily 'tis an equivocal way of speaking. Some will have us always believe what the literal sense imports, with little or no consideration for reason, which they reject as not fit to be employed about the revealed part of religion. Others assert that we may use reason as the instrument but not the rule of our belief. The first contend some mysteries may be, or at least seem to be, contrary to reason, and yet be received by faith. The second, that no mystery is contrary to reason, but that all are "above" it.

On the contrary, we hold that reason is the only foundation of all certitude, and that nothing revealed, whether as to its manner or existence, is more exempted from its disquisitions than the ordinary phenomena of nature. Wherefore, we likewise maintain, according to the title of this discourse, that there is nothing in the Gospel contrary to reason, nor above it; and that no Christian doctrine can be properly called a mystery. . . .

Nothing in nature can come to our knowledge but by some of these four means, viz.: the experience of the senses, the experience of the mind, human and divine revelation.

Now, as we are extremely subject to deception, we may, without some infallible rule, often take a questionable proposition for an axiom, old wives' fables for moral certitude, and human impostures for divine revelation. This infallible rule, or ground of all right persuasion, is evidence, and it consists in the exact conformity of our ideas or thoughts with their objects, or the things we think upon. It is impossible for us to err as long as we take evidence for our guide; and we never mistake, but when we wander from it by abusing our liberty, in denying that of any thing which belongs to it, or attributing to it what we do not see in its idea.

But God the wise creator of all, who has enabled us to perceive things and form judgments of them, has also endued us with the power of suspending our judgments about whatever is uncertain, and of never assenting but to clear perceptions. He is so far from putting us upon any necessity of erring that as he has thus privileged us on the one hand with a faculty of guarding ourselves against prepossession or precipitation, by placing our liberty only in what is indifferent or dubious and obscure, so he provides on the other hand that we should discern and embrace the truth, by taking it out of our power to dissent from an evident proposition. We must necessarily believe that it is impossible the same thing should be and not be at once; nor can all the world persuade us to doubt of it. But we need not admit that there's no void in nature, or that the earth absolves an annual course about the sun, till we get demonstrations to that effect.

Let us cheerfully thank our kind disposer, who has put us under a law of bowing before the light and majesty of evidence. And truly if we might doubt of anything that is clear, or be deceived by distinct conceptions, there could be nothing certain; neither conscience, nor God himself, should be regarded; no society or government could subsist. . . .

I take it to be very intelligible from the precedent section that what is evidently repugnant to clear and distinct ideas, or to our common notions, is contrary to reason. I go on therefore to prove that the doctrines of the Gospel, if it be the word of God, cannot be so. No Christian I know of expressly says reason and the Gospel are contrary to one another. But very many affirm that, though the doctrines of the latter cannot in themselves be contradictory to the principles of the former, as proceeding both from God, yet that according to our conceptions of them they may seem directly to clash. And that though we cannot reconcile them by reason of our corrupt and limited understandings, yet that from the authority of divine revelation we are bound to believe and acquiesce in them; or, as the fathers taught them to speak, to "adore what we cannot comprehend." . . .

Let us enter upon the immediate examen of the opinion itself. The first thing I shall insist upon is that if any doctrine of the New Testament be contrary to reason, we have no manner of idea of it. To say, for instance, that a ball is white and black at once is to say just nothing, for these colors are so incompatible in the same subject as to exclude all possibility of a real positive idea or conception. . . .

If any should think to evade the difficulty by saying that the ideas of certain doctrines may be contrary indeed to common notions, yet consistent with themselves, and I know not what supra-intellectual truths, he's but just where he was. But supposing a little that the thing were so, it still follows that none can understand these doctrines except their perceptions be communicated to him in an extraordinary manner, as by new powers and organs. . . . And since we cannot in this world know anything but by our common notions, how shall we be sure of this pretended consistency between our present seeming contradictions and the theology of the world to come? For as 'tis by reason we arrive at the certainty of God's own existence, so we cannot otherwise discern his revelations but by their conformity with our natural notices of him, which is in so many words to agree with our common notions.

The next thing I shall remark is that those who stick not to say they could believe a downright contradiction to reason, did they find it contained in the Scripture, do justify all absurdities whatsoever, and by opposing one light to another undeniably make God the author of all incertitude. The very supposition that reason might authorize one thing and the Spirit of God another throws us into inevitable skepticism, for we shall be at a perpetual uncertainty which to obey. Nay, we can never be sure which is which. For the proof of the divinity of Scripture depending upon reason, if the clear light of the one might be any way contradicted how shall we be convinced of the infallibility of the other? Reason may err in this point as well as in anything else, and we have no particular promise it shall not.

But if we believe the Scripture to be divine, not upon its own bare assertion but from a real testimony consisting in the evidence of the things contained therein, from undoubted effects and not from words and letters, what is this but to prove it by reason? It has in itself, I grant, the brightest characters of divinity; but 'tis reason finds them out, examines them, and by its principles approves and pronounces them sufficient, which orderly begets in us an acquiescence of faith or persuasion. Now if particulars be thus severely sifted, if not only the doctrine of Christ and his apostles be considered, but also their lives, predictions, miracles, and deaths, surely all this labor would be in vain might we upon any account dispense with contradictions.

The natural result of what has been said is that to believe that divinity of Scripture, or the sense of any passage thereof, without rational proofs and an evident consistency, is a blameable credulity and a temerarious opinion, ordinarily grounded upon an ignorant and willful disposition, but more generally maintained out of a gainful prospect. . . .

I said revelation was not a necessitating motive of assent, but a means of information. We should not confound the way whereby we come to the knowledge of a thing with the grounds we have to believe it. Now such is the nature of a matter of fact that, though it may be conceived possible enough, yet he only can with assurance assert its existence who is himself the author, or by some means of information comes first to the certain knowledge of it. . . .

Thus God is pleased to reveal to us in Scripture several wonderful matters of fact, as the creation of the world, the last judgment, and many other important truths which no man left to himself could ever imagine, no more than any of my fellow-creatures can be sure of my private thoughts. Yet we do not receive them only because they are revealed. For besides the infallible testimony of the revelation from all requisite circumstances, we must see in its subject the indisputable characters of divine wisdom and sound reason, which are the only marks we have to distinguish the oracles and will of God from the impostures and traditions of men.

Whoever reveals anything, that is whoever tells us something we did not know before, his words must be intelligible and the matter possible. This rule holds good, let God or man be the revealer. If we count that person a fool who requires our assent to what is manifestly incredible, how dare we blasphemously attribute to the most perfect being what is an acknowledged defect of one of ourselves? Therefore all matters revealed by God or man must be equally intelligible and possible; so far both revelations agree. But in this they differ, that though the revelation of man should be thus qualified, yet he may impose upon me as to the truth of the thing; whereas what God is pleased to discover to me is not only clear to my reason, but likewise it is always true.

Thus all the doctrines and precepts of the New Testament (if it be indeed divine) must agree with natural reason and our own ordinary ideas.

This every considerate and well-disposed person will find by the careful perusal of it. And whoever undertakes this task will confess the Gospel "not to be hidden from us, nor afar off, but very nigh us, in our mouths, and in our hearts." (Deut. 30:11,14) It affords the most illustrious examples of close and perspicuous ratiocination conceivable, which it is incumbent on me in the explication of its "mysteries" to demonstrate. And though the evidence of Christ's doctrine might claim the approbation of the Gentiles; and its conformity with the types and prophecies of the Old Testament, with all the marks of the Messiah concurring in his person, might justly challenge the assent of his countrymen; yet to leave no room for doubt he proves his authority and Gospel by such works and miracles as the stiff-necked Jews themselves could not deny to be divine. . . .

Nor is there any different rule to be followed in the interpretation of Scripture from what is common to all other books. Whatever unprejudiced person shall use those means will find them notorious deceivers, or much deceived themselves, who maintain the New Testament is written without any order or certain scope, but just as matters came into the apostles' heads. They are strangers to true method who complain of this confusion and disorder. The facility of the Gospel is not confined only to method, for the style is also most easy, most natural, and in the common dialect of those to whom it was immediately consigned. . . .

There remains one objection upon which some lay a mighty stress, though it's like to do them little service. Granting, say they, the Gospel to be as reasonable as you pretend, yet corrupt and depraved reason can neither discern nor receive divine verities. Aye, but that proves not divine verities to be contrary to sound reason. But they maintain that no man's reason is sound. Wherefore I hope so to state this question as to cut off all occasion of dispute from judicious and peaceable men. Reason, taken for the principle of discourse in us, or more particularly for that faculty everyone has of judging of his ideas according to their agreement or disagreement, and so of loving what seems good unto him, and hating what he thinks evil; reason, I say, in this sense is whole and entire in every one whose organs are not accidentally indisposed. 'Tis from it that we are accounted men, and we could neither inform others nor receive improvement ourselves any more than brutes without it.

But if by reason be understood a constant right use of these faculties, viz., if a man never judges but according to clear perceptions, desires nothing but what is truly good for him, nor avoids but what is certainly evil, then, I confess, it is extremely corrupt. We are too prone to frame wrong conceptions and erroneous judgments of things. We generally covet what flatters our senses, without distinguishing noxious from innocent pleasures; and our hatred is as partial. We gratify our bodies so much as to meditate little and think very grossly of spiritual or abstract matters. We are apt to indulge our inclinations, which we term "to follow nature" (I Cor. 2:14); so that the natural man, that is he that gives the swing to his appetites, counts divine things mere folly. But these disorders are so far from being reason that nothing can be more directly contrary to it. We lie under no necessary fate of sinning. There is no defect in our understandings but those of our own creation, that is to say, vicious habits easily contracted but difficultly reformed. . . .

We come at length to inquire whether any doctrine of the Gospel be above, though not contrary to, reason. This expression is taken in a two-fold significance. First, it denotes a thing intelligible of itself, but so covered by figurative words, types and ceremonies that reason cannot penetrate the veil, nor see what is under it till it be removed. Secondly, it is made to signify a thing of its own nature inconceivable, and not to be judged of by our ordinary faculties and ideas, though it be never so clearly revealed. In both these senses "to be above reason" is the same thing with "mystery," and, in effect, they are convertible terms in divinity.

To understand aright what the word "mystery" imports, we must trace the original of it as far back as the theology of the ancient Gentiles. *Myein* in their systems signified "to initiate"; *myesis,* "initiation"; *mystes,* a name afterwards given the priests, denoted the person to be initiated; and "mystery" the doctrine in which he was initiated. . . .

From what has been said it is clear that they understood by "mystery" in those days a thing intelligible of itself, but so veiled by others that it could not be known without special revelation.

But many, not denying what is so plain, yet will have some Christian doctrines to be still "mysterious" in the second sense of the word, that is, inconceivable in themselves however clearly revealed. If I can demonstrate that in the New Testament "mystery" is always used in the first sense of the word, viz., for things naturally very intelligible, but so covered by figurative words or rites that reason could not discover them without special revelation; and that the veil is actually taken away, then it will manifestly follow that the doctrines so revealed cannot now be properly called mysterious.

First, I affirm that nothing can be said to be a mystery because we have not an adequate idea of it, or a distinct view of all its properties at once, for then everything would be a mystery. The knowledge of finite creatures is gradually progressive, as objects are presented to the understanding. We are said to know a thousand things, nor can we doubt of it; yet we never have a full conception of whatever belongs to them. I understand nothing better than this table upon which I am now writing; I conceive it divisible into parts beyond all imagination; but shall I say it is above my reason because I cannot count these parts, nor distinctly perceive their quantity and figures?

Knowing nothing of bodies but their properties, God has wisely provided we should understand no more of these than are useful and necessary for us, which is all our present condition needs. Thus our eyes are not given us to see all quantities, nor perhaps anything as it is in itself, but as it bears some relation to us.

Rightly speaking, then, we are accounted to comprehend anything when its chief properties and their several uses are known to us. It is improper therefore to say a thing is above our reason because we know no more of it than concerns us, and ridiculous to supersede our disquisitions about it upon that score. The most compendious method therefore is neither to trouble ourselves nor others with what is useless, were it known, or what is impossible to be known at all. Since I easily perceive the good or bad effects of rain upon the earth, what should I be the better did I comprehend its generation in the clouds?

The application of this discourse to my subject admits of no difficulty. It is, first, that no Christian doctrine, no more than any ordinary piece of nature, can be reputed a mystery because we have not an adequate or complete idea of whatever belongs to it. Secondly, that what is revealed in religion, as it is most useful and necessary, so it must and may be as easily comprehended, and found as consistent with our common notions, as what we know of wood or stone, of air, of water, or the like. And thirdly, that when we do as familiarly explain such doctrines as what is known of natural things, we may then be as properly said to comprehend the one as the other.

I conclude that neither God himself, nor any of his attributes, are mysteries to us for want of an adequate idea; no, not eternity. Eternity is no more above reason, because it cannot be imagined, than a circle, because it may; for in both cases reason performs its part according to the different natures of the objects, whereof the one is essentially imaginable, the other not.

As we know not all the properties of things, so we can never conceive the essence of any substance in the world. To avoid ambiguity, I distinguish, after an excellent modern philosopher, the nominal from the real essence of a thing. The nominal essence is a collection of those properties or modes which we principally observe in anything. Thus the nominal essence of the sun is a bright, hot, and round body, at a certain distance from us, and that has a constant regular motion. Whoever hears the word "sun" pronounced, this is the idea he has of it. He may conceive more of its properties, or not all these, but it is still a collection of modes or properties that makes his idea. But the real essence is that intrinsic constitution of a thing which is the ground or support of all its properties, and from which they naturally flow or result. Now though we are persuaded that the modes of things must have such a subject to exist in, yet we are absolutely ignorant of what it is.

It follows very plainly that nothing can be said to be a mystery because we are ignorant of its real essence, since it is not more knowable in one thing than in another, and is never conceived or included in the ideas we have of things, or the names we give them. We certainly know as much of the soul as we do of anything else, if not more. We form the clearest conceptions of thinking, knowing, imagining, willing, hoping, loving, and the like operations of the mind. But we are strangers to the subject wherein these operations exist.

As for God, we comprehend nothing better than his attributes. We know not, it's true, the nature of that eternal subject or essence wherein infinite goodness, love, knowledge, power and wisdom coexist; but we are not better acquainted with the real essence of any of his creatures. I remarked in the beginning of this chapter that we knew nothing of things but such of their properties as were necessary and useful. We may say the same of God, for every act of our religion is directed by the consideration of some of his attributes, without ever thinking of his essence. Our love to him is kindled by his goodness, and our thankfulness by his mercy; our obedience is regulated by his justice; and our hopes are confirmed by his wisdom and power.

I think I may now warrantably conclude that nothing is a mystery because we know not its essence, since it appears that it is neither knowable in itself, nor ever thought of by us. So that the divine being himself cannot with more reason be accounted mysterious in this respect than the most contemptible of his creatures. Nor am I very much concerned that these essences escape my knowledge, for I am fixed in the opinion that what infinite goodness has not been pleased to reveal to us, we are either sufficiently capable to discover ourselves, or need not understand at all. . . .

JOSEPH BUTLER (1692–1752)

The Importance of Christianity

But the importance of Christianity will more distinctly appear by considering it more distinctly: first, as a republication, and external institution, of natural or essential religion, adapted to the present circumstances of mankind, and intended to promote natural piety and virtue: and secondly, as containing an account of a dispensation of things, not discoverable by reason, in consequence of which, several distinct precepts are enjoined us. For though natural religion is the foundation and principal part of Christianity, it is not in any sense the whole of it.

Christianity is a republication of natural religion. It instructs mankind in the moral system of the world: that it is the work of an infinitely perfect being, and under his government; that virtue is his law; and that he will finally judge mankind in righteousness, and render to all according to their works, in a future state. And, which is very material, it teaches natural religion, in its genuine simplicity; free from those superstitions, with which, it was totally corrupted, and under which, it was in a manner lost.

Revelation is farther, an authoritative publication of natural religion, and so affords the evidence of testimony for the truth of it. Indeed the miracles and prophecies recorded in Scripture, were intended to prove a particular dispensation of providence, the redemption of the world by the Messiah: but this does not hinder, but they may also prove God's general providence over the world, as our moral governor and judge. And they evidently do prove it; because this character of the author of nature, is necessarily connected with and implied in that particular revealed dispensation of things: it is likewise continually taught expressly, and insisted upon, by those persons, who wrought the miracles and delivered the prophecies. So that indeed natural religion seems as much proved by the Scripture revelation, as it would have been, had the design of revelation been nothing else than to prove it. . . .

Farther: as Christianity served these ends and purposes, when it was first published, by the miraculous publication itself; so it was intended to serve the same purposes, in future ages, by means of the settlement of a visible church: of a society, distinguished from common ones and from the rest of the world, by peculiar religious institutions; by an instituted method of instruction, and an instituted form of external religion. Miraculous powers were given to the first preachers of Christianity, in order to their introducing it into the world: a visible church was established, in order to continue it, and carry it on successively throughout all ages. Had Moses and the Prophets, Christ and his apostles, only taught and by miracles proved, religion to the contemporaries; the benefits of their instructions would have reached but to a small part of mankind. Christianity must have been, in a great degree, sunk and forgot in a very few ages. To prevent this, appears to have been one reason, why a visible church was instituted; to be, like a city upon a hill, a standing memorial to the world of the duty which we owe our maker; to call men continually, both by example and instruction, to attend to it, and by the form of religion, ever before their eyes, remind them of the reality; to be the repository of the oracles of God; and hold up the light of revelation in aid to that of nature, and propagate it throughout all generations to the end of the world—the light of revelation, considered here in no other view, than as designed to enforce natural religion. And in proportion as Christianity is professed and taught in the world, religion, natural or essential religion, is thus distinctly and advantageously laid before mankind; and brought again and again to their thoughts, as a matter of infinite importance. A visible church has also a farther tendency to promote natural religion, as being an instituted method of education, intended to be of more peculiar advantage to those who would conform to it. For one end of the institution was, that by admonition and reproof, as well as instruction, by a general regular discipline, and publick exercises of religion; the body of Christ, as the Scripture speaks, should be edified, i.e. trained up in piety and virtue, for a higher and better state. This settlement then appearing thus beneficial, tending in the nature of things to answer, and in some degree actually answering those ends; it is to be remembered, that the very notion of it implies positive institutions: for the visibility of the church consists in them. Take away every thing of this kind, and you loose the very notion itself. So that if the things now mentioned are advantages, the reason and importance of positive institutions in general, is most obvious; since without them, these advantages could not be secured to the world. And it is mere idle wantonness, to insist upon knowing the reasons, why such particular ones were fixt upon, rather than others.

The benefit arising from this supernatural assistance, which Christianity affords to natural religion, is what some persons are very slow in apprehending. And yet it is a thing distinct in itself, and a very plain obvious one. For will any in good earnest really say, that the bulk of mankind in the heathen world, were in as advantageous a situation with regard to natural religion, as they are now amongst us: that it was laid before them, and enforced upon them, in a manner as distinct, and as much tending to influence their practice? . . .

Christianity is to be considered in a further view; as containing an account of a dispensation of things, not at all discoverable by reason, in consequence of which, several distinct precepts are injoined us. Christianity is not only an external institution of natural religion, and a new promulgation of God's general providence, as righteous governor and judge of the world; but it contains also a revelation of a particular dispensation of providence, carrying on by his Son and Spirit, for the recovery and salvation of mankind, who are represented, in Scripture, to be in a state of ruin. And in consequence of this revelation being made, we are commanded to be baptized, not only in the name of the Father, but also, of the Son and of the Holy Ghost: and other obligations of duty, unknown before, to the Son and the Holy Ghost, are revealed. Now the importance of these duties may be judged of, by observing that they arise, not from positive command merely; but also from the offices, which appear, from Scripture, to belong to those divine persons in the Gospel dispensation; or from the relations, which, we are there informed, they stand in to us. By reason is revealed the relation, which God the Father stands in to us. Hence arises the obligation of duty, which we are under to him. In Scripture are revealed the relations, which the Son and Holy Spirit stand in to us. Hence arise the obligations of Duty, which we are under to them. The truth of the case, as one may speak, in each of these three respects being admitted, that God is the governor of the world, upon the evidence of reason; that Christ is the mediator between God and man, and the Holy Ghost our Guide and Sanctifier, upon the evidence of revelation—the truth of the case, I say, in each of these respects being admitted; it is no more a question, why it should be commanded, that we be baptized in the name of the Son and of the Holy Ghost, than that we be baptized in the name of the Father.

All the general objections against the moral system of nature having been obviated, it is shewn, that there is not any peculiar presumption at all against Christianity considered, either as not discoverable by reason, or as unlike to what is so discovered; nor any worth mentioning, against it as miraculous, if any at all; none certainly, which can render it in the least incredible. It is shewn, that upon supposition of a divine revelation, the analogy of nature renders it, beforehand, highly credible, I think probable, that many things in it, must appear liable to great objections; and that we must be incompetent judges of it, to a great degree. This observation is, I think, unquestionably true, and of the very utmost importance: But it is urged, as I hope it will be understood, with great caution of not vilifying the faculty of reason, which is the candle of the Lord within us (Prov. xx. 27); though it can afford no light, where it does not shine; nor judge, where it has no principles to judge upon. The objections here spoken of, being first answered in the view of Objections against Christianity as a matter of fact, are in the next place considered as urged, more immediately, against the wisdom, justice and goodness of the Christian dispensation. And it is fully made out, that they admit of exactly the like answer, in every respect, to what the like objections against the constitution of nature admit of: that, as partial views give the appearance of wrong to things, which, upon farther consideration and knowledge of their relations to other things, are found just and good; so it is perfectly credible, that the things objected, against the wisdom and goodness of the Christian dispensation, may be rendered instances of wisdom and goodness, by their reference to other things beyond our View: because Christianity is a scheme as much above our comprehension, as that of nature; and, like that, a scheme in which means are made use of to accomplish ends, and which, as is most credible, may be carried on by general laws. And it ought to be attended to, that this is not an answer taken, merely or chiefly, from our ignorance; but from somewhat positive, which our observation shews us. For, to like objections, the like answer is experienced to be just, in numberless parallel cases. The objections against the Christian dispensation, and the method by which it is carried on, having been thus obviated, in general and together; the chief of them are considered distinctly, and the particular things objected to, are shewn credible, by their perfect analogy, each apart, to the constitution of nature. Thus; if mankind be fallen from his primitive state, and to be restored, and infinite wisdom and power engages in accomplishing our recovery: it were to have been expected, it is said, that this should have been effected at once; and not by such a long series of means, and such a various economy of persons and things; one dispensation preparatory to another, this to a farther one, and so on through an indefinite number of Ages, before the end of the scheme proposed can be compleatly accomplished: a scheme conducted by infinite wisdom, and executed by almighty power. But our finding that every thing in the constitution and course of nature, is thus carried on, shews such expectations concerning revelation, to be highly unreasonable; and is a satisfactory answer to them, when urged as objections against the credibility, that the great scheme of providence in the redemption of the world, may be of this kind, and to be accomplished in this manner. As to the particular method of our redemption, the appointment of a mediator between God and man; this is most obviously analogous to the general conduct of nature, i.e. the God of nature, in appointing others to be the instrument of his mercy, as we experience in the daily course of providence. The condition of this world, which the doctrine of our redemption by Christ presupposes, so much falls in with natural appearances, that heathen moralists inferred it from those appearances, inferred that human nature was fallen from its original rectitude, and, in consequence of this, degraded from its primitive happiness. Or, however this opinion came into the world, these appearances must have kept up the tradition, and confirmed the belief of it. And as it was the general opinion under the light of nature, that repentance and reformation, alone and by itself, was not sufficient to do away sin, and procure a full remission of the penalties annext to it; and as the reason of the thing does not at all lead to any such conclusion: so every day's experience shews us, that reformation is not, in any sort, sufficient to prevent the present disadvantages and miseries, which, in the natural course of things, God has annexed to folly and extravagance. Yet there may be ground to think, that the punishments, which, by the general laws of divine government, are annext to vice, may be prevented; that provision may have been, even originally, made, that they should be prevented by some means or other, though they could not by reformation alone. For we have daily instances of such mercy, in the general conduct of nature: compassion for misery, medicines for diseases, friends against enemies. There is provision made, in the original constitution of the world, that much of the natural bad consequences of our follies, which persons themselves alone cannot prevent, may be prevented by the assistance of others; assistance, which nature enables, and disposes, and appoints them to afford. By a method of goodness analogous to this, when the world lay in wickedness and consequently in ruin, God so loved the world, that he gave his only begotten Son to save it. And he being made perfect by suffering, became the author of eternal salvation to all them that obey him (John iii.16, Heb. v.9). Indeed neither reason nor analogy would lead us to think, in particular, that the interposition of Christ in the manner in which he did interpose, would be of that efficacy for recovery of the world, which the Scripture teaches us it was: but neither would reason nor analogy lead us to think, that other particular means would be of the efficacy, which experience shews they are, in numberless instances. And therefore, as the case before us does not admit of experience, so, that neither reason nor analogy can shew, how or in what particular way, the interposition of Christ as revealed in Scripture, is of that efficacy, which it is there represented to be; this is no kind nor degree of presumption against its being really of that efficacy. Farther; the general analogy of nature is an answer to objections against Christianity, from the light of it not being universal, nor its evidence so strong as might possibly have been. That God has made such variety of creatures, is indeed an answer to the former: but that he dispenses his gifts in such variety, both of degrees and kinds, amongst creatures of the same species, and even to the same individuals at different times; is a more obvious and full answer to it. And it is so far from being the method of providence in other cases, to afford us such overbearing evidence, as some require in proof of Christianity, that on the contrary, the evidence upon which we are naturally appointed to act in common matters, throughout a very great part of life, is doubtful in a high degree. And admitting the fact, that God has afforded to some, no more than doubtful evidence of religion; the same account may be given of it, as of difficulties and temptations with regard to practice. But as it is not impossible, surely, that this alledged doubtfulness may be men's own fault; it deserves their most serious consideration, whether it be not so. However, it is certain, that doubting implies a degree of evidence for that, of which we doubt; and that this degree of evidence, as really lays us under obligations, as demonstrative evidence.

The whole then of religion is throughout credible: nor is there, I think, anything relating to the revealed dispensation of things, more different from the experienced constitution and course of nature, than some parts of the constitution of nature are, from other parts of it. And if so, the only question which remains, is, what positive evidence can be alledged for the truth of Christianity. This too in general has been considered, and the objections against it estimated. Deduct then, what is to be deducted from that evidence, upon account of any weight which may be thought to remain in these objections, after what the analogy of nature has suggested in answer to them: and then consider, what are the practical consequences from all this, upon the most sceptical principles, one can argue; for I am writing to persons who entertain these principles. And upon such consideration, it will be obvious, that immorality, as little excuse as it admits of in itself, is greatly aggravated, in persons who have been made acquainted with Christianity, whether they believe it, or not; because the moral system of nature, or natural religion, which Christianity lays before us, approves itself, almost intuitively, to a reasonable mind upon seeing it proposed. In the next place, with regard to Christianity, it will be observed; that there is a middle, between a full satisfaction of the truth of it, and a satisfaction of the contrary. The middle state of mind between these two, consists in a serious apprehension, that it may be true, joined with doubt, whether it be so. And this, upon the best judgment I am able to make, is as far towards speculative infidelity, as any sceptick can at all be supposed to go, who has had true Christianity, with the proper evidence of it, laid before him, and has in any tolerable measure considered them. For I would not be mistaken to comprehend all, who have ever heard of it. Because, as it seems evident that in many countries called Christian, neither Christianity, nor its evidence are fairly laid before men: so in places where both are, there appear to be some, who have very little attended to either, and who reject Christianity with a scorn proportionate to their inattention; and yet are by no means without understanding in other matters. Now it appears, that a serious apprehension that Christianity may be true, lays persons under the strictest obligations of a serious regard to it, throughout the whole of their life: a regard not the same exactly, but in many respects nearly the same, with what a full conviction of its truth would lay them under. Lastly, it will appear, that blasphemy and prophaneness, I mean with regard to Christianity, are absolutely without excuse. For there is no temptation to it, but from the wantonness of vanity or mirth: and these, considering the infinite importance of the subject, are no such temptations as to afford any excuse for it. If this be a just account of things, and yet men can go on to vilify or disregard Christianity, which is to talk and act, as if they had a demonstration of its falsehood; there is no reason to think they would alter their behaviour to any purpose, though there were a demonstration of its truth.

MATTHEW TINDAL (1657–1733)

Christianity as Old as the Creation

A. . . . . I think too great a stress can't be laid on natural religion, which, as I take it, differs not from revealed but in the manner of its being communicated, the one being the internal, as the other the external revelation of the same unchangeable will of a being who is alike at all times infinitely wise and good.

I advance nothing in either of these points without reason. I desire to be informed whether God has not, from the beginning, given mankind some rule, or law, for their conduct? And whether the observing that did not make them acceptable to him? What more can any external revelation do, than render men acceptable to God? Again, if God from the beginning gave men a religion, I ask, was that religion imperfect, or perfect?

B. Most perfect, without doubt, since no religion can come from a being of infinite wisdom and perfection, but what is absolutely perfect.

A. Can, therefore, a religion absolutely perfect admit of any alteration, or be capable of addition, or diminution, and not be as immutable as the author of it? Can revelation, I say, add any thing to a religion thus absolutely perfect, universal, and immutable? Besides, if God at all times was willing all men should come to the knowledge of his truth, could not his infinite wisdom and power at all times find sufficient means for making mankind capable of knowing what his infinite goodness designed they should know?

B. I grant you that God was always willing that all men should come to the knowledge of true religion; and we say that the Christian religion, being the only true and absolutely perfect religion, was what God from the beginning designed for all mankind.

A. If so, it follows that the Christian religion has existed from the beginning; and that God, both then and ever since, has continued to give all mankind sufficient means to know it. So that Christianity, though the name is of a later date, must be as old, and as extensive, as human nature, and as the law of our creation must have been then implanted in us by God himself.

If God never intended mankind should at any time be without religion, or have false religions; and there be but one true religion, which all have been ever bound to believe and profess; I can't see any heterodoxy in affirming that the means to effect this end of infinite wisdom must be as universal and extensive as the end itself; or that all men, at all times, must have had sufficient means to discover whatever God designed they should know and practice. I do not mean by this that all should have equal knowledge, but that all should have what is sufficient for the circumstances they are in.

B. What are those means which, you suppose, God has at all times given the whole race of mankind to enable them to discover what he wills?

A. I freely declare, that the use of those faculties by which men are distinguished from brutes is the only means they have to discern whether there is a God, and whether he concerns himself with human affairs, or has given them any laws, and what those laws are. And as men have no other faculties to judge with, so their using these after the best manner they can must answer the end for which God gave them, and justify their conduct.

A. If God will judge mankind as they are accountable, that is, as they are rational, the judgment must hold an exact proportion to the use they make of their reason. If God designed all mankind should at all times know what he wills them to know; and has given them no other means for this but the use of reason; reason, human reason, must then be that means. For as God has made us rational creatures, and reason tells us that 'tis his will that we act up to the dignity of our natures, so 'tis reason must tell us when we do so. As the eye is the sole judge of what is visible, the ear of what is audible, so reason of what is reasonable. . . .

I shall attempt to show you that men, if they sincerely endeavor to discover the will of God, will perceive that there's a law of nature, or reason, which is so called as being a law which is common, or natural, to all rational creatures; and that this law, like its author, is absolutely perfect, eternal, and unchangeable; and that the design of the Gospel was not to add to, or take from this law, but to free men from that load of superstition which had been mixed with it. So true Christianity is not a religion of yesterday, but what God at the beginning dictated, and still continues to dictate to Christians as well as others. . . .

By natural religion, I understand the belief of the existence of a God, and the sense and practice of those duties which result from the knowledge we, by our reason, have of him and his perfections; and of ourselves, and our own imperfections, and of the relation we stand in to him, and to our fellow-creatures; so that the religion of nature takes in everything that is founded on the reason and nature of things.

I suppose you will allow that it is evident by the light of nature that there is a God, or in other words, a being absolutely perfect, and infinitely happy in himself, who is the source of all other beings; and that what perfections soever the creatures have, they are wholly derived from him. It is equally demonstrable that the creatures can neither add to, nor take away from, the happiness of that being; and that he could have no motive in framing his creatures, or in giving laws to such of them as he made capable of knowing his will, but their own good. It unavoidably follows, nothing can be a part of the divine law, but what tends to promote the common interest and mutual happiness of his rational creatures; and everything that does so must be a part of it.

As God can require nothing of us, but what makes for our happiness; so he, who can't envy us any happiness our nature is capable of, can forbid us those things only which tend to our hurt. From the consideration of these perfections, we cannot but have the highest veneration, nay, the greatest adoration and love for this supreme being, who, that we may not fail to be as happy as possible for such creatures to be, has made our acting for our present, to be the only means of obtaining our future happiness; and that we can't sin against him, but by acting against our reasonable natures.

Our reason, which gives us a demonstration of the divine perfections, affords us the same concerning the nature of those duties God requires, not only with relation to himself, but to ourselves, and one another.

With relation to ourselves, we can't but know how we are to act, if we consider that God has endowed man with such a nature as makes him necessarily desire his own good; and, therefore, he may be sure that God, who has bestowed this nature on him, could not require anything of him in prejudice of it; but on the contrary, that he should do everything which tends to promote the good of it. The health of the body and the vigor of the mind being highly conducing to our good, we must be sensible we offend our maker if we indulge our senses to the prejudice of these. We can't but know we ought to use great moderation with relation to our passions, or, in other words, govern all our actions by reason, that and our true interest being inseparable. And, in a word, whoever so regulates his natural appetites as will conduce most to the exercise of his reason, the health of his body, and the pleasure of his senses, taken and considered together (since herein his happiness consists), may be certain he can never offend his maker.

As to what God expects from men with relation to each other, everyone must know his duty who considers that the common parent of mankind has the whole species alike under his protection, and will equally punish him for injuring others, as he would others for injuring him; and consequently that it is his duty to deal with them, as he expects they should deal with him in the like circumstances. Considering the variety of circumstances men are under, and these continually changing, as well as being for the most part unforeseen, it is impossible to have rules laid down by any external revelation for every particular case. Therefore, there must be some standing rule, discoverable by the light of nature, to direct us in all such cases. And we can't be more certain that it is the will of God that those effects which flow from natural causes should so flow, than we are that it is the will of God that men should observe whatever the nature of things, and the relation they have to one another, make fit to be observed, should be so observed.

And I may add that the better to cause men to observe those rules which make for their mutual benefit, infinite goodness has sown in their hearts seeds of pity, humanity and tenderness, which, without much difficulty, cannot be eradicated; but nothing operates more strongly than that desire men have of being in esteem, credit, and reputation with their fellow creatures, not to be obtained without acting on the principles of natural justice, equity, benevolence, etc. In a word, as a most beneficent disposition in the supreme being is the source of all his actions in relation to his creatures, so he has implanted in man, whom he has made after his own image, a love for his species; the gratifying of which in doing acts of benevolence, compassion and good will, produces a pleasure that never satiates, as on the contrary actions of ill nature, envy, malice, etc., never fail to produce shame, confusion, and everlasting self-reproach.

From these premises, I think, we may boldly draw this conclusion, that if religion consists in the practice of those duties that result from the relation we stand in to God and man, our religion must always be the same. If God is unchangeable, our duty to him must be so too; if human nature continues the same, and men at all times stand in the same relation to one another, the duties which result from those relations must always be the same. And consequently, our duty to God and man must, from the beginning of the world to the end, always be the same, always alike plain and perspicuous, and can neither be changed in whole or part. Consequently, whoever acts what is best for himself, both in a public and private capacity, does all that either God or man can require. Hence I think we may define true religion to consist in a constant disposition of mind to do all the good we can, and thereby render ourselves acceptable to God in answering the end of his creation. . . .

B. There's one difficulty which to me seems insuperable, how to make the faith required by the religion of faith and of the Gospel to have the same views, and tend to the same end.

A. If faith in God himself, no more than in any other act of religion, is required not for God's sake, but our own, can faith in one sent by God be required for any other end? Especially considering, that no person is ever the more known to posterity because his name is transmitted to them. When we say "Caesar" conquered "Pompey," we having no idea of either can only mean somebody conquered somebody. And have we more distinct ideas of "Jesus" and "Pilate"? And though we had a personal idea of the former, he could receive no advantage or disadvantage by what we thought of him. And if faith in him was required for a cause antecedent to his being so sent, founded in his and our nature, and the relation we always stood in to him, would not the eternal reason of things have made it manifest? That which concerned all must be knowable by all, for which reason the apostle says, "that which may be known of God" (and none can know that which may not be known) "was manifest in the Gentiles." (Rom. 1:19)

The end of Christ's coming seems not to teach men new duties, but (repentance being the first thing preached by him and his apostles both to Jews and Gentiles) to repent of the breach of known duties. And Jesus does not say he was "sent" to all "Israel, but to the lost sheep of the house of Israel" (Matt. 15:24); and that the "Son of Man is come to save that which is lost." (Matt. 18:11) And his parable about the lost sheep (Lk. 15:7) supposed all were not lost. And when it was objected to him that he kept company with sinners, he owns the charge and says, "the whole need no physician, but they that are sick" (Matt. 9:12); which would have been an improper answer if he thought that all stood in need of him and his spiritual physic. And to confirm this, he adds, "I am not come to call the righteous, but sinners to repentance." (Matt. 9:13) Which is dividing mankind into two parts, the whole or righteous, and the sick or sinners, and that his business was entirely with the latter. In religion there are no nostrums, or secrets, but all may know what God requires of all; and there is but one universal remedy for all sick persons, repentance and amendment. They, certainly, are whole, and need no physician, who do of themselves what will make them acceptable to him, living as those whom Christ came to reform were taught to live. Is it not absurd to suppose that till then none had sufficient means given them to answer the end for which all were created?

What can be more required than those qualifications as will make Jesus in the last day declare, "Come ye blessed of my Father, inherit the Kingdom prepared for you from the beginning of the world"? (Matt. 25:34) And what are those qualifications, but living up to the law of reason, in exercising acts of benevolence, goodness, etc.? . . .

WILLIAM LAW (1686–1761)

The Limits of Reason

We are not without some natural capacity of judging right of God, of finding out his perfections, and proving what is or is not worthy to be ascribed to him. But what the divine perfections are in themselves, what they imply and contain in their own nature and manner of existence, is altogether mysterious and inconceivable by us at present.

Though we are insufficient for comprehending the reasons on which the particular matter or manner of any divine revelation is founded, yet we may be so far sufficient judges of the reasons for receiving or not receiving a revelation as divine as to make our conduct therein justly accountable to God.

For if God can show a revelation to proceed from him by the same undeniable evidence as he shows the creation to be his work; if he can make himself as visible in a particular extraordinary manner as he is by his general and ordinary providence; then, although we are as unqualified to judge the mysteries of a revelation as we are to judge of the mysteries in creation and providence, yet we may be as fully obliged to receive a revelation as to acknowledge the creation to be the work of God, and as highly criminal for disbelieving it as for denying a general providence.

Adam, Noah, Abraham, and Moses were very incompetent judges of the reasons on which the particular revelations made to them were founded. But this did not hinder their sufficient assurance that such revelations came from God, because they were proved to come from God in the same manner and for the same reasons as the creation is proved to be the work of God.

And if their posterity will let no messages from heaven, no prophecies and miracles persuade them that God can call them to any duties but such as they must enjoin themselves; or to the belief of any doctrines but such as their own minds can suggest; nor to any methods of changing their present state of weakness and disorder for a happy immortality but such as suit their own taste, temper, and way of reasoning; it is because they are grown senseless of the mysteries of creation and providence with which they are surrounded, and forget the awful prerogative of infinite wisdom over the weakest, lowest rank of intelligent beings.

For the excellence of a revelation is to be acknowledged by us for the same reason that we are to acknowledge the excellence of creation and providence; not because they are wholly according to human conception and have no mysteries, but because they are proved to be of God.

And a revelation is to be received as coming from God not because of its internal excellence, or because we judge it to be worthy of God, but because God has declared it to be his, in as plain and undeniable a manner as he has declared creation and providence to be his. For though no revelation can come from God but what is truly worthy of him, and full of every internal excellence, yet what is truly worthy of God to be revealed cannot possibly be known by us but by a revelation from himself. As we can only know what is worthy of God in creation by knowing what he has created, so we can no other way possibly know what is worthy of God to be revealed but by a revelation.

This writer's argument, if it were allowed, leads directly to atheism. For if a revelation cannot be divine if it contains anything mysterious whose fitness and necessity cannot be explained by human reason, then neither creation nor providence can be proved to be divine, for they are both of them more mysterious than the Christian revelation. And revelation itself is therefore mysterious because creation and providence cannot be delivered from mystery. . . .

For if everything is arbitrary whose fitness and expedience human reason cannot prove and explain, then surely an invisible over-ruling providence, that orders all things in a manner and for reasons known only to itself; that subjects human life and human affairs to what changes it pleases; that confounds the best laid designs, and makes great effects arise from folly and imprudence; that gives the race not to the swift, nor the battle to the strong; that brings good men into affliction, and makes the wicked prosperous; surely such a providence must be highly arbitrary. . . .

And therefore if this argument is to be admitted, it leads directly to atheism, and brings us under a greater necessity of rejecting this notion of divine providence, on the account of its mysteries, than of rejecting a revelation that is mysterious in any of its doctrines. There is nothing half so mysterious in the Christian revelation, considered in itself, as there is in that invisible providence which all must hold that believe a God. And though there is enough plain in providence to excite the adoration of humble and pious minds, yet it has often been a rock of atheism to those who make their own reason the measure of wisdom.

The true grounds and reasons on which we are to believe a revelation to be divine are such external marks and signs of God's action and operation as are a sufficient proof of it. And if God has no ways of acting that are peculiar and particular to himself, and such as sufficiently prove his action and operation, then revelation can have no sufficient proof that it comes from God. . . .

I appeal therefore to the miracles and prophecies on which Christianity is founded, as a sufficient proof that it is a divine revelation. Every reason for ascribing the creation to God is the same reason for ascribing such miracles and prophecies to God; and every argument against the certainty of those miracles and prophecies coming from God is the same argument against the certainty of the creation's being the work of God. . . .

As the existence of things is the highest and utmost evidence of God's having created them, and not to be tried by our judgments about the reasonableness and ends of their creation; so a course of plain undeniable miracles, attesting the truth of a revelation, is the highest and utmost evidence of its coming from God, and not to be tried by our judgments about the reasonableness or necessity of its doctrines. . . .

And as miracles thus considered in themselves are the highest and most undeniable evidence of the truth and divinity of any external revelation, so Christianity stands fully distinguished from all other religions by the highest and most undeniable evidence, since it has all the proof that the highest state of miracles can give, and every other religion is without any support from them. . . .

Although common language ascribes a variety of faculties and principles to the soul, yet in strictness of truth everything that is done by us is the action and operation of our reason, and is to be ascribed to it as the sole faculty or principle from whence it proceeded, and by which it is governed and effected. . . .

As our passions not only make us different from other men, but frequently and almost daily different from ourselves, loving and hating under great inconstancy, so our reason is not only different from the reason of other men, but is often different from itself, by a strange inconstancy setting up first one opinion and then another.

So that when we talk of human reason, or a reason common to mankind, we talk of as various, uncertain, and unmeasurable a thing as when we talk of a love, a liking, an aversion, a good nature, or ill nature, common to mankind; for these qualities admit of no variation, uncertainty, or mutability but such as they directly receive from the reason of mankind. For it is as much the reason of man that acts in all these tempers, and makes them to be just what they are, as it is the reason of man that demonstrates a mathematical proposition. . . .

A laudable good nature, or a laudable aversion, is only reason acting in a certain manner; a criminal good nature, or a criminal aversion, is nothing else but an ill-judging reason. But it is still reason or our understanding that is the only agent in our bad passions as well as good passions, and as much the sole agent in all our passions and tempers as in things of mere speculation.

So that the state of reason in human life is nothing else but the state of human tempers and passions. And right reason in morality is nothing else but right love and right aversion.

Brutes are incapable of imprudence and immorality because none of their actions are the actions of reason. Everything therefore that is imprudence, immorality, baseness, or villainy in us must be the act of our reason; otherwise it could no more be imprudent or immoral than the action of brutes. As therefore all that is faithful, just, and wise, can only be attributed to that which is done by our reason, so by plain consequence all that is vain, false, or shameful, can only be imputed to any acts as they are the acts of reason. . . .

All the good, therefore, that there is in any of the desires or aversions of the mere natural man is the good of our reason; and all the evil or blindness that there is in any of our passions is solely the evil and blindness of our reason. So that all that which we call different faculties of the soul, tempers and passions of the heart, strictly speaking means nothing else but the various acts and operations of one and the same rational principle, which has different names according to the objects that it acts upon and the manner of its acting. . . .

To all this it may, perhaps, be objected that our passions and tempers arise from bodily motions, and depend very much upon the state of our blood and animal spirits, and that therefore what we do under their commotions cannot be attributed to our reason. It is readily granted that the body has this share in our passions and tempers; but then the same thing must be granted of the body in all the acts and operations of the mind. For the most abstract thought and calm speculation of the mind has as truly the concurrence and conjunct operation of bodily spirits as our strongest desires or aversions. And it is as much owing to the state of the body that such speculations are what they are, as it is owing to the state of the body that such passions are what they are. . . .

To draw now some plain consequences from the foregoing account. First, if reason be, as above represented, the universal agent in the natural man; if all the difference among such men, either in speculation or practice, is only such a difference as reason makes, then nothing can be more extravagant than to affirm anything concerning the degree of perfection or imperfection of reason as common to man.

Secondly, granting that all matters of religion must be agreeable to right, unprejudiced reason, yet this could be no ground for receiving nothing in religion but what human reason could prove to be necessary, for human reason is no more right unprejudiced reason than a sinner is sinless, or a man an angel.

Granting, again, that a man may go a great way toward rectifying his reason and laying aside its prejudices, yet no particular man can be a better judge of the rectitude of his own reason than he is of the rectitude of his own self-love, the sagacity of his own understanding, the brightness of his own parts, the justness of his own eloquence, and the depth of his own judgment. For there is nothing to deceive him in self-love, in the opinion of his own merit, wit, judgment, and eloquence, but what has the same power to deceive him in the opinion of his own reason.

Thirdly, a man that has his religion to choose, and with this precious privilege, that he need not allow anything to be matter of religion but what his own right reason can prove to be so, is in as fair a way to be governed by his passions, as he that has his condition of life to choose, with the liberty of taking that which his own right reason directs him to.

Does anyone suppose now that nothing but right reason would direct him in the choice of his condition? Or that he would make the better choice because he proceeded upon this maxim, that nothing could be right but that which was agreeable to his reason? Or that his tempers, his prejudices, his self-love, his passions, his partiality, would have no influence upon his choice because he had resigned himself to his own right reason?

For as our choice of a condition of life is not a matter of speculation, but of good and evil, so however it is recommended to our reason, it chiefly excites our passions. And our choice will be just as reasonable as our tempers and passions are. And he that is made the most positive of the sufficiency of his own right reason will be the most likely to be governed by the blindness of his own passions.

Now it is just the same in the choice of a religion as in the choice of a condition of life. As it is not a matter of speculation but of good and evil, so if it is left to be stated and determined by our own reason, it rather appeals to our tempers than employs our reason; and to resign ourselves up to our own reason to tell us what ought or ought not to be a matter of religion is only resigning ourselves up to our tempers, to take what we like and refuse what we dislike in religion.

For it is only natural and easy for him, who believes that nothing can be a part of religion but what his reason can prove necessarily to be so, to take that to be fully proved which is only mightily liked; and all that to be entirely contrary to reason which is only vastly contrary to his tempers.

Lastly, if this be the state of reason, as has been fully proved, then to pretend that our reason is too perfect to be governed by anything but its own light is the same extravagance as to pretend that our love is too pure to be governed by anything but its own inclinations, our hatred too just to be governed by anything but its own motions. For if all that is base and criminal in love, all that is unjust and wicked in hatred, is strictly and solely to be imputed to our reason, then no perfection can be ascribed to our reason but such as is to be ascribed to our love and hatred.

JOHN WESLEY (1703–1791)

On Free Grace

The grace or love of God, whence cometh our salvation, *is free in all, and free for all.*

First: It is free *in all* to whom it is given. It does not depend on any power or merit in man; no, not in any degree, neither in whole nor in part. It does not in any wise depend either on the good works or righteousness of the receiver; not on any thing he has done, or any thing he is. It does not depend on his endeavours. It does not depend on his good tempers, or good desires, or good purposes and intentions; for all these flow from the free grace of God; they are the streams only, not the fountain. They are the fruits of free grace, and not the root. They are not the cause but the effects of it. Whatsoever good is in man or is done by man, God is the author and doer of it. Thus is his grace free in all; that is, no way depending on any power or merit in man, but on God alone, who freely gave us his own Son, and "with him freely giveth us all things."

But is it free *for all,* as well as *in all?* To this some have answered, "No: it is free only for those whom God hath ordained to life; and they are but a little flock. The greater part of mankind God hath ordained to death; and it is not free for them. Them God hateth; and therefore, before they were born, decreed they should die eternally. And this he absolutely decreed; because so was his good pleasure because it was his sovereign will. Accordingly they are born for this, to be destroyed body and soul in hell. And they grow up under the irrevocable curse of God, without any possibility of redemption; for what grace God gives, he gives only for this, to increase, not prevent, their damnation."

This is that decree of predestination. But methinks I hear one say, "This is not the predestination which I hold: I hold only, the election of grace. What I believe is no more than this: that God before the foundation of the world, did elect a certain number of men to be justified, sanctified and glorified. Now all these will be saved, and none else: for the rest of mankind God leaves to themselves; so they follow the imaginations of their own hearts, which are only evil continually, and, waxing worse, are at length justly punished with everlasting destruction."

Is this all the predestination which you hold? Consider: perhaps this is not all. Do not you believe, God ordained them to this very thing? If so, you believe the whole decree; you hold predestination in the full sense, which has been above described. But it may be, you think you do not. Do not you then believe, God hardens the hearts of them that perish? Do not you believe, he (literally) hardened Pharaoh's heart, and that for this end he raised him up, or created him? Why this amounts to just the same thing. If you believe Pharaoh, or any one man upon earth, was created for this end, to be damned, you hold all that has been said of predestination. And there is no need you should add, that God seconds his decree, which is supposed unchangeable and irresistible, by hardening the hearts of those vessels of wrath, whom that decree had before fitted for destruction.

Well; but it may be you do not believe even this: you do not hold any decree of reprobation: you do not think God decrees any man to be damned, nor hardens, irresistibly fits him for damnation: you only say, "God eternally decreed, that all being dead in sin, he would say to some of the dry bones, Live, and to others he would not; that, consequently, these should be made alive, and those abide in death,—these should glorify God by their salvation, and those by their destruction."

Is not this what you mean by the election of grace? If it be, I would ask one or two questions: Are any who are not thus elected, saved? Or, were any, from the foundation of the world? Is it possible any man should be saved, unless he be thus elected? If you say, No; you are but where you were: you are not got one hair's breadth farther: you still believe, that in consequence of an unchangeable, irresistible decree of God, the greater part of mankind abide in death without any possibility of redemption; inasmuch as none can save them but God, and he will not save them. You believe he hath absolutely decreed not to save them; and what is this, but decreeing to damn them? It is, in effect, neither more nor less: it comes to the same thing: for if you are dead, and altogether unable to make yourself alive, then, if God has absolutely decreed he will make only others alive, and not you, he hath absolutely decreed your everlasting death; you are absolutely consigned to damnation. So then, though you use softer words than some, you mean the self same thing; and God's decree concerning the election of grace, according to your own account of it, amounts to neither more nor less than what others call, "God's decree of reprobation."

Call it therefore by whatever name you please, election, preterition, predestination, or reprobation, it comes in the end to the same thing. The sense of all is plainly this: by virtue of an eternal, unchangeable, irresistible decree of God, one part of mankind are infallibly saved, and the rest infallibly damned; it being impossible that any of the former should be damned, or that any of the latter should be saved.

But if this be so, then is all preaching vain. It is needless to them that are elected; for they, whether with preaching or without, will infallibly be saved. Therefore the end of preaching, to save souls, is void with regard to them. And it is useless to them that are not elected, for they cannot possibly be saved. They, whether with preaching or without, will infallibly be damned. The end of preaching is therefore void with regard to them likewise; so that in either case, our preaching is vain, as your hearing also is vain.

This, then, is a plain proof that the doctrine of predestination is not a doctrine of God, because it makes void the ordinance of God: and God is not divided against himself. A second is, that it directly tends to destroy that holiness, which is the end of all the ordinances of God. I do not say, none who hold it are holy; (for God is of tender mercy to those who are unavoidably entangled in errors of any kind;) but that the doctrine itself, —That every man is either elected, or not elected, from eternity and that one must inevitably be saved, and the other inevitably damned,—has a manifest tendency to destroy holiness in general. For it wholly takes away those first motives to follow after it so frequently proposed in Scripture, the hope of future reward and fear of punishment, the hope of heaven and fear of hell. That these shall go away into everlasting punishment, and those into life eternal, is no motive to him to struggle for life, who believes his lot is cast already: it is not reasonable for him so to do, if he thinks he is unalterably adjudged either to life or death. You will say, "But he knows not whether it is life or death." What then?—this helps not the matter: for if a sick man knows that he must unavoidably die, or unavoidably recover, though he knows not which, it is unreasonable for him to take any physic at all. He might justly say, (and so I have heard some speak, both in bodily sickness and in spiritual,) "If I am ordained to life, I shall live; if to death, I shall die: so I need not trouble myself about it." So directly does this doctrine tend to shut the very gate of holiness in general, to hinder unholy men from ever approaching thereto, or striving to enter in thereat.

As directly does this doctrine tend to destroy several particular branches of holiness. Such as meekness and love: love, I mean, of our enemies; of the evil and unthankful. I say not, that none who hold it have meekness and love; (for as is the power of God, so is his mercy;) but that it naturally tends to inspire, or increase, a sharpness or eagerness of temper, which is quite contrary to the meekness of Christ; as then especially appears, when they are opposed on this head. And it as naturally inspires contempt or coldness towards those who we suppose outcasts from God.

"Oh but," you say, "I suppose no particular man a reprobate." You mean, you would not if you could help it. But you cannot help sometimes applying your general doctrine to particular persons: the enemy of souls will apply it for you. You know how often he has done so. But you rejected the thought with abhorrence. True: as soon as you could: but how did it sour and sharpen your spirit in the mean time? You well know it was not the spirit of love which you then felt towards that poor sinner, whom you supposed or suspected, whether you would or no, to have been hated of God from eternity.

Thirdly, this doctrine tends to destroy the comfort of religion, the happiness of Christianity. This is evident as to all those who believe themselves to be reprobated; or who only suspect or fear it. All the great and precious promises are lost to them; they afford them no ray of comfort: for they are not the elect of God; therefore they have neither lot nor portion in them. This is an effectual bar to their finding any comfort or happiness, even in that religion whose ways are designed to be "ways of pleasantness, and all her paths peace."

And as to you who believe yourselves the elect of God, what is your happiness: I hope not a notion; a speculative belief; a bare opinion of any kind; but a feeling possession of God in your heart, wrought in you by the Holy Ghost, or the witness of God's Spirit with your spirit that you are a child of God. This, otherwise termed "the full assurance of faith," is the true ground of a Christian's happiness. And it does indeed imply a full assurance that all your past sins are forgiven, and that you are *now* a child of God. But it does not necessarily imply a full assurance of our future perseverance. I do not say this is never joined to it, but that it is not necessarily implied therein; for many have the one, who have not the other.

Now this witness of the Spirit, experience shows to be much obstructed by this doctrine; and not only in those who, believing themselves reprobated, by this belief thrust it far from them, but even in them that have tasted of that good gift, who yet have soon lost it again, and fallen back into doubts, and fears, and darkness,—horrible darkness, that might be felt! And I appeal to any of you who hold this doctrine, to say, between God and your own hearts, whether you have not often a return of doubts and fears concerning your election or perseverance? If you ask, who has not? I answer, very few of those that hold this doctrine,—but many, very many of those that hold it not, in all parts of the earth, many of those who know and feel they are in Christ today, and "Take no thought for the morrow," who "abide in him" by faith from hour to hour, or rather from moment to moment,—many of these have enjoyed the uninterrupted witness of his Spirit, the continual light of his countenance, from the moment wherein they first believed, for many months or years, to this day. . . .

ON FREE GRACE 197

Fourthly: This uncomfortable doctrine directly tends to destroy our zeal for good works. And this it does, first, as it naturally tends (according to what was observed before) to destroy our love to the greater part of mankind, namely, the evil and unthankful. For whatever lessens our love, must so far lessen our desire to do them good. This it does, secondly, as it cuts off one of the strongest motives to all acts of bodily mercy, such as feeding the hungry, clothing the naked, and the like; viz. the hope of saving their souls from death. For what avails it to relieve their temporal wants, who are just dropping into eternal fire? "Well: but run and snatch them as brands out of the fire."—Nay, this you suppose impossible. They were appointed thereunto, you say, from eternity, before they had done either good or evil. You believe it is the will of God they should die. And "who hath resisted his will?" But you say, you do not know whether these are elected or not. What then? If you know they are the one or the other, that they are either elected, or not elected, all your labour is void and vain. In either case, your advice, reproof, or exhortation, is as needless and useless as our preaching. It is needless to them that are elected; for they will infallibly be saved without it. It is useless to them that are not elected; for with or without it they will infallibly be damned: therefore you cannot, consistently with your principles, take any pains about their salvation. Consequently those principles directly tend to destroy your zeal for good works; for all good works; but particularly for the greatest of all, the saving of souls from death.

But, fifthly, This doctrine not only tends to destroy Christian holiness, happiness, and good works, but hath also a direct and manifest tendency to overthrow the whole Christian revelation. The point which the wisest of the modern unbelievers most industriously labour to prove, is that the Christian revelation is not necessary. They well know, could they once show this, the conclusion would be too plain to be denied, "If it be not necessary, it is not true." Now this fundamental point you give up. For supposing that eternal, unchangeable decree, one part of mankind must be saved though the Christian revelation were not in being, and the other part of mankind must be damned notwithstanding that revelation. And what would an infidel desire more? You allow him all he asks. In making the gospel thus unnecessary to all sorts of men, you give up the whole Christian cause. "Oh tell it not in Gath! Publish it not in the streets of Askelon! lest the daughters of the uncircumcised rejoice"; lest the sons of unbelief triumph! . . .

Yea, the decree is past: and so it was before the foundation of the world. But what decree? Even this: I will set before the sons of men, "life and death, blessing and cursing. And the soul that chooseth life shall live, as the soul that chooseth death shall die." This decree, whereby "whom

God did foreknow, he did predestinate," was indeed from everlasting: this, whereby all who suffer Christ to make them alive are "elect, according to the foreknowledge of God," now standeth fast, even as the moon, and as the faithful witnesses in heaven; and when heaven and earth shall pass away, yet this shall not pass away, for it is as unchangeable and eternal, as is the being of God that gave it. This decree yields the strongest encouragement to abound in all good works, and in all holiness; and it is a well spring of joy, of happiness also, to our great and endless comfort. This is worthy of God: it is every way consistent with all the perfections of his nature. It gives us the noblest view both of his justice, mercy, and truth. To this agrees the whole scope of the Christian revelation, as well as all the parts thereof. To this Moses and all his prophets bear witness, and our blessed Lord and all his apostles. Thus Moses, in the name of his Lord, "I call heaven and earth to record against you this day, that I have set before you life and death, blessing and cursing; therefore choose life, that thou and thy seed may live." Thus Ezekiel (to cite one prophet for all): "The soul that sinneth, it shall die: the son shall not bear [eternally] the iniquity of the father. The righteousness of the righteous shall be upon him, and the wickedness of the wicked shall be upon him" (chap. xviii.20). Thus our blessed Lord: "If any man thirst, let him come unto me and drink" (John vii. 37). Thus his great apostle, St. Paul (Acts xvii.30): "God commandeth all men every where to repent;"—"all men, every where;" every man in every place, without any exception, either of place or person. Thus St. James: "if any of you lack wisdom, let him ask of God, who giveth to all men liberally, and upbraideth not, and it shall be given him" (James i.5). Thus St. Peter (II Pet. iii.9): "The Lord is not willing that any should perish, but that all should come to repentance." And thus St. John: "If any man sin, we have an advocate with the Father: and he is the propitiation for our sins: and not for ours only, but for the sins of the whole world" (I John ii. 2).

Oh hear ye this, ye that forget God! Ye cannot charge your death upon him! "Have I any pleasure at all, that the wicked should die, saith the Lord God?" (Ezek. xviii.23, etc.) "Repent, and turn from all your transgressions: so iniquity shall not be your ruin. Cast away from you all your transgressions whereby ye have transgressed,—for why will ye die, oh house of Israel? For I have no pleasure in the death of him that dieth, saith the Lord God. Wherefore turn yourselves and live ye." "As I live, saith the Lord God, I have no pleasure in the death of the wicked. —Turn ye, turn ye, from your evil ways: for why will ye die, oh house of Israel?" (Ezek. xxxiii.11)

WILLIAM WILBERFORCE (1758–1833)

On Emotion in Religion

The objection of our opponent, that by insisting on the obligation of making our blessed Saviour the object of our religious affections, we are degrading the worship of the understanding, and are substituting and raising up a set of mere feelings in its stead, is one which deserves our most serious consideration. If it be just, it is decisive; for ours must be unquestionably "a reasonable service" (Rom. xii.1). The objector must mean, either that these affections are unreasonable in themselves, or that they are misplaced in religion. He can scarcely however intend that the affections are in their own nature unreasonable. To suppose him to maintain this position, were to suppose him ignorant of what every school-boy knows of the mechanism of the human mind. We shall therefore take it for granted that this cannot be his meaning, and proceed to examine the latter part of the alternative. Here also it may either be intended, that the affections are misplaced in Religion *generally,* or that our blessed Saviour is not the proper object of them. The strain of our objector's language, no less than the objections themselves which he has urged, render it evident (that perhaps without excluding the latter position) the former is in full possession of his mind.

This notion of the affections being out of place in Religion, is indeed an opinion which appears to be generally prevalent. The affections are regarded as the strong holds of enthusiasm. It is therefore judged most expedient to act, as prudent generals are used to do, when they raze the fortress, or spike up the cannon, which are likely to fall into the hands of an enemy. Mankind are apt to be the dupes of misapplied terms; and the progress of persuasion now in question, has been considerably aided by an abuse of language, not sufficiently checked in its first advances, whereby that species of Religion which is opposite to the warm and affectionate kind, has been suffered, almost without disturbance, to usurp to itself the epithet of *rational.* But let not this claim be too hastily admitted. Let the position in question be thoroughly and impartially discussed, and it will appear, if I mistake not, to be a gross and pernicious error. If amputation be indeed indispensable, we must submit to it; but we may surely expect to be heard with patience, or rather with favour and indulgence, while we proceed to shew that there is no need to have recourse to so desperate a remedy. . . .

It cannot, methinks, but afford a considerable presumption against the doctrine which we are about to combat that it proposes to exclude at once from the service of Religion so grand a part of the composition of man; that in this our noblest employment it condemns, as worse than useless, all the most active and operative principles of our nature. One cannot but suppose that like the organs of the body, so the elementary qualities and original passions of the mind were all given us for valuable purposes by our all-wise Creator. It is indeed one of the sad evidences of our fallen condition, that they are now perpetually tumultuating and rebelling against the powers of reason and conscience, to which they should be subject. But even if Revelation had been silent, natural reason might have in some degree presumed, that it would be the effect of a Religion which should come from God, completely to repair the consequences of our super-induced depravity. The schemes of mere human wisdom had indeed tacitly confessed, that this was a task beyond their strength. Of the two most celebrated systems of philosophy, the one expressly confirmed the usurpation of the passions; while the other, despairing of being able to regulate, saw nothing left but to extinguish them. The former acted like a weak government, which gives independence to a rebellious province, which it cannot reduce. The latter formed its boasted scheme merely upon the plan of that barbarous policy, which composes the troubles of a turbulent land by the extermination of its inhabitants. This is the calm, not of order, but of inaction; it is not tranquillity, but the stillness of death; Christianity, we might hope, would not be driven to any such wretched expedients; nor in fact does she condescend to them. They only thus undervalue her strength, who mistake her character, and are ignorant of her powers. It is her peculiar glory, and her main office, to bring all the faculties of our nature into their just subordination and dependence; that so the whole man, complete in all his functions, may be restored to the true ends of his being, and be devoted, entire and harmonious, to the service and glory of God. . . . We can scarcely indeed look into any part of the sacred volume without meeting abundant proofs, that it is the religion of the Affections which God particularly requires. Love, Zeal, Gratitude, Joy, Hope, Trust, are each of them specified; and are not allowed to us as weaknesses, but enjoined on us as our bounden duty, and commended to us as our acceptable worship. Where passages are so numerous, there would be no end of particular citations. Let it be sufficient therefore, to refer the reader to the word of God.

There let him observe too, that as the lively exercise of the passions towards their legitimate object, is always spoken of with praise, so a cold, hard, unfeeling heart is represented as highly criminal. Lukewarmness is stated to be the object of God's disgust and aversion; zeal and love, of his favour and delight; and the taking away of the heart of stone and the implanting of a warmer and more tender nature in its stead is specifically promised as the effect of his returning favour, and the work of his renewing grace. . . . Those modes of worship are set forth and prescribed, which are best calculated to excite the dormant affections, and to maintain them in lively exercise; and the aids of music and singing are expressly superadded to increase their effect. If we look to the most eminent of the Scripture characters, we shall find them warm, zealous, and affectionate. When engaged in their favourite work of celebrating the goodness of their Supreme Benefactor, their souls appear to burn within them, their hearts kindle into rapture; the powers of language are inadequate to the expression of their transports; and they call on all nature to swell the chorus and to unite with them in hallelujahs of gratitude, and joy, and praise. The man after God's own heart most of all abounds in these glowing effusions; and his compositions appear to have been given us in order to set the tone, as it were, to all succeeding generations. . . .

Again, when it pleased God to check the future Apostle of the Gentiles in his wild career, and to make him a monument of transforming grace; was the force of his affections diminished, or was it not only that their direction was changed? He brought his affections entire and unabated into the service of his blessed Master. His zeal now burned even with an increase of brightness; and no intenseness, no continuance of suffering could allay its ardor, or damp the fervors of his triumphant exultations. Finally —The worship and service of the glorified spirits in Heaven, is not represented to us as cold intellectual investigation, but as the worship and service of gratitude and love. And surely it will not be disputed, that it should be even here the humble endeavour of those, who are promised while on earth "to be made meet to be partakers of the inheritance of the saints in light," to bring their hearts into a capacity for joining in those everlasting praises.

But it may not be unadvisable for the writer here to guard against a mistaken supposition, from which the mind of our objector by no means appears exempt, that the force of the religious affections is to be mainly estimated (I had almost said by the thermometer) by the degree of mere animal fervor, by ardors, and transports, and raptures, of which, from constitutional temperament, a person may be easily susceptible; or into which daily experience must convince us, that people of strong conceptions and of warm passions may work themselves without much difficulty, where their hearts are by no means truly or deeply interested. Every tolerable actor can attest the truth of this remark. These high degrees of the passions bad men may experience, good men may want. They may be affected; they may be genuine; but whether genuine or affected, they form not the true standard by which the real nature or strength of the religious affections is to be determined. To ascertain these points, we must examine, whether they appear to be grounded in knowledge, to have their root in strong and just conceptions of the great and manifold excellencies of their object, or to be ignorant, unmeaning, or vague; whether they are natural and easy, or constrained and forced; wakeful and apt to fix on their great objects, delighting in their proper nutriment (if the expression may be allowed) the exercises of prayer and praise, and religious contemplation; or voluntarily omitting offered occasions of receiving it, looking forward on them with little expectation, looking back on them with little complacency, and being disappointed of them with little regret; by observing whether these religious affections are merely occasional visitants, or the abiding inmates of the soul: whether they have got the mastery over the vicious passions and propensities, with which in their origin, and nature, and tendency, they are at open variance; or whether, if the victory be not yet complete, the war is at least constant, and the breach irreconcilable: whether they moderate and regulate all the inferior appetites and desires which are culpable only in their excess, thus striving to reign in the bosom with a settled undisputed predominance: by examining, whether above all they manifest themselves by prompting to the active discharge of the duties of life, the personal, and domestic, and relative, and professional, and social, and civil duties. Here the wideness of their range and the universality of their influence, will generally serve to distinguish them from those partial efforts of diligence and self-denial, to which mankind are prompted by subordinate motives. All proofs, other than this deduced from conduct, are in some degree ambiguous. This, this only, whether we argue from Reason or from Scripture, is a sure, infallible criterion. From the daily incidents of conjugal and domestic life, we learn that a heat of affection occasionally vehement, but superficial and transitory, may consist too well with a course of conduct, exhibiting incontestable proofs of neglect and unkindness. But the passion which alone the holy Scriptures dignify with the name of Love, is a deep, not a superficial feeling; a fixed and permanent, not an occasional emotion. It proves the validity of its title, by actions corresponding with its nature, by practical endeavours to gratify the wishes and to promote the interests of the object of affection. "If a man love me, he will keep my sayings." "This is the love of God, that we keep his commandments." This, therefore, is the best standard by which to try the quality, or the quality being ascertained, to estimate the strength of the religious affections. Without suffering ourselves to derive too much complacency from transient fervors of devotion, we should carefully and frequently prove ourselves by this less dubitable test; impartially examining our daily conduct; and often comparing our actual, with our possible services, the fair amount of our exertions, with our natural or acquired means and opportunities of usefulness.

. . . We are perfectly ready to concede to the objector, whose arguments we have so long been considering, that the religious affections must be expected to be more or less lively in different men, and in the same man at different times, in proportion to natural tempers, ages, situations, and habits of life. But, to found an objection on this ground, would be as unreasonable as it were altogether to deny the obligation of the precepts, which command us to relieve the necessities of the indigent, because the infinitely varying circumstances of mankind must render it impossible to specify beforehand the sum which each individual ought on the whole to allot to this purpose, or to fix in every particular instance, on any determinate measure, and mode of contribution. . . .

He who every where but in Religion is warm and animated, there only phlegmatic and cold, can hardly expect (especially if this coldness be not the subject of unfeigned humiliation and sorrow) that his plea on the ground of natural temper should be admitted; any more than that of a person who should urge his poverty as a justification of his not relieving the wants of the necessitous, at the very time that he should be launching out into expense without restraint, on occasions in which he should be really prompted by his inclinations. In both cases, "it is the *willing* mind which is required." Where that is found, "every man will be judged according to what he hath, and not according to what he hath not" (II Cor. viii.12).

. . . We have every one of us a work to accomplish, wherein our eternal interests are at stake; a work to which we are naturally indisposed. We live in a world abounding with objects which distract our attention and divert our endeavours; and a deadly enemy is ever at hand to seduce and beguile us. If we persevere indeed, success is certain; but our efforts must know no remission. There is a call on us for vigorous and continual resolution, self-denial, and activity. Now man is not a being of mere intellect. . . . The slightest solicitation of appetite is often able to draw us to act in opposition to our clearest judgment, our highest interests, and most resolute determinations. Sickness, poverty, disgrace, and even eternal misery itself, sometimes in vain solicit our regards; they are all excluded from the view, and thrust as it were beyond the sphere of vision, by some poor, unsubstantial, transient object, so minute and contemptible as almost to escape the notice of the eye of reason.

These observations are more strikingly confirmed in our religious concerns than in any other; because in them the interests at stake are of transcendent importance: but they hold equally in every instance according to its measure, wherein there is a call for laborious, painful, and continued exertions, from which any one is likely to be deterred by obstacles, or seduced by the solicitations of pleasure. What then is to be done in the case of any such arduous and necessary undertaking? The answer is obvious— You should endeavour not only to convince the understanding, but also to affect the heart; and for this end, you must secure the reinforcement of the passions. . . .

It is indisputably true, that in religion we have to argue and plead with men for principles of action, the wisdom and expediency of which are universally acknowledged in matters of worldly concern. Frail and "infirm of purpose," we have a business to execute of supreme and indispensable necessity. Solicitations to neglect it every where abound; the difficulties and dangers are numerous and urgent; and the night of death cometh, how soon we know not, "when no man can work." All this is granted. It seems to be a state of things wherein one should look out with solicitude for some powerful stimulants. Mere knowledge is confessedly too weak. The affections alone remain to supply the deficiency. They precisely meet the occasion, and suit the purposes intended. Yet when we propose to fit ourselves for our great undertaking, by calling them in to our help, we are to be told that we are acting contrary to reason. Is this reasonable, to strip us first of our armour of proof, and then to send us to the sharpest of encounters? to summon us to the severest labours, but first to rob us of the precious cordial which should brace our sinews and recruit our strength?

Let these pretended advocates for reason at length then confess their folly, and do justice to the superior wisdom as well as goodness of our heavenly Instructor, who, better understanding our true condition, and knowing our forwardness and inadvertency, has most reasonably as well as kindly pointed out and enjoined on us the use of those aids which may counteract our infirmities; who commanding the effect, has commanded also the means whereby it may be accomplished. . . .

JONATHAN EDWARDS (1703–1758)

Sinners in the Hands of an Angry God

The observation from the words that I would now insist upon is this—
"There is nothing that keeps wicked men at any one moment out of hell,
but the mere pleasure of God."—By the *mere* pleasure of God, I mean his
sovereign pleasure, his arbitrary will, restrained by no obligation, hindered
by no manner of difficulty, any more than if nothing else but God's mere
will had in the least degree, or in any respect whatsoever, any hand in the
preservation of wicked men one moment.—The truth of this observation
may appear by the following considerations.

There is no want of *power* in God to cast wicked men into hell at any
moment. Men's hands cannot be strong when God rises up. The strongest
have no power to resist him, nor can any deliver out of his hands.—He is
not only able to cast wicked men into hell, but he can most easily do it.
Sometimes an earthly prince meets with a great deal of difficulty to subdue
a rebel, who has found means to fortify himself, and has made himself
strong by the numbers of his followers. But it is not so with God. There is
no fortress that is any defence from the power of God. Though hand join
hand, and vast multitudes of God's enemies combine and associate themselves, they are easily broken in pieces. They are as great heaps of light
chaff before the whirlwind; or large quantities of dry stubble before de-
vouring flames. We find it easy to tread on and crush a worm that we see
crawling on the earth; so it is easy for us to cut or singe a slender thread
that any thing hangs by: thus easy is it for God, when he pleases, to cast
his enemies down to hell. What are we, that we should think to stand before him, at whose rebuke the earth trembles, and before whom the rocks
are thrown down?

They *deserve* to be cast into hell; so that divine justice never stands in
the way, it makes no objection against God's using his power at any moment to destroy them. Yea, on the contrary, justice calls aloud for an infinite punishment of their sins. Divine justice says of the tree that brings
forth such grapes of Sodom, "Cut it down, why cumbereth it the ground?"

Luke xiii.7. The sword of divine justice is every moment brandished over their heads, and it is nothing but the hand of arbitrary mercy, and God's mere will, that holds it back.

They are already under a sentence of *condemnation* to hell. They do not only justly deserve to be cast down thither, but the sentence of the law of God, that eternal and immutable rule of righteousness that God has fixed between him and mankind, is gone out against them, and stands against them; so that they are bound over already to hell. John iii.18: "He that believeth not is condemned already." So that every unconverted man properly belongs to hell; that is his place; from thence he is, John viii.23: "Ye are from beneath." And thither he is bound; it is the place that justice, and God's word, and the sentence of his unchangeable law assign to him.

They are now the objects of that very same *anger* and wrath of God, that is expressed in the torments of hell. And the reason why they do not go down to hell at each moment, is not because God, in whose power they are, is not then very angry with them; as he is with many miserable creatures now tormented in hell, who there feel and bear the fierceness of his wrath. Yea, God is a great deal more angry with great numbers that are now on earth; yea, doubtless, with many that are now in this congregation, who it may be are at ease, than he is with many of those who are now in the flames of hell.

So that it is not because God is unmindful of their wickedness, and does not resent it, that he does not let loose his hand and cut them off. God is not altogether such an one as themselves, though they may imagine him to be so. The wrath of God burns against them, their damnation does not slumber; the pit is prepared, the fire is made ready, the furnace is now hot, ready to receive them; the flames do now rage and glow. The glittering sword is whet, and held over them, and the pit hath opened its mouth under them. . . .

It is no security to wicked men for one moment, that there are no visible means of death at hand. It is no security to a natural man, that he is now in health, and that he does not see which way he should now immediately go out of the world by any accident, and that there is no visible danger in any respect in his circumstances. The manifold and continual experience of the world in all ages, shows this is no evidence, that a man is not on the very brink of eternity, and that the next step will not be into another world. The unseen, unthought-of ways and means of persons going suddenly out of the world are innumerable and inconceivable. Unconverted men walk over the pit of hell on a rotten covering, and there are innumerable places in this covering so weak that they will not bear their weight, and these places are not seen. The arrows of death fly unseen at noon-day;

the sharpest sight cannot discern them. God has so many different unsearchable ways of taking wicked men out of the world and sending them to hell, that there is nothing to make it appear, that God had need to be at the expense of a miracle, or go out of the ordinary course of his providence, to destroy any wicked man, at any moment. All the means that there are of sinners going out of the world, are so in God's hands, and so universally and absolutely subject to his power and determination, that it does not depend at all the less on the mere will of God, whether sinners shall at any moment go to hell, than if means were never made use of, or at all concerned in the case.

Natural men's prudence and care to preserve their own lives, or the care of others to preserve them, do not secure them a moment. To this, divine providence and universal experience do also bear testimony. There is this clear evidence that men's own wisdom is no security to them from death; that if it were otherwise we should see some difference between the wise and politic men of the world, and others, with regard to their liableness to early and unexpected death: but how is it in fact? Eccles. ii.16: "How dieth the wise man? even as the fool." . . .

But the foolish children of men miserably delude themselves in their own schemes, and in confidence in their own strength and wisdom; they trust to nothing but a shadow. The greater part of those who heretofore have lived under the same means of grace, and are now dead, are undoubtedly gone to hell; and it was not because they were not as wise as those who are now alive: it was not because they did not lay out matters as well for themselves to secure their own escape. If we could speak with them and inquire of them, one by one, whether they expected, when alive, and when they used to hear about hell, ever to be the subjects of that misery: we doubtless should hear one and another reply, "No, I never intended to come here: I had laid out matters otherwise in my mind; I thought I should contrive well for myself: I thought my scheme good. I intended to take effectual care; but it came upon me unexpected; I did not look for it at that time, and in that manner; it came as a thief: Death outwitted me: God's wrath was too quick for me. Oh, my cursed foolishness! I was flattering myself, and pleasing myself with vain dreams of what I would do; hereafter; and when I was saying, Peace and safety, then destruction came upon me." . . .

Application

The use of this awful subject may be for awakening unconverted persons in this congregation. This that you have heard is the case of every one of you that are out of Christ.—That world of misery, that lake of burning, brimstone, is extended abroad under you. There is the dreadful pit of the glowing flames of the wrath of God; there is hell's wide gaping mouth open; and you have nothing to stand upon, nor any thing to take hold of; there is nothing between you and hell but the air; it is only the power and mere pleasure of God that holds you up. . . .

O sinner! Consider the fearful danger you are in: it is a great furnace of wrath, a wide and bottomless pit, full of the fire of wrath, that you are held over in the hand of that God, whose wrath is provoked and incensed as much against you, as against many of the damned in hell. You hang by a slender thread, with the flames of divine wrath flashing about it, and ready every moment to singe it, and burn it asunder; and you have no interest in any Mediator, and nothing to lay hold of to save yourself, nothing to keep off the flames of wrath, nothing of your own, nothing that you ever have done, nothing that you can do, to induce God to spare you one moment.—And consider here more particularly.

Whose wrath it is: it is the wrath of the infinite God. If it were only the wrath of man, though it were of the most potent prince, it would be comparatively little to be regarded. The wrath of kings is very much dreaded, especially of absolute monarchs, who have the possessions and lives of their subjects wholly in their power, to be disposed of at their mere will. Prov. xx.2: "The fear of a king is as the roaring of a lion: Whoso provoketh him to anger, sinneth against his own soul." The subject that very much enrages an arbitrary prince, is liable to suffer the most extreme torments that human art can invent, or human power can inflict. But the greatest earthly potentates in their greatest majesty and strength, and when clothed in their greatest terrors, are but feeble, despicable worms of the dust, in comparison of the great and almighty Creator and King of heaven and earth. It is but little that they can do, when most enraged, and when they have exerted the utmost of their fury. All the kings of the earth, before God, are as grasshoppers; they are nothing, and less than nothing: both their love and their hatred is to be despised. The wrath of the great King of kings, is as much more terrible than theirs, as his majesty is greater. Luke xii.4,5, "And I say unto you, my friends, Be not afraid of them that kill the body, and after that, have no more that they can do. But I will forewarn you whom you shall fear: fear him, which after he hath killed, hath power to cast into hell; yea, I say unto you, Fear him."

It is the fierceness of his wrath that you are exposed to. We often read of the fury of God; as in Isaiah lix.18, "According to their deeds, accordingly he will repay fury to his adversaries." So Isaiah lxvi.15, "For behold, the Lord will come with fire, and with his chariots like a whirlwind, to render his anger with fury, and his rebuke with flames of fire." And in many other places. So, Rev. xix.15, we read of "the wine press of the fierceness and wrath of Almighty God." The words are exceeding terrible. If it had only been said, "the wrath of God," the words would have implied that which is infinitely dreadful: but it is "the fierceness and wrath of God." The fury of God! the fierceness of Jehovah! Oh, how dreadful must that be! Who can utter what such expressions carry in them! But it is also "the fierceness and wrath of Almighty God." As though there would be a very great manifestation of his almighty power in what the fierceness of his wrath should inflict, as though omnipotence should be as it were enraged, and exerted, as men are wont to exert their strength in the fierceness of their wrath. Oh! then, what will be the consequence? What will become of the poor worms that shall suffer it? Whose hands can be strong? And whose heart can endure? To what a dreadful, inexpressible, inconceivable depth of misery must the poor creature be sunk who shall be the subject of this! . . .

It is *everlasting* wrath. It would be dreadful to suffer this fierceness and wrath of Almighty God one moment; but you must suffer it to all eternity. There will be no end to this exquisite horrible misery. When you look forward, you shall see a long forever, a boundless duration before you, which will swallow up your thoughts, and amaze your soul; and you will absolutely despair of ever having any deliverance, any end, any mitigation, any rest at all. You will know certainly that you must wear out long ages, millions of millions of ages, in wrestling and conflicting with this almighty merciless vengeance; and then when you have so done, when so many ages have actually been spent by you in this manner, you will know that all is but a point to what remains. So that your punishment will indeed be infinite. Oh, who can express what the state of a soul in such circumstances is! All that we can possibly say about it, gives but a very feeble, faint representation of it; it is inexpressible and inconceivable: For "who knows the power of God's anger?"

How dreadful is the state of those that are daily and hourly in the danger of this great wrath and infinite misery! But this is the dismal case of every soul in this congregation that has not been born again, however moral and strict, sober and religious, they may otherwise be. . . .

And now you have an extraordinary opportunity, a day wherein Christ has thrown the door of mercy wide open, and stands in it calling and crying with a loud voice to poor sinners; a day wherein many are flocking to him, and pressing into the kingdom of God. Many are daily coming from the east, west, north and south; many that were very lately in the same miserable condition that you are in, are now in a happy state, with their hearts filled with love to him who has loved them, and washed them from their sins in his own blood, and rejoicing in hope of the glory of God. How awful is it to be left behind at such a day! To see so many others feasting, while you are pining and perishing! To see so many rejoicing and singing for joy of heart, while you have cause to mourn for sorrow of heart and howl for vexation of spirit! How can you rest one moment in such a condition? Are not your souls as precious as the souls of the people at Suffield, where they are flocking from day to day to Christ?

Are there not many who have lived long in the world, and are not to this day born again? and so are aliens from the commonwealth of Israel, and have done nothing ever since they have lived, but treasure up wrath against the day of wrath? Oh, sirs, your case, in an especial manner, is extremely dangerous. Your guilt and hardness of heart is extremely great. Do you not see how generally persons of your years are passed over and left, in the present remarkable and wonderful dispensation of God's mercy? You had need to consider yourselves, and awake thoroughly out of sleep. You cannot bear the fierceness and wrath of the infinite God.—And you, young men, and young women, will you neglect this precious season which you now enjoy, when so many others of your age are renouncing all youthful vanities, and flocking to Christ? You especially have now an extraordinary opportunity; but if you neglect it, it will soon be with you as with those persons who spent all the precious days of youth in sin, and are now come to such a dreadful pass in blindness and hardness.—And you, children, who are unconverted, do not you know that you are going down to hell, to bear the dreadful wrath of that God who is now angry with you every day and every night? Will you be content to be the children of the devil when so many other children in the land are converted, and are become the holy and happy children of the King of kings?

And let every one that is yet of Christ, and hanging over the pit of hell, whether they be old men and women, or middle aged, or young people, or little children, now hearken to the loud calls of God's word and providence. This acceptable year of the Lord, a day of such great favours to some, will doubtless be a day of as remarkable vengeance to others. Men's hearts harden, and their guilt increases apace at such a day as this, if they neglect their souls; and never was there so great a danger of such persons being given up to hardness of heart and blindness of mind. God seems now to be hastily gathering in his elect in all parts of the land; and probably the greater part of adult persons that ever shall be saved, will be brought in now in a little time, and that it will be as it was on the great out-pouring of the Spirit upon the Jews in the apostles' days; the election will obtain, and the rest will be blinded. If this should be the case with you, you will eternally curse this day, and will curse the day that ever you were born, to see such a season of the pouring out of God's Spirit, and will wish that you had died and gone to hell before you had seen it. Now, undoubtedly it is, as it was in the days of John the Baptist, the axe is in an extraordinary manner laid at the root of the trees, that every tree which brings not forth good fruit, may be hewn down and cast into the fire.

Therefore, let every one that is out of Christ, now awake and fly from the wrath to come. The wrath of Almighty God is now undoubtedly hanging over a great part of this congregation: Let every one fly out of Sodom: "Haste and escape for your lives, look not behind you, escape to the mountain, lest you be consumed."

AUGUSTE FRANCKE (1663–1727)

The Love of God Toward Men

. . . But a few general hints displaying this [divine] love, and inviting us to love him again, will suggest to us sufficient matter for our present design.

The marvellous nature and essence of this great and glorious God, as it exceeds the capacity of any of his creatures, so it affords us a constant conviction of his infinite greatness and glory; the Scriptures themselves being very full and expressive of his glory and majesty; of which a large account is set down, Ecclus. xlii.15, and xliii throughout.

But then let us also, in the second place, consider what man is especially after his shameful falling away from God into the service of sin and vanity.

Man is now become a creature unfaithful to his creator, revolted from God, groaning under the sentence of death and the curse of the law. He is filled with sin, both original and actual, and with enmity against so great and gracious a God; he is incapable of all that is good, and prone to what is bad: and thus running himself into all manner of evil, proveth the unhappy contriver of his own ruin and misery.

When you read in the Levitical law, the ordinances God made concerning both the uncleanness of beasts, and the bodily uncleanness of men themselves, . . . then be assured, that all this relateth to the depraved state of men after the fall, which therefore is most lively represented. Hath not David reason then to ask: Lord, what is man, thou takest knowledge of him? or the son of man that thou makest such account of him? Psal. cxliv.3.

Thirdly: Let us also reflect on the great and inconceivable disproportion there is between God who loveth man, and the man himself, who is the object beloved of God.

There seemed to be a vast inequality (at least in the judgment of men,) betwixt Ahasuerus and Esther: But that would be very small, if compared with what we may find betwixt God and man.

For God is the all-perfect Being; and man, as the Psalmist saith, is but a shadow and vanity, (Psal. xxxix.5 and cxliv.4).

God is the most holy; in whose sight even the heavens are not clean, (Job xv.15), when man, on the contrary, is impure and unholy, of a perverse and crooked nature, a rebel against his God, shame and dishonour, and by nature no child of God, but of wrath, (Deut. xxxii.5, Eph. ii.3). And who is now able to express, and sufficiently to set forth, this infinite disproportion?

Fourthly: Consider that there is nothing at all in man, that deserves, or may procure that love which the Lord so freely bestows on him. We ourselves, says the Apostle, were sometimes foolish, disobedient, deceived, serving diverse lusts and pleasures, living in malice and envy, hateful, (or altogether abominable,) and hating one another. And being in this woeful condition, it was then, he says, that the divine philanthropy, or love of God towards men, appeared, (Tit. iii, ver. 3) compared with ver. 4 and Deut. ix.4,5,6.

Fifthly: Do but observe particularly, that there is not only nothing lovely to be met with in man, the object of God's love; but on the contrary, that he is full of everything which may render him odious to the Lord, and bring upon him his just hatred and indignation. And that none should think himself free from so foul and universal a stain, or value himself upon any prerogative whatsoever, the apostle represents both Jews and heathen in most black and detestable colours, and declares them both guilty of most vile and abominable crimes; as plainly appears from the three first chapters of his Epistle to the Romans: To which may be added what is said, (Psal. v and Ezek. xvi), to give us a just sense of the fall of man, and of the horrid corruption of his nature. And even whilst he is in this deplorable state, the love of God begins to work, and calls upon man to return and be saved.

Sixthly: Consider therefore, again and again, that the divine Lover moved to love, not by any worth or dignity he perceiveth in him whom he loveth; but entirely and purely by the motive of his own inconceivable love and compassion. This he hath declared himself, (Jer. xxxi.20). My bowels are troubled for him; I will surely have mercy upon him, saith the Lord. (See also Rom. v.5,6,7.)

Seventhly: Consider that this tender love, which hath its original in the incomprehensible and eternal compassion of God, penetrateth the very abyss of misery, into which man is sunk, in order to deliver him out of it, according to that of Hezekiah: Thou hast in love to my soul delivered it from the pit of corruption, (Isai. xxxviii.17). Consider also, that the end God hath proposed to himself in his love, is no other, than to make man like himself again, who, by his fall, has lost the image of God; and then, after having rescued him from the gulf of perdition, and of all evils attending him here, conduct him at last to the most sublime and glorious perfection.

Eighthly: Remember that the divine love readily bestoweth the greatest of all good things for the saving of man, and for procuring to him unspeakable bliss and happiness. This is no less than the only and beloved Son of God, sent into the world to save and redeem it. And who can doubt, but that it is chiefly with regard to this ineffable love, the Lord himself is called love in the Scripture? It was the tender mercy of God whereby the day-spring from on high hath visited us, to give light to them that sit in darkness and in the shadow of death, (Luk. i.78,79; Joh. iii.16; I Joh. iv.9,10).

Ninethly: Consider that this love employeth all the riches of the goodness of God, of his forebearance and long-suffering; and this for no other reason but that by all possible means he may attain the end which he hath proposed concerning man.

Tenthly: Conclude therefore from thence, that this love is an eternal love, an unsearchable and forever inexhaustible love, altogether sublime and magnificent, most pure, most holy, most perfect, and most divine. For God himself is charity or Love, (I Joh. iv.16).

Eleventhly: Observe that this divine love doth not require of man any merit by works at all, but only a profound acknowledgment of his extreme want and unworthiness, attended with unfeigned grief and repentance for his former wicked and profligate life, whereby he hath deprived himself so long of the enjoyment of this pure and heavenly love. The consequence whereof will be, that, after he hath once regained a sense of so invaluable a love, he will then, with the greater care and concern, watch over it, lest by unbelief or disobedience, he lose again the only comfort of his life. He will suffer, that it may act in him freely, and without opposition. He will be ready to receive it, whenever it offers itself, to quicken his deadish heart, to enflame his cold heart, to melt his icy heart, to cleanse more and more his profane and worldly heart, to diffuse itself in and about it, to display therein its wonderful glory and beauty, and to deliver it at last from all its sin and misery.

Truly, the love and goodness of God will infallibly effect all these marvellous things, provided a man do not hinder its sweet and agreeable operations, by unbelief and self-will; but give himself up to it, as a sick and wounded person to a physician, who is able to procure his health and recovery. Man ought but to humble himself under the hand of God, and, like a patient, quietly wait till he be healed, and relieved by this all-sufficient love; which will not fail to visit him in time, and satiate him forever with the fatness of God's house, and with a river of pleasures.

Twelfthly: Observe that this pure and perfect love of God doth not reject the vilest transgressor that can be, even if he be defiled with the very blood of sin and iniquity. God looks upon a man whilst he is in this miserable condition, with an eye of mercy, and with the tenderest disposition that pity can inspire: And being thus moved with love and compassion, He endeavours to prevent the sinner from farther mischief: He goes forth to meet him in his return, He accepts and receives him, He washes and cleanses him from his filth and impurities. For it is from Him the living waters of the Holy Spirit do proceed, whereby the penitent sinner is regenerated, renewed, made a new man, and rendered acceptable in the sight of God. These and many other graces flowing from the love of God, are most copiously declared (Ezek. xvi.6; Luk. xv.20; Eph. v.25,26,27; I Cor. vi.11; Tit. iii.5,6; Rom. v.5).

Thirteenthly: Consider also the wise and wonderful order, according to which divine love doth proceed in its various works and emanations. First, It gaineth the sinner so far, as to render him thoroughly sensible of the dismal condition into which he hath plunged himself; and then it maketh him groan and breathe after a Redeemer. After the soul hath struggled a while under a woeful sense of her misery, and sees nothing but poverty and nakedness in spirit; 'tis then that the love of God steps in, and clothes her with the robes of grace, and the ornament of salvation, which are the garments of the first-born, wherein the mystical Jacob receives the blessing of his father (Gen. xvii. 15,23,27,29). For it is then that this divine love admits a man into the full possession of Christ, and applies to him his righteousness as his own; that so being justified by his grace, he may be heir of eternal life (Tit. iii.7).

Fourteenthly: Observe that this love produceth a lively hope in man, and that it granteth and giveth the Spirit of adoption, with all other graces that accompany it. And this must needs prove a most valuable engagement, and the very pledge and earnest of that inheritance, which in its proper time, shall be most gloriously displayed. See of this heavenly earnest (Eph. i.14; II Cor. i.21,22, chap. v.5). 'Tis this hope which, as an anchor of the soul, both sure and steadfast, entreth into that which is within the veil, whither Jesus Christ is entered as an High Priest for us (Heb. vi.19,20; Rom. viii.15–25).

Fifteenthly: Remember that the love of God is so free and communicative, as to impart its divine power to man, giving him all things that pertain to life and godliness, by the knowledge of him that hath called him, by his own glory and power (II Pet. i.3). This divine power guardeth him faithfully from the infectious lusts which reign in the world, and maketh him partaker of the divine nature itself; so that he is now no more led by the flesh, but by the spirit; that he walketh now no more after the flesh, but after the spirit, by which he mortifieth the deeds of the body (Rom. viii.1,9,13; Gal. v.22,24,25).

Sixteenthly: Consider, in fine, that this love having once begun a thorough reformation in you, and reclaimed you from your corrupted ways; you ought now to go on steadily in the Lord, and improve his love into a higher degree of sanctification. He is ready to sanctify you more and more, nay, entirely, and render you perfect throughout, that all that is in you, the spirit, soul, and body, may be preserved blameless unto the coming of our Lord Jesus Christ; that you may be presented with gladness before his irreprehensible glory (Phil. i.6; I Thess. v.23,24; Jude, ver. 24). 'Tis then that love arriveth to its final end and perfection, when it conducteth man into the goodly heritage of eternal life, where there will be no more weeping, or lamenting, but a full and constant display of that love which hath been hid here under various crosses and tribulations (I Joh. iii.1,2; Joh. iii.16, chap. xvii.24; Rev., chap. xxi, xxii).

And now, my beloved, remember these things, and meditate thereon with a serene and quiet spirit, which is of so great a price before God; that you may perceive at last, nay taste and feel, to what degree the Lord loveth men. There is no doubt, but this divine fire will soon begin to be kindled within you, after you have mused a while on its various and surprising effects. But then do not rest in a transient taste or view of this love, but let it afford you some matter to higher and more practical observations.

First then, cast an eye upon yourself, and consider what account you have hitherto made of the love of God, and what price you have set upon it: whether you have regarded it as your greatest and most valuable treasure, or whether you have made light of it, as of a thing that cannot give any great satisfaction.

Consider further what place you have afforded it in your heart, whenever it hath presented itself to you, and endeavoured to get admittance into the choicest faculties of your soul.

Consider whether you have suffered it freely to operate, and to effect its divine work in you; whether it hath transformed you into its own nature, and happily united you to its self.

And lastly, I would have you consider, what the present disposition of your soul is in relation to this love: whether your sentiments, thoughts, affections and intentions, discourses and actions; in a word, whether your outward and inward conduct and manner of life doth convince you, that this love hath a real influence upon you, and that it continueth to gain ground in you every day; so that from thence you may conceive a well-grounded hope, that the God of love will also finish his work in his time, and carry it to a happy conclusion at last.

But alas! if you find no such thing as the love of God in your souls, but rather what is contrary to it, I mean the love of sin and vanity; I then beseech you to return betimes, and suffer yourselves to be found and embraced by the love of God: For it seeketh you as a tender mother seeketh her lost child, and waits patiently, that you may receive the comfort it is willing to bestow upon you.

Secondly: You ought well to weigh the nature of that love which you bear to your neighbor and your whole deportment towards him. Consider whether the purity of the love of God towards you, hath wrought you into a pure and disinterested love towards your neighbor: And whether the compassionate tenderness of the divine love hath had so happy an effect upon you, as to clothe you with bowels of mercy towards your neighbour, with kindness and humbleness of mind, with meekness and long-suffering, and other virtues which are wont to accompany that love, which is the bond of perfection (Col. iii.12). For truly the good will and love of God towards us, ought to be the constant model and foundation of that love and affection we ought to bestow on our neighbour, as the apostle doth plainly set forth (Tit. iii.1 compared with ver. 4).

Thirdly and lastly: You ought to consider, that God himself is Love, and that consequently that love is the nearest way to unite you to him forever, who is love in a most universal and essential manner. If you are not able to reach into the bottom of this sea of love, suffer then that a drop of a living faith may fall into this vast ocean, and believe what as yet you cannot see. This sea of love will never be drawn dry, and this ocean will never be fathomed by the narrow dimensions of our understanding: Let therefore your faith sink into that love which passeth knowledge; and let it sink freely, without fear and anxiety. If you lose yourselves in the depth of this love, you shall certainly find yourselves again, and live eternally there, where it will be displayed in its sublimest perfection and lustre.

May the eternal and uncreated Love, that Love which hath so wonderfully manifested itself in Christ Jesus our Lord; plant all these graces in your hearts, and water them constantly by the healing influence of his Spirit!

GOTTHOLD LESSING (1729–1781)

The Education of the Human Race

What education is to the individual man, revelation is to the whole human race. Education is revelation coming to the individual man; and revelation is education which has come, and is still coming, to the human race. Whether it can be of any advantage to the science of instruction to consider education from this point of view I will not here inquire; but in theology it may unquestionably be of great advantage, and may remove many difficulties, if revelation be conceived of as an education of the human race.

Education gives man nothing which he could not also get from within himself; it gives him that which he could get from within himself, only quicker and more easily. In the same way too, revelation gives nothing to the human race which human reason could not arrive at on its own; only it has given, and still gives to it, the most important of these things sooner.

And just as in education, it is not a matter of indifference in what order the powers of a man are developed, as it cannot impart to a man everything at once; so also God had to maintain a certain order and a certain measure in his revelation.

Even though the first man was furnished at once with a conception of the One God; yet it was not possible that this conception, freely imparted and not won by experience, should subsist long in its clearness. As soon as human reason, left to itself, began to elaborate it, it broke up the one immeasurable into many measurables, and gave a distinguishing mark to every one of these parts.

Hence naturally arose polytheism and idolatry. And who can say for how many millions of years human reason would have been lost in these errors, even though at all places and times there were individual men who recognized them *as* errors, had it not pleased God to afford it a better direction by means of a new impulse?

But when he neither could, nor would, reveal himself any more to *each* individual man, he selected an individual people for his special education;

and that the most rude and the most ferocious, in order to begin with it from the very beginning. This was the Hebrew people, about whom we do not even know what kind of divine worship they had in Egypt. For so despised a race of slaves could not have been permitted to take part in the worship of the Egyptians; and the God of their fathers had become entirely unknown to them. . . .

To this rude people God caused himself to be announced at first simply as "the God of their fathers," in order to make them familiar and at home with the idea of God belonging to them too. Following this, through the miracles with which he led them out of Egypt and planted them in Canaan, he testified of himself to them as a God mightier than any other god. And as he continued demonstrating himself to be the mightiest of all, which only one can be, he gradually accustomed them to the idea of the One.

But how far was this conception of the One below the true transcendental conception of the One, which reason, so late, teaches us only to conclude with certainty out of the conception of the infinite!

Although the best of the people were already more or less approaching the true conception of the One, the people as a whole could not for a long time elevate themselves to it. And this was the sole reason why they so often abandoned their one God, and expected to find the One, i.e. the mightiest, in some other god belonging to another people.

But of what kind of moral education was a people so raw, so incapable of abstract thoughts, and so entirely in their childhood, capable? Of none other but such as is adapted to the age of children, an education by rewards and punishments addressed to the senses.

Here too, then, education and revelation come together. As yet God could give to his people no other religion, no other law than one through obedience to which they might hope to be happy, or through disobedience to which they must fear to be unhappy. For as yet they envisaged nothing beyond this life. They knew of no immortality of the soul; they yearned after no life to come. But now to reveal these things, when their reason was so little prepared for them, what would it have been but the same fault in the divine rule as is committed by the vain schoolmaster who chooses to hurry his pupil too rapidly and boast of his progress, rather than thoroughly to ground him? . . .

While God guided his chosen people through all the degrees of a child's education, the other nations of the earth had gone on by the light of reason. The most part had remained far behind the chosen people. Only a few had got in front of them. And this, too, takes place with children, who are allowed to grow up on their own; many remain quite raw; some educate themselves to an astonishing degree.

But as these more fortunate few prove nothing against the use and necessity of education, so the few heathen nations, who hitherto seemed to be ahead of the chosen people even in the knowledge of God, prove nothing against a revelation. The child of education begins with slow but sure footsteps; it is late in overtaking many a more happily placed child of nature; but it *does* overtake it; and thenceforth can never be overtaken by it again. . . .

As yet the Jewish people had worshipped in their Jehovah rather the mightiest than the wisest of all gods; as yet they had rather feared him as a jealous God than loved him: this, too, is a proof that the conceptions which they had of their eternal One God were not exactly the right conceptions which we should have of God. However, now the time was come for these conceptions of theirs to be expanded, ennobled, rectified, to accomplish which God availed himself of a perfectly natural means, a better and more correct measure, by which they got the opportunity of appreciating him.

Instead of, as hitherto, appreciating him in contrast with the miserable idols of the small neighbouring peoples, with whom they lived in constant rivalry, they began, in captivity under the wise Persians, to measure him against the "Being of all Beings" such as a more disciplined reason recognized and worshipped. Revelation had guided their reason, and now, all at once, reason gave clearness to their revelation. . . .

A better instructor must come and tear the exhausted primer from the child's hands—Christ came! That portion of the human race which God had wished to embrace in one plan of education, was ripe for the second great step. He had, however, only wished to embrace in such a plan that part of the human race which by language, habits, government, and other natural and political relationships, was already united in itself.

That is, this portion of the human race had come so far in the exercise of its reason, as to need, and to be able to make use of, nobler and worthier motives for moral action than temporal rewards and punishments, which had hitherto been its guides. The child has become a youth. Sweetmeats and toys have given place to an awakening desire to be as free, as honoured, and as happy as its elder brother.

For a long time, already, the best individuals of that portion of the human race had been accustomed to let themselves be ruled by the shadow of such nobler motives. The Greek and Roman did everything to live on after this life, even if it were only in the memories of their fellow-citizens. It was time that another *true* life to be expected after this one should gain an influence over the youth's actions. And so Christ was the first *reliable, practical* teacher of the immortality of the soul.

The first *reliable* teacher. Reliable, by reason of the prophecies which were fulfilled in him; reliable by reason of the miracles which he achieved;

reliable by reason of his own revival after a death by which he had put the seal to his teaching. Whether we can still *prove* this revival, these miracles, I put aside, as I leave on one side *who* the person of Christ was. All *that* may have been at that time of great importance for the first acceptance of his teaching, but it is now no longer of the same importance for the recognition of the *truth* of his teaching.

The first *practical* teacher. For it is one thing to conjecture, to wish, and to believe in the immortality of the soul, as a philosophic speculation; quite another thing to direct one's inner and outer actions in accordance with it.

And this at least Christ was the first to teach. For although, before him, the belief had already been introduced among many nations, that bad actions have yet to be punished in the life to come; yet they were only such actions as were injurious to civil society, and which had, therefore, already had their punishment in civil society too. To preach an inward purity of heart in reference to another life, was reserved for him alone.

His disciples have faithfully propagated this teaching: and even if they had had no other merit than that of having effected a more general publication among other nations of a truth which Christ had appeared to have destined for the Jews alone, yet if only on that account, they would have to be reckoned among the benefactors and fosterers of the human race.

If, however, they mixed up this one great truth together with other doctrines whose truth was less enlightening, whose usefulness was less considerable, how could it be otherwise? Let us not blame them for this, but rather seriously examine whether these very commingled doctrines have not become a new directing impulse for human reason.

At least, it is already clear from our experience that the New Testament Scriptures, in which these doctrines after some time were found preserved, have afforded, and still afford, the second, better primer for the race of man. For seventeen hundred years past they have occupied human reason more than all other books, and enlightened it more, were it even only through the light which human reason itself put into them.

It would have been impossible for any other book to become so generally known among such different nations: and indisputably, the fact that modes of thought so completely diverse from each other have turned their attention to this same book, has assisted human reason on its way more than if every nation had had its *own* primer specially for itself.

It was also most necessary that each people should for a time consider this book as the *non plus ultra* of their knowledge. For the youth must believe his primer to be the first of all books, so that his impatience to be finished with it may not hurry him on to things for which he has not yet laid the foundations. . . .

As we by this time can dispense with the Old Testament for the doctrine of the unity of God, and as we are gradually beginning also to be less dependent on the New Testament for the doctrine of the immortality of the soul: might there not be mirrored in this book also other truths of the same kind, which we are to gaze at in awe as revelations, just until reason learns to deduce them from its other demonstrated truths, and to connect them with them?

For instance, the doctrine of the Trinity, How if this doctrine should in the end, after countless waverings to one side or the other, merely bring human reason on the path to recognizing that God cannot possibly be One in the sense in which finite things are one, that even his unity must be a transcendental unity which does not exclude a sort of plurality? Must not God at least have the most perfect conception of himself, i.e. a conception which contains everything which is in him? But would everything be contained in it which is in him, if it contained merely a conception, merely the possibility even of his necessary reality, as well as of his other qualities? This possibility exhausts the being of his other qualities. Does it exhaust that of his necessary reality? I think not. Consequently either God can have no perfect conception of himself at all, or this perfect conception is just as necessarily real (i.e. actually existent) as he himself is. Admittedly the image of myself in the mirror is nothing but an empty representation of me, because it only has that of me which is reflected by rays of light falling on its surface. If, however, this image contained everything, everything without exception, which is contained in me, would it then still be a mere empty representation, or not rather a true double of myself? When I believe that I recognize in God a similar reduplication, I perhaps do not so much err, as that my language is insufficient for my ideas: and so much at least remains for ever incontrovertible, that those who want to make the idea acceptable to the popular intelligence could scarcely have expressed themselves in a more apt and comprehensible form than by giving the name of a Son whom God begets from eternity.

And the doctrine of original sin. How if finally everything were to convince us that man, standing on the first and lowest step of his humanity, is by no means so much master of his actions that he is *able* to obey moral laws?

And the doctrine of the Son's satisfaction. How if everything finally compelled us to assume that God, in spite of that original incapacity of man, chose rather to give him moral laws, and forgive him all transgressions in consideration of his Son, i.e. in consideration of the living embodiment of all his own perfections, compared with which, and in which, all imperfections of the individual disappear, than *not* to give him those laws, and thus to exclude him from all moral bliss, which cannot be conceived of without moral laws? . . .

And why should not we too, by means of a religion whose historical truth, if you will, looks dubious, be led in a similar way to closer and better conceptions of the divine Being, of our own nature, of our relation to God, which human reason would never have reached on its own?

It is not true that speculations upon these things have ever done harm or been injurious to civil society. Reproach is due, not to these speculations, but to the folly and tyranny which tried to keep them in bondage; a folly and tyranny which would not allow men to develop their own thoughts.

On the contrary, though they may in individual instances be found wanting, speculations of this sort are unquestionably the most fitting exercises of the human reason that exist, just as long as the human heart, as such, is capable to the highest degree of loving virtue for its eternal blessed consequences.

For this selfishness of the human heart, which wishes to exercise its understanding only on that which concerns our bodily needs, succeeds in blunting rather than in sharpening it. It is absolutely necessary for it to be exercised on spiritual objects, if it is to attain its perfect illumination, and bring out that purity of heart which makes us capable of loving virtue for its own sake alone.

Or is the human species never to arrive at this highest step of illumination and purity?—Never? Never?—Let me not think this blasphemy. All Merciful! Education has its goal, in the race, no less than in the individual. That which is educated is educated for a purpose. The flattering prospects which are opened to the youth, the honour and well-being which are held out to him, what are they more than means of educating him to become a man, who, when these prospects of honour and well-being have vanished, shall be able to do his *duty?*

This is the aim of *human* education, and does the divine education not extend as far? Is nature not to succeed with the whole, as art succeeded with the individual? Blasphemy! Blasphemy! No! it will come! it will assuredly come! the time of the perfecting, when man, the more convinced his understanding feels about an ever better future, will nevertheless not need to borrow motives for his actions from this future; for he will do right because it *is* right, not because arbitrary rewards are set upon it, which formerly were intended simply to fix and strengthen his unsteady gaze in recognizing the inner, better rewards of well-doing. It will assuredly come! the time of a new eternal gospel, which is promised us in the primers of the New Covenant itself! . . .

IMMANUEL KANT (1724–1804)

The Postulates of Pure Practical Reason

Happiness is the condition of a rational being in the world with whom everything goes according to his wish and will; it rests, therefore, on the harmony of physical nature with his whole end, and likewise with the essential determining principle of his will. Now the moral law as a law of freedom commands by determining principles, which ought to be quite independent of nature and of its harmony with our faculty of desire (as springs). But the acting rational being in the world is not the cause of the world and of nature itself. There is not the least ground, therefore, in the moral law for a necessary connexion between morality and proportionate happiness in a being that belongs to the world as part of it, and therefore dependent on it, and which for that reason cannot by his will be a cause of this nature, nor by his own power make it thoroughly harmonize, as far as his happiness is concerned, with his practical principles. Nevertheless, in the practical problem of pure reason, i.e. the necessary pursuit of the *summum bonum,* such a connexion is postulated as necessary: we ought to endeavour to promote the *summum bonum,* which, therefore, must be possible. Accordingly, the existence of a cause of all nature, distinct from nature itself, and containing the principle of this connexion, namely of the exact harmony of happiness with morality, is also postulated. Now, this supreme cause must contain the principle of the harmony of nature, not merely with a law of the will of rational beings, but with the conception of this law, in so far as they make it the supreme determining principle of the will, and consequently not merely with the form of morals, but with their morality as their motive, that is, with their moral character. Therefore, the *summum bonum* is possible in the world only on the supposition of a Supreme Being having a causality corresponding to moral character. Now a being that is capable of acting on the conception of laws is an *intelligence* (a rational being), and the causality of such a being according to this conception of laws is his *will;* therefore the supreme cause of nature, which must be presupposed as a condition of the *summum bonum,* is a being which is the cause of nature by *intelligence* and *will,* consequently its author, that is God. It follows that the postulate of the possibility of the *highest derived good* (the best world) is likewise the postulate of the reality of a *highest original good,* that is to say, of the existence of God. Now it was seen to be a duty for us to promote the *summum bonum;* consequently it is not merely allowable, but it is a necessity connected with duty as a requisite, that we should presuppose the possibility of this *summum bonum;* and as this is possible only on condition of the existence of God, it inseparably connects the supposition of this with duty; that is, it is morally necessary to assume the existence of God.

It must be remarked here that this moral necessity is *subjective,* that is, it is a want, and not *objective,* that is, itself a duty, for there cannot be a duty to suppose the existence of anything (since this concerns only the theoretical employment of reason). Moreover, it is not meant by this that it is necessary to suppose the existence of God as a *basis of all obligation in general* (for this rests, as has been sufficiently proved, simply on the autonomy of reason itself). What belongs to duty here is only the endeavour to realize and promote the *summum bonum* in the world, the possibility of which can therefore be postulated; and as our reason finds it not conceivable except on the supposition of a supreme intelligence, the admission of this existence is therefore connected with the consciousness of our duty, although the admission itself belongs to the domain of speculative reason. Considered in respect of this alone, as a principle of explanation, it may be called a *hypothesis,* but in reference to the intelligibility of an object given us by the moral law (the *summum bonum*), and consequently of a requirement for practical purposes, it may be called *faith,* that is to say a pure *rational faith,* since pure reason (both in its theoretical and its practical use) is the sole source from which it springs. . . .

The doctrine of Christianity, even if we do not yet consider it as a religious doctrine, gives, touching this point, a conception of the *summum bonum* (the kingdom of God) which alone satisfies the strictest demand of practical reason. The moral law is holy (unyielding) and demands holiness of morals, although all the moral perfection to which man can attain is still only virtue, that is, a rightful disposition arising from *respect* for the law, implying consciousness of a constant propensity to transgression, or at least a want of purity, that is, a mixture of many spurious (not moral) motives of obedience to the law, consequently a self-esteem combined with humility. In respect, then, of the holiness which the Christian law requires, this leaves the creature nothing but a progress *in infinitum,* but for that very reason it justifies him in hoping for an endless duration of his existence. The *worth* of a character *perfectly* accordant with the moral law is infinite, since the only restriction on all possible happiness in the judgment of a wise and all-powerful distributor of it is the absence of conformity of rational beings to their duty. But the moral law of itself does not *promise* any happiness, for according to our conceptions of an order of nature in general, this is not necessarily connected with obedience to the law. Now Christian morality supplies this defect (of the second indispensable element of the *summum bonum*) by representing the world, in which rational beings devote themselves with all their soul to the moral law, as a *kingdom of God,* in which nature and morality are brought into a harmony foreign to each of itself, by a holy Author who makes the derived *summum bonum* possible. *Holiness* of life is prescribed to them as a rule even in this life, while the welfare proportioned to it, namely, *bliss,* is represented as attainable only in an eternity; because the *former* must always be the pattern of their conduct in every state, and progress towards it is already possible and necessary in this life; while the *latter,* under the name of happiness, cannot be attained at all in this world (so far as our own power is concerned), and therefore is made simply an object of hope. Nevertheless, the Christian principle of *morality* itself is not theological (so as to be heteronomy), but is autonomy of pure practical reason, since it does not make the knowledge of God and His will the foundation of these laws, but only of the attainment of the *summum bonum,* on condition of following these laws, and it does not even place the proper *spring* of this obedience in the desired results, but solely in the conception of duty, as that of which the faithful observance alone constitutes the worthiness to obtain those happy consequences.

In this manner the moral laws lead through the conception of the *summum bonum* as the object and final end of pure practical reason to *religion,* that is, to the *recognition of all duties as divine commands, not as sanctions, that is to say arbitrary ordinances of a foreign will and contingent in themselves,* but as essential *laws* of every free will in itself, which, nevertheless, must be regarded as commands of the Supreme Being, because it is only from a morally perfect (holy and good) and at the same time all-powerful will, and consequently only through harmony with this will, that we can hope to attain the *summum bonum* which the moral law makes it our duty to take as the object of our endeavours. Here again, then, all remains disinterested and founded merely on duty; neither fear nor hope being made the fundamental springs, which if taken as principles would destroy the whole moral worth of actions. The moral law commands me to make the highest possible good in a world the ultimate object of all my conduct. But I cannot hope to effect this otherwise than by the harmony of my will with that of a holy and good Author of the world; and although the conception of the *summum bonum* as a whole, in which the greatest happiness is conceived as combined in the most exact proportion with the highest degree of moral perfection (possible in creatures), includes *my own happiness,* yet it is not this that is the determining principle of the will which is enjoined to promote the *summum bonum,* but the moral law, which, on the contrary, limits by strict conditions my unbounded desire of happiness.

Hence also morality is not properly the doctrine how we should *make* ourselves happy, but how we should become *worthy* of happiness. It is only when religion is added that there also comes in the hope of participating some day in happiness in proportion as we have endeavoured to be not unworthy of it.

A man is *worthy* to possess a thing or a state when his possession of it is in harmony with the *summum bonum.* We can now easily see that all worthiness depends on moral conduct, since in the conception of the *summum bonum* this constitutes the condition of the rest (which belongs to one's state), namely, the participation of happiness. Now it follows from this that *morality* should never be treated as a *doctrine of happiness,* that is, an instruction how to become happy; for it has to do simply with the rational condition (*conditio sine qua non*) of happiness, not with the means of attaining it. But when morality has been completely expounded (which merely imposes duties instead of providing rules for selfish desires), then first, after the moral desire to promote the *summum bonum* (to bring the kingdom of God to us) has been awakened, a desire founded on a law, and which could not previously arise in any selfish mind, and when for the behoof of this desire the step to religion has been taken, then this ethical doctrine may be also called a doctrine of happiness because the *hope* of happiness first begins with religion only.

We can also see from this that, when we ask what is *God's ultimate end* in creating the world, we must not name the *happiness* of the rational beings in it, but the *summum bonum,* which adds a further condition to that wish of such beings, namely, the condition of being worthy of happiness, that is, the *morality* of these same rational beings, a condition which alone contains the rule by which only they can hope to share in the former at the hand of a *wise* Author. For as *wisdom* theoretically considered signifies *the knowledge of the summum bonum,* and practically *the accordance of the will with the summum bonum,* we cannot attribute to a supreme independent wisdom an end based merely on *goodness.* For we cannot conceive the action of this goodness (in respect of the happiness of rational beings) as suitable to the highest original good, except under the restrictive conditions of harmony with the holiness of His will. Therefore those who placed the end of creation in the glory of God (provided that this is not conceived anthropomorphically as a desire to be praised) have perhaps hit upon the best expression. For nothing glorifies God more than that which is the most estimable thing in the world, respect for His command, the observance of the holy duty that His law imposes on us, when there is added thereto His glorious plan of crowning such a beautiful order of things with corresponding happiness. If the latter (to speak humanly) makes Him worthy of love, by the *former* He is an object of adoration. Even men can never acquire respect by benevolence alone, though they may gain love, so that the greatest beneficence only procures them honour when it is regulated by worthiness.

That in the order of ends, man (and with him every rational being) is *an end in himself,* that is, that he can never be used merely as a means by any (not even by God) without being at the same time an end also himself, that therefore *humanity* in our person must be *holy* to ourselves, this follows now of itself because he is the *subject of the moral law,* in other words, of that which is holy in itself, and on account of which and in agreement with which alone can anything be termed holy. For this moral law is founded on the autonomy of his will, as a free will which by its universal laws must necessarily be able to agree with that to which it is to submit itself.

Of the Postulates of Pure Practical Reason in General

They all proceed from the principle of morality, which is not a postulate but a law, by which reason determines the will directly, which will, because it is so determined as a pure will, requires these necessary conditions of obedience to its precept. These postulates are not theoretical dogmas, but suppositions practically necessary; while then they do not extend our speculative knowledge, they give objective reality to the ideas of speculative reason in general (by means of their reference to what is practical), and give it a right to concepts, the possibility even of which it could not otherwise venture to affirm.

These postulates are those *of immortality, freedom* positively considered (as the causality of a being so far as he belongs to the intelligible world), and the *existence of God.* The *first* results from the practically necessary condition of a duration adequate to the complete fulfilment of the moral law; the *second* from the necessary supposition of independence on the sensible world, and of the faculty of determining one's will according to the law of an intelligible world, that is, of freedom; the *third* from the necessary condition of the existence of the *summum bonum* in such an intelligible world, by the supposition of the supreme independent good, that is, the existence of God.

Thus the fact that respect for the moral law necessarily makes the *summum bonum* an object of our endeavours, and the supposition thence resulting of its objective reality, lead through the postulates of practical reason to conceptions which speculative reason might indeed present as problems, but could never solve. Thus it leads— 1. To that one in the solution of which the latter could do nothing but commit *paralogisms* (namely that of immortality), because it could not lay hold of the character of permanence, by which to complete the psychological conception of an ultimate subject necessarily ascribed to the soul in self-consciousness, so as to make it the real conception of a substance, a character which practical reason furnishes by the postulate of a duration required for accordance with the moral law in the *summum bonum,* which is the whole end of the practical reason. 2. It leads to that of which speculative reason contained nothing but *antinomy,* the solution of which it could only found on a notion problematically conceivable indeed, but whose objective reality it could not prove or determine, namely, the *cosmological* idea of an intelligible world and the consciousness of our existence in it, by means of the postulate of freedom (the reality of which it lays down by virtue of the moral law), and with it likewise the law of an intelligible world, to which speculative reason could only point, but could not define its conception. 3. What speculative reason was able to think, but was obliged to leave undetermined as a mere transcendental *ideal,* viz. the *theological* conception of the First Being, to this it gives significance (in a practical view, that is, as a condition of the possibility of the object of a will determined by that law), namely, as the supreme principle of the *summum bonum* in an intelligible world, by means of moral legislation in it invested with sovereign power.

Is our knowledge, however, actually extended in this way by pure practical reason, and is that *immanent* in practical reason which for the speculative was only *transcendent?* Certainly, but *only in a practical point of view.* For we do not thereby take knowledge of the nature of our souls, nor of the intelligible world, nor of the Supreme Being, with respect to what they are in themselves, but we have merely combined the conceptions of them in the *practical* concept of the *summum bonum* as the object of our will, and this altogether *a priori,* but only by means of the moral law, and merely in reference to it, in respect of the object which it commands. But how freedom is possible, and how we are to conceive this kind of causality theoretically and positively, is not thereby discovered; but only that there is such a causality is postulated by the moral law and in its behoof. It is the same with the remaining ideas, the possibility of which no human intelligence will ever fathom, but the truth of which, on the other hand, no sophistry will ever wrest from the conviction even of the commonest man.

THE NINETEENTH CENTURY
Introduction

The characteristic note of the nineteenth century was progress. In all areas of human life it was a century of rapid, unprecedented change from that which had always been to that which had hardly even been imagined. Social revolution was in process of replacing monarchy and divine right with democracy and popular will. Science was harnessing nature to man's ever growing demand for control of the earth's resources. Knowledge was exploding as communication and travel between past and present, East and West, Europe and America, provided the interchange of more and more resources with which the human mind could work.

In the confrontation with this development Protestant thought found its task. Increasingly, as the century wore on, that task was seen as the need to come to terms with the age. The challenge was to find in the spirit of the age the tools that would allow the Christian thinker to reformulate his message in currently comprehensible terms. The traditional thought patterns, the perennial modes of expression, the assumptions and presuppositions until then unquestioned, all seemed no longer adequate vehicles for communicating the Christian faith. Nineteenth-century Protestant thought became a search for relevance, or perhaps, more accurately, an attempt to find in the ancient faith and its expression, place for all the insights of the new age.

The selections in this section attempt to illustrate the specifics of this search under several categories: biblical criticism, liberal theology, and theological developments in Scandinavia, England, and America.

BIBLICAL CRITICISM

Perhaps the most startling example of the nineteenth century's determination to submit all the traditional elements of Christian thought to radical reexamination occurred in the field of scriptural studies. In previous centuries whatever might have been the diversity in understanding the meaning of Christianity, all Christian thinkers had agreed that the Bible was the Word of God. However different the interpretations of that book by the various Christian churches might be, it was the solid rock on which Christian belief rested. As God's Word it was true, inerrant, exempt from the fallibility of human thought and expression.

A hundred years of scientific investigation undermined this privileged position of Scripture. Although the scholars at the end of the century still viewed the Bible as God's Word, and therefore as having much to teach men about the religious meaning of life and its moral direction, nevertheless belief in the inerrancy of Scripture had disappeared. The realization grew that these books had been written by limited and fallible human authors who were circumscribed, as all men are, by the circumstances and limitations, the thought modes and world view, of the times in which they wrote.

The new situation grew out of applying to Scripture the newly developed methods of historical criticism. The books of the Bible were subjected to the same questions as the literary critics were asking about the works of Homer, Virgil, and Shakespeare. Who were the authors of these books? What were the authors' purposes in writing them? What style of language, mode of expression, literary structure did they use? How are the various books related to each other and to the historical situation in which they were written?

Out of such questioning, unprecedented and disturbing answers came. Moses was not the single author of the Pentateuch; this set of books was the product of several authors, written in several different historical periods. The Genesis story of creation also manifested the presence of several distinct traditions, and each one had introduced its own details and its own pedagogical purposes into the narrative. Many prophecies, upon investigation, were recognized as written after, not before, the event predicted. As the list of such discoveries grew, the inescapable conclusion grew along with it that these books were products of particular men, of particular times and places, and each evidenced the limitations and fallibilities that such conditions entail.

The sector of the Bible which drew most attention was the New Testament and within it the life and teaching of Jesus. Here the task was seen as the separation of fact from fiction, substance from form, historical event from myth and legend. How much of what the gospel writers described as objective, historical fact about Jesus was critically verifiable?

One example of how this question was handled was David Strauss's *Life of Jesus*. Strauss's key concept in examining the narrative was the notion of myth. His conviction was that in the Jewish world of the time the dominant religious influence was an imminently expected Messiah. This expectation colored the Jewish view of all contemporary events. It was natural, then, that the life and teaching of Jesus of Nazareth, who though extraordinary was still only a man, would make a strong impression on those whom he gathered around him. With his death, the process of divinizing him began. He became, in the mythical interpretation of his disciples, the Messiah, the Redeemer, and ultimately, in St. John's account, the Son of God. Myth had, in Strauss's view, taken the historical Jesus and made of him the Christ of faith.

The century produced a succession of investigators of the life of Jesus. The objective of all of them was, in Schweitzer's words, "the quest of the historical Jesus." The works varied in quality of scholarship as well as in the value and radicalness of their conclusions. But the overall effect was to produce a growing scepticism about the reliability of the scriptural testimony to Jesus. Could he really be the Son of God? What assent ought to be given to the church's teaching about him?

The search ended in inconclusiveness. Albert Schweitzer summed up the results of the quest at the turn of the century. His posing of the problem and his assessment of the results achieved comprise the second selection. He found that the men who studied Scripture with the newly discovered historical consciousness forgot to turn the same scrutiny upon themselves and their time as they did upon biblical times. Jesus became "a figure designed by rationalism, endowed with life by liberalism, and clothed by modern theology in an historical garb." Nineteenth-century biblical scholars did much to advance the scientific study of the Bible. Their basic weakness was that in searching for the historical Jesus they tended to be looking in a mirror.

LIBERAL THEOLOGY

The second line along which the reinterpretation of Christianity proceeded in the nineteenth century was that of liberal Protestant theology. The fundamental premise on which this movement rested was that Christianity must adapt itself and the presentation of its message to the contemporary world. Such adaptation meant different things to different thinkers. Selections from three of the century's most influential thinkers are presented here. Their modes of rethinking the Christian faith from within the cultural and intellectual patterns of the age were the most typical, most successful, and most influential expressions of liberalism's attempt at adaptation and relevance.

Friedrich Schleiermacher's idea of what constituted the essence of religion is represented in the passage from his work *Religion: Speeches to Its Cultured Despisers*. Schleiermacher believed that if man would but analyze his own consciousness he would discover there a sense of absolute dependence, of creatureliness and finitude. Further analysis would lead him to conclude to the existence of One who was absolutely independent. Dependence, in a word, implied independence. In this feeling lies the heart of religion. All else is derived from this. Mankind has from its beginnings attempted to give rational expression to this awareness. Thus is creed and dogma born. These, however, are derivative; they are not the essence of religion. What sets one religion apart from another, therefore, is not its religious experience—this is the same in all men—but its formulation of that experience in rationally articulated systems and creeds of belief. Christianity is no exception to this rule. As Schleiermacher conceived Christianity, it was a loftier and purer expression of religion, yet it differed from the other religions not so much in kind as in its explicitation of the basic feeling of dependence.

Schleiermacher had caught one of the key motifs of his age, man's burgeoning sense of himself. Man was on center stage in the nineteenth century because of his enormously successful drive towards knowledge and domination over nature. Schleiermacher took that centrality and presented faith, and Christianity in particular, as but the religious expression of man's growing self-awareness. The movement was launched towards a Christianity more anthropologically than theologically focused. Thus what Schleiermacher asserted was that God was present in man's understanding of himself.

Equal in stature and influence to Schleiermacher was Albert Ritschl, the second great figure of nineteenth-century liberalism. The point at which he chose to confront the spirit of the age was the thought of Immanuel Kant. Ritschl accepted Kant's insistence that the human mind was incapable of arriving at a metaphysical knowledge of God. His own conclusion from this agreement was that Christianity ought to cease laying such heavy emphasis on theoretical knowledge of God. It ought rather to present itself as a value system for man's will. The appeal of Christianity should be based on moral and ethical norms of conduct rather than on rational appeals to the intellect.

With this perspective as his starting point Ritschl developed an interpretation of Christianity as based on, and creating for man, a series of value judgments. The details of his approach are worked out in his chief work, *The Christian Doctrine of Justification and Reconciliation*. The excerpts given illustrate what he meant by his thesis that Christianity is based on value judgments. Ritschl's basic point is that in reflection on himself man becomes aware of his own superior worth or value in contrast with the rest of created reality. He makes a value judgment of himself. Further reflection leads him to affirm the existence of God, who is responsible for the presence of this sense of worth in all men.

It is also clear to Ritschl that God Himself appeals to this human tendency to make value judgments in His dealing with men. In Jesus Christ, for example, He has given men an embodiment of the highest set of values to which men can commit themselves. What matters about Christ for the Christian is not, then, metaphysical speculation about his two natures but rather acceptance of the ideals he offers for human living.

Ritschl rethought the whole of Christianity in terms of this concept of value. In so doing, he turned the attention of a significant segment of subsequent Protestant thought in the direction of the ethical and social implications of the Christian faith.

The third giant of nineteenth-century Protestant liberalism was Adolf von Harnack. He epitomized in his work liberalism's response to a further aspect of the spirit of the age, its growing concern for historical consciousness. The passage from *What Is Christianity?* expresses Harnack's approach to the reinterpretation of Christianity.

Harnack was an historical theologian; his interest was in uncovering the process by which Christianity passed from its primitive simplicity in the New Testament to the subtlety and complexity of that faith as found in later centuries. He concluded that Greek philosophy was responsible for that change. To learn what Christianity is in essence it will be necessary to strip away the Hellenic philosophical accretions. Only then will it be possible to uncover the initial simplicity of the gospel message. Harnack proceeded to this task and, when finished, he discovered that the basic message of Christianity could be simply put: God is our Father; through Jesus He calls us to union with Himself in love.

Although later scholars might read the evidence differently, they did learn from Harnack historical perspective and method. His legacy to subsequent thought was the premise that each age interprets and presents the Christian faith in its own terms. And thus each age needs to reexamine, in the light of its own historical context, the past history of the Christian faith. History is, in a word, an inescapable and important dimension of all Christian theology.

DEVELOPMENTS IN OTHER SECTORS OF WESTERN CHRISTIANITY

Theological leadership was centered in Germany in the nineteenth century, but there were significant voices speaking elsewhere in Western Christendom. They too were responding to the age as they encountered its spirit in their own countries. By so doing, they too were not only contributing to the shaping of nineteenth-century Protestant thought but were also setting the directions that thought would take in the twentieth century. Five men are chosen here to illustrate these responsive and predictive lines of development.

In Denmark, Søren Kierkegaard was writing during the second quarter of the century. His thought, largely ignored in his day, would emerge a century later as one of the essential ingredients in the contemporary philosophy of existentialism. Kierkegaard's abiding question in much of his work was: What does it mean to be a Christian in this day and age? His answer was always in terms of the individual person. A man must know himself and what he ought to be. Life was then to be spent bringing oneself into conformity with this self-knowledge. The price of a life thus spent would be, in Kierkegaard's view, a high one, because when the Christian read his New Testament and saw there the demands that Christianity made on him, he would understand that life could be lived only in complete rejection of all that society and church stood for. Becoming Christian—and for Kierkegaard this was life's purpose—meant loneliness and alienation.

One could expect no help from the church in one's pursuit of true Christianity. The church was, rather, by reason of her total capitulation to the world and its standards, the chief enemy to that pursuit. A selection is included from Kierkegaard's *Attack upon "Christendom,"* in which the impossibility of becoming Christian within the institutional church is spelled out in a scathing denunciation of the empty formalism of the official Christian church. Kierkegaard is here foreshadowing what will be a strong emphasis in the twentieth century, the necessity of a faith rooted and lived in personally meaningful convictions coupled with a vehement criticism of the church for making the living of Christianity so difficult.

England, too, produced during the middle decades of the century a religious thinker destined to have greater influence on posterity than on his contemporaries, Frederick Denison Maurice. One of Maurice's principal preoccupations in much of his writing was with the problem of "the reconciliation of all the Christian sects." He is in this sense one of the early pioneers of the ecumenical movement. His *Kingdom of Christ* is represented here as an illustration of his concern with finding an interpretation of Christianity acceptable to the widest possible Christian audience. His understanding of Christianity, though aimed at reunion, was not, however, a bland, generalized presentation of a Christian faith stripped down to the point where it would be universally acceptable. He argues carefully and in precise theological terms, not relying on concession so much as on the conformity of his view with the best of Christian tradition. He was persuaded that theological speculation conscientiously exercised could serve the cause of reconciliation.

In *The Kingdom of Christ* Maurice argues that the church is essential to universal Christian brotherhood. Only there is true unity to be found. One of the strongest bonds forging that unity is dogmatic truth, the common acceptance of the tenets of the Christian faith. As Maurice conceives the role of the church and her teaching, therefore, doctrine is made not the stone that shatters unity but the rock that establishes and guarantees it.

America was, in the nineteenth century, beginning to come to maturity as a nation. This growing consciousness of self-identity manifested itself in most aspects of the country's life and thought. It was natural, therefore, that the religious thought should reflect this same emphasis. Three examples of nineteenth-century American religious thought are included: a passage from Horace Bushnell's works, a sermon by Theodore Parker, and a selection from the writings of Walter Rauschenbusch. Each of these men illustrates in his own way the emergence of American thought as a significant influence in modern Protestantism.

Prior to the Civil War, American Protestantism almost inevitably had given the bulk of its energy and attention to two major concerns, first, the establishment of religion in the new country, and second, in the period after the Revolution, the winning of Americans to a faith for the first time to be freely chosen rather than imposed by establishment. In both tasks the most successful instrument had been the series of revivals that swept the country periodically during the century and a half before the war between the states.

One major effect of the use of the revival technique was that little attention had been paid to serious theological effort. The revivalist approach tended to be long on emotion but short on doctrinal content. In consequence, much of American Protestantism was emotional and superficial, with little solid intellectual substratum. Aside from Jonathan Edwards, the new country had produced few religious thinkers of stature.

By the middle decades of the nineteenth century this situation began to change and theological tradition began to establish itself. The movement towards a more temperate and intellectually rigorous presentation of Christianity was on. Both Horace Bushnell and Theodore Parker are typical figures of this period of American Protestant thought.

Bushnell's thought has been aptly termed "a progressive orthodoxy." The phrase captures his approach to theology: an ability to blend the traditional Calvinism of America's initial period with the new insights being developed by the more recent Unitarian and Transcendentalist expressions of Christianity. On most of the basic Christian doctrines he reached a position mediate between traditional orthodoxy and radical newness. Thus, for example, in his thinking on the Trinity he saw no difficulty in holding that God in His inner life was one, but that in the revelation of Himself to men He decided upon a threefold mode of self-disclosure under the names Father, Son, and Spirit. In such an interpretation it was possible for a Christian to be both unitarian and trinitarian in his belief.

The passage cited from his work, *The Vicarious Sacrifice,* applies his mode of theologizing to the doctrine of the redemption. Christ's death ought not to be conceived of as a manifestation of the justice of God; it ought rather to be seen as revealing the love of God. For Bushnell, the emphasis in understanding Christ rests on seeing what He tells us of God's love for men, not in concentrating on what it tells us of men and their sinfulness. He retains the traditional view that man needs a Savior but prefers to see that Savior as a manifestation of divine love rather than as a proof of divine justice.

Theodore Parker, a second typical figure of nineteenth-century American Protestantism, is represented by one of his sermons, *The Transient and the Permanent in Christianity.* The sermon mirrors Parker's Unitarian view of the Christian faith. This school of theology took as its basic norm for the interpretation of Christianity that "the truth of religion does not depend on tradition nor historical facts, but has an unerring witness in the soul." On the basis of this principle, Unitarianism tended to set aside such traditional Christian notions as original sin, miracles, the Trinity, and the divinity of Christ. All these were thought of as "the transient" elements in Christianity, man-made doctrines developed by the "folly, the uncertain wisdom and the impiety of man." Over against these were the abiding elements of the Christian faith, its "permanent" truths, representing the eternal wisdom of God. These the human spirit could intuit because of its innate capacity to seek and find God. Unitarianism is perhaps best understood if it is seen as the American version of the rationalism that dominated religious thought in eighteenth-century Europe.

Towards the end of the nineteenth century American Protestant thought began to enter a new phase, represented here by the person of Walter Rauschenbusch. In this phase, emphasis was put on the need for a social dimension in one's Christian faith. The title of the selection from Rauschenbusch, *Social Christianity and Personal Religion,* suggests the new emphasis. It is not enough that the Christian lead a good personal life; he must be open to the demands of social Christianity.

This new approach to an interpretation of Christianity grew out of the needs of the time in which it developed. The industrial revolution had, by the late nineteenth century, begun to establish itself in America. In its train it brought a whole host of social ills: poverty, slums, child labor, alcoholism, crime. The nation sought an answer to these problems, and Protestant Christianity attempted to supply that answer in the Social Gospel movement. Rauschenbusch is the outstanding representative of that school. Fundamentally, his thought and that of the movement he led ran along three lines. First, the heart of the gospel message was interpreted to be the call to establish the kingdom of God. Secondly, this meant in concrete terms the establishment of a just social order. Thirdly, such an establishment could only be achieved through the serious study of social disorders and the development of the best programs possible to remedy these ills.

There was much in the Social Gospel movement that smacked of a naive social optimism, the belief that man had only to learn the nature of his problems to be well on his way to solving them. This defect would finds its corrective in the sobering realism of Reinhold Niebuhr, who points out that sin is an enduring element in human nature which guarantees the ambiguity of any solution man develops for his problems. But what the movement did accomplish was to turn Protestantism away from its accent on individual salvation towards concern for man as a social being. By so doing it prepared Protestantism for a more realistic confrontation with the twentieth century and its problems.

DAVID STRAUSS (1808–1874)

On Myth in the Bible

Perhaps it may be admitted that there is a possibility of unconscious fiction, even when an individual author is assigned to it, provided that the mythical consists only in the filling up and adorning some historical event with imaginary circumstances: but that where the whole story is invented, and not any historical nucleus is to be found, this unconscious fiction is impossible. Whatever view may be taken of the heathen mythology, it is easy to show with regard to the New Testament, that there was the greatest antecedent probability of this very kind of fiction having arisen respecting Jesus without any fraudulent intention. The expectation of a Messiah had grown up amongst the Israelitish people long before the time of Jesus, and just then had ripened to full maturity. And from its beginning this expectation was not indefinite, but determined, and characterized by many important particulars. Moses was said to have promised his people a prophet like unto himself (Deut. xviii.15), and this passage was in the time of Jesus applied to the Messiah (Acts iii.22; vii.37). Hence the rabbinical principle: as the first redeemer, so shall be the second; which principle was carried out into many particulars to be expected in the Messiah after his prototype Moses. Again, the Messiah was to come of the race of David, and as a second David take possession of his throne (Matt. xxii.42; Luke i.32; Acts ii.30): and therefore in the time of Jesus it was expected that he, like David, should be born in the little village of Bethlehem (John vii.42; Matt. ii.5f.). In the above passage Moses describes the supposed Messiah as a prophet; so in his own idea, Jesus was the greatest and last of the prophetic race. But in the old national legends the prophets were made illustrious by the most wonderful actions and destiny. How could less be expected of the Messiah? Was it not necessary beforehand, that his life should be adorned with that which was most glorious and important in the lives of the prophets? Must not the popular expectation give him a share in the bright portion of their history, as subsequently the sufferings of himself and his disciples were attributed by Jesus, when he appeared as the

Messiah, to a participation in the dark side of the fate of the prophets (Matt. xxiii.29ff.; Luke xiii.33ff.; comp. Matt. v.12)? Believing that Moses and all the prophets had prophesied of the Messiah (John v.46; Luke iv.21; xxiv.27), it was as natural for the Jews, with their allegorizing tendency, to consider their actions and destiny as types of the Messiah, as to take their sayings for predictions. In general the whole Messianic era was expected to be full of signs and wonders. The eyes of the blind should be opened, the ears of the deaf should be unclosed, the lame should leap, and the tongue of the dumb praise God (Isa. xxxv.5f.; xlii.7; comp. xxxii.3,4). These merely figurative expressions soon came to be understood literally (Matt. xi.5; Luke vii.21f.), and thus the idea of the Messiah was continually filled up with new details, even before the appearance of Jesus. Thus many of the legends respecting him had not to be newly invented; they already existed in the popular hope of the Messiah, having been mostly derived with various modifications from the Old Testament, and had merely to be transferred to Jesus, and accommodated to his character and doctrines. In no case could it be easier for the person who first added any new feature to the description of Jesus, to believe himself its genuineness, since his argument would be: Such and such things must have happened to the Messiah; Jesus was the Messiah; therefore such and such things happened to him.

Truly it may be said that the middle term of this argument, namely, that Jesus was the Messiah, would have failed in proof to his contemporaries all the more on account of the common expectation of miraculous events, if that expectation had not been fulfilled by him. But the following critique on the Life of Jesus does not divest it of all those features to which the character of miraculous has been appropriated: and besides we must take into account the overwhelming impression which was made upon those around him by the personal character and discourse of Jesus, as long as he was living amongst them, which did not permit them deliberately to scrutinize and compare him with their previous standard. The belief in him as the Messiah extended to wider circles only by slow degrees; and even during his lifetime the people may have reported many wonderful stories of him (comp. Matt. xiv.2). After his death, however, the belief in his resurrection, however that belief may have arisen, afforded a more than sufficient proof of his Messiahship; so that all the other miracles in his history need not be considered as the foundation of the faith in this, but may rather be adduced as the consequence of it.

It is however by no means necessary to attribute this same freedom from all conscious intention of fiction, to the authors of all those narratives in the Old and New Testament which must be considered as unhistorical. In every series of legends, especially if any patriotic or religious party interest is associated with them, as soon as they become the subject of free poetry or any other literary composition, some kind of fiction will be intentionally mixed up with them. The authors of the Homeric songs could not have believed that every particular which they related of their gods and heroes had really happened; and just as little could the writer of the Chronicles have been ignorant that in his deviation from the books of Samuel and of the Kings, he was introducing many events of later occurrence into an earlier period; or the author of the book of Daniel that he was modelling his history upon that of Joseph, and accommodating prophecies to events already past; and exactly as little may this be said of all the unhistorical narratives of the Gospels, as for example, of the first chapter of the third, and many parts of the fourth Gospel. But a fiction, although not undesigned, may still be without evil design. It is true, the case is not the same with the supposed authors of many fictions in the Bible, as with poets properly so called, since the latter write without any expectation that their poems will be received as history: but still it is to be considered that in ancient times, and especially amongst the Hebrews, and yet more when this people was stirred up by religious excitement, the line of distinction between history and fiction, prose and poetry, was not drawn so clearly as with us. It is a fact also deserving attention that amongst the Jews and early Christians, the most reputable authors published their works with the substitution of venerated names, without an idea that they were guilty of any falsehood or deception by so doing.

The only question that can arise here is whether to such fictions, the work of an individual, we can give the name mythi? If we regard only their own intrinsic nature, the name is not appropriate; but it is so when these fictions, having met with faith, come to be received amongst the legends of a people or religious party, for this is always a proof that they were the fruit, not of any individual conception, but of an accordance with the sentiments of a multitude.

A frequently raised objection remains, for the refutation of which the remarks above made, upon the date of the origin of many of the gospel mythi, are mainly important: the objection, namely, that the space of about thirty years, from the death of Jesus to the destruction of Jerusalem during which the greater part of the narratives must have been formed; or even the interval extending to the beginning of the second century, the most distant period which can be allowed for the origin of even the latest of these gospel narratives, and for the written composition of our gospels;—is much too short to admit of the rise of so rich a collection of mythi. But, as we have shown, the greater part of these mythi did not arise during that period, for their first foundation was laid in the legends of the Old Testament, before and after the Babylonish exile; and the transference of these legends with suitable modifications to the expected Messiah, was made in the course of the centuries which elapsed between that exile and the time of Jesus. So that for the period between the formation of the first Christian community and the writing of the Gospels, there remains to be effected only the transference of Messianic legends, almost all ready formed, to Jesus, with some alterations to adapt them to Christian opinions, and to the individual character and circumstances of Jesus: only a very small proportion of mythi having to be formed entirely new.

Definition of the Evangelical Mythus and Its Distinctive Characteristics

The precise sense in which we use the expression *mythus,* applied to certain parts of the gospel history, is evident from all that has already been said; at the same time the different kinds and gradations of the mythi which we shall meet with in this history may here by way of anticipation be pointed out.

We distinguish by the name *evangelical mythus* a narrative relating directly or indirectly to Jesus, which may be considered not as the expression of a fact, but as the product of an idea of his earliest followers: such a narrative being mythical in proportion as it exhibits this character. The mythus in this sense of the term meets us, in the Gospel as elsewhere, sometimes in its pure form, constituting the substance of the narrative, and sometimes as an accidental adjunct to the actual history.

The *pure mythus* in the Gospel will be found to have two sources, which in most cases contributed simultaneously, though in different proportions, to form the mythus. The one source is, as already stated, the Messianic ideas and expectations existing according to their several forms in the Jewish mind before Jesus, and independently of him; the other is that particular impression which was left by the personal character, actions, and fate of Jesus, and which served to modify the Messianic idea in the minds of his people. The account of the Transfiguration, for example, is derived almost exclusively from the former source; the only amplification taken from the later source being—that they who appeared with Jesus on the Mount spake of his decease. On the other hand, the narrative of the rending of the veil of the temple at the death of Jesus seems to have had its origin in the hostile position which Jesus, and his church after him, sustained in relation to the Jewish temple worship. Here already we have something historical, though consisting merely of certain general features of character, position, etc.; we are thus at once brought upon the ground of the historical mythus.

The *historical mythus* has for its groundwork a definite individual fact which has been seized upon by religious enthusiasm, and twined around with mythical conceptions culled from the idea of the Christ. This fact is perhaps a saying of Jesus such as that concerning "fishers of men" or the barren fig-tree, which now appear in the Gospels transmuted into marvellous histories: or, it is perhaps a real transaction or event taken from his life; for instance, the mythical traits in the account of the baptism were built upon such a reality. Certain of the miraculous histories may likewise have had some foundation in natural occurrences, which the narrative has either exhibited in a supernatural light, or enriched with miraculous incidents.

All the species of imagery here enumerated may justly be designated as mythi, even according to the modern and precise definition of George, inasmuch as the unhistorical which they embody—whether formed gradually by tradition, or created by an individual author—is in each case the product of an *idea*. But for those parts of the history which are characterized by indefiniteness and want of connexion, by misconstruction and transformation, by strange combinations and confusion,—the natural results of a long course of oral transmission; or which, on the contrary, are distinguished by highly coloured and pictorial representations, which also seem to point to a traditionary origin;—for these parts the term *legendary* is certainly the more appropriate.

Lastly. It is requisite equally to distinguish from the mythus and the legend, that which, as it serves not to clothe an idea on the one hand, and admits not of being referred to tradition on the other, must be regarded as the *addition of the author,* as purely individual, and designed merely to give clearness, connexion, and climax, to the representation.

It is to the various forms of the unhistorical in the Gospels that this enumeration exclusively refers: it does not involve the enunciation of the *historical* which they may likewise contain.

ALBERT SCHWEITZER (1875–1965)

The Quest of the Historical Jesus

The Problem

It is only at first sight that the absolute indifference of early Christianity towards the life of the historical Jesus is disconcerting. When Paul, representing those who recognize the signs of the times, did not desire to know Christ after the flesh, that was the first expression of the impulse of self-preservation by which Christianity continued to be guided for centuries. It felt that with the introduction of the historic Jesus into its faith, there would arise something new, something which had not been foreseen in the thoughts of the Master Himself, and that thereby a contradiction would be brought to light, the solution of which would constitute one of the great problems of the world.

Primitive Christianity was therefore right to live wholly in the future with the Christ who was to come, and to preserve of the historic Jesus only detached sayings, a few miracles, His death and resurrection. By abolishing both the world and the historical Jesus it escaped the inner division described above and remained consistent in its point of view. We, on our part, have reason to be grateful to the early Christians that, in consequence of this attitude they have handed down to us, not biographies of Jesus but only Gospels, and that therefore we possess the Idea and the Person with the minimum of historical and contemporary limitations.

But the world continued to exist, and its continuance brought this one-sided view to an end. The supra-mundane Christ and the historical Jesus of Nazareth had to be brought together into a single personality at once historical and raised above time. That was accomplished by Gnosticism and the Logos Christology. Both, from opposite standpoints, because they were seeking the same goal, agreed in sublimating the historical Jesus into the supra-mundane Idea. The result of this development, which followed on the discrediting of eschatology, was that the historical Jesus was again introduced into the field of view of Christianity, but in such a way that all justification for, and interest in, the investigation of His life and historical personality were done away with.

Greek theology was as indifferent in regard to the historical Jesus who lives concealed in the Gospels as was the early eschatological theology. More than that, it was dangerous to Him; for it created a new supernatural-historical Gospel, and we may consider it fortunate that the Synoptics were already so firmly established that the Fourth Gospel could not oust them; instead, the Church, as though from the inner necessity of the antitheses which now began to be a constructive element in her thought, was obliged to set up two antithetic Gospels alongside of one another.

When at Chalcedon the West overcame the East, its doctrine of the two natures dissolved the unity of the Person, and thereby cut off the last possibility of a return to the historical Jesus. The self-contradiction was elevated into a law. But the Manhood was so far admitted as to preserve, in appearance, the rights of history. Thus by a deception the formula kept the life prisoner and prevented the leading spirits of the Reformation from grasping the idea of a return to the historical Jesus.

This dogma had first to be shattered before men could once more go out in quest of the historical Jesus, before they could even grasp the thought of His existence. That the historic Jesus is something different from the Jesus Christ of the doctrine of the Two Natures seems to us now self-evident. We can, at the present day, scarcely imagine the long agony in which the historical view of the life of Jesus came to birth. And even when He was once more recalled to life, He was still, like Lazarus of old, bound hand and foot with grave-clothes—the grave-clothes of the dogma of the Dual Nature. . . .

The historical investigation of the life of Jesus did not take its rise from a purely historical interest; it turned to the Jesus of history as an ally in the struggle against the tyranny of dogma. Afterwards when it was freed from this *pathos* it sought to present the historic Jesus in a form intelligible to its own time. . . . Thus each successive epoch of theology found its own thoughts in Jesus; that was, indeed, the only way in which it could make Him live.

But it was not only each epoch that found its reflection in Jesus; each individual created Him in accordance with his own character. There is no historical task which so reveals a man's true self as the writing of a Life of Jesus. No vital force comes into the figure unless a man breathes into it all the hate or all the love of which he is capable. The stronger the love, or the stronger the hate, the more lifelike is the figure which is produced. For hate as well as love can write a Life of Jesus, and the greatest of them are written with hate: that of Reimarus, the Wolfenbüttel Fragmentist, and that of David Friedrich Strauss. It was not so much hate of the Person of

Jesus as of the supernatural nimbus with which it was so easy to surround Him, and with which He had in fact been surrounded. They were eager to picture Him as truly and purely human, to strip from Him the robes of splendor with which He had been apparelled, and clothe Him once more with the coarse garments in which He had walked in Galilee.

And their hate sharpened their historical insight. They advanced the study of the subject more than all the others put together. But for the offense which they gave, the science of historical theology would not have stood where it does today. . . .

But the others, those who tried to bring Jesus to life at the call of love, found it a cruel task to be honest. The critical study of the life of Jesus has been for theology a school of honesty. The world had never seen before, and will never see again, a struggle for truth so full of pain and renunciation as that of which the Lives of Jesus of the last hundred years contain the cryptic record. . . .

The personal character of the study is not only due, however, to the fact that a personality can only be awakened to life by the touch of a personality; it lies in the essential nature of the problem itself. For the problem of the life of Jesus has no analogue in the field of history. No historical school has ever laid down canons for the investigation of this problem, no professional historian has ever lent his aid to theology in dealing with it. Every ordinary method of historical investigation proves inadequate to the complexity of the conditions. The standards of ordinary historical science are here inadequate, its methods not immediately applicable. The historical study of the life of Jesus has had to create its own methods for itself. In the constant succession of unsuccessful attempts, five or six problems have emerged side by side which together constitute the fundamental problem. There is, however, no direct method of solving the problem in its complexity; all that can be done is to experiment continuously, starting from definite assumptions; and in this experimentation the guiding principle must ultimately rest upon historical intuition.

The cause of this lies in the nature of the sources of the life of Jesus, and in the character of our knowledge of the contemporary religious world of thought. It is not that the sources are in themselves bad. When we have once made up our minds that we have not the materials for a complete Life of Jesus, but only for a picture of His public ministry, it must be admitted that there are few characters of antiquity about whom we possess so much indubitably historical information, of whom we have so many authentic discourses. The position is much more favorable, for instance, than in the case of Socrates; for he is pictured to us by literary men who exercised their creative ability upon the portrait. Jesus stands much more immediately before us, because He was depicted by simple Christians without literary gift.

But at this point there arises a twofold difficulty. There is first the fact that what has just been said applies only to the first three Gospels, while the fourth, as regards its character, historical data, and discourse material, forms a world of its own. It is written from the Greek standpoint, while the first three are written from the Jewish. And even if one could get over this, and regard, as has often been done, the Synoptics and the Fourth Gospel as standing in something of the same relation to one another as Xenophon does to Plato as sources for the life of Socrates, yet the complete irreconcilability of the historical data would compel the critical investigator to decide from the first in favor of one source or the other. Once more it is found true that "No man can serve two masters." This stringent dilemma was not recognized from the beginning; its emergence is one of the results of the whole course of experiment.

The second difficulty regarding the sources is the want of any thread of connection in the material which they offer us. While the Synoptics are only collections of anecdotes (in the best, historical sense of the word), the Gospel of John—as stands on record in its closing words—only professes to give a selection of the events and discourses.

From these materials we can only get a Life of Jesus with yawning gaps. How are these gaps to be filled? At the worst with phrases, at the best with historical imagination. There is really no other means of arriving at the order and inner connection of the facts of the life of Jesus than the making and testing of hypotheses. If the tradition preserved by the Synoptists really includes all that happened during the time that Jesus was with his disciples, the attempt to discover the connection must succeed sooner or later. It becomes more and more clear that this presupposition is indispensable to the investigation. If it is merely a fortuitous series of episodes that the Evangelists have handed down to us, we may give up the attempt to arrive at a critical reconstruction of the life of Jesus as hopeless. . . .

Results

Those who are fond of talking about negative theology can find their account here. There is nothing more negative than the result of the critical study of the Life of Jesus.

The Jesus of Nazareth who came forward publicly as the Messiah, who preached the ethic of the Kingdom of God, who founded the Kingdom of Heaven upon earth, and died to give His work its final consecration, never had any existence. He is a figure designed by rationalism, endowed with life by liberalism, and clothed by modern theology in an historical garb.

This image has not been destroyed from without, it has fallen to pieces, cleft and disintegrated by the concrete historical problems which came to the surface one after another, and in spite of all the artifice, art, artificiality, and violence which was applied to them, refused to be planed down to fit the design on which the Jesus of the theology of the last hundred and thirty years had been constructed, and were no sooner covered over than they appeared again in a new form. The thoroughgoing sceptical and the thoroughgoing eschatological school have only completed the work of destruction by linking the problems into a system and so making an end of the *Divide et impera* of modern theology, which undertook to solve each of them separately, that is, in a less difficult form. Henceforth it is no longer permissible to take one problem out of the series and dispose of it by itself, since the weight of the whole hangs upon each.

Whatever the ultimate solution may be, the historical Jesus of whom the criticism of the future, taking as its starting point the problems which have been recognized and admitted, will draw the portrait, can never render modern theology the services which it claimed from its own half-historical, half-modern Jesus. He will be a Jesus, who was Messiah, and lived as such, either on the ground of a literary fiction of the earliest Evangelist, or on the ground of a purely eschatological Messianic conception.

In either case, He will not be a Jesus Christ to whom the religion of the present can ascribe, according to its long-cherished custom, its own thoughts and ideas, as it did with the Jesus of its own making. Nor will He be a figure which can be made by a popular historical treatment so sympathetic and universally intelligible to the multitude. The historical Jesus will be to our time a stranger and an enigma. . . . .

Modern lives of Jesus are too general in their scope. They aim at influencing, by giving a complete impression of the life of Jesus, a whole community. But the historical Jesus, as He is depicted in the Gospels, influenced individuals by the individual word. They understood Him so far as it was necessary for them to understand, without forming any conception of His life as a whole, since this in its ultimate aims remained a mystery even for the disciples.

Because it is thus preoccupied with the general, the universal, modern theology is determined to find its world-accepting ethic in the teaching of Jesus. Therein lies its weakness. The world affirms itself automatically; the modern spirit cannot but affirm it. But why on that account abolish the conflict between modern life, with the world-affirming spirit which inspires it as a whole, and the world-negating spirit of Jesus? Why spare the spirit of the individual man its appointed task of fighting its way through the world-negation of Jesus, of contending with Him at every step over the value of material and intellectual goods—a conflict in which it may never rest? For the general, for the institutions of society, the rule is: affirmation of the world, in conscious opposition to the view of Jesus, on the ground that the world has affirmed itself! This general affirmation of the world, however, if it is to be Christian, must in the individual spirit be Christianized and transfigured by the personal rejection of the world which is preached in the sayings of Jesus. It is only by means of the tension thus set up that religious energy can be communicated to our time. There was a danger that modern theology, for the sake of peace, would deny the world-negation in the sayings of Jesus, with which Protestantism was out of sympathy, and thus unstring the bow and make Protestantism a mere sociological instead of a religious force. There was perhaps also a danger of inward insincerity, in the fact that it refused to admit to itself and others that it maintained its affirmation of the world in opposition to the sayings of Jesus, simply because it could not do otherwise.

For that reason it is a good thing that the true historical Jesus should overthrow the modern Jesus, should rise up against the modern spirit and send upon earth, not peace, but a sword. He was not a teacher, not a casuist; He was an imperious ruler. It was because He was so in His inmost being that He could think of Himself as the Son of Man. That was only the temporally conditioned expression of the fact that He was an authoritative ruler. The names in which men expressed their recognition of Him as such, Messiah, Son of Man, Son of God, have become for us historical parables. We can find no designation which expresses what He is for us.

He comes to us as One unknown, without a name, as of old, by the lake-side, He came to those men who knew Him not. He speaks to us the same word: "Follow thou me!" and sets us to the tasks which He has to fulfill for our time. He commands. And to those who obey Him, whether they be wise or simple, He will reveal himself in the toils, the conflicts, the sufferings which they shall pass through in His fellowship, and, as an ineffable mystery, they shall learn in their own experience Who He is.

FRIEDRICH SCHLEIERMACHER (1763–1834)

On the Nature of Religion

In order to make quite clear to you what is the original and characteristic possession of religion, it resigns, at once, all claims on anything that belongs either to science or morality. Whether it has been borrowed or bestowed it is now returned. What then does your science of being, your natural science, all your theoretical philosophy, in so far as it has to do with the actual world, have for its aim? To know things, I suppose, as they really are; to show the peculiar relations by which each is what it is; to determine for each its place in the Whole, and to distinguish it rightly from all else; to present the whole real world in its mutually conditioned necessity; and to exhibit the oneness of all phenomena with their eternal laws. This is truly beautiful and excellent, and I am not disposed to depreciate. Rather, if this description of mine, so slightly sketched, does not suffice, I will grant the highest and most exhaustive you are able to give.

And yet, however high you go; though you pass from the laws to the Universal Lawgiver, in whom is the unity of all things; though you allege that nature cannot be comprehended without God, I would still maintain that religion has nothing to do with this knowledge, and that, quite apart from it, its nature can be known. Quantity of knowledge is not quantity of piety. Piety can gloriously display itself, both with originality and individuality, in those to whom this kind of knowledge is not original. They may only know it as everybody does, as isolated results known in connection with other things. The pious man must, in a sense, be a wise man, but he will readily admit, even though you somewhat proudly look down upon him, that, in so far as he is pious, he does not hold his knowledge in the same way as you.

Let me interpret in clear words what most pious persons only guess at and never know how to express. Were you to set God as the apex of your science, as the foundation of all knowing as well as of all knowledge, they would accord praise and honor, but it would not be their way of having and knowing God. From their way, as they would readily grant, and as is easy enough to see, knowledge and science do not proceed.

It is true that religion is essentially contemplative. You would never call anyone pious who went about in impervious stupidity, whose sense is not open for the life of the world. But this contemplation is not turned, as your knowledge of nature is, to the existence of a finite thing, combined with and opposed to another finite thing. It has not even, like your knowledge of God—if for once I might use an old expression—to do with the nature of the first cause, in itself and in its relation to every other cause and operation. The contemplation of the pious is the immediate consciousness of the universal existence of all finite things, in and through the Infinite, and of all temporal things in and through the Eternal. Religion is to seek this and find it in all that lives and moves, in all growth and change, in all doing and suffering. It is to have life and to know life in immediate feeling, only as such an existence in the Infinite and Eternal. Where this is found religion is satisfied, where it hides itself there is for her unrest and anguish, extremity and death. Wherefore it is a life in the infinite nature of the Whole, in the One and in the All, in God, having and possessing all things in God, and God in all. Yet religion is not knowledge and science, either of the world or of God. Without being knowledge, it recognizes knowledge and science. In itself it is an affection, a revelation of the Infinite in the finite, God being seen in it and it in God. . . .

What can man accomplish that is worth speaking of, either in life or in art, that does not arise in his own self from the influence of this sense for the Infinite? Without it, how can anyone wish to comprehend the world scientifically, or if, in some distinct talent, the knowledge is thrust upon him, how should he wish to exercise it? What is all science, if not the existence of things in you, in your reason? what is all art and culture if not your existence in the things to which you give measure, form and order? And how can both come to life in you except in so far as there lives immediately in you the eternal unity of Reason and Nature, the universal existence of all finite things in the Infinite?

Wherefore, you will find every truly learned man devout and pious. Where you see science without religion, be sure it is transferred, learned up from another. It is sickly, if indeed it is not that empty appearance which serves necessity and is no knowledge at all. And what else do you take this deduction and weaving together of ideas to be, which neither live nor correspond to any living thing? Or in ethics, what else is this wretched uniformity that thinks it can grasp the highest human life in a single dead formula? The former arises because there is no fundamental feeling of that living nature which everywhere presents variety and individuality, and the latter because the sense fails to give infinity to the finite by determining its nature and boundaries only from the Infinite. Hence the dominion of the mere notion; hence the mechanical erections of your systems instead of an organic structure; hence the vain juggling with analytical formulas, in which, whether categorical or hypothetical, life will not be fettered. Science is not your calling, if you despise religion and fear to surrender yourself to reverence and aspiration for the primordial. Either science must become as low as your life, or it must be separated and stand alone, a division that precludes success. If man is not one with the Eternal in the unity of intuition and feeling which is immediate, he remains in the unity of consciousness which is derived, for ever apart. . . .

What we feel and are conscious of in religious emotions is not the nature of things, but their operation upon us. What you may know or believe about the nature of things is far beneath the sphere of religion. The Universe is ceaselessly active and at every moment is revealing itself to us. Every form it has produced, everything to which, from the fullness of its life, it has given a separate existence, every occurrence scattered from its fertile bosom is an operation of the Universe upon us. Now religion is to take up into our lives and to submit to be swayed by them, each of these influences and their consequent emotions, not by themselves but as a part of the Whole, not as limited and in opposition to other things, but as an exhibition of the Infinite in our life. Anything beyond this, any effort to penetrate into the nature and substance of things, is no longer religion, but seeks to be a science of some sort. . . .

The sum total of religion is to feel that, in its highest unity, all that moves us in feeling is one; to feel that aught single and particular is only possible by means of this unity; to feel that is to say, that our being and living is a being and living in and through God. But it is not necessary that the Deity should be presented as also one distinct object. To many this view is necessary, and to all it is welcome, yet it is always hazardous and fruitful in difficulties. It is not easy to avoid the appearance of making Him susceptible of suffering like other objects. It is only one way of characterizing God, and, from the difficulties of it, common speech will probably never rid itself. But to treat this objective conception of God just as if it were a perception, as if apart from His operation upon us through the world the existence of God before the world, and outside the world, though for the world, were either by or in religion exhibited as science is, so far as religion is concerned, vain mythology. What is only a help for presentation is treated as a reality. It is a misunderstanding very easily made, but it is quite outside the peculiar territory of religion. . . .

If then this, that I trust I have indicated clearly enough for you all, is really the nature of religion, I have already answered the questions, Whence do those dogmas and doctrines come that many consider the essence of religion? Where do they properly belong? And how do they stand related to what is essential in religion? They are all the result of that contemplation of feeling, of that reflection and comparison of which we have already spoken. The conceptions that underlie these propositions are, like your conceptions from experience, nothing but general expressions for definite feelings. They are not necessary for religion itself, scarcely even for communicating religion, but reflection requires and creates them. Miracle, inspiration, revelation, supernatural intimations, much piety can be had without the need of any one of these conceptions. But when feeling is made the subject of reflection and comparison they are absolutely unavoidable. In this sense all these conceptions do certainly belong to the sphere of religion, and indeed belong without condition or the smallest limit to their application. . . .

What is a miracle? What we call miracle is everywhere else called sign, indication. Our name, which means a wonder, refers purely to the mental condition of the observer. It is only in so far appropriate that a sign, especially when it is nothing besides, must be fitted to call attention to itself and to the power in it that gives it significance. Every finite thing, however, is a sign of the Infinite, and so these various expressions declare the immediate relation of a phenomenon to the Infinite and the Whole. But does that involve that every event should not have quite as immediate a relation to the finite and to nature? Miracle is simply the religious name for event. Every event, even the most natural and usual, becomes a miracle, as soon as the religious view of it can be the dominant. To me all is miracle. In your sense the inexplicable and strange alone is miracle, in mine it is no miracle. The more religious you are, the more miracle would you see everywhere. All disputing about single events, as to whether or not they are to be called miraculous, gives me a painful impression of the poverty and wretchedness of the religious sense of the combatants. One party show it by protesting everywhere against miracle, whereby they manifest their wish not to see anything of immediate relationship to the Infinite and to the Deity. The other party display the same poverty by laying stress on this and that. A phenomenon for them must be marvellous before they will regard it as a miracle, whereby they simply announce that they are bad observers.

What is revelation? Every original and new communication of the Universe to man is a revelation, as, for example, every such moment of conscious insight as I have just referred to. Every intuition and every original feeling proceeds from revelation. As revelation lies beyond consciousness, demonstration is not possible, yet we are not merely to assume it generally, but each one knows best himself what is repeated and learned elsewhere, and what is original and new. If nothing original has yet been generated in you, when it does come it will be a revelation for you also, and I counsel you to weigh it well.

What is inspiration? It is simply the general expression for the feeling of true morality and freedom. But do not mistake me. It is not that marvellous and much-praised morality and freedom that accompany and embellish actions with deliberations. It is that action which springs from the heart of man, despite of, or at least, regardless of, all external occasion. In the same measure in which this action is freed from all earthly entanglement, it is felt as divine and referred to God.

What is prophecy? Every religious anticipation of the other half of a religious event, one half being given, is prophecy. It was very religious of the ancient Hebrews to measure the divineness of a prophet, neither by the difficulty of predicting, nor by the greatness of the subject, but, quite simply, by the issue, for we cannot know from one thing how complete the feeling is in everything, till we see whether the religious aspect of this one special circumstance has been rightly comprehended.

What is operation of grace? Nothing else manifestly than the common expression for revelation and inspiration, for interchange between the entrance of the world into man, through intuition and feeling, and the outgoing of man into the world, through action and culture. It includes both, in their originality and in their divine character, so that the whole life of the pious simply forms a series of operations of divine grace.

You see that all these ideas, in so far as religion requires, or can adopt ideas, are the first and the most essential. They indicate in the most characteristic manner a man's consciousness of his religion, because they indicate just what necessarily and universally must be in it. The man who does not see miracles of his own from the standpoint from which he contemplates the world, the man in whose heart no revelation of his own arises, when his soul longs to draw in the beauty of the world, and to be permeated by its spirit; the man who does not, in supreme moments, feel, with the most lively assurance, that a divine spirit urges him, and that he speaks and acts from holy inspiration, has no religion. The religious man must, at least, be conscious of his feelings as the immediate product of the Universe; for less would mean nothing. He must recognize something individual in them, something that cannot be imitated, something that guarantees the purity of their origin from his own heart. To be assured of this possession is the true belief. . . .

This then is my view of these subjects. The usual conception of God as one single being outside of the world and behind the world is not the beginning and the end of religion. It is only one manner of expressing God, seldom entirely pure and always inadequate. Such an idea may be formed from mixed motives, from the need for such a being to console and help, and such a God may be believed in without piety, at least in my sense, and I think in the true and right sense. If, however, this idea is formed, not arbitrarily, but somehow by the necessity of a man's way of thinking, if he needs it for the security of his piety, the imperfections of his idea will not cumber him nor contaminate his piety. Yet the true nature of religion is neither this idea nor any other, but immediate consciousness of the Deity as He is found in ourselves and in the world. Similarly the goal and character of the religious life is not the immortality desired and believed in by many—or what their craving to be too wise about it would suggest—pretended to be believed in by many. It is not the immortality that is outside of time, behind it, or rather after it, and which still is in time. It is the immortality which we can now have in this temporal life; it is the problem in the solution of which we are for ever to be engaged. In the midst of finitude to be one with the Infinite and in every moment to be eternal is the immortality of religion.

ALBERT RITSCHL (1822–1889)

On Value Judgment in Christianity

How, then, is *religious knowledge* related to theoretical or philosophical knowledge? This question, indeed, has already been raised by the very fact of Greek Philosophy; still, much more tangible and comprehensive reasons for raising it are to be found in the mutual relations of Christianity and philosophy. Accordingly, it is best that we should limit the question to Christianity in so far as it is a religion, intelligible as such from the characteristics noted above. The possibility of both kinds of knowledge mingling, or, again, colliding, lies in this, that they deal with the same object, namely, the world. Now we cannot rest content with the amiable conclusion that Christian knowledge comprehends the world as a whole, while philosophy fixes the special and universal laws of nature and spirit. For with this task every philosophy likewise combines the ambition to comprehend the universe under one supreme law. And for Christian knowledge also one supreme law is the form under which the world is comprehensible as a whole under God. Even the thought of God, which belongs to religion, is employed in some shape or other by every non-materialistic philosophy. Thus no principle of discrimination between the two kinds of knowledge is, at least provisionally, to be found in the object with which they deal.

Now, in order to elicit the distinction between the two from the realm of the subject, I recall the twofold manner in which the mind (*Geist*) further appropriates the sensations aroused in it. They are determined, according to their value for the Ego, by the feeling of pleasure or pain. Feeling is the basal function of mind, inasmuch as in it the Ego is originally present to itself. In the feeling of pleasure or pain, the Ego decides whether a sensation, which touches the feeling of self, serves to heighten or depress it. On the other hand, through an idea the sensation is judged in respect of its cause, the nature of the latter, and its connection with other causes: and by means of observation, etc., the knowledge of things thus gained is extended until it becomes scientific. The two functions of spirit mentioned are always in operation simultaneously, and always also in some degree mutually related, even though it be in the inverse ratio of prominence. In particular, it must not be forgotten that all continuous cognition of the things which excite sensation is not only accompanied, but likewise guided, by feeling. For in so far as attention is necessary to attain the end of knowledge, will, as representing the desire for accurate cognition, comes in between; the proximate cause of will, however, is feeling as expressing the consciousness that a thing or an activity is worth desiring, or that something ought to be put away. Value-judgments therefore are determinative in the case of all connected knowledge of the world, even when carried out in the most objective fashion. Attention during scientific observation, and the impartial examination of the matter observed, always denote that such knowledge has a value for him who employs it. This fact makes its presence all the more distinctly felt when knowledge is guided through a richly diversified field by attention of a technical or practical kind.

But even if we have made up our mind that religious knowledge in general, and therefore Christian knowledge too, consists of value-judgments, such a definition is as lacking in precision as it would be to describe philosophical knowledge contrariwise as disinterested. For without interest we do not trouble ourselves about anything. We have therefore to distinguish between *concomitant* and *independent* value-judgments. The former are operative and necessary in all theoretical cognition, as in all technical observation and combination. But all perceptions of moral ends or moral hindrances are *independent* value-judgments, in so far as they excite moral pleasure or pain, or, it may be, set in motion the will to appropriate what is good or repel the opposite. If the other kinds of knowledge are called "disinterested" this only means that they are without these moral effects. But even in them pleasure or pain must be present, according as they succeed or fail. Religious knowledge forms another class of independent value-judgments. That is, it cannot be traced back to the conditions which mark the knowledge belonging to moral will, for there exists religion which goes on without any relation whatever to the moral conduct of life. Besides, in many religions, religious pleasure is of a purely natural kind, and is independent of those conditions which lift religious above natural pleasure. For only at the higher stages do we find religion combined with the ethical conduct of life. Religious knowledge moves in independent value-judgments, which relate to man's attitude to the world, and call forth feelings of pleasure or pain, in which man either enjoys the dominion over the world vouchsafed him by God, or feels grievously the lack of God's help to that end. This theory is almost more easily intelligible if it be tested by religions which possess no moral character. Orgiastic worships represent contending natural feelings with extraordinary intensity and with abrupt changes, in virtue of their recognition of the value which the identity of the Godhead with the vegetation as it decays and again revives, has for the man who modifies his attitude towards the world of nature in sympathy with the Godhead which he adores. The peculiar nature of religious value-judgments is less clear in the case of religions of an explicitly ethical character. Nevertheless, in Christianity we can distinguish between the religious functions which relate to our attitude towards God and the world, and the moral functions which point directly to men, and only indirectly to God, Whose end in the world we fulfil by moral service in the Kingdom of God. In Christianity the religious motive of ethical action lies here, that the Kingdom of God, which it is our task to realise, represents also the highest good which God destines for us as our supramundane goal. For here there emerges the value-judgment that our blessedness consists in that elevation above the world in the Kingdom of God which accords with our true destiny. This is a religious judgment, inasmuch as it indicates the value of this attitude taken up by believers towards the world, just as those judgments are religious in which we set our trust in God, even when He condemns us to suffering.

In its day the Hegelian philosophy represented theoretical knowledge as not merely the most valuable function of spirit, but likewise the function which has to take up the problem of religion and solve it. To this Feuerbach opposed the observation that in religion the chief stress falls upon the wishes and needs of the human heart. But as the latter philosopher also continued to regard professedly pure and disinterested knowledge as the highest achievement of man, religion, and especially the Christian religion —which he held to be the expression of a purely individual and therefore egoistic interest, and a self-delusion in respect of its object, God—was by him declared to be worthless, as compared not merely with the knowledge of philosophic truth, but also with purely moral conduct. But an interest in salvation in the Christian sense, when rightly understood, is incompatible with egoism. Egoism is a revolt against the common tasks of action. Now, people might say that faith in God for our salvation, and a dutiful public spirit towards our fellows, have nothing to do with one another, and that therefore there is no conceivable reason why religion, as a rule, should not be egoistic. But in Christianity precisely faith in God and moral duty within the Kingdom of God *are* related to one another. As a rule, therefore, it is impossible that Christian faith in God should be egoistic. On the other hand, theoretical knowledge in itself, as has been shown, is not disinterested; but moral conduct is still less so. For in the latter domain the vital point is that one realises as one's own interest the interest of others to whom the service is rendered. The moral disposition can nowhere strike root save in such motives. It is true that, contrary to the rule, faith in God may be combined with egoistic arrogance towards others. But the same danger attaches to both of the other kinds of activity which have been compared. It is possible for one occupied with theoretical knowledge to be vain and haughty, and for one devoted to the moral service of others to be tyrannical or sycophantic.

Scientific knowledge is accompanied or guided by a judgment affirming the worth of impartial knowledge gained by observation. In Christianity, religious knowledge consists in independent value-judgments, inasmuch as it deals with the relation between the blessedness which is assured by God and sought by man, and the whole of the world which God has created and rules in harmony with His final end. Scientific knowledge seeks to discover the laws of nature and spirit through observation, and is based on the presupposition that both the observations and their arrangement are carried out in accordance with the ascertained laws of human cognition. Now the desire for scientific knowledge carries with it no guarantee that, through the medium of observation and the combination of observations according to known laws, it will discover the supreme universal law of the world, from which, as a starting-point, the differentiated orders of nature and spiritual life, each in its kind, might be explained, and understood as forming one whole. On the contrary, the intermingling and collision of religion and philosophy always arises from the fact that the latter claims to produce in its own fashion a unified view of the world. This, however, betrays rather an impulse religious in its nature, which philosophers ought to have distinguished from the cognitive methods they follow. For in all philosophical systems the affirmation of a supreme law of existence, from which they undertake to deduce the world as a whole, is a departure from the strict application of the philosophic method, and betrays itself as being quite as much an object of the intuitive imagination, as God and the world are for religious thought. . . .

The aim of the Christian is conceived as the attainment of eternal life. This means the consistent realisation of the personal self-end, of which the test is that the whole world does not compare in worth with the personal life, and that by the acquisition of spiritual lordship over the world, this, the true worth of life, is vindicated. Now this religious vocation of the members of the Christian community is prefigured in the person of its Founder, and rests upon His person as its abiding source of strength for all imitation of Him, because He Himself made God's supreme purpose of the union of men in the Kingdom of God the aim of His own personal life; and thereby realised in His own experience that independence toward the world which through Him has become the experience of the members of His community. This ideal, the true development of the spiritual personality, cannot be rightly or fully conceived apart from contemplation of Him Who is the prototype of man's vocation. Thus what in the historically complete figure of Christ we recognise to be the real worth of His existence, gains for ourselves, through the uniqueness of the phenomenon and its normative bearing upon our own religious and ethical destiny, the worth of an abiding rule, since we at the same time discover that only through the impulse and direction we receive from Him, is it possible for us to enter into His relation to God and to the world. . . .

There is yet another reason why the Person of Christ maintains its place in the Christian view of the world. Christ founds His religion with the claim that He brings the perfect revelation of God, so that beyond what He brings no further revelation is conceivable or is to be looked for. Whoever, therefore, has a part in the religion of Christ in the way Christ Himself intended, cannot do other than regard Christ as the Bearer of the final revelation of God. . . . The claim Christ makes to the perfect revelation of God in Himself is only defined . . . by the fact that on the ground of his peculiar relation to God, Christ lived a life of mastery over the world, such as makes possible the community in which each Christian is to attain the similar destiny of the life eternal. Because this goal is not the reward of fulfilling a statutory law, Christ does not count, like Mohammed, merely as a lawgiver. On the contrary, since the aim of the Christian is to be attained under the form of personal freedom, therefore the twofold significance we are compelled to ascribe to Christ as being at once the perfect revealer of God and the manifest (*offenbar*) type of spiritual lordship over the world, finds expression in the single predicate of His Godhead. . . .

But if Christ by what He has done and suffered for my salvation is my Lord, and if, by trusting for my salvation to the power of what He has done for me, I honour Him as my God, then that is a value-judgment of a direct kind. It is not a judgment which belongs to the sphere of disinterested scientific knowledge, like the formula of Chalcedon. When, therefore, my opponents demand in this connection a judgment of the latter sort, they reveal their own inability to distinguish scientific from religious knowledge, which means that they are not really at home in the sphere of religion. Every cognition of a religious sort is a direct judgment of value. The nature of God and the Divine we can only know in its essence by determining its value for our salvation. Let him who denies this see to it how he reconciles his position . . . with the fact that we know God only by revelation, and therefore also must understand the Godhead of Christ, if it is to be understood at all, as an attribute revealed to us in His saving influence upon ourselves. We must first be able to prove the Godhead that is revealed before we take account of the Godhead that is eternal. My opponents, however, being bent on getting first an acknowledgment of the latter, imagine that they can establish the Godhead of Christ upon the basis of a scientific idea, that is, through an act of disinterested cognition, previous to all possible experience, and apart from all religious experience of the matter. And as representatives of a scientific conception of the Godhead of Christ, they pursue an impracticable method, inasmuch as their conception of the Word of God, eternally begotten by God before the world, rests only on tradition, detached from all the circumstances of its origin. Accordingly, they would have us make confession of the Godhead of Christ in this particular formula, before ever His Godhead has been proved to us in His saving influence upon ourselves, aye even although the said influence cannot possibly prove His Godhead in the aspects of it here concerned. These teachers must first of all be good enough to tell us what Christ's Godhead in its eternal essence is—what it is in its eternal relation to God; then it will be time enough to discuss whether and in what way this attribute is for us savingly effective and actually revealed. The method of cognition herein applied is false, and Luther's warning against teachers who would determine the things of God *a priori*, from above downwards, previous to all definite Divine revelation, holds good for this problem also. . . .

The religious estimate of Christ, which finds expression under definite conditions in the predicate of His Godhead, must approve itself in the connection between Christ's visible conduct and His religious convictions and ethical motives; it does not stand in any direct relation to the presumable endowment of His Person with inborn qualities or powers. For not in this latter relation but in the former does He exert an influence upon us. The religious estimate of His Person will stand related to His moral conduct in so far as the latter is the test and counterpart of His own conviction that He enjoys a unique fellowship with God. . . .

Jesus is the bearer of the perfect spiritual religion, which consists in mutual fellowship with God, the Author of the world and its final goal. In the idea of God as the final goal of all things lies the reason why Jesus recognises as binding upon Himself for God's sake the widest conceivable aim of moral effort, namely, the union of mankind through love; while in the idea of God as the Author of the world lies the reason why Jesus for His own personal life repudiates every motive that is individual, worldly, and therefore less than Divine. But inasmuch as Jesus desired His own attitude to God to be shared by the rest of mankind, He laid upon His disciples, as their aim also, the union of mankind through love, or, in other words, the realisation of the Kingdom of God; and through His own personal freedom in relation to the world, He led His disciples, in accepting their view of the world from Him, to the assured conviction that human life is of more worth than all the world. By making the aim of His own life the aim of mankind, who are to be called into the fellowship of His community, He is before all else the Founder of a religion and the Redeemer of men from the dominion of the world. He is the author of a moral code only in so far as the raising of men above the world, and their fellowship in this relation, carries with it the ordering of their conduct towards each other in the Kingdom of God. But since this end is served by setting up the universal principle of brotherly love, it is not any defect in the moral code of Jesus as such that the ordering of the separate provinces of moral life is left to the free application of this supreme principle. Had Jesus directed His attention to the ethical regulation of the separate provinces of human life, the result would have been—since He meant to be the Founder of a community—that He would have drawn up definite legal enactments.

ADOLF VON HARNACK (1851–1930)

What Is Christianity?

If, however, we take a general view of Jesus' teaching, we shall see that it may be grouped under three heads. They are each of such a nature as to contain the whole, and hence it can be exhibited in its entirety under any one of them. Firstly, the kingdom of God and its coming. Secondly, God the Father and the infinite value of the human soul. Thirdly, the higher righteousness and the commandment of love.

That Jesus' message is so great and so powerful lies in the fact that it is so simple and on the other hand so rich; so simple as to be exhausted in each of the leading thoughts which he uttered; so rich that every one of these thoughts seems to be inexhaustible and the full meaning of the sayings and parables beyond our reach. But more than that—he himself stands behind everything that he said. His words speak to us across the centuries with the freshness of the present. . . .

The Kingdom of God and Its Coming

Jesus' message of the kingdom of God runs through all the forms and statements of the prophecy which, taking its color from the Old Testament, announces the day of judgment and the visible government of God in the future, up to the idea of an inward coming of the kingdom, starting with Jesus' message and then beginning. His message embraces these two poles, with many stages between them that shade off one into another. At the one pole the coming of the kingdom seems to be a purely future event, and the kingdom itself to be the external rule of God; at the other, it appears as something inward, something which is already present and making its entrance at the moment. You see, therefore, that neither the conception of the kingdom of God, nor the way in which its coming is represented, is free from ambiguity. Jesus took it from the religious traditions of his nation, where it already occupied a foremost place; he accepted various aspects of it in which the conception was still a living force, and he added

new ones. Eudaemonistic expectations of a mundane and political character were all that he discarded.

Jesus, like those of his own nation who were really in earnest, was profoundly conscious of the great antithesis between the kingdom of God and
that kingdom of the world in which he saw the reign of evil and the evil
one. This was no mere image or empty idea; it was a truth which he saw
and felt most vividly. He was certain then, that the kingdom of the world
must perish and be destroyed. But nothing short of a battle can effect it.
With dramatic intensity battle and victory stand like a picture before his
soul, drawn in those large firm lines in which the prophets had seen them.
At the close of the drama he sees himself seated at the right hand of his
Father and his twelve disciples on thrones judging the twelve tribes of Israel; so objective was this picture to him, so completely in harmony with
the ideas of his time. Now we may take the view—and not a few of us
take it—that in these dramatic pictures, with their hard colors and con-
trasts, we have the actual purport of Jesus' message and the fundamental
form which it took; and that all his other statements of it must be simply
regarded as secondary. We may say that they are all variations of it more
or less edifying, variations which were added, perhaps, only by later re-
porters; but that the only positive factor is the dramatic hope for the future. In this view I cannot concur. It is considered a perverse procedure in
similar cases to judge eminent, epoch-making personalities first and foremost by what they share with their contemporaries, and on the other hand
to put what is great and characteristic in them into the background. The
tendency as far as possible to reduce everything to one level, and to efface
what is special and individual, may spring in some minds from a praise-
worthy sense of truth, but it has proved misleading. More frequently, however, we get the endeavor, conscious or unconscious, to refuse greatness
any recognition at all, and to throw down anything that is exalted. There
can be no doubt about the fact that the idea of the two kingdoms, of God
and of the devil, and their conflicts, and of that last conflict at some future
time when the devil, long since cast out of heaven, will be also defeated on
earth, was an idea which Jesus simply shared with his contemporaries. He
did not start it, but he grew up in it and he retained it. The other view,
however, that the kingdom of God "cometh not with observation," that it is
already here, was his own.

For us, gentlemen, today, it is difficult to reconcile, nay, it is scarcely
possible to bridge over, such an opposition as is involved, on the one side
in a dramatic picture of God's kingdom existing in the future, and on the
other in the announcement that "it is in the midst of you," a still and
mighty power in the hearts of men. But to understand why it was that with
other historical traditions and other forms of culture no opposition was felt

to exist between these views, nay, that both were able to exist side by side, we must reflect, we must steep ourselves in the history of the past. I imagine that a few hundred years hence there will be found to exist in the intellectual ideas which we shall have left behind us much that is contradictory; people will wonder how we put up with it. They will find much hard and dry husk in what we took for the kernel; they will be unable to understand how we could be so short-sighted, and fail to get a sound grasp of what was essential and separate it from the rest. Some day the knife will be applied and pieces will be cut away where as yet we do not feel the slightest inclination to distinguish. Let us hope that then we may find fair judges, who will measure our ideas not by what we have unwittingly taken over from tradition and are neither able nor called upon to correct, but by what was born of our very own, by the changes and improvements which we have effected in what was handed down to us or was commonly prevalent in our day.

Truly the historian's task of distinguishing between what is traditional and what is peculiar, between kernel and husk, in Jesus' message of the kingdom of God is a difficult and responsible one. How far may we go? We do not want to rob this message of its innate character and color; we do not want to change it into a pale scheme of ethics. On the other hand, we do not want to lose sight of its peculiar character and strength, as we should do were we to side with those who resolve it into the general ideas prevailing at the time. The very way in which Jesus distinguished between the traditional elements—he left out none in which there was a spark of moral force, and he accepted none which encouraged the selfish expectations of his nation—this very discrimination teaches us that it was from a deeper knowledge that he spoke and taught. But we possess testimonies of a much more striking kind. If anyone wants to know what the kingdom of God and the coming of it meant in Jesus' message, he must read and study his parables. He will then see what it is that is meant. The kingdom of God comes by coming to the individual, by entering into his soul and laying hold of it. True, the kingdom of God is the rule of God; but it is the rule of the holy God in the hearts of individuals; *it is God Himself in His power*. From this point of view everything that is dramatic in the external and historical sense has vanished; and gone, too, are all the external hopes for the future. Take whatever parable you will, the parable of the sower, of the pearl of great price, of the treasure buried in the field—the God of God, God Himself, is the kingdom. It is not a question of angels and devils, thrones and principalities, but of God and the soul, the soul and its God.

God the Father and the Infinite Value of the Human Soul

To our modern way of thinking and feeling, Christ's message appears in the clearest and most direct light when grasped in connection with the idea of God the Father and the infinite value of the human soul. Here the elements which I would describe as the restful and restgiving in Jesus' message, and which are comprehended in the idea of our being children of God, find expression. I call them *restful* in contrast with the impulsive and stirring elements; although it is just they that are informed with a special strength. But the fact that the whole of Jesus' message may be reduced to these two heads—God as the Father, and the human soul so ennobled that it can and does unite with him—shows us that the Gospel is in no wise a positive religion like the rest; that it contains no statutory or particularistic elements; *that it is, therefore, religion itself.* It is superior to all antithesis and tension between this world and a world to come, between reason and ecstasy, between work and isolation from the world, between Judaism and Hellenism. It can dominate them all, and there is no factor of earthly life to which it is confined or necessarily tied down. Let us, however, get a clearer idea of what being children of God, in Jesus' sense, means, by briefly considering . . . the Lord's Prayer. . . .

It was communicated by Jesus to his disciples at a particularly solemn moment. They had asked him to teach them how to pray, as John the Baptist had taught his disciples. Thereupon he uttered the Lord's Prayer. It is by their prayers that the character of the higher religions is determined. But this prayer was spoken—as everyone must feel who has ever given it a thought in his soul—by one who has overcome all inner unrest, or overcomes it the moment that he goes before God. The very apostrophe of the prayer, "Our Father," exhibits the steady faith of the man who knows that he is safe in God, and it tells us that he is certain of being heard. Not to hurl violent desires at heaven or to obtain this or that earthly blessing does he pray, but to preserve the power which he already possesses and strengthen the union with God in which he lives. No one, then, can utter this prayer unless his heart is in profound peace and his mind wholly concentrated on the inner relation of the soul with God. All other prayers are of a lower order, for they contain particularistic elements, or are so framed that in some way or other they stir the imagination in regard to the things of sense as well; whilst this prayer leads us away from everything to the height where the soul is alone with its God. And yet the earthly element is not absent. The whole of the second half of the prayer deals with earthly relations, but they are placed in the light of the Eternal. In vain will you look for any request for particular gifts of grace, or special blessings, even of a spiritual kind. "All else shall be added unto you." The name of God, His will, and His kingdom—these elements of rest and permanence are poured out over the earthly relations as well. Everything that is small and selfish melts away, and only four things are left with regard to which it is worth while to pray—the daily bread, the daily trespass, the daily temptations, and the evil in life. There is nothing in the Gospels that tells us more certainly what the Gospel is, and what sort of disposition and temper it produces, than the Lord's Prayer. With this prayer we ought also to confront all those who disparage the Gospel by representing it as an ascetic or ecstatic or sociological pronouncement. It shows the Gospel to be the Fatherhood of God applied to the whole of life; to be an inner union with God's will and God's kingdom, and a joyous certainty of the possession of eternal blessings and protection from evil. . . .

The Higher Righteousness and the Commandment of Love

This is the third head, and the whole of the Gospel is embraced under it. To represent the Gospel as an ethical message is no depreciation of its value. The ethical system which Jesus found prevailing in his nation was both ample and profound. To judge the moral ideas of the Pharisees solely by their childish and casuistical aspects is not fair. By being bound up with religious worship and petrified in ritual observance, the morality of holiness had, indeed, been transformed into something that was the clean opposite of it. But all was not yet hard and dead; there was some life still left in the deeper parts of the system. To those who questioned him Jesus could still answer: "You have the law, keep it; you know best yourselves what you have to do; the sum of the law is, as you yourselves say, to love God and your neighbor." Nevertheless, there is a sphere of ethical thought which is peculiarly expressive of Jesus' Gospel. Let us make this clear by citing four points.

Firstly: Jesus severed the connection existing in his day between ethics and the external forms of religious worship and technical observance. He would have absolutely nothing to do with the purposeful and self-seeking pursuit of "good works" in combination with the ritual of worship. He exhibited an indignant contempt for those who allow their neighbors, nay, even their parents, to starve, and on the other hand send gifts to the temple. He will have no compromise in the matter. Love and mercy are ends in themselves; they lose all value and are put to shame by having to be anything else than the service of one's neighbor.

Secondly: in all questions of morality he goes straight to the root, that is, to the disposition and the intention. It is only thus that what he calls the "higher righteousness" can be understood. The "higher righteousness" is the righteousness that will stand when the depths of the heart are probed. Here, again, we have something that is seemingly very simple and self-evident. Yet the truth, as he uttered it, took the severe form: "It was said of old . . . but I say unto you." After all, then, the truth was something new; he was aware that it had never yet been expressed in such a consistent form and with such claims to supremacy. A large portion of the so-called Sermon on the Mount is occupied with what he says when he goes in detail through the several departments of human relationships and human failings so as to bring the disposition and intention to light in each case, to judge a man's works by them, and on them to hang heaven and hell.

Thirdly: what he freed from its connection with self-seeking and ritual elements, and recognized as the moral principle, he reduces to *one* root and to *one* motive—love. He knows of no other, and love itself, whether it takes the form of love of one's neighbor or of one's enemy, or the love of the Samaritan, is of one kind only. It must completely fill the soul; it is what remains when the soul dies to itself. In this sense of love is the new life already begun. But it is always the love which *serves,* and only in this function does it exist and live.

Fourthly: we saw that Jesus freed the moral element from all alien connections, even from its alliance with the public religion. Therefore to say that the Gospel is a matter of ordinary morality is not to misunderstand him. And yet there is one all-important point where he combines religion and morality. It is a point which must be felt; it is not easy to define. In view of the Beatitudes it may, perhaps, best be described as *humility.* Jesus made love and humility one. Humility is not a virtue by itself; but it is pure receptivity, the expression of inner need, the prayer for God's grace and forgiveness, in a word, the opening up of the heart to God. In Jesus' view, this humility, which is the love of God of which we are capable—take, for instance, the parable of the Pharisee and the publican—is an abiding disposition towards the good, and that out of which everything that is good springs and grows. "Forgive us our trespasses even as we forgive them that trespass against us" is the prayer at once of humility and of love. This, then, is the source and origin of the love of one's neighbor; the poor in spirit and those who hunger and thirst after righteousness are also the peacemakers and the merciful.

It was in this sense that Jesus combined religion and morality, and in this sense religion may be called the soul of morality, and morality the body of religion. We can thus understand how it was that Jesus could place the love of God and the love of one's neighbor side by side; the love of one's neighbor is the only practical proof on earth of that love of God which is strong in humility.

In thus expressing his message of the higher righteousness and the new commandment of love in these four leading thoughts, Jesus defined the sphere of the ethical in a way in which no one before him had ever defined it. But should we be threatened with doubts as to what he meant, we must steep ourselves again and again in the Beatitudes of the Sermon on the Mount. They contain his ethics and his religion, united at the root, and freed from all external and particularistic elements.

SØREN KIERKEGAARD (1813–1855)

Attack upon "Christendom"

The Religious Situation

The religious situation in our country is: Christianity (that is, the Christianity of the New Testament—and everything else is not Christianity, least of all by calling itself such), Christianity does not exist—as almost anyone must be able to see as well as I.

We have, if you will, a complete crew of bishops, deans, and priests; learned men, eminently learned, talented, gifted, humanly well-meaning; they all declaim—doing it well, very well, eminently well, or tolerably well, or badly—but not one of them is in the character of the Christianity of the New Testament. But if such is the case, the existence of this Christian crew is so far from being, Christianly considered, advantageous to Christianity that it is far rather a peril, because it is so infinitely likely to give rise to a false impression and the false inference that when we have such a complete crew we must of course have Christianity, too. A geographer, for example, when he has assured himself of the existence of this crew, would think that he was thoroughly justified in putting into his geography the statement that the Christian religion prevails in the land.

We have what one might call a complete inventory of churches, bells, organs, benches, alms-boxes, foot-warmers, tables, hearses, etc. But when Christianity does not exist, the existence of this inventory, so far from being, Christianly considered, an advantage, is far rather a peril, because it is so infinitely likely to give rise to a false impression and the false inference that when we have such a complete Christian inventory we must of course have Christianity, too. A statistician, for example, when he had assured himself of the existence of this Christian inventory, would think that he was thoroughly justified in putting into his statistics the statement that the Christian religion is the prevailing one in the land.

We are what is called a "Christian" nation—but in such a sense that not a single one of us is in the character of the Christianity of the New Testament, any more than I am, who again and again have repeated and do now repeat, that I am only a poet. The illusion of a Christian nation is due doubtless to the power which number exercises over the imagination. I have not the least doubt that every single individual in the nation will be honest enough with God and with himself to say in solitary conversation, "If I must be candid, I do not deny that I am not a Christian in the New Testament sense; if I must be honest, I do not deny that my life cannot be called an effort in the direction of what the New Testament calls Christianity, in the direction of denying myself, renouncing the world, dying from it, etc.; rather the earthly and the temporal become more and more important to me with every year I live." I have not the least doubt that everyone will, with respect to ten of his acquaintances, let us say, be able to hold fast to the view that they are not Christians in the New Testament sense, and that their lives are not even an effort in the direction of becoming such. But when there are 100,000, one becomes confused—they tell a ludicrous story about an innkeeper, a story moreover which is related incidentally by one of my pseudonyms, but I would use it again because it has always seemed to me to have a profound meaning. It is said that he sold his beer for a cent less than he paid for it; and when a certain man said to him, "How does that balance the account? That means to spend money," he replied, "No, my friend, it's the big number that does it"—big number, that also in our time is the almighty power. When one has laughed at this story, one would do well to take to heart the lesson which warns against the power which number exercises over the imagination. For there can be no doubt that this innkeeper knew very well that one bottle of beer which he sold for 3 cents meant a loss of 1 cent when it cost him 4 cents. Also with regard to ten bottles the innkeeper will be able to hold fast that it is a loss. But 100,000 bottles! Here the big number stirs the imagination, the round number runs away with it, and the innkeeper becomes dazed—it's a profit, says he, for the big number does it. So also with the calculation which arrives at a Christian nation by adding up units which are not Christian, getting the result by means of the notion that the big number does it. For true Christianity this is the most dangerous of all illusions, and at the same time it is of all illusions precisely the one to which every man is prone; for number (the high number, when it gets up to 100,000, into the millions) tallies precisely with the imagination. But Christianly of course the calculation is wrong, and a Christian nation composed of units which honestly admit that they are not Christians, *item* honestly admit that their life cannot in any sense be called an effort in the direction of what the New Testament understands by Christianity—such a Christian nation is an impossibility. On the other hand, a knave could not wish to find a better hiding-place than behind such phrases as "the nation is Christian," "the people are making a Christian endeavor," since it is almost as difficult to come to close quarters with such phrases as it would be if one were to say, "N.N. is a Christian, N.N. is engaged in Christian endeavor."

But inasmuch as Christianity is spirit, the sobriety of spirit, the honesty of eternity, there is of course nothing which to its detective eye is so suspicious as are all fantastic entities: Christian states, Christian lands, a Christian people, and (how marvelous!) a Christian world. And even if there were something true in this talk about Christian people and states—but, mind you, only when all mediating definitions, all divergencies from the Christianity of the New Testament, are honestly and honorably pointed out and kept in evidence—yet it is certain that at this point a monstrous criminal offense has been perpetrated, yea, everything this world has hitherto seen in the way of criminal affairs is a mere bagatelle in comparison with this crime, which has been carried on from generation to generation throughout long ages, eluding human justice, but has not yet got beyond the arm of divine justice.

This is the religious situation. And to obviate if possible a waste of time I will at once anticipate a turn which one will perhaps give the matter. Let me explain by means of another case. If there were living in the land a poet who in view of the ideal of what it is to love talked in this fashion: "Alas, I must myself admit that I cannot truly be said to be in love; neither will I play the hypocrite and say that I am endeavoring more and more in this direction, for the truth unfortunately is that things are rather going backward with me. Moreover, my observation convinces me that in the whole land there is not a single person who can be said to be truly in love"—then the inhabitants of the land could reply to him, and in a certain degree with justice: "Yes, my good poet, that may be true enough with your ideals; but we are content, we find ourselves happy with what we call being in love, and that settles it." But such can never be the case with Christianity. The New Testament indeed settles what Christianity is, leaving it to eternity to pass judgment upon us. In fact the priest is bound by an oath upon the New Testament—so it is not possible to regard that as Christianity which men like best and prefer to call Christianity. As soon as we assume that we may venture to give the matter this turn, Christianity is *eo ipso* done away with, and the priest's oath . . . but here I break off, I do not wish to draw the inference before they constrain me further to do so, and even then I do not wish to do it. But if we do not dare to give the matter this turn, there are only two ways open to us: either (as I propose) honestly and honorably to make an admission as to how we are related to the Christianity of the New Testament; or to perform artful tricks to conceal the true situation, tricks to conjure up the vain semblance that Christianity is the prevailing religion in the land. . . .

What Christ's Judgment Is about Official Christianity

. . . But what then is "Christendom"? Is not "Christendom" the most colossal attempt at serving God, not by following Christ, as He required, and suffering for the doctrine, but instead of that, by "building the sepulchers of the prophets and garnishing the tombs of the righteous" and saying, "If we had been in the days of our fathers, we should not have been partakers with them in the blood of the prophets"?

It is of this sort of divine service I used the expression that, in comparison with the Christianity of the New Testament, it is playing Christianity. The expression is essentially true and characterizes the thing perfectly. For what does it mean to play, when one reflects how the word must be understood in this connection? It means to imitate, to counterfeit, a danger when there is no danger, and to do it in such a way that the more art is applied to it, the more delusive the pretense is that the danger is present. So it is that soldiers play war on the parade grounds; there is no danger, one only pretends that there is, and the art essentially consists in making everything deceptive, just as if it were a matter of life and death. And thus Christianity is played in "Christendom." Artists in dramatic costumes make their appearance in artistic buildings—there is really no danger at all, anything but that: the teacher is a royal functionary, steadily promoted, making a career—and now he dramatically plays Christianity, in short, he plays comedy. He lectures about renunciation, but he himself is being steadily promoted; he teaches all that about despising worldly titles and rank, but he himself is making a career; he describes the glorious ones ("the prophets") who were killed, and the constant refrain is: If we had been in the days of our fathers, we should not have been partakers with them in the blood of the prophets—we who build their sepulchers and garnish their tombs. So they will not go so far even as to do what I have constantly, insistently and imploringly proposed, that they should at least be so truthful as to admit that they are not a bit better than those who killed the prophets. No, they take advantage of the circumstance that they are not in fact contemporary with them to assert mendaciously of themselves that they are far, far better than those who killed the prophets, entirely different beings from those monsters—they in fact build the sepulchers of the men so unjustly killed and garnish their tombs.

However, this expression, "to play Christianity," could not be used by the Authoritative Teacher; He has a different way of talking about it.

Christ calls it (O give heed!), He calls it "hypocrisy." And not only that, but He says (now shudder!), He says that this guilt of hypocrisy is as great, precisely as great a crime as that of killing the prophets, so it is blood-guilt. Yea, if one could question Him, He would perhaps make answer that this guilt of hypocrisy, precisely because it is adroitly hidden and deliberately carried on through a whole lifetime, is a greater crime than theirs who in an outburst of rage killed the prophets.

This then is the judgment, Christ's judgment upon "Christendom." Shudder; for if you do not, you are implicated in it. It is so deceptive: must not we be nice people, true Christians, we who build the sepulchers of the prophets and garnish the tombs of the righteous, must not we be nice people, especially in comparison with those monsters who killed them? And besides, what else shall we do? We surely cannot do more than be willing to give of our money to build churches, etc., not be stingy with the priest, and go ourselves to hear him. The New Testament answers: What thou shalt do is to follow Christ, to suffer, suffer for the doctrine; the divine service thou wouldst like to carry on is hypocrisy; what the priests, with family, live on is that thou art a hypocrite, or they live by making thee a hypocrite, by keeping thee a hypocrite.

"Your fathers killed them, and ye build their tombs: so ye are witnesses and consent unto the works of your fathers." Luke 11:48.

Yes, Sunday Christianity and the huge gang of tradesmen-priests may indeed become furious at such a speech, which with one single word closes all their shops, quashes all this royally authorized trade, and not only that, but warns against their divine worship as against blood-guilt.

However, it is Christ who speaks. So profoundly does hypocrisy inhere in human nature that just when the natural man feels at his best, has got a divine worship fixed up entirely to his own liking, Christ's judgment is heard: This is hypocrisy, it is blood-guilt. It is not true that while on weekdays thy life is worldliness, the good thing about thee is that after all on Sundays thou goest to church, the church of official Christianity. No, no, official Christianity is much worse than all thy weekday worldliness, it is hypocrisy, it is blood-guilt.

At the bottom of "Christendom" there is this truth, that man is a born hypocrite. The Christianity of the New Testament was truth. But man shrewdly and knavishly invented a new kind of Christianity which builds the sepulchers of the prophets and garnishes the tombs of the righteous, and says, "If we had been in the days of our fathers." And this is what Christ calls blood-guilt.

What Christianity wants is . . . the following of Christ. What man does not want is suffering, least of all the kind of suffering which is properly the Christian sort, suffering at the hands of men. So he dispenses with "following," and consequently with suffering, the peculiarly Christian suffering, and then builds the sepulchers of the prophets. That is one thing. And then he says, lyingly before God, to himself and to others, that he is better than those who killed the prophets. That is the second thing. Hypocrisy first and hypocrisy last—and according to the judgment of Christ . . . blood-guilt.

Imagine that the people are assembled in a church in Christendom, and Christ suddenly enters the assembly. What dost thou think He would do?

He would turn upon the *teachers* (for of the *congregation* He would judge as He did of yore, that they were led astray), He would turn upon them who "walk in long robes," tradesmen, jugglers, who have made God's house, if not a den of robbers, at least a shop, a peddler's stall, and would say, "Ye hypocrites, ye serpents, ye generation of vipers"; and likely as of yore He would make a whip of small cords and drive them out of the temple.

Thou who readest this, if thou knowest nothing more about Christianity than is to be learned from the Sunday twaddle—I am thoroughly prepared for thee to be shocked at me, as though I were guilty of the cruelest mockery of God by representing Christ in this way, "putting such words into His mouth: serpents, generation of vipers. That is so dreadful. These indeed are words one never hears from the mouth of a cultivated person; and to make Him repeat them several times, that is so dreadfully common; and to turn Christ into a man who uses violence."

My friend, thou canst look it up in the New Testament. But when what has to be attained by preaching and teaching Christianity is an agreeable, a pleasurable life in a position of prestige, then the picture of Christ must be altered considerably. As for "garnishing"—no, there will be no sparing on that: gold, diamonds, rubies, etc. No, the priest is glad to see that and makes men believe that this is Christianity. But severity, the severity which is inseparable from the seriousness of eternity, that must go. Christ thus becomes a languishing figure, the impersonation of insipid human kindliness. This is related to the consideration that the plate must be passed during the sermon and the congregation must be in a mood to spend something, to shell out freely; and above all it is related to the desire prompted by fear of men to be on good terms with people, whereas the Christianity of the New Testament is: in the fear of God to suffer for the doctrine at the hands of men.

But "woe unto you, who build the sepulchers of the prophets" (teaching the people that this is the Christianity of the New Testament) "and garnish the tombs of the righteous" (constantly setting Money and Christianity together by the ears) and say, "If we"—yea, if ye had lived in the time of the prophets, ye would have put them to death, that is, ye would have done, as actually was done, hiddenly prompted the people to do it and bear the guilt. But in vain ye hide yourselves behind "Christendom," for what is hidden becomes revealed when the Truth pronounces the judgment: "Wherefore ye bear witness to yourselves that ye are the sons of them that killed the prophets, and ye fill up the measure of your fathers; for they killed the prophets, and ye garnish their tombs." In vain ye set yourselves up as holy, in vain ye think that precisely by building the tombs of the righteous ye prove yourselves better than the ungodly men who put them to death. Ah, the impotence of hypocrisy to hide itself! Ye are seen through and through. Precisely the building of the tombs of the righteous and saying, "If we," precisely this is to kill them, to be the true children of those ungodly men, doing the same thing as they, it is to bear witness to the fathers' deeds and to consent to them, to fill up the measure of your fathers, that is, to do what is far worse.

FREDERICK MAURICE (1805–1872)

On the Nature of the Church

It seems to me, that whatever may be the temper or education of theological students, and thoughtful men generally, in this day, or to whatever point they mean to direct their studies, the questions—Is there a Catholic Church? what are its principles and constitution?—inevitably force themselves upon their attention, and in some sense take precedence of all others. We have most of us known persons who determined, at the outset of their course, that the cultivation of personal religion in themselves and their brethren, should be the sole object of their solicitude. "Some men," they said, "might be needful to defend the out-works of Christianity; in general, those who had least right to be esteemed in the church, the most to be honoured in the world, would take that office upon themselves; the Christian who understands the secret moving in his own heart, the temptations to which he is liable, the aids and deliverances which he may expect, has a higher and more awful vocation. To watch over the seeds of life which are planted within him, till they have taken root downwards, and borne fruit upwards, and are fit to be transplanted into another soil, and, so far as he may, to teach others how they may exercise like care and husbandry; this is his task, from which he must on no account turn aside to notice the movements of the world without, or to investigate the mechanism of visible institutions." Some use this language from lively convictions, sustained by little knowledge of themselves; in some it is the utterance of a deliberate, inward conviction, of which greater experience may modify the shape, but cannot alter the substance. The former soon discover how little they counted the cost; what mighty influences are at work to urge them out of the quiet haven of contemplation into outward and definite action; what plausible excuses there are for yielding to these influences; how impossible it is to preserve the texture of their spirits in that fineness and delicacy which they once thought so necessary, but which they now hardly think desirable; how needful it is to act upon vulgar men, by vulgar motives which alone they can understand; how dextrous and cunning it is to turn the instruments which the world has invented, and of which it deems highly, to the service of that religion which it hates. But the other class are led, by nearly the same experience, to very different reflections. They perceive that it is, in some important sense, the condition of our receiving wisdom, that we should impart it; they wonder, if there be such a law, how it happens that the spiritual energy and vitality of each person, should be diminished by the pains which he takes to quicken his brethren; they inquire whether there is no divine scheme which shall accomplish both purposes at once—no great machine, the wheels of which move, because the Spirit of the living creature is in them? In other words, whether there is not, or has not been, or shall not be, a Catholic Church?

Again, a man starts from the very opposite position to that which we have been considering. He regards the phrases spiritual and personal religion with some suspicion. Though he is aware that they have an important meaning, he fancies that they are often indexes of a restless and factious temper; he thinks that they express a discontent with what is quiet and orderly, an inclination to what is exciting, piquant, and exclusive; he thinks it best for individuals, that there should be a certain established tone of mind, to which they should conform themselves; and essential for society, that a love for peculiar notions should not set the different portions of it at war with each other. At different periods, different methods may be useful to check this tendency. Toleration may do that most effectually to-day, which restraint and severity would have been used to accomplish in times gone by. The principle in both cases is the same—to prevent the order and harmony of society from being disturbed by the friction of individual sentiments and speculations. Now, if we suppose this habit of mind not to be the result of mere constitutional laziness, but, as it certainly must often be, of a hearty and honest reverence, and even passion for order—a reverence and passion which manifest themselves in a faithful fulfilment of the ordinary relations of life—and if we suppose it to be accompanied, as it generally is, with somewhat of practical shrewdness and observation, it must, I should think, be much assaulted by such reflections as these:—"After all the contrivances that men have resorted to for the purpose of hindering these outbreakings, which I feel to be so dangerous, what have they accomplished? Persecution provoked the spirit which it strove to extinguish. Have compromise and liberality succeeded in repressing it? Is this age, in which all opinions are so commonly believed to be indifferently true, less fruitful of party notions and animosities than any previous one? Do men find fewer excuses now than formerly, for quarrelling with each other, and hating each other? Would it not be more correct to say, that our modern liberalism means permission to men to quarrel with and hate each other as much as they please; a tacit repeal of the edict, which had been found in all ages so troublesome, but had never before been formally abrogated, that each man should love his neighbour as himself? If this be the case, what is the meaning of that order of which I have dreamed? Was I altogether wrong in fancying that it was possible? If so, everything within me and without me is a contradiction; confusion and perplexity lose their names and their natures—they become the law of the world. But if there be such an order, must it not be deeper than all these outward edicts and decrees, which have been constantly asserting its necessity, and have been utterly unable to preserve its existence? Till I understand the principles of this order, is it possible to understand why any of the rules which depend upon them are violated, or how they may be maintained? Is it not a childish sentimentalism, utterly unworthy of a practical man, to whine because men choose courses for themselves, when I have not yet ascertained whether there be any constitution with which there were meant to be an agreement, and what it is?" Thus, men of this class, also, are led to inquire, whether there be any divinely ordained and universal society for men, which is superior to all mere positive law and arbitrary convention; in other words, they are led to examine into the nature and principles of the Catholic Church.

Once more: There are some who have been led to perceive, that all the mighty machinery of the world around us, and the more subtle and wonderful machinery of the world within us, cannot exist merely for their own sakes and for ours. "To cultivate the religious principle in ourselves, to preserve society from falling into disorder, may be great objects, but they cannot be the ultimate object; for the glory of God, for the manifestation of his character, the system of nature, the operations of mind, and the course of history must have been contrived. This is the only end which can account for the existence of all inanimate nature; this is the only end in which the conscious and voluntary creation can find satisfaction and repose. If we would enter into the designs of God, if we would not live in a constant contradiction with ourselves, we must forget all minor considerations, we must count as secondary and subordinate, the education of our hearts, and the regulation of society; we must draw all our thoughts, desires, and hopes to this centre." A man who had adopted this grand and unselfish principle, for the rule of his inward and outward life, is likely for a time to acquiesce in it as something which not only surpasses, but supersedes all other feelings and speculations. But after a while, he is compelled to perceive, that there is a danger in this case too, of substituting words for realities, and of making his principle abortive, by making it exclusive. If there be no great scheme through which God is manifesting forth his own glory; if we are to invent the schemes for promoting that glory, we soon become the objects of our own worship. If it be merely in nature that God hath made a manifestation of himself, we may see power and order; goodness and truth we cannot see. But it is questionable whether even this power and order be not discernible there, because we have had indications of them on some other ground; whether we do not impute them to nature, because they are necessary to man. If, again, the manifestation of goodness and truth, as the foundation of order and power, be only made to a few minds here and there, then also the principle is set at nought; the glory of God cannot be the end implied in the constitution of man. Is there not, then, some spiritual order, answering in universality to the order of nature, in and through which it has pleased God to manifest his perfections? Is there a Catholic Church?

In these three cases (and I think it will be allowed that they include most of the forms of thought which prevail among us), we have seen that men who would have been naturally indisposed to consider the subject of these letters, are nevertheless drawn to it by the circumstances of the age in which they live, and by the necessity of following out their own principles. Let us next consider in how many ways the question which is excited in their minds is wont to be answered. The words *respice, circumspice, prospice,* contain the three dogmas of our day respecting the church. "Look back," says one class of thoughtful and intelligent divines, "look back to the centuries which immediately followed the coming of our Lord in the flesh. In these ages lived the men who conversed with Christ's own apostles, received their traditions, imbibed their spirit, suffered their persecutions; then the church was one in itself; the heretics who rose up within it were distinguished from its true members, and soon cast out; then men received mysteries without speculating upon them; then they understood their great powers, and proclaimed them to the world; then doctrines were believed because the church asserted them; then the ministers spoke as those who had authority and the people thought that it was their only function to receive the words which they heard, and to bring forth the fruits of them in their lives; then sacraments were reckoned of mighty dignity, and the ordination of the priest, and the consecration of the elements, gave them their validity; then the conditions and methods of a holy life were understood, and men who desired spiritual blessings fashioned themselves according to the rule of the church, and not according to their own caprice. Then the church was indeed a church, then it was indeed Catholic. Since then it has fallen into divisions; the Eastern has been opposed to the Western; the Western has become split into Papists and Protestants; each of these, especially the latter, into numberless other divisions; the vestiges of a Catholic Church are scarcely discernible. But it may be restored; the early ages are the pattern in the Mount, after which it is to be built again; all modern innovations must be discarded, all modern speculation restrained, and men must labour to arrive at the unreasoning innocence of childhood."

"Look around you," say the teachers of another school, "and wonder at the amazing blessings and privileges of the age in which you live. Now first is the church showing herself in her real freedom and power; now have men learned to combine, for the promotion of great spiritual objects, the barriers which superstition and prejudice raised to the progress of the Gospel, the notions of a particular sanctity in places, forms, and offices are gradually disappearing, and all that machinery which has been found so useful in forwarding secular purposes is converted to the service of the sanctuary. We have failed to secure uniformity of opinion, but we are beginning to secure uniformity of purpose; all is not yet as it should be, for a number of inconvenient usages and antiquated restrictions stand in our way; but all is becoming right. We have at last got into the true line and scheme of action; the church is approaching every day nearer to the condition of a great co-operative society, aiming at the conversion of the world, and certain, at no distant time, to accomplish its aim."

"Look forward," say a third party; "every thing behind you except in the days of the apostles, is dark; everything around you is cheerless; the church began to decline when its first preachers left the earth; it has been degenerating ever since, and has reached its lowest point of degradation now. But a new dispensation is at hand; the prophecies which by one class of critics have been supposed to be fulfilled in the first coming of our Lord and the establishment of the church, by another have been turned to mere private and personal uses, all point to its arrival; then, indeed, a kingdom will be set up on earth, then, indeed, Christ will reign among his ancients gloriously. Our present duty is to wait and wish for the time; to keep aloof from all institutions and societies, by whatever name they may be called, whether confessedly of human origin, or claiming apostolic derivations, which have been defiled by earthly sin. In due time a church will appear; the new Jerusalem will descend from above, as a bride adorned for her husband; and, by terrible judgments, the earth shall be purged of the enemies of her and of her Lord, and shall thenceforth be the obedient subject of those over whom she has been the cruel tyrant."

Now, for those who do not feel the necessity of examining into the nature of Christ's church and kingdom, I do not write; for those who are perfectly contented with any of those views which I have described, I do not write; lastly, for those who want some new and startling view to set them all aside, I do not write. But in saying this, I believe that I do not exclude any very considerable number of readers. I have explained why I think that very few considerate men are indifferent to the subject. I am persuaded that almost as few are so content with the system which they prefer, that they are not at times ready to abandon it as untenable, and at times to see a reasonableness in each of the others; and I feel quite sure that most men are sufficiently weary of systems and schemes, to resist the intrusion of any new one, affecting to displace its predecessors. What remains? I answer, to look at the facts of the case as they are presented to us by these disputants, and to see whether they do not give us some hints of an older and simpler doctrine, which excludes neither the *respice,* the *circumspice,* nor the *prospice;* but declares that, only in the union of the three can we find a church which shall satisfy the wants of a creature who looks before and after, shall present the image of an order abiding from generation to generation, and be a mirror of the glory of him which was, and which is, and which is to come.

My object, then, is only to trace the "hints" of this doctrine. A learned treatise is necessary for the justification of either of those particular views on which I have commented; a learned treatise would be necessary to expound some original view which should set them aside; but what seems to me most necessary, for the circumstances of our time, and the wants of our minds, is, that we should be taught how to profit by the writings of men who have seen certain sides of truth very strongly; how we may be prevented from rejecting what they rejected. At present, most of our books are written against some past or prevailing notion; Papists write against Protestants, Protestants against Popery; the supporters of the *Via Media* against both. It is impossible for men holding one view to read the words written on the opposite hypothesis, except for the purpose of finding fault with them. It is impossible for those who adopt none of the views to gain quiet and comfortable instruction from the writers who have defended them. Thus three-fourths of our time for reading is spent in finding out what we may abuse; and numbers seem ready to abandon reading altogether, because they find so little with which they may agree. Surely this state of feeling is most mischievous; surely there must be that in the writings of all the three classes which I have described, from which we might derive a blessing; and there may be a blessing in each one, which the other cannot give. What we want, is to be brought into a point of view, in which the fair and illuminated side of each doctrine, and not its dark side, may be presented to us. When we have been familiarized to its beauty, its deformity will be far more disagreeable and appalling to us than it ever can be while we are perpetually conversing with it alone.

How easy it is to misrepresent this desire, and to give it the most odious character, I am well aware. By the very slight and moderate injustice of representing the student as one who wishes to place himself above all sects and parties, that from a calm elevation he may behold their errors, and smile at them with the complacency of the great Epicurean poet, and not as one who wishes to place himself where he may receive the light from them all, because he feels himself so dark and ignorant that he cannot spare one ray of it, he may very plausibly be described as the most self-conceited of human creatures. . . .

I have not complained of the antiquarian theologians, because they reverence that which is past; but because they are cold and discouraging in their treatment of the desires which men feel in the present day, and cheerless respecting the future. I have not complained of those who look with admiration upon the present age, because they think that God has a great work for it to do, and has endowed it with gifts suitable to that end; but because, by rejecting the wisdom of former ages, and making light of man's pantings after something better than the routine of things around him, they forget their function, and make abortive their gifts. I have not complained of those whose eyes are wearily watching for the morning, because their hopes are too bright and gorgeous; but because they will not acknowledge that the day which they long for is already risen, and will be seen whenever it please God to disperse the mists and fogs by which the eyes of men have been hindered from discovering it. To show that the half-scholastic, half-popular decrees by which the realm of theological thought has been portioned out into the two provinces of "doctrine" and "discipline," and practical Christianity into the two provinces of the "inward" or "spiritual," and the "formal" or "ecclesiastical," rest on no adequate foundation of authority or of reason; that we must go back to the old principle of the church being a kingdom, and steadily keep that principle in sight, in all our studies respecting it—that the Gospel is indeed the revelation of a kingdom within us, a kingdom, of which the heart and spirit of man can alone take cognizance, and yet of a kingdom which ruleth over all, and to which all other kingdoms, even now, are reluctantly doing homage, while they most struggle to resist it—that the outward badges of this kingdom are not inconsistent with its spiritual character, but uphold that character, which would perish so soon as they were removed—that this universal kingdom or church is not the adversary of national order and family life, but is the sustainer and consummation of them both—that this church is not the adversary of man's reason and will, but is the appointed trainer of them both, for a state and a knowledge which, without her, they could never acquire; that she forgets her commission and underrates her powers, when she strives to crush them, and not rather to bring them forth, and give them the highest development of which they are capable; and that they sink into a low, grovelling, despicable condition, when they refuse her guidance, and do not aspire after the glory to which she promises to lead them—this I thought not a needless undertaking in these days, and yet one in which a person who is himself only seeking for knowledge and light, might be profitable to others; because he who is willing to state his own difficulties; and sympathize with ours, is sometimes better able to help us, than those who are so much above us as to be surprised at our ignorance, and impatient of our dullness.

HORACE BUSHNELL (1802–1876)

On the Meaning of Vicarious Sacrifice

Our first point must be to settle a just and true conception of vicarious sacrifice, or of what is the real undertaking of Christ in the matter of such sacrifice. . . .

This word *vicarious,* that has made so conspicuous a figure in the debates of theology, it must be admitted is no word of the Scripture. The same is true, however, of *free agency, character, theology,* and of the many other terms which the conveniences of use have made common. If a word appears to be wanted in Christian discussions or teachings, the fact that it is not found in the Scripture is no objection to it; we have only to be sure that we understand what we mean by it. In the case, too, of this particular word *vicarious,* a special care is needed, lest we enter something into the meaning, from ourselves, which is not included in the large variety of Scripture terms and expressions the word is set to represent.

Thus we have—"made a curse for us"—"bare our sins"—"hath laid on him the iniquity of us all"—"made to be sin for us"—"offered to bear the sins of many"—"borne our griefs and carried our sorrows"—"wounded for our transgressions, bruised for our iniquities"—"tasted death for every man." The whole Gospel is a texture, thus of vicarious conceptions, in which Christ is represented, in one way or another, as coming into our place, substituted in our stead, bearing our burdens, answering for us, and standing in a kind of suffering sponsorship for the race.

Now the word *vicarious* is chosen to represent, and gather up into itself, all these varieties of expression. It is the same word, in the root, as the word *vice* in vice-regent, viceroy, vicar, vicar-general, vice-president, and the like. It is a word that carries always a face of substitution, indicating that one person comes in place, somehow, of another. Thus a vice-president is one who is to act in certain contingencies, as and for the president; a viceroy, for the king. . . .

Then if we speak of "sacrifice," any person acts in a way of "vicarious sacrifice," not when he burns upon an altar in some other's place, but when he makes loss for him, even as he would make loss for himself, in the offering of a sacrifice for his sin. The expression is a figure, representing that the party making such sacrifice for another, comes into burden, pain, weariness, or even to the yielding up of life for his sake. The word "vicarious" does not say all, nor the word "sacrifice," but the two together make out the true figure of Christ and his Gospel.

In this sense it is that Christianity or the Christian salvation is a vicarious sacrifice. It does not mean simply that Christ puts himself into the case of man as a helper; one man helps another without any vicarious relationship implied or supposed. Neither does it mean that Christ undertakes for man in a way of influence; one man tries to influence another, without coming at all into his place. Neither does the vicarious sacrifice imply that he simply comes under common liabilities with us, as when every citizen suffers for the wrongs and general misconduct and consequent misgovernment of the community to which he belongs. Nor that he simply comes into the track of those penal retributions which outrun the wrongs they chastise, passing over upon the innocent, as the sins of fathers propagate their evils in the generations of their children coming after. The idea of Christ's vicarious sacrifice is not matched by any of these lighter examples, though it has something in common with them all. . . .

On the other hand, we are not to hold the Scripture terms of vicarious sacrifice, as importing a literal substitution of places, by which Christ becomes a sinner for sinners, or penally subject to our deserved penalties. That is a kind of substitution that offends every strongest sentiment of our nature. He can not become guilty for us. Neither, as God is a just being, can he be any how punishable in our place—all God's moral sentiments would be revolted by that. And if Christ should himself consent to such punishment, he would only ask to have all the most immovable convictions, both of God's moral nature and our own, confounded, or eternally put by.

Excluding now all these under-stated and over-stated explanations we come to the true conception, which is that Christ, in what is called his vicarious sacrifice, simply engages, at the expense of great suffering and even of death itself, to bring us out of our sins themselves and so out of their penalties; being himself profoundly identified with us in our fallen state, and burdened in feeling with our evils. Nor is there anything so remote, or difficult, or violent, in this vicarious relation, assumed by Christ, as many appear to suppose. It would rather be a wonder if, being what he is, he did not assume it. For we are to see and make our due account of this one fact, that a good being is, by the supposition, ready, just according to his goodness, to act vicariously in behalf of any bad, or miserable being whose condition he is able to restore. For a good being is not simply one who gives bounties and favors, but one who is in the principle of love; and it is the nature of love, universally, to insert itself into the miseries, and take upon its feeling the burdens of others. Love does not consider the ill desert of the subject; he may even be a cruel and relentless enemy. It does not consider the expense of toil, and sacrifice, and suffering the intervention may cost. It stops at nothing but the known impossibility of relief, or benefit; asks for nothing as inducement, but the opportunity of success. Love is a principle essentially vicarious in its own nature, identifying the subject with others, so as to suffer their adversities and pains, and taking on itself the burden of their evils. It does not come in officiously and abruptly, and propose to be substituted in some formal and literal way that overturns all the moral relations of law and desert, but it clings to the evil and lost man as in feeling, afflicted for him, burdened by his ill deserts, incapacities and pains, encountering gladly any loss or suffering for his sake. Approving nothing wrong in him, but faithfully reproving and condemning him in all sin, it is yet made sin—plunged, so to speak, into all the fortunes of sin, by its friendly sympathy. In this manner it is entered vicariously into sacrifice on his account. So naturally and easily does the vicarious sacrifice commend itself to our intelligence, by the stock ideas and feelings out of which it grows.

How it was with Christ, and how he bore our sins, we can see exactly, from a very impressive and remarkable passage in Matthew's Gospel, where he conceives that Christ is entered vicariously into men's diseases, just as he is elsewhere shown to bear, and to be vicariously entered into, the burden of their sins. I produce the passage, . . . because of the very great and decisive importance it has; for it is remarkable as being the one Scripture citation that gives, beyond a question, the exact *usus loquendi* of all the vicarious and sacrificial language of the New Testament.

Christ has been pouring out his sympathies, all day, in acts of healing, run down, as it were, by the wretched multitudes crowding about him and imploring his pity. No humblest, most repulsive creature is neglected or fails to receive his tenderest, most brotherly consideration. His heart accepts each one as a burden upon its feeling, and by that feeling he is inserted into the lot, the pain, the sickness, the sorrow of each. And so the evangelist, having, as we see, no reference whatever to the substitution for sin, says—"That it might be fulfilled, which was spoken by Esaias the prophet, saying—'Himself took our infirmities and bare our sicknesses.' " And the test is the more remarkable that the passage he cites from Isaiah, is from his liii chapter, which is, in fact, a kind of stock chapter, whence all the most vicarious language of the New Testament is drawn. Besides the word *bare* occurs in the citation; a word that is based on the very same figure of carrying as that which is used in the expression, "bare our sins," "bare the sins of many," and is moreover precisely the same word which is used by the Apostle when he says . . . "bear ye one another's burdens, and so fulfill the law of Christ." If then we desire to know exactly what the substitution of Christ for sin was, and how far it went—what it means for example that he bare our sin—we have only to revert back to what is here said of his relation to sicknesses, and our question is resolved.

What then does it mean that Christ "bare our sicknesses"? Does it mean that he literally had our sicknesses transferred to him, and so taken off from us? Does it mean that he became blind for the blind, lame for the lame, a leper for the lepers, suffering in himself all the fevers and pains he took away from others? No one had ever such a thought. How then did he bear our sicknesses, or in what sense? In the sense that he took them on his feeling, had his heart burdened by the sense of them, bore the disgusts of their loathsome decays, felt their pains over again, in the tenderness of his more than human sensibility. Thus manifestly it was that he bare our sicknesses—his very love to us put him, so far, in a vicarious relation to them, and made him, so far, a partaker in them.

Here then we have the true law of interpretation, when the vicarious relation of Christ to our sins comes into view. It does not mean that he takes them literally upon him, as some of the old theologians and a very few moderns appear to believe; it does not mean that he took their ill desert upon him by some mysterious act of imputation, or had their punishment transferred to his person. A sickness might possibly be transferred, but a sin can not by any rational possibility. It does not mean that he literally came into the hell of our retributive evils under sin, and satisfied, by his own suffering, the violated justice of God; for that kind of penal suffering would satisfy nothing but the very worst injustice. No, but the bearing of our sins does mean, that Christ bore them on his feeling, became inserted into their bad lot by his sympathy as a friend, yielded up himself and his life, even, to an effort of restoring mercy; in a word that he bore our sins in just the same sense that he bore our sicknesses. Understand that love itself is an essentially vicarious principle, and the solution is no longer difficult. . . .

Thus it is that every sort of love is found twining its feeling always into the feeling, and loss, and want, and woe, of whatever people, or person, or even enemy, it loves; thus that God himself takes our sinning enmity upon his heart, painfully burdened by our broken state, and travailing, in all the deepest feeling of his nature, to recover us to himself. And this it is which the cross and vicarious sacrifice of Jesus signify to us, or outwardly express. Such a God in love, must be such a Saviour in suffering—he could not well be other or less. There is a Gethsemane hid in all love, and when the fit occasion comes, no matter how great and high the subject may be, its heavy groaning will be heard—even as it was in Christ. He was in an agony, exceeding sorrowful even unto death. By that sign it was that God's love broke into the world, and Christianity was born!

Here, then, as I conceive, is the true seed principle of the Christian salvation. What we call the vicarious sacrifice of Christ is nothing strange as regards the principle of it, no superlative, unexampled, and therefore unintelligible grace. It only does and suffers, and comes into substitution for, just what any and all love will, according to its degree. And, in this view, it is not something higher in principle than our human virtue knows, and which we ourselves are never to copy or receive, but it is to be understood by what we know already, and is to be more fully understood by what we are to know hereafter, when we are complete in Christ. Nothing is wanting to resolve the vicarious sacrifice of Jesus, but the commonly known, always familiar principle of love, accepted as the fundamental law of duty, even by mankind. Given the universality of love, the universality of vicarious sacrifice is given also. Here is the center and deepest spot of good, or goodness, conceivable. At this point we look into heaven's eye itself, and read the meaning of all heavenly grace.

How much to be regretted then is it that Christianity has been made so great an offense, to so many ingenuous and genuinely thoughtful souls, at just this point of vicarious sacrifice, where it is noblest to thought, and grandest, and most impressive to feeling. There ought never to be a question over its reality and truth to nature, more than over a mother's watch and waiting for her child. And yet there has been kept up, for centuries, what a strain of logical, or theological endeavor—shall I call it high, or shall I call it weak and low—to make out some formal, legal, literal account of substitution and vicarious sacrifice, in which all God's quickening motivity and power are taken away from the feeling, and nothing left but a sapless wood, or dry stubble of reason, for a mortal sinner's faith to cling to. Nothing is so simple, and beautiful, and true, and close to feeling, as this same blessed truth—Jesus the Lord in vicarious sacrifice; and yet there is made of it, I know not what, or how many riddles, which to solve, were it possible, were only to miss of its power; much more which to miss of solving, is only to be lost in mazes and desert windings where even faith itself is only turned to jangling. How often has the innate sense of justice in men been mocked by the speculated satisfactions of justice, or schemes of satisfaction, made up for God; how often has the human feeling that would have been attracted and melted, by the gracious love of Jesus, coming to assume our nature and bear our sin, been chilled, or revolted, by some account of his death, that turns it to a theologic fiction, by contriving how he literally had our sin upon him, and was therefore held to die retributively on account of it.

At the same time, there have been thrown off into antagonism, a great many times, whole sects of disciples, who could see no way to escape the revolting theories of vicarious sacrifice, but to formally deny the fact; and then what evidence have they given of the fact, as a distinctive integral element of Christianity, by their utter inability, in the way of denial, to maintain the vitality and propagating power of Christian society without it. If God's love has no vicarious element, theirs of course will have as little; if he simply stands by law and retribution, if he never enters himself into human evils and sins, so as to be burdened by them, never identifies himself with souls under evil, to bear them—enemies and outcasts though they be—then it will be seen that they, as believers, are never in affliction for the sin of others, never burdened as intercessors for them; for there was in fact no such mind in Christ Jesus himself. On the contrary, as God stands off, waiting only by the laws of duty and abstract justice, moved vicariously to no intervention, so will they lose out the soul bond of unity and religious fellowship with their kind, dropping asunder into atoms of righteous individuality, and counting it even a kind of undignified officiousness to be overmuch concerned for others. Christian society is by that time gone. The sense of God, translating himself into the evils and fallen fortunes of souls, in the vicarious love and passion of his Son, was the root of it; and that being gone, the divine life takes no headship in them, they no membership of unity with each other. They are only incommunicable monads—the Christian *koinonia* is lost or abolished. "I will take care of myself, answer for myself, and let every other do the same"—that is the Christianity left—it is duty, self-care, right living atomically held before moral standards. As to the church, or the church life, it no longer exists; Christ is the head of nothing, because he has never come into the cause, or feeling, or life of any, by coming into their lot. So necessary is the faith of a vicarious sacrifice to the maintenance of any genuine Christian life and society. Without and apart from it individualities are never bridged, never made coalescent, or common to each other. The chill that follows must in due time be fatal. No such mode of necessary unfellowship can live.

By this experimental proof, it can be clearly seen how necessary to the living Gospel and church of Christ is the faith, in some true sense, of a vicarious sacrifice. And what that sense may be it is not difficult, I think, to find. We have already found that love itself contains the fact and is the sufficient and easy solution.

But there is an objection to be encountered even here, before the solution will be satisfactory to some; it is that if love, love in God, and love in all beings created and uncreated, is an essentially vicarious element or principle; if it moves to the certain identification of the loving party with evil minds and their pains, and the assuming of them, to be a burden on its feeling, or even a possible agony in it; then, as long as there is any such thing as evil and death, love must be a cause of unhappiness, a lot of suffering and sorrow. In one view it must, in another it will be joy itself, the fullest, and profoundest, and sublimest joy conceivable. There was never a being on earth so deep in his peace and so essentially blessed as Jesus Christ. Even his agony itself is scarcely an exception. There is no joy so grand as that which has a form of tragedy, and there is besides, in a soul given up to loss and pain for love's sake, such a consciousness of good—it is so far ennobled by its own great feeling—that it rises in the sense of magnitude and majesty, and Godlikeness, and has thoughts breaking out in it as the sound of many waters, joys that are full as the sea. And this, too, corresponds exactly with our human experience. We are never so happy, so essentially blessed as when we suffer well, wearing out our life in sympathies spent on the evil and undeserving, burdened heavily in our prayers, struggling on through secret Gethsemanes and groaning before God in groanings audible to God alone, for those who have no mercy on themselves. What man of the race ever finds that in such love as this he has been made unhappy? As Christ himself bequeathed his joy to such, so has he found it to be a most real and dear bequest, and that when he has been able, after Christ's example, to bear most and be deepest in sacrifice for others—even painful sacrifice—then has he been raised to the highest pitch of beatitude. The compensations of such a life transcend, how sublimely, the losses. As they did with Christ, so they do with us, so they will in all beings and worlds. Therefore when we say that love is a principle of vicarious sacrifice, how far off are we from casting any shade of gloom on the possibilities and fortunes of this love. We only magnify its joy and brighten its prospect. . . .

This one thing is clear, that love is a vicarious principle, bound by its own nature itself to take upon its feeling, and care, and sympathy, those who are down under evil and its penalties. Thus it is that Jesus takes our nature upon him, to be made a curse for us and to bear our sin. Holding such a view of vicarious sacrifice, we must find it belonging to the essential nature of all holy virtue. We are also required of course, to go forward and show how it pertains to all other good beings, as truly as to Christ himself in the flesh—how the eternal Father before Christ, and the Holy Spirit coming after, and the good angels both before and after, all alike have borne the burdens, struggled in the pains of their vicarious feeling for men; and then, at last, how Christianity comes to its issue, in begetting in us the same vicarious love that reigns in all glorified and good minds of the heavenly kingdom; gathering us in after Christ our Master, as they that have learned to bear his cross, and be with him in his passion. Then having seen how Christ, as a power on character and life, renews us in this love, we shall be able to consider the very greatly inferior question, how far and in what manner he becomes our substitute, before the law violated by our transgression. . . . .

THEODORE PARKER (1810–1860)

On the Transient and the Permanent in Christianity

In actual Christianity—that is, in that portion of Christianity which is preached and believed—there seems to have been, ever since the time of its earthly founder, two elements, the one transient, the other permanent. The one is the thought, the folly, the uncertain wisdom, the theological notions, the impiety of man; the other, the eternal truth of God. . . .

It must be confessed, though with sorrow, that transient things form a great part of what is commonly taught as religion. An undue place has often been assigned to forms and doctrines, while too little stress has been laid on the divine life of the soul, love to God and love to man. Religious forms may be useful and beautiful. They are so, whenever they speak to the soul, and answer a want thereof. In our present state some forms are perhaps necessary. But they are only the accident of Christianity, not its substance. They are the robe, not the angel, who may take another robe quite as becoming and useful. One sect has many forms; another, none. Yet both may be equally Christian, in spite of the redundance or the deficiency. They are a part of the language in which religion speaks, and exist, with few exceptions, wherever man is found. In our calculating nation, in our rationalizing sect, we have retained but two of the rites so numerous in the early Christian Church, and even these we have attenuated to the last degree, leaving them little more than a spectre of the ancient form. Another age may continue or forsake both; may revive old forms, or invent new ones to suit the altered circumstances of the times, and yet be Christians quite as good as we, or our fathers of the dark ages. Whether the Apostles designed these rites to be perpetual, seems a question which belongs to scholars and antiquarians; not to us, as Christian men and women. So long as they satisfy or help the pious heart, so long they are good. Looking behind or around us, we see that the forms and rites of the Christians are quite as fluctuating as those of the heathens, from whom some of them have been, not unwisely, adopted by the earlier church.

Again, the doctrines that have been connected with Christianity, and taught in its name, are quite as changeable as the form. This also takes place unavoidably. . . . Now there can be but one religion which is absolutely true, existing in the facts of human nature and the ideas of Infinite God. That, whether acknowledged or not, is always the same thing, and never changes. So far as a man has any real religion—either the principle or the sentiment thereof—so far he has that, by whatever name he may call it. For, strictly speaking, there is but one kind of religion, as there is but one kind of love, though the manifestations of this religion, in forms, doctrines, and life, be never so diverse. It is through these men approximate to the true expression of this religion. Now, while this religion is one and always the same thing, there may be numerous systems of theology or philosophies of religion. These, with their creeds, confessions, and collections of doctrines, deduced by reasoning upon the facts observed, may be baseless and false, either because the observation was too narrow in extent, or otherwise defective in point of accuracy, or because the reasoning was illogical, and therefore the deduction spurious. Each of these three faults is conspicuous in the systems of theology. . . .

Any one who traces the history of what is called Christianity, will see that nothing changes more from age to age than the doctrines taught as Christian, and insisted on as essential to Christianity and personal salvation. What is falsehood in one province passes for truth in another. The heresy of one age is the orthodox belief and "only infallible rule" of the next. Now Arius, and now Athanasius, is lord of the ascendant. Both were excommunicated in their turn, each for affirming what the other denied. Men are burned for professing what men are burned for denying. . . .

This transitoriness of doctrines appears in many instances, of which two may be selected for a more attentive consideration. First, the doctrine respecting the origin and authority of the Old and New Testament. There has been a time when men were burned for asserting doctrines of natural philosophy which rested on evidence the most incontestable, because those doctrines conflicted with sentences in the Old Testament. Every word of that Jewish record was regarded as miraculously inspired, and therefore as infallibly true. . . .

But modern criticism is fast breaking to pieces this idol which men have made out of the scriptures. It has shown that here are the most different works thrown together; that their authors, wise as they sometimes were, pious as we feel often their spirit to have been, had only that inspiration which is common to other men equally pious and wise; that they were by no means infallible, but were mistaken in facts or in reasoning—

uttered predictions which time has not fulfilled; men who in some measure partook of the darkness and limited notions of their age, and were not always above its mistakes or its corruptions. . . .

Another instance of the transitoriness of doctrines taught as Christian is found in those which relate to the nature and authority of Christ. One ancient party has told us that he is the infinite God; another, that he is both God and man; a third, that he was a man, the son of Joseph and Mary—born as we are, tempted like ourselves, inspired, as we may be, if we will pay the price. Each of the former parties believed its doctrine on this head was infallibly true, and formed the very substance of Christianity, and was one of the essential conditions of salvation, though scarce any two distinguished teachers, of ancient or modern times, agree in their expression of this truth.

Almost every sect that has ever been makes Christianity rest on the personal authority of Jesus, and not the immutable truth of the doctrines themselves, or the authority of God who sent him into the world. Yet it seems difficult to conceive any reason why moral and religious truths should rest for their support on the personal authority of their revealer, any more than the truths of science on that of him who makes them known first or most clearly. It is hard to see why the great truths of Christianity rest on the personal authority of Jesus, more than the axioms of geometry rest on the personal authority of Euclid or Archimedes. The authority of Jesus, as of all teachers, one would naturally think, must rest on the truth of his words, and not their truth on his authority. . . .

In respect of doctrines as well as forms, we see all is transitory. "Everywhere is instability and insecurity." Opinions have changed most on points deemed most vital. Could we bring up a Christian teacher of any age—from the sixth to the fourteenth century, for example, though a teacher of undoubted soundness of faith, whose word filled the churches of Christendom—clergymen would scarce allow him to kneel at their altar, or sit down with them at the Lord's table. His notions of Christianity could not be expressed in our forms, nor could our notions be made intelligible to his ears. The questions of his age, those on which Christianity was thought to depend—questions which perplexed and divided the subtle doctors—are no questions to us. The quarrels which then drove wise men mad, now only excite a smile or a tear, as we are disposed to laugh or weep at the frailty of man. We have other straws of our own to quarrel for. Their ancient books of devotion do not speak to us; their theology is a vain word. To look back but a short period, the theological speculations of our fathers during the last two centuries, their "practical" divinity, even the sermons written by genius and piety, are, with rare exceptions, found unreadable; such a change is there in the doctrines. . . .

But while this change goes on, while one generation of opinions passes away, and another rises up, Christianity itself, that pure religion which exists eternal in the constitution of the soul and the mind of God, is always the same. The word that was before Abraham, in the very beginning, will not change, for that word is truth. From this Jesus subtracted nothing; to this he added nothing. But he came to reveal it as the secret of God, that cunning men could not understand, but which filled the souls of men meek and lowly of heart. This truth we owe to God; the revelation thereof to Jesus, our elder brother, God's chosen son. . . .

Christianity is a simple thing, very simple. It is absolute, pure morality; absolute, pure religion; the love of man, the love of God acting without let or hindrance. The only creed it lays down is the great truth which springs up spontaneous in the holy heart—there is a God. Its watchword is, Be perfect as your Father in heaven. The only form it demands is a divine life; doing the best thing in the best way, from the highest motives; perfect obedience to the great law of God. Its sanction is the voice of God in your heart; the perpetual presence of him who made us and the stars over our heads; Christ and the Father abiding within us. All this is very simple—a little child can understand it; very beautiful—the loftiest mind can find nothing so lovely. Try it by reason, conscience, and faith—things highest in man's nature—we see no redundance, we feel no deficiency. Examine the particular duties it enjoins—humility, reverence, sobriety, gentleness, charity, forgiveness, fortitude, resignation, faith, and active love; try the whole extent of Christianity, so well summed up in the command, "Thou shalt love the Lord thy God with all thy heart, and with all thy soul, and with all thy mind—thou shalt love thy neighbor as thyself"; and is there anything therein that can perish? No, the very opponents of Christianity have rarely found fault with the teachings of Jesus. The end of Christianity seems to be to make all men one with God as Christ was one with him; to bring them to such a state of obedience and goodness that we shall think divine thoughts and feel divine sentiments, and so keep the law of God by living a life of truth and love. Its means are purity and prayer; getting strength from God, and using it for our fellow-men as well as ourselves. It allows perfect freedom. It does not demand all men to *think* alike, but to think uprightly, and get as near as possible at truth; not all men to *live* alike, but to live holy, and get as near as possible to a life perfectly divine. Christ set up no pillars of Hercules, beyond which men must not sail the sea in quest of truth. He says, "I have many things to say unto you, but ye cannot bear them now. . . ."

In an age of corruption, as all ages are, Jesus stood and looked up to God. There was nothing between him and the Father of all; no old world, be it of Moses or Esaias, of a living rabbi, or sanhedrin of rabbis; no sin or perverseness of the finite will. As the result of this virgin purity of soul and perfect obedience, the light of God shone down into the very depths of his soul, bringing all of the Godhead which flesh can receive. He would have us do the same; worship with nothing between us and God; act, think, feel, live, in perfect obedience to him; and we never are *Christians* as he was the *Christ,* until we worship, as Jesus did, with no mediator, with nothing between us and the Father of all. He felt that God's word was in him; that he was one with God. He told what he saw, the truth; he lived what he felt, a life of love.The truth he brought to light must have been always the same before the eyes of all-seeing God, nineteen centuries before Christ, or nineteen centuries after him. A life supported by the principle and quickened by the sentiment of religion, if true to both, is always the same thing in Nazareth or New England. Now that divine man received these truths from God, was illumined more clearly by "the light that lighteneth every man," combined or involved all the truths of religion and morality in his doctrine, and made them manifest in his life. Then his words and example passed into the world, and can no more perish than the stars be wiped out of the sky. The truths he taught; his doctrines respecting man and God; the relation between man and man, and man and God, with the duties that grow out of that relation—are always the same, and can never change till man ceases to be man, and creation vanishes into nothing. No; forms and opinions change and perish, but the word of God cannot fail. The form religion takes, the doctrines wherewith she is girded, can never be the same in any two centuries or two men; for since the sum of religious doctrines is both the result and the measure of a man's total growth in wisdom, virtue, and piety, and since men will always differ in these respects, so religious *doctrines* and *forms* will always differ, always be transient, as Christianity goes forth and scatters the seed she bears in her hand. But the *Christianity holy men feel in the heart,* the Christ that is born within us, is always the same thing to each soul that feels it. This differs only in degree, and not in kind, from age to age, and man to man. . . .

Such, then, is the transient and such the permanent in Christianity. What is of absolute value never changes; we may cling round it and grow to it for ever. No one can say his notions shall stand. But we may all say, the truth as it is in Jesus shall never pass away. Yet there are always some, even religious men, who do not see the permanent element, so they rely on the fleeting, and, what is also an evil, condemn others for not doing the same. They mistake a defence of the truth for an attack upon the holy of holies, the removal of a theological error for the destruction of all religion. Already men of the same sect eye one another with suspicion, and lowering brows that indicate a storm, and, like children who have fallen out in their play, call hard names, Now, as always, there is a collision between these two elements. The question puts itself to each man, "Will you cling to what is perishing, or embrace what is eternal?" This question each must answer for himself. . . .

WALTER RAUSCHENBUSCH (1861–1918)

Social Christianity and Personal Religion

Personal religion has a supreme value for its own sake, not merely as a feeder of social morality, but as the highest unfolding of life itself, as the blossoming of our spiritual nature. Spiritual regeneration is the most important fact in any life history. A living experience of God is the crowning knowledge attainable to a human mind. Each one of us needs the redemptive power of religion for his own sake, for on the tiny stage of the human soul all the vast world tragedy of good and evil is re-enacted. . . .

If, therefore, our personal religious life is likely to be sapped by our devotion to social work, it would be a calamity second to none. But is it really likely that this will happen? The great aim underlying the whole social movement is the creation of a free, just, and brotherly social order. This is the greatest moral task conceivable. Its accomplishment is the manifest will of God for this generation. Every Christian motive is calling us to it. If it is left undone, millions of lives will be condemned to a deepening moral degradation and to spiritual starvation. Does it look probable that we shall lose our contact with God if we plunge too deeply into this work? Does it stand to reason that we shall go astray from Jesus Christ when we engage in the unequal conflict with organized wrong? What kind of "spirituality" is it which is likely to get hurt by being put to work for justice and our fellow-men?

Some of the anxiety about personal religion is due to a subtle lack of faith in religion. Men think it is a fragile thing that will break up and vanish when the customs and formulas which have hitherto encased and protected it are broken and cast aside. Most of us have known religion under one form, and we suppose that it can have no other. But religion is the life of God in the soul of man, and is God really so fragile? Will the tongue of fire sputter and go out unless we shelter it under a bushel? Let the winds of God roar through it, and watch it! Religion unites a great variability of form with an amazing constancy of power. The Protestant Reformation changed the entire outward complexion of religion in the nations of northern Europe. All the most characteristic forms in which Christianity had expressed itself and by which its strength had hitherto been gauged were swept away. No pope, no priest, no monk, no mass, no confessional, no rosary, no saints, no images, no processions, no pilgrimages, no indulgences! It was a clean sweep. What was left of religion? Religion itself! At least your Puritans and Huguenots seemed to think they had personal religion; more in fact, than ever before. Catholics thought it was the destruction of personal religion: really it was the rise of a new type of religion. In the same way the social Christianity of today is not a dilution of personal religion, but a new form of experimental Christianity, and its religious testimony will have to be heard henceforth when "the varieties of religious experience" are described.

Nevertheless, conservative Christian men are not frightened by their own imaginings when they fear that the progress of the social interest will mean a receding of personal religion. They usually have definite cases in mind in which that seemed to be the effect, and it is well worth while to examine those more closely.

In the first place, personal religion collapses with some individuals, because in their case, it had long been growing hollow and thin. . . . As long as their life goes on in the accustomed way, they maintain their religious connections and expressions, and do so sincerely, but if they move to another part of the country, or if a new interest turns their minds forcibly in some other direction, the frayed bond parts and they turn from their Church and religion. If it is the social interest which attracts them, it may seem to them and others that this has extinguished their devotional life. In reality there was little personal religion to lose, and that little would probably have been lost in some other way. This would cover the inner history of some ministers as well as of church members.

In other cases we must recognize that men become apathetic about church activities in which they have been interested, because they have found something better. The Hebrew prophets turned in anger from the sacrificial doings of their people; Jesus turned away from the long prayers of the Pharisees, who were the most pious people of his day; the Reformers repudiated many of the most devout activities of medieval Catholicism. Wherever there is a new awakening of spiritual life, there is a discarding of old religious forms, and it is to the interest of personal religion that there should be. Is there nothing petty, useless, and insipid in the Catholic or Protestant church life of our day from which a soul awakened to larger purposes ought really to turn away? Is it reprehensible if some drop out of a dress parade when they hear the sound of actual fighting just across the hills?

It is also true that in this tremendous awakening and unsettlement some turn away in haste from things which have lasting value. Few men and few movements have such poise that they never overshoot the mark. When the Reformation turned its back on medieval superstition, it also smashed the painted windows of the cathedrals and almost banished art and music from its services. When mystics feel the compelling power of the inner word of God, they are apt to slight the written word. So when religious souls who have been shut away from social ideals and interests and pent up within a fine but contracted religious habitation get the new outlook of the social awakening, it sweeps them away with new enthusiasms. Their life rushes in to fill the empty spaces. Their mind is busy with a religious comprehension of a hundred new facts and problems, and the old questions of personal religion drop out of sight. In such cases we can safely trust to experience to restore the equilibrium. . . .

The question takes a wider meaning when we turn to the alienation of entire classes from religion. There is no doubt that in all the industrialized nations of Europe, and in our own country, the working classes are dropping out of connection with their churches and synagogues, and to a large extent are transferring their devotion to social movements, so that it looks as if the social interest displaced religion. But here, too, we must remember that solid masses of the population of continental Europe have never had much vital religion to lose. Their religion was taught by rote and performed by rote. It was gregarious and not personal. Detailed investigations have been made of the religious thought world of the peasantry or industrial population of limited districts, and the result always is that the centuries of indoctrination by the Church have left only a very thin crust of fertile religious conviction and experience behind. This is not strange, for whenever any spontaneous and democratic religion has arisen among the people, the established churches have done their best to wet-blanket and suppress it, and they have succeeded finely. When these people cut loose from their churches, they may not be getting much farther away from God. Usually these unchurched people still have a strong native instinct for religion, and when the vital issues and convictions of their own life are lifted into the purer light of Jesus Christ and set on fire by religious faith, they respond. . . .

Those who fear the influence of the social interest on personal religion are not, therefore, wholly wrong. In any powerful spiritual movement, even the best, there are yeasty, unsettling forces which may do good in the long run but harm in the short run. Atheistic socialism may influence the religious life of great classes as deforestation affects a mountain side.

On the other hand, where the new social spirit combines harmoniously with the inherited Christian life, a new type of personal religion is produced which has at least as good a right to existence as any other type.

Jesus was not a theological Christian, nor a churchman, nor an emotionalist, nor an ascetic, nor a contemplative mystic. A mature social Christian comes closer to the likeness of Jesus Christ than any other type.

In religious individualism, even in its sweetest forms, there was a subtle twist of self-seeking which vitiated its Christlikeness. Thomas à Kempis' *Imitation of Christ* and Bunyan's *Pilgrim's Progress* are classical expressions of personal religion, the one Roman Catholic and monastic, the other Protestant and Puritan. In both piety is self-centered. In both we are taught to seek the highest good of the soul by turning away from the world of men. . . .

It is charged that those who become interested in "social work" lose interest in "personal work." Doubtless there is truth in that, and it is a regrettable one-sidedness. It is only fair to remember, however, that they share this loss of interest with the entire American Church. Evangelism itself had long become so one-sided, mechanical, and superficial in its gospel and methods that the present apathy can be explained only as a reaction from it. . . . Those who add the new social intelligence to the old religious love of man's soul will take every man in his own social place and his own human connections, will try to understand his peculiar sin and failure from his own point of view, and see by what means salvation can effectively be brought to him. Such an evangelism would be more truly personal than the old; it would have more sense of the individuality of each man. . . .

Christianity must offer every man a full salvation. The individualistic gospel never did this. Its evangelism never recognized more than a fractional part of the saving forces at work in God's world. Salvation was often whittled down to a mere doctrinal proposition; assent to that, and you were saved. Social Christianity holds to all the real values in the old methods, but rounds them out to meet all the needs of human life. . . .

Sin is a social force. It runs from man to man along the lines of social contact. Its impact on the individual becomes more overwhelming when sin is most completely socialized. Salvation, too, is a social force. It is exerted by groups that are charged with divine will and love. It becomes durable and complete in the measure in which the individual is built into a social organism that is ruled by justice, cleanness, and love. A full salvation demands a Christian social order which will serve as the spiritual environment of the individual. . . .

I claim that social Christianity is by all tokens the great highway by which this present generation can come to God.

For one thing, it puts an end to most of the old conflicts between religion and science. The building of the Kingdom of God on earth requires surprisingly little dogma and speculative theology, and a tremendous quantity of holy will and scientific good sense. It does not set up a series of propositions which need constant modernizing and which repel the most active intellects, but it summons all to help in transforming the world into a reign of righteousness, and men of good will are not very far apart on that. That kind of religion has no quarrel with science. It needs science to interpret the universe which Christianity wants to transform. Social Christianity sets up fewer obstacles for the intellect and puts far heavier tasks on the will, and all that is sound in modern life will accept that change with profound relief.

Social Christianity would also remove one other obstacle which bars even more men out of religion than the scientific difficulties of belief. The most effective argument against religion today is that religion has been "against the people." The people are coming to their own at last. For a century and a half at least they have been on the upgrade, climbing with inexpressible toil and suffering toward freedom, equality, and brotherhood. The spirit of Christ has been their most powerful ally; but the official Church, taking Christendom as a whole, has thrown the bulk of its great resources to the side of those who are in possession, and against those who were in such deadly need of its aid. This is the great scandal which will not down. Scientific doubt may alienate thousands, but the resentment against the Church for going over to the enemy has alienated entire nations. Nothing would so expiate that guilt and win back the lost respect for religion, as determined coöperation on the part of the Church in creating a social order in which the just aspirations of the working class will be satisfied. Those Christian men who are the outstanding and bold friends of the people's cause are today the most effective apologists of Christianity. . . .

THE TWENTIETH CENTURY
Introduction

The Protestant thought of the present century had its beginnings in World War I and in the reactions of Christian thinkers to that war. Until the eve of the war the dominant thrust in Protestant writing, preaching, and social involvement rested on nineteenth-century liberalism and its unqualified endorsement of man's inherent goodness. Given proper education and direction, there was no limit to what human nature could and would attain in building a better world.

The war and its aftermath shattered this dream by making it clear that there was a dark side to man's nature. Sin, in particular man's inhumanity to man, remained a necessary component in any realistic appraisal of the human situation. New perspectives were needed to correct liberalism's myopia.

In 1918 the first of the new voices was heard. Karl Barth brought out his *Epistle to the Romans* in that year. Its message, to be constantly reiterated in the years ahead, was that only in Scripture could man learn who he was, who God was, and what was the nature of their relationship. Of man Scripture said: sinner; of God it said: Wholly Other than man conceives Him. Their relationship is defined in terms of man's radical and total dependence on God and of the divine judgment on all human achievements.

For Barth, Christian thought could begin only with God. Man is not the focus of religion; God is. This fact too is clear in Scripture. Using as his source only the Word of God, Barth developed over the ensuing long years of his life a theology calculated to destroy man's self-complacency and return him to a necessary sense of his sinfulness and dependence on God for salvation.

In later years Barth came to temper his initially pessimistic view of the human condition before God. Whereas his first works had stressed the absolute transcendence of God and the severity of the divine judgment on all things human, he came in later life to see that the figure of Christ provided a necessary corrective for his early thought. In Christ, God became human; in Jesus, God indicated that His final judgment on man was mercy and forgiveness. Man continues to remain in total dependence; he is still inescapably sinner. But the figure of Christ demands that the final judgment on man's fate be optimistic. A selection chosen from *The Humanity of God,* written in 1954, chronicles the history of Barth's thought from its first rejection of liberalism up to the point when the person of Jesus Christ brought him to rethink his theology in a more balanced and hopeful form.

Barth's neo-orthodoxy, his new insistence that only a thought based exclusively on the Word of God could call itself orthodox, is both the foundation and the catalyst of much of twentieth-century Protestant thought. He was agreed with or challenged, but in any case his work set the direction for much of what was to follow.

Barthian thought came to the United States in the late twenties in the person of Reinhold Niebuhr. Niebuhr's early ministry in a parish in industrial Detroit brought him to as somber a view of man's sinfulness as Barth had reached. Daily confrontation with the suffering and tragedy that man visited upon man in an industrial society provided him with the raw materials of his Christian Realism. His thought was Christian because rooted in Scripture and the tradition of the Christian church. It was realism because it insistently demanded that the Christian faith face the real world and its problems, admit its own insufficiency to provide definitive solutions for those problems, yet never cease striving for practical and limited attempts to confront these problems.

Niebuhr's thought rests on his analysis of man in *The Nature and Destiny of Man.* The passages excerpted here from that work summarize his balanced view of man as at once image of God, creature, and sinner. Most of his other writings, which tend to be more socially and politically than theologically oriented, spell out the specifics of his vision of man in the arenas of politics, race, war, social reform, and international relations. Niebuhr is the first of the breed of contemporary Christian thinkers dedicated primarily to the social implementation of Christianity. His realism in confronting the Christian faith with political and social actualities set the tone for much of the American theological work that developed during and after World War II.

Standing alongside Karl Barth as one of the great seminal thinkers of this century is the figure of Rudolf Bultmann. His concern was with Scripture and its relevancy for contemporary man. The New Testament was written for first-century man, and it adopted his world as the structure within which it would communicate to him its religious message. The men of that time saw the world as a three-storied house—heaven, earth, and hell. Each of these stories was inhabited by its own beings—angels, men, and demons. Miracles altered the course of nature; God intervened in human history in dramatic and unpredictable ways.

Bultmann believes that this world of myth and wonder and miracle makes no sense to modern man. Nor is this strange, since the world of the twentieth century has its own completely different view of the universe. Science has learned to subject material reality to man's needs. There is neither necessity nor evidence for an invisible world peopled by supernatural beings nor for divine intervention and miraculous events.

The tragedy, Bultmann believes, is that in rejecting the Scripture's world view, today's man makes the mistake of also rejecting its religious message. That message is as valid now as it was for any past age. What needs to be done is to disentangle that message from its mythological framework. This task Bultmann calls the process of demythologizing.

Once this process is accomplished it becomes possible to ask the New Testament the questions it was written to answer. Man must learn to ask such questions in terms meaningful to himself. For Bultmann the questions that have perennially engaged man's attention are those of the meaning of human existence: Who am I, whence am I, where am I going, what does life mean? Every man asks and seeks answers to these queries. These are the questions to which the New Testament addresses itself.

To frame these questions in meaningful terms for contemporary man Bultmann relies on the philosophy of Martin Heidegger with its emphasis on analyzing the difference between authentic human existence and inauthentic living. In Heidegger's view inauthentic existence is rooted in one's willingness to be made by other people and other things. Authentic existence, on the other hand, starts with the decision to shape one's own life and being.

It is to this question of authentic versus inauthentic existence that Bultmann believes the gospel addresses itself. It is his contention that the Bible's essential revelation is that man is incapable of authentic existence relying solely on his own resources. Only God can provide him with the power to achieve it. Man has need of God if he is to be truly himself.

Many of these basic themes are developed in the selection from Bultmann's *Jesus Christ and Mythology,* the need and purpose of demythologization, the meaning and attaining of authentic existence. The specific details of how the New Testament yields its message in response to these Heideggerian questions are spelled out in Bultmann's many books of scriptural interpretation. Like Barth's, Bultmann's work has been determinative in its effect on twentieth-century Protestant thought. Those who come after him in scriptural study may go beyond him, but he is their unavoidable starting point.

Barth represents twentieth-century Protestantism's return to an exclusively revelation-based theology. Bultmann initiates the same thought's preoccupation with developing a contemporaneously acceptable interpretation of the Word of God. Paul Tillich is the century's most influential philosopher-theologian. Philosophy meant for Tillich the understanding of the human situation by a wide-ranging study of all the cultural forms in which man expresses his understanding of himself. Philosophy, art, history, depth psychology, literature, politics, were all areas through which Tillich moved to learn who modern man is. That man he came to see as lonely and anxious, alienated from his true existence and helpless to escape his state. Once the Christian theologian has completed this absolutely inescapable cultural work, he is in a position to correlate the human questions implicit in that culture with the answers that Christianity offers to man. The answers cannot, however, be given until the questions are known. Once they are known, the theologian must use the language that man uses in putting the questions to frame the Christian answers. In short, Tillich's fundamental operating assumption is that religion and culture interpenetrate and influence each other. "The substance of culture is religion; the form of religion is culture."

To the human sense of anxiety and alienation Christianity responds, in Tillich's terms, by providing the divine answer to the human plight. To man God promises in Christ the power of "new being," the ability to overcome his separated state and return to his true existence, the acceptance of dependence upon God.

Tillich's sermon *You Are Accepted* is included here because it expands on his notion of how man comes to new life by his acceptance of Christian faith. That faith once affirmed puts man on the road to wholeness, empowers him to accept himself for what he is, enables him to begin a life rooted in God, the ultimate ground of his being and of all being.

Tillich's work defies summary because very few areas of contemporary culture are absent from his vision. It is, likewise, this many-faceted character of his writing that makes most subsequent Christian thinkers indebted to him. He continues to exercise a creative influence on present thought precisely because of his mastery in probing man's cultural situation.

Barth, Bultmann, Niebuhr, and Tillich set the mood and charted the course for this century's Protestant thought until well into the fifties. At that point the theological focus began to shift away from their concerns; new perspectives began to develop in the light of new problems. The overriding concern of current Christian thought is the problem of God. The problem has many aspects. The last selections chosen for this century focus on one or other of these aspects. Finally, two selections, one from John Cobb, Jr., the other from Harvey Cox, are offered to indicate some of the directions in which Protestant thought will probably go in the years ahead.

Dietrich Bonhoeffer is the pivotal figure in the swing of Protestant thought away from the concerns of Barth, Tillich, and Bultmann. Essentially a conservative Lutheran theologian in his early years, Bonhoeffer came, through his active involvement in the anti-Nazi underground and the two years of imprisonment that ended in his death by hanging in 1945, to a radical questioning of traditional Christianity. In his *Letters and Papers from Prison* he formulates some of those questions: Who is Christ for us today? what does it mean to believe in God in the twentieth century? Indeed, is such belief possible? what role, if any, is the Christian church called upon to play today? The excerpts presented from his *Letters* indicate the beginnings of his answers to these questions. Unfortunately he did not live to work out his insights in detail. His legacy is tantalizingly fragmentary. What he did accomplish was the fundamental reorientation of Protestant thought after him.

By the late fifties other theologians began to pick up Bonhoeffer's questions and to explore them. John Robinson, Bishop of Woolwich in South London, is the first such thinker represented here. His *Honest to God,* published in 1963, put into popular language what have since been theology's primary questions: the possibility of belief in God, the contemporary meaning of Christ, the relevance of the Christian church. His own essay on the need for contemporary man to be atheist which is presented here is taken from his *The New Reformation,* the sequel to *Honest to God.* The impossibility of retaining the traditional supernaturalist view of God is presented, and then, paradoxically, the bishop argues that a new faith must and can be built on the ashes of the old.

The questioning of the validity of traditional Christianity is approached from a different perspective by Edward Schweizer. Not quite so radical as Robinson in his assessment of Christianity, Schweizer is typical of the contemporary biblical scholar. He does not blink at the radical questioning of Scripture in today's thinking but argues that it is possible to produce a meaningful Christianity by an honest attempt to let present thought, past tradition, and the initial Word of God interact with and correct each other. It is in this direction that much of present scriptural work is moving. The concentration is particularly on the problem of hermeneutics, the proper method of interpreting Scripture.

Working on the same problem: what ought to be the present understanding of the Christian faith, the systematic theologians are essaying modes of presenting Christianity which attempt to embody the developments of twentieth-century thought. John Macquarrie's *Principles of Christian Theology* offers an understanding of Christianity which relies heavily on Bultmann, Heidegger, Tillich—indeed, most of the century's significant religious and philosophical thinkers. The excerpt illustrates the thrust of his own thought. This is basically to develop a new perspective in speaking of the Christian faith. Within that perspective Macquarrie believes that talk of God and the supernatural needs to become indirect or "symbolic." His book is the beginning of systematic theology's answer to the questions raised by Bonhoeffer and Robinson.

Such, then, is the contemporary situation in Protestant thought. The last two selections summarize that situation and speak, each in its own way, to the problem of the future: Where does Protestantism and Christian thought in general go from here? Both selections are basically optimistic about that future. Cobb sees real hope for a theological renascence in the process thinking of Alfred North Whitehead and the cosmic vision of Teilhard de Chardin. His startling proposal is for a revolutionary approach to thought about God done in the context of a frank acceptance of the relativity of all human thought.

Cox pins his hope to a theology of the future. His conviction is that past and present are prelude. Hope lies with the future and with a theological stance that accepts "man-as-promise" and "the ontology of the not-yet" as its fundamental categories of thought.

Prophecy is a hazardous vocation. But if the arrow tips of present thought point anywhere it is towards a thoroughly secularized, this-worldly Christianity which will use a language to speak of God and Christ that will sound foreign to many a present Christian ear and wherein the institutional church will have a far different form than it presently has.

The future of present attempts to come to grips with the current problems of Christianity will clarify whether the presently popular expression "We live in a post-Christian world" is to be interpreted as a death notice or a reproclamation of the original Easter message.

KARL BARTH (1886–1969)

The Humanity of God

What began forcibly to press itself upon us about forty years ago was not so much the humanity of God as His *deity*—a God absolutely unique in His relation to man and the world, overpoweringly lofty and distant, strange, yes even wholly other. Such was the God with whom man has to do when he takes the name of God upon his lips, when God encounters him, when he enters into relation with God. We were confronted by the mystery comparable only to the impenetrable darkness of death, in which God veils Himself precisely when He unveils, announces, and reveals Himself to man, and by the judgment man must experience because God is gracious to him, because He wills to be and is his God. What we discovered in the change which occurred at that time was the majesty of the crucified, so evident in its full horror, just as Grünewald saw and depicted Him. We saw the finger of John the Baptist, by the same artist, pointing with authority to this holy One: "He must increase but I must decrease."

Unmistakably for us the *humanity* of God at that time moved from the center to the periphery, from the emphasized principal clause to the less emphasized subordinate clause. . . .

Evangelical theology almost all along the line, certainly in all its representative forms and tendencies, had become *religionistic, anthropocentric,* and in this sense humanistic. What I mean to say is that an external and internal disposition and emotion of man, namely his piety—which might well be Christian piety—had become its object of study and its theme. Around this it revolved and seemed compelled to revolve without release. This was true of evangelical theology in its doctrine of principles, in its presentation of the Christian past and its practical understanding of the Christian present, in its ethics and in that which perhaps was to be regarded as its dogmatics, in the proclamation and instruction of the Church determined by it—above all, however, in its interpretation of the Bible. What did it know and say of the *deity* of God? For this theology, to think about God meant to think in a scarcely veiled fashion about man, more exactly about the religious, the Christian religious man. To speak about God meant to speak in an exalted tone but once again and more than ever about this man—his revelations and wonders, his faith and his works. There is no question about it: here man was made great at the cost of God —the divine God who is someone other than man, who sovereignly confronts him, who immovably and unchangeably stands over against him as the Lord, Creator, and Redeemer. This God who is also man's free partner in a history inaugurated by Him and in a dialogue ruled by Him was in danger of being reduced, along with this history and this dialogue, to a pious notion—to a mystical expression and symbol of a current alternating between a man and his own heights or depths. But whatever truth was gained in this way could be only that of a monologue.

At this point some of us were appalled after we, along with everyone else, had drained the different chalices of this theology to the last drop. We then concluded (from approximately the middle of the second decade of our century on) that we could not side with it any longer. Why? . . .

. . . was it . . . the discovery that the theme of the Bible, contrary to the critical and to the orthodox exegesis which we inherited, certainly could not be man's religion and religious morality and certainly not his own secret divinity? The stone wall we first ran up against was that the theme of the Bible is the deity of *God,* more exactly God's *deity*—God's independence and particular character, not only in relation to the natural but also to the spiritual cosmos; God's absolutely unique existence, might, and initiative, above all, in His relation to man. Only in this manner were we able to understand the voice of the Old and New Testaments. Only with this perspective did we feel we could henceforth be theologians, and in particular, preachers—ministers of the divine Word. . . .

It must now quite frankly be granted that we were at that time only partially in the right, even in reference to the theology which we inherited and from which we had to disengage ourselves—partially right in the same sense in which all preponderantly critical-polemic movements, attitudes, and positions, however meaningful they may be, are usually only partially in the right. What expressions we used—in part taken over and in part newly invented!—above all, the famous "wholly other" breaking in upon us "perpendicularly from above," the not less famous "infinite qualitative distinction" between God and man, the vacuum, the mathematical point, and the tangent in which alone they must meet. . . . There was also the bold assurance that there is in the Bible only *one* theological interest, namely, that in God; that only *one* way appears, namely, that from above downwards; that only *one* message can be heard, namely, that of an immediate forgiveness of sins both in prospect and in retrospect. The problem of ethics was identified with man's sickness unto death; redemption was viewed as consisting in the abolition of the creatureliness of the creature, the swallowing of immanence by transcendence, and in conformity with these the demand for a faith like a spring into the abyss, and more of the like! All this, however well it may have been meant and however much it may have mattered, was nevertheless said somewhat severely and brutally, and moreover—at least according to the other side—in part heretically. How we cleared things away! And we did almost nothing but clear away! Everything which even remotely smacked of mysticism and morality, of pietism and romanticism, or even of idealism, was suspected and sharply interdicted or bracketed with reservations which sounded actually prohibitive! What should really have been only a sad and friendly smile was a derisive laugh! . . .

Where did we really go astray? Where was and is the starting point for the new change of direction? . . . I believe it consisted in the fact that we were wrong exactly where we were right, that at first we did not know how to carry through with sufficient care and thoroughness the new knowledge of the *deity* of God which was so exciting both to us and to others. It was certainly good and proper to return to it and to make it known with greater power. . . .

It is nevertheless true that it was pre-eminently the image and concept of a "wholly other" that fascinated us and which we, though not without examination, had dared to identify with the deity of Him who in the Bible is called Yahweh-Kyrios. We viewed this "wholly other" in isolation, abstracted and absolutized, and set it over against man, this miserable wretch —not to say boxed his ears with it—in such fashion that it continually showed greater similarity to the deity of the God of the philosophers than to the deity of the God of Abraham, Isaac, and Jacob. . . .

But did it not appear to escape us by quite a distance that the *deity* of the *living* God—and we certainly wanted to deal with Him—found its meaning and its power only in the context of His history and of His dialogue with *man,* and thus in His *togetherness* with man? Indeed—and this is the point back of which we cannot go—it is a matter of *God's* sovereign togetherness with man, a togetherness grounded in Him and determined, delimited, and ordered through Him alone. Only in this way and in this context can it take place and be recognized. It is a matter, however, of God's *togetherness* with man. Who God is and what He is in His deity He proves and reveals not in a vacuum as a divine being-for-Himself, but precisely and authentically in the fact that He exists, speaks, and acts as the *partner* of man, though of course as the absolutely superior partner. He who does *that* is the living God. And the freedom in which He does *that* is His deity. It is the deity which as such also has the character of humanity. In this and only in this form was—and still is—our view of the deity of

God to be set in opposition to that earlier theology. There must be positive acceptance and not unconsidered rejection of the elements of truth, which one cannot possibly deny to it even if one sees all its weaknesses. It is precisely God's *deity* which, rightly understood, includes his *humanity*. . . .

How do we come to know that? What permits and requires this statement? It is a *Christological* statement, or rather one grounded in and to be unfolded from Christology. A second change of direction after that first one would have been superfluous had we from the beginning possessed the presence of mind to venture the whole inevitable counterthrow from the Christological perspective and thus from the superior and more exact standpoint of the central and entire witness of Holy Scripture. Certainly in *Jesus Christ,* as He is attested in Holy Scripture, we are not dealing with man in the abstract: not with the man who is able with his modicum of religion and religious morality to be sufficient unto himself without God and thus himself to be God. But neither are we dealing with *God* in the abstract: not with one who in His deity exists only separated from man, distant and strange and thus a non-human if not indeed an inhuman God. In Jesus Christ there is no isolation of man from God or of God from man. Rather, in Him we encounter the history, the dialogue, in which God and man meet together and are together, the reality of the covenant *mutually* contracted, preserved, and fulfilled by them. Jesus Christ is in His one Person, as true *God, man's* loyal partner, and as true *man, God's.* He is the Lord humbled for communion with man and likewise the Servant exalted to communion with God. He is the Word spoken from the loftiest, most luminous transcendence and likewise the Word heard in the deepest, darkest immanence. He is both, without their being confused but also without their being divided; He is wholly the one and wholly the other. Thus in this oneness Jesus Christ is the Mediator, the Reconciler, between God and man. Thus He comes forward to *man* on behalf of *God* calling for and awakening faith, love, and hope, and to *God* on behalf of *man,* representing man, making satisfaction and interceding. Thus He attests and guarantees to man God's free *grace* and at the same time attests and guarantees to God man's free *gratitude.* Thus He establishes in His Person the justice of God vis-à-vis man and also the justice of man before God. Thus He is in His Person the covenant in its fullness, the Kingdom of heaven which is at hand, in which God speaks and man hears, God gives and man receives, God commands and man obeys, God's glory shines in the heights and thence into the depths, and peace on earth comes to pass among men in whom He is well pleased. Moreover, exactly in this way Jesus Christ, as this Mediator and Reconciler between God and man, is also the *Revealer* of them both. We do not need to engage in a free-ranging investigation to seek out and construct who and what God truly is, and who and what man truly is, but only to read the truth about both where it resides, namely, in the fullness of their togetherness, their covenant which proclaims itself in Jesus Christ.

Who and what *God* is—this is what in particular we have to learn better and with more precision in the new change of direction in the thinking and speaking of evangelical theology, which has become necessary in the light of the earlier change. But the question must be, who and what is God *in Jesus Christ,* if we here today would push forward to a better answer.

Beyond doubt God's *deity* is the first and fundamental fact that strikes us when we look at the existence of Jesus Christ as attested in the Holy Scripture. And God's deity in Jesus Christ consists in the fact that God Himself in Him is the *subject* who speaks and acts with sovereignty. *He* is the free One in whom all freedom has its ground, its meaning, its prototype. *He* is the initiator, founder, preserver, and fulfiller of the covenant. *He* is the sovereign Lord of the amazing relationship in which He becomes and is not only different from man but also one with him. *He* is also the creator of him who is His partner. *He* it is through whose faithfulness the corresponding faithfulness of His partner is awakened and takes place. The old Reformed Christology worked that out especially clearly in its doctrine of the "hypostatic union": God is on the throne. In the existence of Jesus Christ, the fact that God speaks, gives, orders, comes absolutely first—that man hears, receives, obeys, can and must only follow this first act. In Jesus Christ man's freedom is wholly enclosed in the freedom of God. Without the condescension of God there would be no exaltation of man. As the Son of God and not otherwise, Jesus Christ is the Son of Man. This sequence is irreversible. God's independence, omnipotence, and eternity, God's· holiness and justice and thus God's deity, in its original and proper form, is the power leading to this effective and visible sequence in the existence of Jesus Christ: superiority preceding subordination. Thus we have here no universal deity capable of being reached conceptually, but this concrete deity—real and recognizable in the *descent* grounded in that sequence and peculiar to the existence of Jesus Christ.

But here there is something even more concrete to be seen. God's high freedom in Jesus Christ is His freedom for *love.* The divine capacity which operates and exhibits itself in that superiority and subordination is manifestly also God's capacity to bend downwards, to attach Himself to another and this other to Himself, to be together with him. This takes place in that irreversible sequence, but in it is completely real. In that sequence there arises and continues in Jesus Christ the highest communion of God with man. God's deity is thus no prison in which He can exist only in and for Himself. It is rather His freedom to be in and for Himself but also with and for us, to assert but also to sacrifice Himself, to be wholly exalted but also completely humble, not only almighty but also almighty mercy, not only Lord but also servant, not only judge but also Himself the judged, not only man's eternal king but also his brother in time. And all that without in the slightest forfeiting His deity! All that, rather, in the highest proof and proclamation of His deity! He who *does* and manifestly *can* do all that, He and no other is the living God. So constituted is His deity, the deity of the God of Abraham, Isaac, and Jacob. In Jesus Christ it is in this way operative and recognizable. If He is the Word of Truth, then the truth of *God* is exactly this and nothing else.

It is when we look at Jesus Christ that we know decisively that God's deity does not exclude, but includes His *humanity*. Would that Calvin had energetically pushed ahead on this point in his Christology, his doctrine of God, his teaching about predestination, and then logically also in his ethics! His Geneva would then not have become such a gloomy affair. His letters would then not have contained so much bitterness. It would then not be so easy to play a Heinrich Pestalozzi and, among his contemporaries, a Sebastian Castellio off against him. How could God's deity exclude His humanity, since it is God's freedom for love and thus His capacity to be not only in the heights but also in the depths, not only great but also small, not only in and for Himself but also with another distinct from Him, and to offer Himself to him? In His deity there is enough room for communion with man. Moreover God has and retains in His relation to this other one the unconditioned priority. It is His act. *His* is and remains the first and decisive Word, *His* the initiative, *His* the leadership. How could we see and say it otherwise when we look at Jesus Christ in whom we find man taken up into communion with God? No, God requires no exclusion of humanity, no non-humanity, not to speak of inhumanity, in order to be truly God. But we may and must, however, look further and recognize the fact that actually His deity *encloses humanity in itself*. This is not the fatal Lutheran doctrine of the two natures and their properties. On the contrary, the essential aim of this doctrine is not to be denied at this point but to be adopted. It would be the false deity of a false God if in His deity His humanity did not also immediately encounter us. Such false deities are by Jesus Christ once for all made a laughingstock. In Him the fact is once for all established that God does not exist without man.

It is not as though God stands in need of another as His partner, and in particular of man, in order to be truly God. "What is man, that thou art mindful of him, and the son of man that thou dost care for him?" Why should God not also be able, as eternal Love, to be sufficient unto Himself? In His life as Father, Son, and Holy Spirit He would in truth be no lonesome, no egotistical God even without man, yes, even without the whole created universe. And He must more than ever be not *for* man; He *could*—one even thinks He *must*—rather be against him. But that is the mystery in which He meets us in the existence of Jesus Christ. He wants in His freedom actually not to be without man but *with* him and in the same freedom not against him but *for* him, and that apart from or even counter to what man deserves. He wants in fact to be man's partner, his almighty and compassionate Saviour. He chooses to give man the benefit of His power, which encompasses not only the high and the distant but also the deep and the near, in order to maintain communion with him in the realm guaranteed by His deity. He determines to love him, to be his God, his Lord, his compassionate Preserver and Saviour to eternal life, and to desire his praise and service.

In this divinely free volition and election, in this sovereign decision (the ancients said, in His decree), God is *human*. His free affirmation of man, His free concern for him, His free substitution for him—this is God's humanity. We recognize it exactly at the point where we also first recognize His deity. Is it not true that in Jesus Christ, as He is attested in the Holy Scripture, genuine deity includes in itself genuine humanity? There is the father who cares for his lost son, the king who does the same for his insolvent debtor, the Samaritan who takes pity on the one who fell among robbers and in his thoroughgoing act of compassion cares for him in a fashion as unexpected as it is liberal. And this is the act of compassion to which all these parables as parables of the Kingdom of heaven refer. The very One who speaks in these parables takes to His heart the weakness and the perversity, the helplessness and the misery, of the human race surrounding Him. He does not despise men, but in an inconceivable manner esteems them highly just as they are, takes them into His heart and sets Himself in their place. He perceives that the superior will of God, to which He wholly subordinates Himself, requires that He sacrifice Himself for the human race, and seeks His honor in doing this. In the mirror of this humanity of Jesus Christ the humanity of God enclosed in His deity reveals itself. Thus God is as He is. Thus He affirms man. Thus He is concerned about him. Thus He stands up for him. The God of Schleiermacher cannot show mercy. The God of Abraham, Isaac, and Jacob can and does. If Jesus Christ is the Word of Truth, the "mirror of the fatherly heart of God," then Nietzsche's statement that man is something that must be overcome is an impudent lie. Then the truth of God is, as Titus 3:4 says, His loving-kindness and nothing else.

REINHOLD NIEBUHR (1892–   )

The Christian View of the Nature of Man: Image of God, Creature, Sinner

The Christian view of man is sharply distinguished from all alternative views by the manner in which it interprets and relates three aspects of human existence to each other: (1) It emphasizes the height of self-transcendence in man's spiritual stature in its doctrine of "image of God." (2) It insists on man's weakness, dependence, and finiteness, on his involvement in the necessities and contingencies of the natural world, without, however, regarding this finiteness as, of itself, a source of evil in man. In its purest form the Christian view of man regards man as a unity of God-likeness and creatureliness in which he remains a creature even in the highest spiritual dimensions of his existence and may reveal elements of the image of God even in the lowliest aspects of his natural life. (3) It affirms that the evil in man is a consequence of his inevitable though not necessary unwillingness to acknowledge his dependence, to accept his finiteness and to admit his insecurity, an unwillingness which involves him in the vicious circle of accentuating the insecurity from which he seeks escape. . . .

Man as Image of God

Implicit in the human situation of freedom and in man's capacity to transcend himself and his world is his inability to construct a world of meaning without finding a source and key to the structure of meaning which transcends the world beyond his own capacity to transcend it. The problem of meaning, which is the basic problem of religion, transcends the ordinary rational problem of tracing the relation of things to each other as the freedom of man's spirit transcends his rational faculties.

This problem is not solved without the introduction of a principle of meaning which transcends the world of meaning to be interpreted. If some vitality of existence, or even some subordinate principle of coherence is used as the principle of meaning, man is involved in idolatry. He lifts some finite and contingent element of existence into the eminence of the divine. He uses something which itself requires explanation as the ultimate principle of coherence and meaning. The most obvious forms of idolatry are those in which the world of meaning is organized around a center of natural or historical vitality, such as the life of a tribe or nation which is patently contingent and not ultimate. More covert forms of idolatry are achieved if a subordinate principle of coherence and meaning is regarded as the ultimate principle. The causal sequences of nature represent one such subordinate principle. If the effort is made to comprehend the meaning of the world through the principle of natural causation alone, the world is conceived in terms of a mechanistic coherence which has no place for the freedom which reveals itself in human consciousness. Rational principles of coherence represent another, somewhat higher, and yet inadequate system of meaning. Every effort to identify meaning with rationality implies the deification of reason. That such an identification represents idolatry and that the laws of reason and logic are incapable of fully comprehending the total meaning of the world, is attested by the fact that life and history are full of contradictions which cannot be resolved in terms of rational principles. Furthermore a mind which transcends itself cannot legitimately make itself the ultimate principle of interpretation by which it explains the relation of mind to the world. The fact of self-transcendence leads inevitably to the search for a God who transcends the world. Augustine accurately describes the logic of this procedure in the words: "I dive on this side and on that as far as I can see and there is no end. . . . I will pass beyond this power of mine which is called memory; yea, I will pass beyond it that I may approach unto Thee."

Though the religious faith through which God is apprehended cannot be in contradiction to reason in the sense that the ultimate principle of meaning cannot be in contradiction to the subordinate principle of meaning which is found in rational coherence, yet, on the other hand, religious faith cannot be simply subordinated to reason or made to stand under its judgment. When this is done the reason which asks the question whether the God of religious faith is plausible has already implied a negative answer in the question because it has made itself God and naturally cannot tolerate another. The usual procedure in purely rational and intellectual judgments upon religion is to find the God of religious faith essentially identical with the god of reason, with the distinction that religious faith is regarded as a somewhat crude form of apprehending what reason apprehends more purely.

The real situation is that man who is made in the image of God is unable, precisely because of those qualities in him which are designated as "image of God," to be satisfied with a god who is made in man's image. By virtue of his capacity for self-transcendence he can look beyond himself sufficiently to know that a projection of himself is not God. This does not mean that he will not commit idolatry and make God in his own image. Man is constantly tempted to the sin of idolatry and constantly succumbs to it because in contemplating the power and dignity of his freedom he forgets the degree of his limitations. Yet the rigorous efforts of mystic religions to escape the sin of idolatry and to overcome the error of defining God in finite and contingent terms attest to a transcendent perspective in the human spirit from which the sin of idolatry is apprehended.

The ability to be conscious of and uneasy about the sin of idolatry, which is revealed in mystic spirituality, does not, of course, solve the problem of man's self-transcendence on the one hand and finiteness on the other. Without the presuppositions of the Christian faith, men run into the Charybdis of life-denial and acosmism in the effort to escape the Scylla of idolatry. Either they make some contingent and relative vitality or coherence into the unconditioned principle of meaning or they negate the whole of temporal and historical existence because it is involved in contingency. . . .

Man as Creature

The Christian view of the goodness of creation is solidly anchored in a very simple word of Scripture: "And God saw every thing that he had made, and behold, it was very good" (Gen. 1:31). The doctrine does not of course depend merely upon the authority of this estimate of creation in Genesis. The whole Biblical interpretation of life and history rests upon the assumption that the created world, the world of finite, dependent and contingent existence, is not evil by reason of its finiteness. . . .

The Biblical view is that the finiteness, dependence and the insufficiency of man's mortal life are facts which belong to God's plan of creation and must be accepted with reverence and humility. In one of the most beautiful Biblical expositions of the glory and majesty of God the brevity of man is presented merely as a contrast to and proof of that Majesty: "All flesh is grass and all the goodliness thereof is as the flower of the field; The grass withereth, the flower fadeth: . . . but the word of our God shall stand forever." Even man's collective and national life, which so frequently offers him the illusion of an immortality and eternity transcending his individual finiteness, is rightly seen to be involved in the same finiteness: "Behold, the nations are as a drop of a bucket, and are counted as the small dust of the balance: . . . all nations before him are as nothing;

and they are counted to him less than nothing" (Is. 40). The fragmentary character of human life is not regarded as evil in Biblical faith because it is seen from the perspective of a center of life and meaning in which each fragment is related to the plan of the whole, to the will of God. The evil arises when the fragment seeks by its own wisdom to comprehend the whole or attempts by its own power to realize it. All Biblical theism contains the suggestion that God's will and wisdom must be able to transcend any human interpretation of its justice and meaning, or it would be less than the center of that inclusive meaning which alone can comprehend the seeming chaos of existence into a total harmony. . . .

It is important to recognize how basic the Christian doctrine of the goodness of creation is for a conception of man in which human finiteness is emphasized but not deprecated. In the Biblical view the contrast between the created world and the Creator, between its dependent and insufficient existence and His freedom and self-sufficiency, is absolute. But this contrast never means that the created world is evil by reason of the particularization and individualization of its various types of existence. It is never a corruption of an original divine unity and eternity, as in Neo-Platonism; nor is it evil because of the desire and pain which characterize all insufficient and dependent life, as in Buddhism.

The whole import of the Christian doctrine of creation for the Christian view of man is really comprehended in the Christian concept of individuality. The individual is conceived of as a creature of infinite possibilities which cannot be fulfilled within terms of this temporal existence. But his salvation never means the complete destruction of his creatureliness and absorption into the divine. On the other hand, though finite individuality is never regarded as of itself evil, its finiteness, including the finiteness of the mind, is never obscured. The self, even in the highest reaches of its self-consciousness, is still the finite self, which must regard the pretensions of universality, to which idealistic philosophies for instance tempt it, as a sin. It is always a self, anxious for its life and its universal perspectives qualified by its "here and now" relation to a particular body. Though it surveys the whole world and is tempted to regard its partial transcendence over its body as proof of its candidature for divinity, it remains in fact a very dependent self. . . .

Man as Sinner

. . . the uniqueness of the Biblical approach to the human problem lies in its subordination of the problem of finiteness to the problem of sin. It is not the contradiction of finiteness and freedom from which Biblical religion seeks emancipation. It seeks redemption from sin; and the sin from which it seeks redemption is occasioned, though not caused, by this contradiction in which man stands. Sin is not caused by the contradiction because, according to Biblical faith, there is no absolute necessity that man should be betrayed into sin by the ambiguity of his position, as standing in and yet above nature. But it cannot be denied that this is the occasion for his sin.

Man is insecure and involved in natural contingency; he seeks to overcome his insecurity by a will-to-power which overreaches the limits of human creatureliness. Man is ignorant and involved in the limitations of a finite mind; but he pretends that he is not limited. He assumes that he can gradually transcend finite limitations until his mind becomes identical with universal mind. All of his intellectual and cultural pursuits, therefore, become infected with the sin of pride. Man's pride and will-to-power disturb the harmony of creation. The Bible defines sin in both religious and moral terms. The religious dimension of sin is man's rebellion against God, his effort to usurp the place of God. The moral and social dimension of sin is injustice. The ego which falsely makes itself the center of existence in its pride and will-to-power inevitably subordinates other life to its will and thus does injustice to other life.

Sometimes man seeks to solve the problem of the contradiction of finiteness and freedom, not by seeking to hide his finiteness and comprehending the world into himself, but by seeking to hide his freedom and by losing himself in some aspect of the world's vitalities. In that case his sin may be defined as sensuality rather than pride. Sensuality is never the mere expression of natural impulse in man. It always betrays some aspect of his abortive effort to solve the problem of finiteness and freedom. Human passions are always characterized by unlimited and demonic potencies of which animal life is innocent. . . .

In short, man, being both free and bound, both limited and limitless, is anxious. Anxiety is the inevitable concomitant of the paradox of freedom and finiteness in which man is involved. Anxiety is the internal precondition of sin. It is the inevitable spiritual state of man, standing in the paradoxical situation of freedom and finiteness. Anxiety is the internal description of the state of temptation. It must not be identified with sin because there is always the ideal possibility that faith would purge anxiety out of the tendency toward sinful self-assertion. The ideal possibility is that faith in the ultimate security of God's love would overcome all immediate insecurities of nature and history. That is why Christian orthodoxy has consistently defined unbelief as the root of sin, or as the sin which precedes pride. . . .

Yet anxiety is not sin. It must be distinguished from sin partly because it is its precondition and not its actuality, and partly because it is the basis of all human creativity as well as the precondition of sin. Man is anxious not only because his life is limited and dependent and yet not so limited that he does not know of his limitations. He is also anxious because he does not know the limits of his possibilities. He can do nothing and regard it perfectly done, because higher possibilities are revealed in each achievement. All human actions stand under seemingly limitless possibilities. There are, of course, limits but it is difficult to gauge them from any immediate perspective. There is therefore no limit of achievement in any sphere of activity in which human history can rest with equanimity.

It is not possible to make a simple separation between the creative and destructive elements in anxiety; and for that reason it is not possible to purge moral achievement of sin as easily as moralists imagine. The same action may reveal a creative effort to transcend natural limitations, and a sinful effort to give unconditioned value to contingent and limited factors in human existence. Man may, in the same moment, be anxious because he has not become what he ought to be; and also anxious lest he cease to be at all. . . .

Anxiety about perfection and about insecurity are thus inexorably bound together in human actions, and the errors which are made in the search for perfection are never due merely to the ignorance of not knowing the limits of conditioned values. They always exhibit some tendency of the agent to hide his own limits, which he knows only too well. Obviously the basic source of temptation is, therefore, not the inertia of "matter" or "nature" against the larger and more inclusive ends which reason envisages. It resides in the inclination of man, either to deny the contingent character of his existence (in pride and self-love) or to escape from his freedom (in sensuality). Sensuality represents an effort to escape from the freedom and infinite possibilities of spirit by becoming lost in the detailed processes, activities and interests of existence, an effort which results inevitably in unlimited devotion to limited values. Sensuality is man "turning inordinately to mutable goods" (Aquinas).

Anxiety, as a permanent concomitant of freedom, is thus both the source of creativity and a temptation to sin. It is the condition of the sailor, climbing the mast (to use a simile), with the abyss of the waves beneath him and the "crow's nest" above him. He is anxious about both the end toward which he strives and the abyss of nothingness into which he may fall. The ambition of man to be something is always partly prompted by the fear of meaninglessness which threatens him by reason of the contingent character of his existence. His creativity is therefore always corrupted by some effort to overcome contingency by raising precisely what is contingent to absolute and unlimited dimensions. This effort, though universal, cannot be regarded as normative. It is always destructive. Yet obviously the destructive aspect of anxiety is so intimately involved in the creative aspects that there is no possibility of making a simple separation between them. The two are inextricably bound together by reason of man being anxious both to realize his unlimited possibilities and to overcome and to hide the dependent and contingent character of his existence.

When anxiety has conceived it brings forth both pride and sensuality. Man falls into pride, when he seeks to raise his contingent existence to unconditioned significance; he falls into sensuality when he seeks to escape from his unlimited possibilities of freedom, from the perils and responsibilities of self-determination, by immersing himself into a "mutable good," by losing himself in some natural vitality.

RUDOLF BULTMANN (1884–   )

The Christian Message and the Modern World View

An objection often heard against the attempt to demythologize is that it takes the modern world-view as the criterion of the interpretation of the Scripture and the Christian message and that Scripture and Christian message are not allowed to say anything that is in contradiction with the modern world-view.

It is, of course, true that demythologizing takes the modern world-view as a criterion. To demythologize is to reject not Scripture or the Christian message as a whole, but the world-view of Scripture, which is the world-view of a past epoch, which all too often is retained in Christian dogmatics and in the preaching of the Church. To demythologize is to deny that the message of Scripture and of the Church is bound to an ancient world-view which is obsolete.

The attempt to demythologize begins with this important insight: Christian preaching, in so far as it is preaching of the Word of God by God's command and in His name, does not offer a doctrine which can be accepted either by reason or by a *sacrificium intellectus*. Christian preaching is kerygma, that is, a proclamation addressed not to the theoretical reason, but to the hearer as a self. In this manner Paul commends himself to every man's conscience in the sight of God (II Cor. 4:2). Demythologizing will make clear this function of preaching as a personal message, and in doing so it will eliminate a false stumbling-block and bring into sharp focus the real stumbling-block, the word of the cross.

For the world-view of the Scripture is mythological and is therefore unacceptable to modern man whose thinking has been shaped by science and is therefore no longer mythological. Modern man always makes use of technical means which are the result of science. In case of illness modern man has recourse to physicians, to medical science. In case of economic and political affairs, he makes use of the results of psychological, social, economic and political sciences, and so on. Nobody reckons with direct intervention by transcendent powers.

Of course, there are today some survivals and revivals of primitive thinking and superstition. But the preaching of the Church would make a disastrous mistake if it looked to such revivals and conformed to them. The nature of man is to be seen in modern literature, as for instance, in the novels of Thomas Mann, Ernst Jünger, Thornton Wilder, Ernest Hemingway, William Faulkner, Graham Greene and Albert Camus, or in the plays of Jean-Paul Sartre, Jean Anouilh, Jean Giraudoux, etc. Or let us think simply of the newspapers. Have you read anywhere in them that political or social or economic events are performed by supernatural powers such as God, angels or demons? Such events are always ascribed to natural powers, or to good or bad will on the part of men, or to human wisdom or stupidity.

The science of today is no longer the same as it was in the nineteenth century, and to be sure, all the results of science are relative, and no world-view of yesterday or today or tomorrow is definitive. The main point, however, is not the concrete results of scientific research and the contents of a world-view, but the method of thinking from which world-views follow. For example, it makes no difference in principle whether the earth rotates round the sun or the sun rotates round the earth, but it does make a decisive difference that modern man understands the motion of the universe as a motion which obeys a cosmic law, a law of nature which human reason can discover. Therefore, modern man acknowledges as reality only such phenomena or events as are comprehensible within the framework of the rational order of the universe. He does not acknowledge miracles because they do not fit into this lawful order. When a strange or marvelous accident occurs, he does not rest until he has found a rational cause.

The contrast between the ancient world-view of the Bible and the modern world-view is the contrast between two ways of thinking, the mythological and the scientific. The method of scientific thinking and inquiry is in principle the same today as it was at the beginning of methodical and critical science in ancient Greece. It begins with the question about the origin from which the world is conceivable as unity, as systematic order and harmony. It begins therefore also with the attempt to give reasonable proofs for every statement. These principles are the same in modern science, and it does not matter that the results of scientific research are changing over and over again, since the change itself results from the permanent principles.

Certainly it is a philosophical problem whether the scientific world-view can perceive the whole reality of the world and of human life. There are reasons for doubting whether it can do so. . . . But for present purposes it is enough to say that the thinking of modern men is really shaped by the scientific world-view, and that modern men need it for their daily lives.

Therefore, it is mere wishful thinking to suppose that the ancient world-view of the Bible can be renewed. It is the radical abandonment and the conscious critique of the mythological world-view of the Bible which brings the real stumbling-block into sharp focus. This stumbling-block is that the Word of God calls man out of all man-made security. The scientific world-view engenders a great temptation, namely, that man strive for mastery over the world and over his own life. He knows the laws of nature and can use the powers of nature according to his plans and desires. He discovers more and more accurately the laws of social and of economic life, and thus organizes the life of the community more and more effectively. . . .

Thus modern man is in danger of forgetting two things: first, that his plans and undertakings should be guided not by his own desires for happiness and security, usefulness and profit, but rather by obedient response to the challenge of goodness, truth and love, by obedience to the commandment of God which man forgets in his selfishness and presumption; and secondly, that it is an illusion to suppose that real security can be gained by men organizing their own personal and community life. There are encounters and destinies which man cannot master. He cannot secure endurance for his works. His life is fleeting and its end is death. History goes on and pulls down all the towers of Babel again and again. There is no real, definitive security, and it is precisely this illusion to which men are prone to succumb in their yearning for security.

What is the underlying reason for this yearning? It is the sorrow, the secret anxiety which moves in the depths of the soul at the very moment when man thinks that he must obtain security for himself.

It is the Word of God which calls man away from his selfishness and from the illusory security which he has built up for himself. It calls him to God, who is beyond the world and beyond scientific thinking. At the same time, it calls man to his true self. For the self of man, his inner life, his personal existence is also beyond the visible world and beyond rational thinking. The Word of God addresses man in his personal existence and thereby it gives him freedom from the world and from the sorrow and anxiety which overwhelm him when he forgets the beyond. By means of science men try to take possession of the world, but in fact the world gets possession of men. We can see in our times to what degree men are dependent on technology, and to what degree technology brings with it terrible consequences. To believe in the Word of God means to abandon all merely human security and thus to overcome the despair which arises from the attempt to find security, an attempt which is always vain.

Faith in this sense is both the demand of and the gift offered by preaching. Faith is the answer to the message. Faith is the abandonment of man's own security and the readiness to find security only in the unseen beyond, in God. This means that faith is security where no security can be seen; it is, as Luther said, the readiness to enter confidently into the darkness of the future. Faith in God who has power over time and eternity, and who calls me and who has acted and now is acting on me—this faith can become real only in its "nevertheless" against the world. For in the world nothing of God and of his action is visible or can be visible to men who seek security in the world. We may say that the Word of God addresses man in his insecurity and calls him into freedom, for man loses his freedom in his very yearning for security. This formulation may sound paradoxical, but it becomes clear when we consider the meaning of freedom.

Genuine freedom is not subjective arbitrariness. It is freedom in obedience. The freedom of subjective arbitrariness is a delusion, for it delivers man up to his drives, to do in any moment what lust and passion dictate. This hollow freedom is in reality dependence on the lust and passion of the moment. Genuine freedom is freedom from the motivation of the moment; it is freedom which withstands the clamor and pressure of momentary motivations. It is possible only when conduct is determined by a motive which transcends the present moment, that is, by law. Freedom is obedience to a law of which the validity is recognized and accepted, which man recognizes as the law of his own being. This can only be a law which has its origin and reason in the beyond. We may call it the law of spirit or, in Christian language, the law of God.

This idea of freedom, constituted by law, this free obedience or obedient freedom, was well known both to ancient Greek philosophy and to Christianity. In modern times, however, this conception vanished and was replaced by the illusory idea of freedom as subjective arbitrariness which does not acknowledge a norm, a law from beyond. There ensues a relativism which does not acknowledge absolute ethical demands and absolute truths. The end of this development is nihilism.

There are several reasons for this development. The first is the development of science and technology which procures the illusion that man is master over the world and his life. Then there is the historical relativism which grew out of the Romantic Movement. It contends that our reason does not perceive eternal or absolute truths but is subject to historical development, that every truth has only a relative validity for a given time, race or culture, and thus, in the end, the search for truth becomes meaningless.

There is still another reason for the change from genuine freedom to the freedom of subjectivism. This deepest reason is anxiety in the face of real freedom, the yearning for security. Genuine freedom, it is true, is freedom within laws, but it is not freedom in security, because it is always freedom gained in responsibility and decision, and therefore it is freedom in insecurity. Freedom of subjective arbitrariness believes itself to be secure precisely because it is not responsible to a transcendent power, because it believes itself to be master of the world through science and technology. Subjective freedom grows out of the desire for security; it is in fact anxiety in the face of genuine freedom.

Now it is the Word of God which calls man into genuine freedom, into free obedience, and the task of demythologizing has no other purpose but to make clear the call of the Word of God. It will interpret the Scripture, asking for the deeper meaning of mythological conceptions and freeing the Word of God from a bygone world-view.

Thus it follows that the objection is raised by a mistake, namely, the objection that demythologizing means rationalizing the Christian message, that demythologizing dissolves the message into a product of human rational thinking, and that the mystery of God is destroyed by demythologizing. Not at all! On the contrary, demythologizing makes clear the true meaning of God's mystery. The incomprehensibility of God lies not in the sphere of theoretical thought but in the sphere of personal existence. Not what God is in Himself, but how he acts with men, is the mystery in which faith is interested. This is a mystery not to theoretical thought, but to the natural wills and desires of men.

God's Word is not a mystery to my understanding. On the contrary, I cannot truly believe in the Word without understanding it. But to understand does not mean to explain rationally. I can understand, for example, what friendship, love and faithfulness mean, and precisely by genuine understanding I know that the friendship, love and faithfulness which I personally enjoy are a mystery which I cannot but thankfully receive. For I perceive them neither by my rational thinking, nor by psychological, nor by anthropological analysis but only in open readiness to personal encounters. In this readiness I can understand them in a certain way already before I am given them because my personal existence needs them. Then I understand them in searching for them, in asking for them. Nevertheless, the fact itself that my yearning is fulfilled, that a friend comes to me, remains a mystery.

In the same manner I can understand what God's grace means, asking for it as long as it does not come to me, accepting it thankfully when it does come to me. The fact that it comes to me, that the gracious God is my God, remains forever a mystery, not because God performs in an irrational manner something that interrupts the natural course of events, but because it is inconceivable that He should encounter me in His Word as the gracious God.

PAUL TILLICH (1886–1965)

You Are Accepted

Moreover the law entered, that the offence might abound. But where sin abounded, grace did much more abound. (Romans 5:20)

These words of Paul summarize his apostolic experience, his religious message as a whole, and the Christian understanding of life. To discuss these words, or to make them the text of even several sermons, has always seemed impossible to me. I have never dared to use them before. But something has driven me to consider them during the past few months, a desire to give witness to the two facts which appeared to me, in hours of retrospection, as the all-determining facts of our life: the abounding of sin and the greater abounding of grace.

There are few words more strange to most of us than "sin" and "grace." They are strange, just because they are so well-known. During the centuries they have received distorting connotations, and have lost so much of their genuine power that we must seriously ask ourselves whether we should use them at all, or whether we should discard them as useless tools. But there is a mysterious fact about the great words of our religious tradition: they cannot be replaced. All attempts to make substitutions, including those I have tried myself, have failed to convey the reality that was to be expressed; they have led to shallow and impotent talk. There are no substitutes for words like "sin" and "grace." But there *is* a way of rediscovering their meaning, the same way that leads us down into the depth of our human existence. In that depth these words were conceived; and *there* they gained power for all ages; *there* they must be found again by each generation, and by each of us for himself. Let us therefore try to penetrate the deeper levels of our life, in order to see whether we can discover in them the realities of which our text speaks.

Have the men of our time still a feeling of the meaning of sin? Do they, and do we, still realize that sin does *not* mean an immoral act, that "sin" should never be used in the plural, and that not our sins, but rather our *sin* is the great, all-pervading problem of our life? Do we still know that it is arrogant and erroneous to divide men by calling some "sinners" and others "righteous"? For by way of such a division, we can usually discover that we ourselves do not *quite* belong to the "sinners," since we have avoided heavy sins, have made some progress in the control of this or that sin, and have been even humble enough not to call ourselves "righteous." Are we still able to realize that this kind of thinking and feeling about sin is far removed from what the great religious tradition, both within and outside the Bible, has meant when it speaks of sin?

I should like to suggest another word to you, not as a substitute for the word "sin," but as a useful clue in the interpretation of the word "sin": "separation." Separation is an aspect of the experience of everyone. Perhaps the word "sin" has the same root as the word "asunder." In any case, *sin is separation*. To be in the state of sin is to be in the state of separation. And separation is threefold: there is separation among individual lives, separation of a man from himself, and separation of all men from the Ground of Being. This threefold separation constitutes the state of everything that exists; it is a universal fact; it is the fate of every life. And it is our human fate in a very special sense. For *we* as men know that we are separated. We not only suffer with all other creatures because of the self-destructive consequences of our separation, but also know *why* we suffer. We know that we are estranged from something to which we really belong, and with which we *should* be united. We know that the fate of separation is not merely a natural event like a flash of sudden lightning, but that it is an experience in which we actively participate, in which our whole personality is involved, and that, as fate, it is also *guilt*. Separation which is fate *and* guilt constitutes the meaning of the word "sin." It is *this* which is the state of our entire existence, from its very beginning to its very end. Such separation is prepared in the mother's womb, and before that time, in every preceding generation. It is manifest in the special actions of our conscious life. It reaches beyond our graves into all the succeeding generations. It is our existence itself. *Existence is separation!* Before sin is an act, it is a state.

We can say the same things about grace. For sin and grace are bound to each other. We do not even have a knowledge of sin unless we have already experienced the unity of life, which is grace. And conversely, we could not grasp the meaning of grace without having experienced the separation of life, which is sin. Grace is just as difficult to describe as sin. For some people, grace is the willingness of a divine king and father to forgive over and again the foolishness and weakness of his subjects and children. We must reject such a concept of grace; for it is a merely childish destruction of a human dignity. For others, grace is a magic power in the dark places of the soul, but a power without any significance for practical life, a quickly vanishing and useless idea. For others, grace is the benevolence that we may find beside the cruelty and destructiveness in life. But then, it does not matter whether we say "life goes on," or whether we say "there is grace in life"; if grace means no more than this, the word should, and will disappear. For other people, grace indicates the gifts that one has received from nature or society, and the power to do good things with the help of those gifts. But grace is more than gifts. In grace something is overcome; grace occurs "in spite of" something; grace occurs in spite of separation and estrangement. Grace is the *re*union of life with life, the *re*conciliation of the self with itself. Grace is the acceptance of that which is rejected. Grace transforms fate into a meaningful destiny; it changes guilt into confidence and courage. There is something triumphant in the word "grace": in spite of the abounding of sin grace abounds much more.

And now let us look down into ourselves to discover there the struggle between separation and reunion, between sin and grace, in our relation to others, in our relation to ourselves, and in our relation to the Ground and aim of our being. If our souls respond to the description that I intend to give, words like "sin" and "separation," "grace" and "reunion," may have a new meaning for us. But the words themselves are not important. It is the response of the deepest levels of our being that is important. If such a response were to occur among us this moment, we could say that we have known grace.

Who has not, at some time, been lonely in the midst of a social event? The feeling of our separation from the rest of life is most acute when we are surrounded by it in noise and talk. We realize then much more than in moments of solitude how strange we are to each other, how estranged life is from life. Each one of us draws back into himself. We cannot penetrate the hidden centre of another individual; nor can that individual pass beyond the shroud that covers our own being. Even the greatest love cannot break through the walls of the self. Who has not experienced that disillusionment of all great love? If one were to hurl away his self in complete self-surrender, he would become a nothing, without form or strength, a self without a self, merely an object of contempt and abuse. Our generation knows more than the generation of our fathers about the hidden hostility in the ground of our souls. Today we know much about the profusive aggressiveness in every being. Today we can confirm what Immanuel Kant, the prophet of human reason and dignity, was honest enough to say: there is something in the misfortune of our best friends which does not displease us. Who amongst us is dishonest enough to deny that this is true also of him? Are we not almost always ready to abuse everybody and everything, although often in a very refined way, for the pleasure of self-elevation, for an occasion for boasting, for a moment of lust? To know that we are ready is to know the meaning of the separation of life from life, and of "sin abounding."

The most irrevocable expression of the separation of life from life today is the attitude of social groups within nations towards each other, and the attitude of nations themselves towards other nations. The walls of distance, in time and space, have been removed by technical progress; but the walls of estrangement between heart and heart have been incredibly strengthened. The madness of the German Nazis and the cruelty of the lynching mobs in the South provide too easy an excuse for us to turn our thoughts from our own selves. But let us just consider ourselves and what we feel, when we read, this morning and tonight, that in some sections of Europe all children under the age of three are sick and dying, or that in some sections of Asia millions without homes are freezing and starving to death. The strangeness of life to life is evident in the strange fact that we can know all this, and yet can live today, this morning, tonight, as though we were completely ignorant. And I refer to the most sensitive people amongst us. In both mankind and nature, life is separated from life. Estrangement prevails among all things that live. Sin abounds.

It is important to remember that we are not merely separated from each other. For we are also separated from ourselves. *Man Against Himself* is not merely the title of a book, but rather also indicates the rediscovery of an age-old insight. Man is split within himself. Life moves against itself through aggression, hate, and despair. We are wont to condemn self-love; but what we really mean to condemn is contrary to self-love. It is that mixture of selfishness and self-hate that permanently pursues us, that prevents us from loving others, and that prohibits us from losing ourselves in the love with which we are loved eternally. He who is able to love himself is able to love others also; he who has learned to overcome self-contempt has overcome his contempt for others. But the depth of our separation lies in just the fact that we are not capable of a great and merciful divine love towards ourselves. On the contrary, in each of us there is an instinct of self-destruction, which is as strong as our instinct of self-preservation. In our tendency to abuse and destroy others, there is an open or hidden tendency to abuse and to destroy ourselves. Cruelty towards others is always also cruelty towards ourselves. Nothing is more obvious than the split in both our unconscious life and conscious personality. Without the help of modern psychology, Paul expressed the fact in his famous words, "For I do not do the good I desire, but rather the evil that I do not desire." And then he continued in words that might well be the motto of all depth psychology: "Now if I should do what I do not wish to do, it is not I that do it, but rather sin which dwells within me." The apostle sensed a split between his conscious will and his real will, between himself and something strange within and alien to him. He was estranged from himself; and that estrangement he called "sin." He also called it a strange "law in his limbs," an irresistible compulsion. How often we commit certain acts in perfect consciousness, yet with the shocking sense that we are being controlled by an alien power! That is the experience of the separation of ourselves from ourselves, which is to say "sin," whether or not we like to use that word.

Thus, the state of our whole life is estrangement from others and ourselves, because we are estranged from the Ground of our being, because we are estranged from the origin and aim of our life. And we do not know where we have come from, or where we are going. We are separated from the mystery, the depth, and the greatness of our existence. We hear the voice of that depth; but our ears are closed. We feel that something radical, total, and unconditioned is demanded of us; but we rebel against it, try to escape its urgency, and will not accept its promise.

We cannot escape, however. If that something is the Ground of our being, we are bound to it for all eternity, just as we are bound to ourselves and to all other life. We always remain in the power of that from which we are estranged. That fact brings us to the ultimate depth of sin; separated and yet bound, estranged and yet belonging, destroyed and yet preserved, the state which is called despair. Despair means that there is no escape. Despair is "the sickness unto death." But the terrible thing about the sickness of despair is that we cannot be released, not even through open or hidden suicide. For we all know that we are bound eternally and inescapably to the Ground of our being. The abyss of separation is not always visible. But it has become more visible to our generation than to the preceding generations, because of our feeling of meaninglessness, emptiness, doubt and cynicism—all expressions of despair, of our separation from the roots and the meaning of our life. Sin in its most profound sense, sin as despair, abounds amongst us.

"Where sin abounded, grace did more abound," says Paul in the same letter in which he describes the unimaginable power of separation and self-destruction within society and the individual soul. He does not say these words because sentimental interests demand a happy ending for everything tragic. He says them because they describe the most overwhelming and determining experience of his life. In the picture of Jesus as the Christ, which appeared to him at the moment of his greatest separation from other men, from himself and God, he found himself accepted in spite of his being rejected. And when he found that he was accepted, he was able to accept himself and to be reconciled to others. The moment in which grace struck him and overwhelmed him, he was reunited with that to which he belonged, and from which he was estranged in utter strangeness. Do we know what it means to be struck by grace? It does *not* mean that we suddenly believe that God exists, or that Jesus is the Saviour, or that the Bible contains the truth. To believe that something *is,* is almost contrary to the meaning of grace. Furthermore, grace does not mean simply that we are making progress in our moral self-control, in our fight against special faults, and in our relationships to men and to society. Moral progress may be a fruit of grace; but it is not grace itself, and it can even prevent us from receiving grace. For there is too often a graceless acceptance of Christian doctrines and a graceless battle against the structures of evil in our personalities. Such a graceless relation to God may lead us by necessity either to arrogance or to despair. It would be better to refuse God and the Christ and the Bible than to accept Them without grace. For if we accept without grace, we do so in the state of separation, and can only succeed in deepening the situation. We cannot transform our lives, unless we allow them to be transformed by that stroke of grace. It happens; or it does not happen. And certainly it does *not* happen if we try to force it upon ourselves, just as it shall not happen so long as we think, in our self-complacency, that we have no need of it. Grace strikes us when we are in great pain and restlessness. It strikes us when we walk through the dark valley of a meaningless and empty life. It strikes us when we feel that our separation is deeper than usual, because we have violated another life, a life which we loved, or from which we were estranged. It strikes us when our disgust for our own being, our indifference, our weakness, our hostility, and our lack of direction and composure have become intolerable to us. It strikes us when, year after year, the longed-for perfection of life does not appear, when the old compulsions reign within us as they have for decades, when despair destroys all joy and courage. Sometimes at that moment a wave of light breaks into our darkness, and it is as though a voice were saying: "You are accepted. *You are accepted,* accepted by that which is greater than you, and the name of which you do not know. Do not ask for the name now; perhaps you will find it later. Do not try to do anything now; perhaps later you will do much. Do not seek for anything; do not perform anything; do not intend anything. *Simply accept the fact that you are accepted!*" If that happens to us, we experience grace. After such an experience we may not be better than before, and we may not believe more than before. But everything is transformed. In that moment, grace conquers sin, and reconciliation bridges the gulf of estrangement. And nothing is demanded of this experience, no religious or moral or intellectual presupposition, nothing but *acceptance.*

In the light of this grace we perceive the power of grace in our relation to others and to ourselves. We experience the grace of being able to look frankly into the eyes of another, the miraculous grace of reunion of life with life. We experience the grace of understanding each other's words. We understand not merely the literal meaning of the words, but also that which lies behind them, even when they are harsh or angry. For even then there is a longing to break through the walls of separation. We experience the grace of being able to accept the life of another, even if it be hostile and harmful to us, for through grace, we know that it belongs to the same Ground to which we belong, and by which we have been accepted. We experience the grace which is able to overcome the tragic separation of the sexes, of the generations, of the nations, of the races, and even the utter strangeness between man and nature. Sometimes grace appears in all these separations to reunite us with those to whom we belong. For life belongs to life.

And in the light of this grace we perceive the power of grace in our relation to ourselves. We experience moments in which we accept ourselves, because we feel that we have been accepted by that which is greater than we. If only more such moments were given to us! For it is such moments that make us love our life, that make us accept ourselves, not in our goodness and self-complacency, but in our certainty of the eternal meaning of our life. We cannot force ourselves to accept ourselves. We cannot compel anyone to accept himself. But sometimes it happens that we receive the power to say "yes" to ourselves, that peace enters into us and makes us whole, that self-hate and self-contempt disappear, and that our self is reunited with itself. Then we can say that grace has come upon us.

"Sin" and "grace" are strange words; but they are not strange things. We find them whenever we look into ourselves with searching eyes and longing hearts. They determine our life. They abound within us and in all of life. May grace more abound within us!

DIETRICH BONHOEFFER (1906–1945)

Contemporary Christianity

The Problem

The thing that keeps coming back to me is, what *is* Christianity, and indeed what *is* Christ, for us today? The time when men could be told everything by means of words, whether theological or simply pious, is over, and so is the time of inwardness and conscience, which is to say the time of religion as such. We are proceeding towards a time of no religion at all: men as they are now simply cannot be religious any more. Even those who honestly describe themselves as "religious" do not in the least act up to it, and so when they say "religious" they evidently mean something quite different. Our whole nineteen-hundred-year-old Christian preaching and theology rests upon the "religious premise" of man. What we call Christianity has always been a pattern—perhaps a true pattern—of religion. But if one day it becomes apparent that this *a priori* "premise" simply does not exist, but was an historical and temporary form of human self-expression, i.e. if we reach the stage of being radically without religion—and I think this is more or less the case already, else how is it, for instance, that this war, unlike any of those before it, is not calling forth any "religious" reaction?—what does that mean for "Christianity"?

It means that the linchpin is removed from the whole structure of our Christianity to date, and the only people left for us to light on in the way of "religion" are a few "last survivals of the age of chivalry," or else one or two who are intellectually dishonest. Would they be the chosen few? Is it on this dubious group and none other that we are to pounce, in fervor, pique, or indignation, in order to sell them the goods we have to offer? Are we to fall upon one or two unhappy people in their weakest moment and force upon them a sort of religious coercion?

If we do not want to do this, if we had finally to put down the western pattern of Christianity as a mere preliminary stage to doing without religion altogether, what situation would result for us, for the Church? How can Christ become the Lord even of those with no religion? If religion is no more than the garment of Christianity—and even that garment has had very different aspects at different periods—then what is a religionless Christianity? . . .

The questions needing answers would surely be: What is the significance of a Church (church, parish, preaching, Christian life) in a religionless world? How do we speak of God without religion, i.e. without the temporally-influenced presuppositions of metaphysics, inwardness, and so on? How do we speak (but perhaps we are no longer capable of speaking of such things as we used to) in secular fashion of God? In what way are we in a religionless and secular sense Christians, in what way are we the *Ekklesia,* "those who are called forth," not conceiving of ourselves religiously as specially favored, but as wholly belonging to the world? Then Christ is no longer an object of religion, but something quite different, indeed and in truth the Lord of the world. Yet what does that signify? What is the place of worship and prayer in an entire absence of religion? Does the secret discipline, or, as the case may be, the distinction (which you have met with me before) between penultimate and ultimate, at this point acquire fresh importance? . . .

Religious people speak of God when human perception is (often just from laziness) at an end, or human resources fail: it is really always the *Deus ex machina* they call to their aid, either for the so-called solving of insoluble problems or as support in human failure—always, that is to say, helping out human weakness or on the borders of human existence. Of necessity that can only go on until men can, by their own strength, push those borders a little further, so that God becomes superfluous as a *Deus ex machina.* I have come to be doubtful even about talking of "borders of human existence." Is even death today, since men are scarcely afraid of it any more, and sin, which they scarcely understand any more, still a genuine borderline? It always seems to me that in talking thus we are only seeking frantically to make room for God. . . .

The movement beginning about the thirteenth century (I am not going to get involved in any arguments about the exact date) towards the autonomy of man (under which head I place the discovery of the laws by which the world lives and manages in science, social and political affairs, art, ethics and religion) has in our time reached a certain completion. Man has learned to cope with all questions of importance without recourse to God as a working hypothesis. In questions concerning science, art, and even ethics, this has become an understood thing which one scarcely dares to tilt at any more. But for the last hundred years or so it has been increasingly true of religious questions also: it is becoming evident that everything gets along without "God," and just as well as before. As in the scientific field, so in human affairs generally, what we call "God" is being more and more edged out of life, losing more and more ground.

Catholic and Protestant historians are agreed that it is in this development that the great defection from God, from Christ, is to be discerned, and the more they bring in and make use of God and Christ in opposition to this trend, the more the trend itself considers itself to be anti-Christian. The world which has attained to a realization of itself and of the laws which govern its existence is so sure of itself that we become frightened. False starts and failures do not make the world deviate from the path and development it is following; they are accepted with fortitude and detachment as part of the bargain, and even an event like the present war is no exception. Christian apologetic has taken the most varying forms of opposition to this self-assurance. Efforts are made to prove to a world thus come of age that it cannot live without the tutelage of "God." Even though there has been surrender on all secular problems, there still remain the so-called ultimate questions—death, guilt—on which only "God" can furnish an answer, and which are the reason why God and the Church and the pastor are needed. Thus we live, to some extent, by these ultimate questions of humanity. But what if one day they no longer exist as such, if they too can be answered without "God"? . . .

The attack by Christian apologetic upon the adulthood of the world I consider to be in the first place pointless, in the second ignoble, and in the third un-Christian. Pointless, because it looks to me like an attempt to put a grown-up man back into adolescence, i.e. to make him dependent on things on which he is not in fact dependent any more, thrusting him back into the midst of problems which are in fact not problems for him any more. Ignoble, because this amounts to an effort to exploit the weakness of man for purposes alien to him and not freely subscribed to by him. Un-Christian, because for Christ himself is being substituted one particular stage in the religiousness of man, i.e. a human law. . . .

The Answer

. . . how wrong it is to use God as a stop-gap for the incompleteness of our knowledge. For the frontiers of knowledge are inevitably being pushed back further and further, which means that you only think of God as a stop-gap. He also is being pushed back further and further, and is in more or less continuous retreat. We should find God in what we do know, not in what we don't; not in outstanding problems, but in those we have already solved. This is true not only for the relation between Christianity and science, but also for wider human problems such as guilt, suffering and death. It is possible nowadays to find answers to these problems which leave God right out of the picture. It just isn't true to say that Christianity alone has the answers. In fact the Christian answers are no more conclusive or compelling than any of the others. Once more, God cannot be used as a stop-gap. We must not wait until we are at the end of our tether: he must be found at the center of life: in life, and not only in death; in health and vigor, and not only in suffering; in activity, and not only in sin. The ground for this lies in the revelation of God in Christ. Christ is the center of life, and in no sense did he come to answer our unsolved problems. From the center of life certain questions are seen to be wholly irrelevant, and so are the answers commonly given to them. . . .

Unlike the other Oriental religions the faith of the Old Testament is not a religion of salvation. Christianity, it is true, has always been regarded as a religion of salvation. But isn't this a cardinal error, which divorces Christ from the Old Testament and interprets him in the light of the myths of salvation? Of course it could be urged that under Egyptian and later, Babylonian influence, the idea of salvation became just as prominent in the Old Testament—e.g. Deutero-Isaiah. The answer is, the Old Testament speaks of *historical* redemption, i.e. redemption on this side of death, whereas the myths of salvation are concerned to offer men deliverance from death. Israel is redeemed out of Egypt in order to live before God on earth. The salvation myths deny history in the interests of an eternity after death. Sheol and Hades are no metaphysical theories, but images which imply that the past, while it still exists, has only a shadowy existence in the present. It is said that the distinctive feature of Christianity is its proclamation of the resurrection hope, and that this means the establishment of a genuine religion of salvation, in the sense of release from this world. The emphasis falls upon the far side of the boundary drawn by death. But this seems to me to be just the mistake and the danger. Salvation means salvation from cares and need, from fears and longing, from sin and death into a better world beyond the grave. But is this really the distinctive feature of Christianity as proclaimed in the Gospels and St. Paul? I am sure it is not. The difference between the Christian hope of resurrection and a mythological hope is that the Christian hope sends a man back to his life on earth in a wholly new way which is even more sharply defined than it is in the Old Testament.

The Christian, unlike the devotees of the salvation myths, does not need a last refuge in the eternal from earthly tasks and difficulties. But like Christ himself ("My God, my God, why hast thou forsaken me?") he must drink the earthly cup to the lees, and only in his doing that is the crucified and risen Lord with him, and he crucified and risen with Christ. This world must not be prematurely written off. In this the Old and New Testaments are at one. Myths of salvation arise from human experiences of the boundary situation. Christ takes hold of a man in the center of his life. . . .

And the only way to be honest is to recognize that we have to live in the world *etsi deus non daretur*. And this is just what we do see—before God! So our coming of age forces us to a true recognition of our situation *vis-à-vis* God. God is teaching us that we must live as men who can get along very well without him. The God who is with us is the God who forsakes us (Mark 15.34). The God who makes us live in this world without using him as a working hypothesis is the God before whom we are ever standing. Before God and with him we live without God. God allows himself to be edged out of the world and on to the cross. God is weak and powerless in the world, and that is exactly the way, the only way, in which he can be with us and help us. Matthew 8.17 makes it crystal clear that it is not by his omnipotence that Christ helps us, but by his weakness and suffering.

This is the decisive difference between Christianity and all religions. Man's religiosity makes him look in his distress to the power of God in the world; he uses God as a *Deus ex machina*. The Bible, however, directs him to the powerlessness and suffering of God; only a suffering God can help. To this extent we may say that the process we have described by which the world came of age was an abandonment of a false conception of God, and a clearing of the decks for the God of the Bible, who conquers power and space in the world by his weakness. This must be the starting point for our "worldly" interpretation.

JOHN ROBINSON (1919–   )

Can a Truly Contemporary Person Not Be an Atheist?

In fact I want to treat the question of atheism as a very serious one for those of us who would call ourselves Christians. So I have deliberately posed it, for myself as well as for you, in the form: "Can a truly contemporary person *not* be an atheist?" For I believe there is an important sense in which a person who is fully a man of our times *must*—or, at any rate, *may*—be an atheist before he can be a Christian. That is to say, there is so much in the atheist's case which is true that for many people today the only Christian faith which can be valid *for them* is one that takes over *post mortem dei*, after the death of God as "God" has traditionally been understood. I put this strongly—and can afford to put it strongly—as I shall insist equally strongly on the faith. But it is a faith which I suspect for increasing numbers of our contemporaries will only be possible through, and out the other side of, the atheist critique. The Christian should therefore take atheism seriously, not only so that he may be able to "answer" it, but so that he himself may still be able to be a believer in the mid-twentieth century.

With this in mind, I would ask you to expose yourselves to the three thrusts of modern atheism. These are not so much three types of atheism —each is present, in varying degree, in any representative type—so much as three motives which have impelled men, particularly over the past hundred years, to question the God of their upbringing and ours. They may be represented by three summary statements: (1) God is intellectually superfluous. (2) God is emotionally dispensable. (3) God is morally intolerable. Let us consider each of them in turn.

1. *God is intellectually superfluous.* "I have no need of that hypothesis": so Laplace, the great astronomer, replied to Napoleon, when asked where God fitted into his system. Within the terms of an astronomical system, he was clearly correct. To bring in God to fill the gaps in our science

or to deal with life at the point at which things get beyond human explanation or control is intellectual laziness or practical superstition. And yet, ever since the scientific and technological revolution which created our modern world, the defense of Christianity has in fact been bound up with staving off the advance of secularization, whose effect is precisely to close the gaps in the circle of explanation and control. . . .

God is an "x" in the equation whom we cannot get on without, a cause, controller or designer whom we are bound to posit or allow room for— this hypothesis seems to men today more and more superfluous. There is nothing that *disproves* it. It is simply, in the words of Anthony Flew, the linguistic philosopher, being "killed by inches"; it is dying "the death of a thousand qualifications". . . .

And what is true at the level of explanation is equally true at the level of control. Neither to account for sickness nor to deal with it does it occur to men today to bring in "God." Or if it does occur to them, it is when they have reached the end of their tether and "turn to prayer." But this simply confirms the judgment of Werner Pelz that "When we use the word 'God' we are talking about something which no longer connects with anything in most people's life, except with whatever happens to be left over when all the vital connections have been made." Most of us today are practical atheists. The "god-hypothesis" is as irrelevant for running an economy or coping with the population as it was for Laplace's system. As a factor you must take into account in the practical business of living, God is "out"—and no amount of religious manipulation can force him back in. He is peripheral, redundant, incredible—and therefore *as God* displaced: in Julian Huxley's words, "not a ruler, but the last fading smile of a cosmic Cheshire Cat."

I am very far from saying this is the whole truth or that all the atheist's arguments on this front, or any other, are valid (many of them reflect a very superficial or crudely tendentious understanding even of the traditional theology). What I am urging is that we allow ourselves to feel the full force of this attack rather than spend our time looking for yet another hole in the wire fence. . . .

2. *God is emotionally dispensable.* According to this line of attack religion is a prop or a sop. It is not merely something incredible and superfluous; it is a dangerous illusion which can prevent men facing reality and shouldering responsibility. This lies at the heart of the Freudian critique of religion as the universal neurosis or the Marxist attack on it as "the opium of the people." God and the gods are the projection of men's fears, insecurities and longings. They act as a debilitating crutch which men must have the courage to discard if they are to grow up and shake off the sense of helplessness which religion both induces and sanctions.

The call of atheism here is to man to cut the strings, to move out of the shadow of the Father-figure, to cease treating God as a peg, or a refuge, or a compensation for miseries which he should be fighting. Secularization means that man must accept responsibility for his own destiny, neither trying to blame it on the gods nor expecting some providence to relieve him of it or see him through.

Again I believe we must recognize the essential truth of this attack. Whatever as Christians we may wish to add or come back with, we should not be caught trying to defend this God or save him from death by artificial respiration. . . .

In varying degrees we all *need* religion, and nowhere more than here is the thrust of atheism seen as a threat. The tearing down of the traditional structure in which "the good Lord provides" and surrounds the whole of life with the protective comfort of the womb is viewed as an act of sacrilege which must be withstood, if not for our own sake, at any rate for the sake of the weaker brethren to whose pastoral care we hasten. Or, as an alternative line of defense, we seek to dismiss those who try, as someone has put it, to "destroy my grandmother's religion with my grandfather's science." But if we are honest, our "grandmother's religion" probably plays a much larger role in our conscious and unconscious life than we care to admit. . . .

Men need to be weaned, however painfully, from refusal to accept the burden of responsibility. A God who relieves them of this requires killing.

This clamor for the death of a God who keeps men languid and dispossessed, associated with Feuerbach before Marx, Engels and Freud developed it in their different ways, leads directly into the even more strident protest which expresses itself in the third statement.

3. *God is morally intolerable.* This reverses Voltaire's dictum that "If God did not exist, we should have to invent him." It says rather, "If God did exist, we should have to abolish him." This is the tradition that derives again from Feuerbach, and runs through Bakunin, Proudhon and Nietzsche to Camus and Sartre. It represents the real quick of twentieth-century atheism, in contrast with its dying nerves—if one may dare to thus speak of Marxism, as I think one can, as somewhat dated. It is what Jacques Maritain has called "positive atheism." It centers in the determination that God must *die* if man is to *live*. It is not content with accepting the negative absence of God and carrying on as though everything remained the same. It is concerned positively in living in a "world without God"—creating the justice and the meaning and the freedom which God, the great blood-sucker, has drained away.

But we should be careful not to state it in too emotive language. It would be easy to discredit this whole protest as the titanism of a Nietzsche or the outburst of a few intellectuals. But if this was once true, it is certainly true no longer. Camus spoke for an entire emerging generation. There is a dispassionate quality about modern atheism, of a piece with our whole urban-secular civilization. It is not vindictive or despairing, and it is noticeably losing its overtones of an anti-religion. . . .

[This particular form of atheism] . . . has a moral nerve which must not be cut, if it is to continue to purge and purify. For it draws its strength from the seriousness with which it takes the problem of evil. A God who "causes" or "allows" the suffering of a single child is morally intolerable. So the debate ranges, back and forth, in some of the great dialogues of modern literature—in Dostoievski's *Brothers Karamazov,* in Camus's *The Plague* and, most recently, in Peter de Vries's *The Blood of the Lamb* (describing the agony of a father watching his girl die of leukemia). But, of course, this is no intellectuals' debate. It is the root of atheism in most ordinary people, and today it is openly asserted even by the young. . . .

God does not solve the problem of suffering; he only magnifies it. To push off evil on to God simply makes him into a Devil—and in any case represents a cowardly evasion. Men must carry the can and refuse the temptation to dissociation or transference.

I believe that this is a profoundly moral response, and one that must be taken with the utmost seriousness. Any glib notion of a God who "causes" cancer or "sends" the streptococcus *is* a blasphemy. Most traditional theodicy, so far from justifying the ways of God to man, has the effect of strengthening atheism. . . . Atheism has done its purifying work. For there is nothing that provokes our generation to doubt or blasphemy more than the idea of a Being who sends such events into the lives of individuals. One of the liberating effects of secularization is that *this* idea of divine causation has at any rate been discredited. People rightly look for natural rather than supernatural causes. *But they still assume that Christians teach otherwise*—and their God is dismissed with them with indignation and disgust.

After the Death of God—can a truly contemporary person *not* be an atheist? It is a very real question. Not all people will feel the force of each of these thrusts. Their God may survive any or indeed all of them. I would certainly not want to suggest that a contemporary Christian *must* go through the mill of first being an atheist. But I firmly believe that he *may,* and that increasingly many will.

But *post mortem dei,* what? Is, in fact, faith possible out the other side? I believe that it is, and that not merely despite the death of God but even because of it. For this, after all, is no new situation for the people of God. The faith of Abraham, the father of faith, was born, as St. Paul reminds us, out of "contemplating his own body, now as good as dead, and the deadness of Sarah's womb." The faith of Job was possible to him only after all that he trusted in had first been removed. Even Jesus himself had to go through the process of the death of God—of the One who allowed it all to happen, "with a million angels watching, and they never move a wing." But, above all, Christianity itself was "born in the grave". . . . : it could only come into being at all *post mortem dei*. And for each one of us in some degree the Resurrection can only happen after the death of God. Though it looks as if everything is taken away—even the body of the Lord —yet this is not the destruction of Christianity but its liberation.

For—with all metaphysical security shattered, with even the word "God" of doubtful currency, with no theodicy of our own that we can establish—we find that we still cannot get shot of God; after his death he is disturbingly alive. . . .

Is not the situation of many of us today that we feel we *must* be atheists, and yet we *cannot* be atheists? God as we have been led to posit him *is* intellectually superfluous, *is* emotionally dispensable, *is* morally intolerable—and yet, in grace and demand, he *will not* let us go. The hound of heaven still dogs us, the "beyond in our midst" still encounters us, when all the images, all the projections, even all the words, for God have been broken. . . .

In dealing with other people it is possible for us to treat them simply as things—to use them, control them, manipulate them. This is what John Macmurray calls the *instrumental* relationship. Or, if for no other reason than that we soon discover they are not wholly amenable to such treatment, we can relate ourselves to them in what he calls the *functional* relationship, of co-operation with them. This is the most common relation we have with others, in which we treat them often as means to an end but never merely as means. But, thirdly, we can give ourselves to them in pure personal relationship, responding to them in love and trust for their own sakes. And ultimately it is only in this relationship that we can know them —and we ourselves be known—*as persons*.

To transfer this analogy to the universe, to life as a whole, we can respond to it in a purely instrumental, scientific, relationship—at the level of its mathematical regularities. We can regard reality as ultimately nothing more than a collocation of atoms, and we can even try to run history as a piece of social engineering. But there are few purely mechanistic materialists today. Much more common are those whose ultimate frame of reference is a functional one—humanists, whether dialectical, evolutionary or idealistic. And the atheist is the man who in his attitude to life stops there —for whom nothing finally is absolute or unconditional, for whom all is a means (though not merely a means).

The man who finds himself compelled to acknowledge the reality of

God, whatever he may call him or however he may image him, is the man who, through the mathematical regularities and through the functional values, is met by the same grace and the same claim that he recognizes in the I-Thou relation with another person. It may come to him through nature, through the claims of artistic integrity or scientific truth, through the engagements of social justice or of personal communion. Yet always it comes with an overmastering givenness and demand such as no other thing or person has the power to convey or the right to require. Like the child Samuel in the Temple, confusing the call of God with the voice of Eli, he may think at first that it can simply be identified with or contained within the finite relationship by which it is mediated. He may not be able to tell what to make of it, he may find it profoundly disturbing, but he knows it in the end to be inescapable and unconditional. In this relationship, too, he discovers himself known and judged and accepted for what ultimately he is. He finds in it for himself the way, the truth and the life. And if he is a Christian, he recognizes and acknowledges this grace and claim supremely in the person of Jesus Christ, the definition at one and the same time of a genuinely human existence and of this intangible, ineffable reality of "God." He agrees, passionately, with the atheist that such a reality cannot be *used* or *needed.* A God like that *is* superfluous, dispensable, intolerable. In fact it is *no God.* And then, when that God is dead, the Lord appears. . . .

How, then, does it stand in relation to the three thrusts we examined before? In the first place, God remains intellectually superfluous, in the sense that he does not need to be "brought in." There is no "place" for him in the system—or for that matter on its edge. The ring has been closed in which before an opening was left for God. Secularization must be gladly accepted—and no attempt made to find another hole in the fence or to reinstate him outside it. . . .

As a factor introduced to make the system work he is redundant. In that sense it is possible to answer every question without God—even the ones that before were thought to admit only of a religious solution. And at the level of control things get along, for good or for ill, just as well without him. It is not necessary to bring him in.

But in another sense it is not possible to leave him out—any more than it is possible to run an economy or cope with the population explosion without in the last analysis treating persons as persons, without reckoning with the dimension of the "Thou." God is a reality of life whom one cannot ultimately evade. . . . The one who is superfluous as a hypothesis becomes all too present as a subject in encounter.

Then, secondly, God continues to be emotionally dispensable. The returning Lord does not come as compensation for the gap left by the God of the gaps. There is no solace to restore the old relationships. The crutches are broken, and it remains "good for you that I go away." Nothing relieves of responsibility those who have to live by the Spirit.

Yet man come of age is still called to be a son. It is a mark of our religious immaturity that the "Father" image inextricably suggests emotional dependence, if not domination. The son never seems to grow up. Yet in fact for the New Testament "sonship" is a figure for freedom and stands precisely for man who has passed out of his minority and come of age. The Christian faith, so far from seeking to keep men in strings, calls them to maturity, not the maturity of the adolescent revolting *against* a father, but of the "full-grown man" entering into the responsible freedom of the son and heir.

There is nothing in the God of the New Testament—nor indeed in the God who said to the prophet, "Son of man, stand upon your feet and I will speak with you"—which would keep men languid or dispossessed. The call is to bear and to share the terrible freedom of love. And faith in the fatherly reality to which sonship is the response is not a belief in anything that undercuts this. . . .

This brings us, lastly, to the third charge, that God is morally intolerable. Again, it is a charge that stands. A Being who "sends" the worst into the lives of individuals or who stands aside to "permit" it is a God who must die. But that is precisely what the Christian faith proclaims happened at Calvary. The God who could have sent "twelve legions of angels" and did not is exposed as the God who failed even his Son. The obituary read by the atheist is valid, even if sometimes shrill.

Nothing in the Christian faith implies the rehabilitation of that God. Yet the Christian, as he looks back on the Cross from the other side of the Resurrection, sees not a world without God at its borders but a world with God at its center. What it means to believe in love as the final reality is to be discerned not in the absentee controller who allows the suffering but in the crucified transfiguring figure who bears it. The New Testament "answer" to the problem of evil is given, not majestically out of the whirlwind but agonizingly out of the darkness. As Bonhoeffer saw, in that situation "only a suffering God can help." The God of the Christian faith, who alone can be "our" God, can ultimately be revealed and responded to only as love which *takes* responsibility for evil—transformingly and victoriously.

For men to adjust to life in a world with that as its central reality is no intellectual exercise: it is, in Bonhoeffer's words again, to "range themselves with God in his suffering." That is the test he saw distinguishing Christians from unbelievers. And even among professed unbelievers there may at the point of dereliction, where the choice of our ultimate allegiance stands forth most starkly, be many who find that they cannot rail.

"For Christians, heathens alike, he hangeth dead." Such is the reality Bonhoeffer recognized as the common presupposition of our age—replacing what he called "the religious premise." Atheists and Christians start there together. And on their walk from the tomb, sharing the disenchantment of other more facile hopes, the dialogue can begin.

EDWARD SCHWEIZER (1913–   )

The Relation of Scripture, Church Tradition and Modern Interpretation

If I understand the situation in modern New Testament research correctly, it seems that it is no longer possible to consider the Bible as a kind
of quarry out of which the Church orders the foundation stones for its
dogmatic buildings, the proof texts for its doctrinal statements. Even if we
went back in history to the first credal statements of the early Church or to
the genuine words of Jesus, it is impossible to find a pure expression of
the truth like some kind of distilled water cleansed from all foreign sub-
stances. Luckily enough this is so. For, as we know, distilled water, deprived of its minerals and salts, no longer quenches our thirst. A "distilled" truth, not affected by the way of thinking, the insights and errors,
needs and hopes of its respective time, would be but an ineffable mystery
available for god-like beings only, and of no help for us. *The* truth encounters us in the body of the truth for the hearers of Jesus, for the Pales-
tinian churches in 30 AD, for the Hellenistic communities of the fifties, for
the church in Rome in 400, for the Reformation time, for the church of
1963 in U.S.A., etc. All these truths are undoubtedly different, and yet
only different bodies of one truth. What enables us to preach confidently
the truth for our time and our country, without going astray? Where is
truth, and where is untruth?

History and Tradition

1. *The Origin of the Tradition in Easter and Pentecost.* The basis of
the New Testament writings is the Easter event. Even the gospels are written in the light of Easter so that the earthly Jesus and the post-Easter
Christ become one.

What does Easter mean? According to John 20:21–23 Easter is also
Pentecost. On Easter the risen Lord breathes the Holy Spirit on His disci-

ples and sends them into the world. But also for Matthew the Easter event is the beginning of the mission of the disciples, and the promise of the heavenly Lord to be with them to the close of the age is actually the gift of the Spirit. For Paul, seeing the risen Lord and becoming His apostle was the same event (I Cor. 9:1; Gal. 1:16). Luke is the only one who distinguishes between Easter and Pentecost, but even he sees the two events very closely connected; for it is the risen Lord who, on Easter day, gives the commandment of the proclamation of the gospel to all nations and the promise of the Spirit. Even if we had the best sound film of a Jerusalem newsreel of the year 30 AD (or whatever it was), it would not help us much, since it could not show what really happened on that day. Only Easter, the revelation of the Spirit, shows what really happened.

It is therefore absolutely appropriate when the author of Revelation introduces his letters to the seven churches as the words of Christ, just because they are the words of the Spirit. Hence the introductory formula always refers to the heavenly Christ, the closing formula to the Holy Spirit as the real author of these letters. Revelation only explicitly states what, in the Synoptic or Johannine tradition of the deeds and words of Jesus, went on for decades. In new situations, the heavenly Lord, through His Spirit, explained His former words and reinterpreted them in a new situation. The authority of the heavenly Lord could certainly not be less than that of the earthly Jesus. Why, therefore, should the New Testament hesitate to formulate His words so that they meant in the very situation of the Church of that time what they were to mean from the beginning? Probably nobody purposely and consciously altered the words of Jesus; they only heard them in such a way that they spoke directly into their own problems and their own time.

We may formulate our point 1: *The New Testament never severs the earthly Jesus from the risen Lord. It is the risen Lord only who, speaking through the Spirit, gives meaning to the words or deeds of the earthly Jesus.*

2. *The Relation of a Fact to Its Understanding.* Modern physicists know about the problems which we touch, even in the area of physical facts. The questions which we ask alter the result of an experiment. This is certainly even more true in the area of history. There is evidently some difference, at least in degree, between facts in the area of history and human encounter, and facts in the area of physics. The role that our understanding plays is greater in the former area than in the latter. A cancer, for instance, has its effects whether we know about it or not; it can be removed by surgery, and it does not affect the healing if we do not know that it was cancer. Quite differently, a deed of love usually has its effect on us only if we know about and interpret it as was meant. It is possible

that someone loves us for years without our knowing. In this case such a love would not affect us or change our situation. It is equally possible that someone does something for us out of mere love, but we misunderstand his motive and are driven into inferiority complexes or even hate. Therefore a historical positivism which puts historical facts on exactly the same level as physical facts is impossible. It forgets that, in the area of human encounter, the interpretation and understanding of a fact is sometimes even more important than the fact itself. This may be true, for instance, for the history of the conquest of the West and its interpretation in movies and television.

This, I think, may help us to find our way towards a solution of the problem of "scripture and tradition." Let us choose a very simple example. Let us assume that a girl pays all the debts of her boy friend, because she loves him and wants to give him a new start. Let us assume that they marry. The problem of their matrimony will be how he copes with what his wife has done for him. His feelings of inferiority towards her may grow more and more. Even doubts may arise whether she really did it out of love or, perhaps, out of sheer calculation. Hence, the task of this girl will be to accompany her husband in a continuing love in order to interpret her initial deed to him and to "bring it home" to him. This leads to our point 2: *A deed of love and the continuing interpretation by love belong closely together. . . .*

The Danger of Not Being Modern Enough

1. *The First Mark of the Spirit: His Affection for Modern Men.* What is the standard by which to test the utterances of the Spirit and to separate right and wrong tradition? In the pre-Pauline church, the Spirit was naively identified with an extraordinary power for healings, prophecies, etc. This led, in Hellenistic congregations, to an extreme preference for ecstatic phenomena. The only alternative to this was an ecclesiastical institutionalism, as it was probably to be found in Jerusalem under James, after the persecution in 44, and the departure of Peter. Paul was the first to reflect carefully about the nature of the Spirit of God. He points to the fact that the Spirit speaks "for the common good" (I Cor. 12:7). He speaks so that He "edifies the Church" (14:4). He speaks in such a way that every member of the Church understands Him (14:2,6–12). This means: the Spirit of God is always directed towards contemporaries. He is always speaking in modern language. If this were not the case, it would be best to put the sermons of Paul and Peter on a tape recording and to play them in our services, instead of training ministers who are, in spite of their expensive training, not always on the level of Paul and Peter. A sermon without

burning love towards modern men, a sermon in an outlived language, no longer understandable in a modern world, is probably no sermon of the Holy Spirit. Thus let us keep in mind point 1: *It is the sign of the Holy Spirit that He does not speak into the air, but in modern language to modern men, knowing their needs, their hopes and their dangers.*

2. *His Criticism of a Petrified Tradition.* . . . There is no doubt that Paul reads his Bible very carefully, and that he finds the new life of the Spirit in this very Bible. Long passages of his letters are interpretations of the Scripture. But when the Scripture is used, as it is used in a fundamentalist theology, in a legalistic way, it becomes the "written code" against which Paul fights so vehemently. Against some groups of Jewish Christians, Paul fights vigorously for his thesis that, in his mission to the Gentiles, the history of salvation goes on, although it seems to be in contradiction to some words of Jesus if literally understood. Whatever the roots of the Johannine tradition be, it is certain that it is a totally new interpretation of Jesus' words and deeds by the post-Easter Spirit which has not much to do with a literal repetition of the sayings of Jesus. Even Matthew, who is rather close to the conception of a new law, and for whom Jesus is, first of all, the teacher of a new righteousness, in many respects offers a new interpretation for new needs. Besides, it is exactly Matthew who emphasizes that the Church has the power of binding and loosing (18:18), i.e. of creating new law or invalidating old law, and of forgiving or keeping sins. Luke distinguishes different periods of a continuing history of God, in which the Spirit leads the Church to new insights. A petrified tradition which can no longer be developed by the living Spirit into new insights is legalism which kills instead of bringing into life, even if it were the tradition of the genuine sayings of Jesus.

Hence our point 2: *An orthodoxy which replaces the life in the Spirit by an acceptance of the historicity of Biblical facts and a legal authority of Biblical words or of credal formulas would be a killing legalism.* . . .

The Danger of a Christianity Losing Its Roots in History

1. *The Second Mark of the Spirit: His Testimony to Jesus.* The other standard for judging the utterances of the Spirit which Paul mentions is the testimony to Jesus the Lord. Whoever witnesses to Jesus as the Lord is moved by the Spirit, and whoever denies this is far from the Spirit of God (I Cor. 12:3). Christianity, unlike all other religions, is shaped by the fact that the preached Word of God is but the vehicle by which the incarnate Word of God meets us. If we lose this basis in history, we shall have lost

the content of the gospel. God is not to be restricted to His actual speaking in the preaching of our time. His Word to the world is a man of flesh and blood, so real that he was hanged. A spiritualized preaching, severed from the history of Palestine in the first three decades of our era, would be like a tree whose roots were pulled out of the soil which gave it life. Our point 1 therefore understands *the gospel not as a doctrine about eternally unchangeable ideas, but as the praising proclamation of God's deeds which in Jesus Christ, once for all, changed the situation of the world.*

2. *The Affinity of the Spirit to History and Tradition.* For Paul himself, the fact of the crucifixion of Jesus was so scandalous that he was never in danger of forgetting that Jesus was a real, historic person. This was different for Greek congregations which were living far away from the historical facts of about 30 AD in Jerusalem. They were in a real danger of developing into a gnosticism as we know it from groups of the second century AD. Gnosticism presents a comprehensive doctrine of salvation, containing even a myth which tells about the descent from and the ascent to heaven of a man-like saviour, but here only the kerygma matters. The myth is but an illustration of the eternally unchangeable truth. Therefore it does not matter at all whether uneducated people believe that all this really happened in distant primitive times, or more educated people take this myth as a mere image for the truth. Against such tendencies John formulates what Paul had written in a simpler form in I Cor. 12:3: "Every spirit which confesses that Jesus Christ has come in the flesh is of God, and every spirit which does not confess Jesus is not of God" (I John 4:2f.). Even more important is the fact that, when some time had elapsed and the real historical figure of Jesus of Nazareth was in danger of fading away, four Gospels were written in order to defend the gospel against being converted into gnosticism. The historical facts are nothing without their interpretation by the post-Easter Spirit—therefore all the Gospels present the earthly Jesus in the light of the risen Christ. However, this interpretation, in and of itself, is equally meaningless if not understood as the interpretation of these facts.

To sum up point 2: *The New Testament writers are not concerned with a distinction between the so-called historical Jesus and the risen Lord speaking through the Spirit, but they are certainly concerned with the distinction between a mere doctrine or a mere myth and a history interpreted by the Spirit. . . .*

The Relation between Jesus Christ, the New Testament, the Tradition and the Proclamation of the Church Today

1. *The Third Mark of the Spirit: A Gift to the Whole Church.* According to Paul, it is extremely important that the whole congregation understands the message of the Spirit and is able to agree with its "Amen" (I Cor. 14:16). Therefore the prophet speaking in the Spirit must be judged by the congregation (v. 29). The Spirit is given to all believers. "Any one who does not have the Spirit of Christ does not belong to him" (Rom. 8:9). "You shall receive the gift of the Holy Spirit; for the promise is to . . . every one whom the Lord our God calls to him" (Acts 2:38f.). In the New Testament, the Spirit is always the gift to the whole Church. This means that the preaching of the Spirit is always subject to control by the members of the Church. I, therefore, always prepare my sermons together with a group of church members, listening for an hour and a half to their discussion of the text. Thus our point 1 will be *that the Spirit is given to the Church and is therefore controlled by all the brethren.*

2. *The Role of the Tradition.* God cannot contradict Himself. Therefore we must listen carefully to all our brethren and, if we disagree, ask ourselves whether we are not hard of hearing for the voice of the Spirit. But the Church did not start in 1963, and the Spirit did not begin to speak in 1963. There are brethren throughout all the centuries of church history. Some of these brethren are in an outstanding position. They have suffered and died for the truth that they proclaimed, and/or they have proclaimed that truth not as individuals but as Church, in common agreement. This is the case, for instance, with the declaration of Barmen in the Confessing Church of Germany in 1934, or with the Heidelberg Catechism, in 1563.

This is one reason for listening to the tradition, but there is another one. Past centuries had their own way of thinking. On the one hand, being men of another century we are usually quite aware of the errors which were involved in their thinking. In the discussion of the Lord's Supper, for instance, Lutherans and Calvinists thought in categories totally foreign to the New Testament, because they had a conception of matter or substance conceived in the Middle Ages, but unknown in New Testament times. Hence it goes without saying that we must read the tradition with a critical mind, avoiding their inappropriate categories of thinking as far as possible. On the other hand, being men of our century, we are usually blind to the inappropriate categories of our own century. And here, the tradition renders us the most necessary service of helping us to see the limits of our own thinking. It may, for instance, be impossible for us to repeat literally the clause in the first answer of the Heidelberg Catechism that Jesus Christ paid with his dear blood completely for my sin and redeemed me from all power of the devil. And yet, it reminds us that there is dimension in the New Testament message which is not yet covered, if we consider Jesus mainly as a teacher of ethical example or even the messenger of justification by faith. We may therefore formulate point 2: *It is the advantage of tradition that we, while better aware of its limits and errors than of those of our contemporary thinking, may see in its light the deficiencies of our own theology.*

3. *The Role of the Scripture.* What is the particular position of the New Testament within this tradition? A first answer would be that what is true for the Heidelberg Catechism or the declaration of Barmen is even truer for the New Testament. It is surrounded by a cloud of martyrs who died witnessing to its truth. It is a team work in an excellent way, and its acceptance by the whole Church is without parallel. However, all this is only a difference in degree.

A second answer starts from the fact that the New Testament distinguishes the first encounter of the risen Lord with the apostles clearly and definitely from later visions by which the heavenly Lord gives some guidance to the believer. Paul's encounter with the risen Lord near Damascus is the basis of all his preaching and is referred to in Gal. 1:16 and I Cor. 9:1, also in Rom. 1:1 and similar places. The vision of II Cor. 12 with its extraordinary ascent to heaven should not be mentioned at all, since it is a more personal experience without any importance for the Church as a whole. Luke draws a strict line between the appearance of the risen Lord within the first forty days and heavenly visions like the one before Peter in Joppa.

Easter is the event which always reminds us that it is God Himself who gave us this understanding, once for all, unchangeable in its essence. The New Testament is certainly not identical with this understanding that God Himself gave to men. It is written in Greek, and every human language involves necessarily quite a lot of categories of thinking which are partly appropriate, partly inappropriate for expressing the divine truth. It is written by men who understood and misunderstood what God wanted them to understand. And yet, the New Testament is, first, historically the closest to the event of the incarnate Word of God. Second, it has been tested by time, and again by the whole Church. Third, it stood the test in the sufferings of the Church before and after its acceptance as the canon of the Church. Therefore, the canon is still open. However, this would be a merely theoretical thesis. Theoretically also a gentle stroke on the hand of a child is the same as a whipping which leaves a cripple, since both are fundamentally corporal punishment; but actually there is all the difference in the world between the two. And yet, it is impossible to draw a mathematically clear line. Therefore we may close point 3: *The New Testament is part of the tradition, therefore necessarily expressed in human language, limited by contemporary possibilities of understanding, imperfect, and yet standing in a unique position as the beginning of the tradition, historically close to the incarnate Word of God and sign for its "once-for-all-ness."*

JOHN MACQUARRIE (1919–   )

Symbolic Theology

. . . We come now to specifically Christian theology, to the explicitation of that faith which centers in the revelation given in the person and work of Jesus Christ. This revelation has been transmitted in the Christian community, primarily in the scriptures of the community, but also in the community's tradition of life and thought, in which the revelation has already been developed and explicated in ways that have become part of the community's identity, so that they could scarcely be discarded without destroying the continuity of the community. The whole issue of tradition will demand fuller discussion when we come to talk about the nature of the community itself, but for the present it is simply being claimed that any explication of the Christian faith, while it must be rooted in the Bible as the primary testimony to the primordial revelation, cannot leap straight back across the centuries to the New Testament but must take account of the way in which the Church, in its creeds, in the decisions of its ecumenical councils (especially those of the early centuries), and, generally, in its collective wisdom and universal teaching, has understood and interpreted the faith which it holds and of which it is the guardian. . . .

All our talk of God must be indirect, because our language is primarily adapted for talking about beings, so that when we want to talk about Being, we have to stretch the everyday usages of language. We saw how, in various ways, beings and our talk about beings can open up for us insights into Being. The most general way of describing indirect language of this kind is to call it "symbolic," though we have seen that some parts of it might be more accurately called "analogical," some "paradoxical," and the undifferentiated language out of which these arise, "mythical."

There may, however, be some resistance to the expression "symbolic theology" on the ground that it may seem to take away reality from what is talked about, or again that it may seem to deny any genuine knowledge of whatever reality there may be. Our whole exposition of symbols should have made it clear that such fears are unfounded. It was shown that symbols, so far from being mere empty ciphers, have Being "present-and-manifest" in them, as was repeatedly said. They are not just ideas floating in our minds but are the concrete ways in which Being (God) accomplishes its self-giving and self-manifestation. Furthermore, it was shown that symbolic language is not just a poetic language of images, but does throw light on actual structures. The typical language of symbolic theology is a mixed one in which both images and concepts play their part. We should remember Paul Tillich's good advice: "One should never say, 'only a symbol,' but one should say, 'not less than a symbol.'" So we should be far from despising symbols, for they have an indispensable part to play in our knowing, providing the only way in which we can attain insight into and talk about Being.

What then is the symbolic material in which the Christian revelation has found expression? It should be remembered that the theological interest lies primarily in verbal expression, that is to say, in articulating the faith in words, though the expression of faith in life and worship is at least equally important, perhaps more so, and has its own implied theology which we must not allow to slip out of sight. But we have already indicated where the verbal symbols of the Church's faith are to be found, namely, in the Bible and in the subsequent development of the Church's thought. These are the vehicles by which the content of the primordial revelation, so far as this could be put into words, has been passed on. A examination of this material will show us what the distinctively Christian symbols are, and what special marks, if any, may belong to these symbols as a whole.

While it would be impossible to attempt anything like a classification of this mass of material—the work of form-critics shows how complicated is the task of classifying even a small segment of the material—nevertheless some major categories may be recognized, and it is important that we should take note of them before embarking on the task of a theological explicitation of the material.

1. First among these categories may be mentioned *myth*, that is to say, material displaying all the characteristics which were earlier listed as belonging to the mythical mode of discourse. There are in fact very few straightforward mythical narratives in the Bible, for the criticism of myth has already begun. The story of the creation of Adam and the subsequent fall comes within the category of myth, and there are allusions to older myths. But while intact myths are rare, mythological ideas are all-pervasive both in the Bible and in subsequent theology. Eschatological ideas derived from myths about the end color the whole of the gospel narrative, for instance.

2. Next may be mentioned a vast amount of imagery which may per-

haps be broadly designated *analogical*. It differs from myth in that it is used with full consciousness of its symbolic character, and also in that it has much more of an *ad hoc* character and does not constitute in itself a cosmic story or series of stories. This miscellaneous material includes analogues, similes, metaphors, parables, allegories, and whatever other ways are employed of trying to point to God and to illuminate his meaning for human existence.

3. Very important and distinctive for the Christian revelation is *history*. In the Old Testament, God makes himself known in the history of Israel, which is interpreted as his deliverances and his judgments; while the New Testament message has as its center the history of Jesus Christ, and especially his death and resurrection. But while we rightly acknowledge the centrality of history in the biblical revelation, we must also acknowledge that it is history of a peculiar kind. It is not a scientific reconstruction of past events, as many modern scholars would understand history. Just as revelation, in order to be revelation, must include the reception and appropriation of the revelation by the person or community to whom it is directed, so history, considered as a vehicle of revelation, is already presented to us in an interpreted form, with the historical happenings represented as divine acts. Hence the historical material in Christianity tends to be incorporated into the mythical framework, and also to be embellished by legendary material illustrative of what is taken to be the "meaning" of the history. In many cases, it has become impossible to know what the facts of the matter were—just what would have been seen by a person present, or just what would have been heard. The question of history and its interpretation is one that is constantly arising in the context of Christian theology, and in various ways it will engage our attention. For the present, however, we simply note that Christianity differs from many religions in placing its revelation within the course of world history rather than in a timeless myth.

4. Yet another category of material is dogma—and it was indicated that although we propose to drop the adjective "dogmatic" and the expression "dogmatic theology," it might still be found useful to retain the noun "dogma." There is little dogma in the New Testament itself, but the formulation of dogmas, creeds, and definitions of belief became a major concern of the Church at quite an early stage in its existence. A dogma would seem to have at least three distinguishing marks: it has its basis in the revelation; it is proposed by the Church, as expressing the mind of the community on a particular issue; and it has a conceptual and propositional form, being often expressed in a philosophical terminology. As is well known, dogmas were usually formulated when there was a threat that the Church's teaching in some area might be gravely distorted, and it had be-

come necessary to state more precisely than had ever been done before just what the Church's teaching in this matter might be. Thus dogmas are interpretations. For historical reasons, some areas of the Church's teaching (such as the doctrine of the person of Christ) were interpreted rather precisely, while other areas (such as the doctrine of the work of Christ) were much less closely interpreted. In any case, however, what may have been an interpretation in the fourth century of our era will almost certainly stand in need of reinterpretation today, especially if it uses the language of an outmoded philosophy. So when it was said earlier in this section that the modern theologian cannot turn his back on credal symbols that have become elements in the community's identity, this certainly did not mean that he is simply to repeat these unaltered. This would be quite unintelligent deference to tradition. He is not to reject symbols that declare the Church's common mind, but he must, by what has earlier been described as "repetitive thinking," penetrate behind the possibly quaint and even alien language of the dogma to the existential issues that agitated the Church at the time of the dogma's formulation, and appropriate for our own time and in our own language the essential insight which the dogma sought to express. Every interpretation, in course of time, demands a new act of interpretation. When it is remembered further that dogmas were usually formulated to exclude particular errors, so that they are frequently more explicit in what they rule out than in what they affirm, it will be understood that the formulation of a dogma does not mean that some final point has been reached and that future generations are excused from reflecting any more on the matter. The point has been well put by Karl Rahner, with special reference to christological dogma: "The clearest formulations, the most sanctified formulas, the classic condensations of the centuries-long work of the Church in prayer, reflection and struggle concerning mysteries; all these derive their life from the fact that they are not end but beginning, not goals but means, truths which open the way to the ever greater Truth."

5. We must also notice the vast amount of what may be called *practical* material in the sources for symbolic theology. Under this category we include all the ethical material on the conduct of life, and also all the directions and counsels on prayer, worship, the community, and so on. This is not to be dismissed as *merely* practical, as if it had nothing to do with theology. We have repeatedly observed that theology is *one* way in which faith expresses itself, but there are other and probably more important ways. Yet these ways are not to be separated, for ideally they are only aspects of the total expression of faith in the whole existence of man. What he does implies a theology, while theological convictions in turn have their influence on action. The practical side of Christian teaching is to be kept in view if the existential dimension of theology is to be maintained, and it is to be prevented from lapsing into an arid scholasticism.

This brief characterization of the major categories of material to which we must pay attention in any attempt at a theological explication of the specifically Christian revelation does not pretend to be exhaustive. Yet perhaps we are able to perceive from it something of the distinctive character of Christian symbolism as a whole. There is a preference, though not an exclusive preference, for the dynamic and dramatic, the temporal and historical, over generalized timeless truths. Even the traditional dogmas, with their abstract metaphysical terminology, were used to elucidate the person of Christ, or again the differentiated and fundamentally dynamic "life" of the triune God. This distinctive character of the Christian symbols will become more apparent as our symbolic theology is developed.

The Method of Symbolic Theology

The transition from philosophical theology to symbolic theology involves also a shift in method, already hinted at in our general introductory remarks on method. The shift is not, of course, a total one, but it may be expressed by saying that in this middle division of the work, interpretation will be our major concern, just as description played the principal role in the first division. But no sharp distinction can be made between them. Every description tends to become an interpretation, while any securely based interpretation must begin from a full and accurate description of what is to be interpreted—that is to say, from exposure to the matter itself, which is indeed the explicit aim of phenomenology.

It is worth noting that in the most recent discussions of hermeneutics increasing stress seems to be laid just on this very business of letting ourselves be exposed to the matter itself, rather than on concerning ourselves too much with our actual methods or with the prior understanding which in every case we undoubtedly bring to the tasks of interpretation. There is stress on the need to return to the sources, to listen and to let ourselves hear what is said in the classic expositions of the Christian revelation, rather than to allow these to be obscured for us by centuries of intervening and sometimes distorting transmission. As with so much else in contemporary theology, we can see here the influence of Heidegger (quite explicit in such students of hermeneutic method as Fuchs and Ebeling) and his doctrine of a repetitive thinking which reaches back and enters into the thinking of the text to be interpreted. In offering an interpretation of a passage from Sophocles, Heidegger prefaces it by saying: "We must attempt to hear only what is said. But . . . we are inexperienced at such hearing, and our ears are full of things that prevent us from hearing properly."

Because of this need to hear what is said, the systematic theologian must continually pay attention to what can be learned from biblical theology and historical theology since these presumably do conduct us back to the sources and light them up for us. But now we must be on our guard against an exaggerated respect for these classic expositions of the Christian revelation, whether in the New Testament or in the thought of some great period of the Church's history, such as the Middle Ages or the Reformation. There is a tendency among scholars to retreat into one or other of these periods, and even if these scholars are hearing with perfect clarity what was being said, this does not make them in the slightest degree interpreters unless they can come back to their own time and speak the same matter in the language and categories of our day. Biblical and historical theology can have merely an antiquarian interest unless they subserve the task of a contemporary exposition of faith. Let us remember Rahner's remark that a classical formulation is not an end but a beginning.

It was claimed (in a previous section) that an existential-ontological language would be an appropriate one for theological interpretation, though this had still to be shown. We are now in a position to evaluate the claim that was made then, for we have seen how a philosophical theology beginning from the analysis of human existence finds within that existence itself the question of being, and the development of this question leads in turn into a descriptive natural theology. Since we have seen that for an act of interpretation we require two parallel languages that can throw light on each other, we see how an existential-ontological language, describing universal structures and experiences of the human existent, can serve as the interpretative parallel for the symbolic language of a particular revelation. Much of our symbolic theology will in fact be an interpretation of the Christian symbols in terms of the language of the philosophical theology developed in the first division. But we shall expect to find that as usual the process of interpretation involves a two-way traffic. If the existential-ontological language provides a frame of reference that will help us to locate and understand the symbols, these concrete symbols will from their side enrich and vivify the relatively abstruse language of existence and being.

We are also in a position to understand better why the appropriate interpretative language should have been designated by the hyphenated expression "existential-ontological"—an expression which, it must be confessed, is clumsy enough. The excuse for this expression must be that it points to two aspects in the interpretation, both of which we take to be indispensable. The symbolic material to be interpreted must be related on the one hand to our existence, and on the other to Being, and we must firmly resist erroneous interpretations which swing out either on the one side or on the other.

Thus, we not only embrace the demythologizing method of Bultmann, and also the general method of existential interpretation which can be applied to material that would not strictly fall within the category of myth, but we reject any attempt at a purely existential theology. Bultmann too rejects such an extreme development of his position, but there are and have been theologians and philosophers of religion who think of Christianity's symbolic material as setting forth nothing more than a manner of existence or a way of life for man. On this view, even statements about God are taken to be veiled statements about existence or possibly commands to act in a certain way. Religion becomes a purely practical matter, dogmas are interpreted as rules for the conduct of life, and the idea of God is taken to stand not for any independence or prior reality over against man but simply as a symbol of ideal existence. Our own exposition of the revelatory situation . . . makes it clear that while indeed we acknowledge and indeed lay great stress on the existential dimension in theology, we have never thought of an existential interpretation as offering an exhaustive account of the content of faith. It has been consistently maintained that religion is more than a practical matter and yields insight into the transhuman and, indeed, primordial reality which we call God or Being. So existential interpretation (including interpretation in terms of an existentially conceived history) can never constitute a *complete* theological method, though it is certainly an indispensable element in any adequate theological method, and we may be glad that this is so clearly recognized at the present time.

So, on the other hand, our interpretation will be ontological in the sense that it will seek to elucidate from the symbolic material new and deeper understanding of Being. But here we must guard against the temptation of treating theology as if it were metaphysics and as if our aim were to provide just an intellectually satisfying account of God, the world, and man. With the rise of dogma in the early Church, concrete and existentially significant symbols tended to be edged out in favor of an abstract vocabulary of "substance," "nature," and the like. This kind of language does indeed serve to interpret and clarify the symbols, but then the dogmas come to be thought of as objective, neutrally descriptive truths. Then from time to time we get protests against the excessive intellectualizing of faith, and against the transforming of the God of religion into the God of the philosophers, the living God into a metaphysical construct. Luther, Pascal, Kierkegaard, Harnack, and a host of others have in the modern period recalled theology from metaphysical speculation to its existential dimensions. The peril today, however, is not that faith will be understood in intellectual terms but that this whole side of theology will be obscured and that the current antipathy to metaphysics will crush out the ontological aspect of theology. In Gogarten and his followers, for instance, history and metaphysics are set up in a dualistic opposition to each other, and it is implied that the theologian must choose between the historical and the metaphysical method. Here it is important, I think, to see that ontology and metaphysics, though they have often been identical enterprises, are not always so. Heidegger thinks of his own inquiry into Being as an "overcoming of metaphysics," and it is clear that there is certainly a major difference between what he is doing and the old style metaphysic. The latter was a rational inquiry, proceeding by strictly logical demonstration. Heidegger's inquiry, on the other hand, is existentially oriented throughout; it considers Being not objectively but by way of our own participation in Being; its appeal is not to deductive logic, but to the insights that we attain in such states of mind as anxiety. The objections to ontology in a theological interpretation rest on a failure to distinguish contemporary ontology from old style metaphysics. There need be no sharp dualism between history and ontology, and indeed if there is, it is fatal to the theological enterprise. Our own discussion of Being in the earlier parts of this book was, following Heidegger, always existentially rooted and oriented. As such, it was in no danger of becoming an abstract speculative metaphysic. Provided that we continue to avoid this danger, the ontological aspect of theological interpretation must be as firmly maintained as the existential aspect.

Another way of pointing to the inseparability of the two aspects of existential-ontological interpretation is to remind ourselves of the meaning of the word "God," as this became clear to us in the earlier discussion. The word "God," we have seen, is not just a synonym for "Being," for it is not a neutral designation. It never means less than "holy Being," that is to say, Being that impinges on our beings, demanding, judging, and sustaining, and Being to which in turn we give our allegiance. So any talk of God demands for its interpretation nothing less than an existential-ontological language.

JOHN COBB, JR. (1925–   )

From Crisis Theology to the
Post-Modern World

Our culture, the culture in which we do and must live, is characterized by the death of God. We cannot but understand ourselves and our beliefs historically and hence relativistically.

These two problems are intimately interconnected. The death of God is caused in part by the historicizing of all our thinking. Since we understand an idea by understanding how it arises and develops, we can no longer view the idea as having a one-to-one correlation with reality. We can talk seriously about ideas of God but are not able to speak directly of God. More broadly, we can enter imaginatively into many ways of perceiving reality, but just for that reason we cannot affirm any of them as true. Indeed, the word "true" we are forced to place in quotes, not knowing any longer what we can mean by it.

It is also the case that the death of God is a *cause* of a relativism. As long as God's reality remained a fixed pole for thought, the relativity of human experience and belief could be understood as reflecting varying ways of grasping one ultimate reality. Truth was found in God's knowledge, and even though we might not claim any final criteria for identifying the content of truth, that there existed a final truth about all things was clear. With the death of God, however, truth and reality are alike relativized. They exist nowhere.

This world in which God is dead and truth and reality are without meaning is indeed our world. Yet it is not our total world. If it were, no such statement about it could be understood. If God were wholly and unequivocally dead for us, the statement that it is so would not be made. Indeed, all discourse would be at an end. Every statement assumes that it somehow transcends total relativism, that it points to some kind of reality, that it participates in some kind of truth. We do still live in a world formed by a past that remains alive even in its decay.

I do not mean to seize the point that total relativism is self-contradictory as a basis for setting relativism aside. The *affirmation* of total relativism is self-contradictory, but there is a sense in which relativism can be lived unspoken. The complete relativist would never apply the term relativism to his own thought, for he would not think in such universals. It is the reality of lived relativism, not its philosophical defense, that seems to lie ahead for our world.

I do not mean to say, however, that the reality of the death of God and of the concomitant relativism does not exhaust our contemporary world. If we take seriously the historical consciousness which we have already seen play such havoc with traditional forms of faith and theology, we must also see that the death of God and the concomitant relativism are likewise a function of time and place, one way of being among others, in themselves neither absolute nor final. History shows us that just at that point at which a *Zeitgeist* seems to have swept all before it, it may already be giving way in the minds of the most creative and authentic persons to something quite different, something that certainly will not repeat the past, but something which may yet recover out of the past just what seemed in greatest danger of being destroyed. Perhaps even today at the point at which all rational structure and all human meaning seems to be evaporating, new structures and new meanings may be emerging.

If this is so, and I earnestly hope that it is so, then we may escape the desperate choice indicated above between affirming the modern world and reacting against it defensively. We may refuse the modern world not by defending the past but in the name of the new world which *may* be born. We cannot of course know that it will be born. We cannot even know whether our decision for it may help it to be born. But we can affirm it, and in doing so we can repudiate the modern world in the name of the world we will to be the post-modern world.

The picture I am proposing may be sketched as follows. The *Zeitgeist* of our world is one in which God is dead and all truth and reality have collapsed in relativity. That *Zeitgeist* is working its way into ever more consistent expression in thought, art, and existence. It leads to the death of man in the sense of self-conscious, responsible, historical, individual man. Its chief obstacle to total victory is the vast deposit of centuries of Christian thought, art, and existence which, partly consciously but more largely unconsciously, is expressing itself in a still powerful humanism. This is our contemporary post-Christian situation.

If this were the total situation, I have argued above, then the theologian could only decide between throwing his lot with the new and reacting defensively against it by appealing to the authority of the past. He has learned, as many of his colleagues have not, that there is no resting place in the mid-way point of rationalistic or romantic humanisms. But I am suggesting now that this is not the total situation. In addition to the remnants of Christendom and to the demonic powers released by the death of God, there are other thrusts here and there, thrusts which are as authentically modern as any nihilism, but which refuse nihilism in the name of truth.

These emergent claims upon the future are endlessly varied, and there is no place to stand from which one may judge the likelihood of the success of one or another. Nor is there a place to stand from which one may safely baptize one or another such thrust as Christian. Yet I believe that, ignoring the question of success and risking the danger of apostasy, the Christian thinker today must reach out for a novelty that disdains all appeal to the authority of the past and dares to think creatively and constructively in the present.

Teilhard de Chardin is a recent figure who represents such daring. The world he knew, however strange, was surely authentic, genuinely contemporary. He discounted nothing of the magnificent intellectual achievements of science. He did not appeal to the authority of the past. He took the risk of apostasy. Whether in the end his vision is durable we cannot yet know, but that it struck a responsive chord in the minds of many is clear. That it *could* point to a new world, the beginnings of a new *Zeitgeist,* cannot be denied. For my part I would far rather live in that world than in the world being fashioned by dominant modernity.

The work of Teilhard is instructive in that though it fundamentally eschews the authority of the past it affirms Jesus Christ as the center of reality. Sceptics will understandably regard this as a nostalgic remnant of inherited faith or as a concession aimed at placating the church. But I do not believe this. Whether by historic accident or by supernatural purpose, there is an absoluteness in Jesus Christ which can speak not only through the continuity of Christendom but also across the gulf of centuries.

I mention the work of Teilhard de Chardin not to hold it up as the one great hope for the future or for the theologian. On the contrary, I find it often vague, confusing, and unsatisfactory. But it represents a mood which challenges the predominant *Zeitgeist* on its own terms, defending nothing on the ground that "it is written" or that "it is Christian," avidly open to all truth—yet still *believing.* This mood is one with which I can identify myself as theologian, as Christian, as man.

My own effort to share in the work to which this mood gives rise is directed toward thinking into the new world opened up in the philosophy of Alfred North Whitehead. To enter Whitehead's world is to experience a psychic revolution as great or greater than the Cartesian and Kantian revolutions. To experience that revolution is to enter into possibilities of thought and self-understanding at which Whitehead himself barely hinted. I believe that from within this new Whiteheadian world one can appropriate also the world of Teilhard de Chardin—as of other revolutionary thinkers of our day—with greater clarity than they themselves could achieve.

Although any serious exposition of Whitehead's thought is beyond the scope of this paper, it is appropriate that some indication be given of the aspects of his thought which seem relevant to this context. Whitehead himself speaks of his speculative philosophy as like a poem, mutely appealing for understanding. One cannot begin with terms and objects as defined within some other vision of reality and then state unambiguously that which Whitehead intends. This procedure is impossible wherever there is genuine novelty of sensibility and vision. Hence, all the more, a few brief paragraphs on his thought can hardly hope to be intelligible. Yet, one must try.

Whitehead alters the locus of concreteness as over against modern common sense. Especially with the decay of idealism, modernity has identified concreteness either with things presented to us in sense experience or with the sense data themselves. Whitehead declares this to be the "fallacy of misplaced concreteness." What is concrete is experience as such, just as it occurs in each particularized moment. . . .

Whitehead . . . sees the whole physical world as itself composed of "actual occasions of experience" and of societies of such occasions. There is and can be no object which is not itself a subject or a society of subjects. The physical is one dimension of all experiences including the human, but it is not at all the name of a realm over against that of experience. Whitehead also . . . [perceives] experience as a momentary becoming and perishing rather than as a continuum of becoming.

The profoundly distinctive character of Whitehead's vision is apparent in his understanding of relations. All real relations are the re-enactment in new experiences of elements of old experiences. All causality is to be understood in this way. Through its causal efficacy the past always profoundly affects the becoming present but never determines exactly how it will become. Causal influence and free self-determination alike characterize every entity in the world.

In terms of these briefly identified principles almost all the traditional problems of thought receive new answers or new versions of old answers. Furthermore, light is shed upon the special problems of modern mathematics and physics that relate these disciplines to human existence in a quite new way. In this context, however, we can note only the relevance of Whitehead's thought for the two acute problems previously discussed—the death of God and universal relativism. . . .

Whitehead's doctrine of God has many points of contact with traditional Christian thought—more, I think, than either he or his critics generally recognize. Nevertheless, it is profoundly new. It has been transformed by modern science and mathematics, on the one hand, and by the revolutionary vision of the world as a society of societies of occasions of experiences, on the other. The understanding of God's relation to the world is further transformed by the new understanding of space-time and of relation as a re-enactment and by Whitehead's special doctrine of God's providing each momentary occasion with its ideal aim. After generations in which theologians and religious philosophers have struggled to defend some one relation in which God's importance for the world can be argued, we are confronted with a new world of thought in which all manner of modes of relatedness to God are affirmed. Within the Whiteheadian context we can understand both the Person-to-person encounter of modern Protestantism and the mysticisms of both East and West. We can agree with those who have seen the relation of man to God in the ethical dimension and those who have reasoned to God from the order and directionality of nature. We can see both the reality and the all-determinativeness of grace and also the freedom and responsibility of man. But we see all this in a frame of reference that to some degree transforms the meanings of all the traditional terms and problems.

The point of the above is not to explain Whitehead's doctrine of God —that again would be impossible in a few paragraphs—but simply to stress that once one enters the strange new world of Whitehead's vision, God becomes very much alive. The understanding of the world begins and ends with him to a far greater extent than Whitehead himself made explicit in his writings. Insofar as I come existentially to experience myself in terms of the world to which Whitehead introduces us, I experience myself in God; God as in me; God as law, as love, as grace; and the whole world as grounded in him. And I experience this not as in some separation from or tension with what I know of myself physiologically and psychologically, but precisely as illuminative of the fragmentary knowledge afforded by these and all other disciplines. If Whitehead's vision should triumph in the years ahead, the "death of God" would indeed turn out after all to have been only the "eclipse of God."

The problem of the relation of Whitehead's vision to the encompassing relativism of our time is still more complex. Obviously his vision is one among many, conditioned by time, place, and circumstance, subject to interpretation biographically, psychologically, and historically. Unlike most philosophers, Whitehead's philosophy articulates itself as just such a relative undertaking and achievement. One cannot *prove* its truth; one can only display its extraordinary coherence, relevance, and adequacy. And, of course, even the acceptance of such criteria is also conditioned and relative. There is and can be no escape from the circularity of all thinking.

Yet if we take seriously also the conditionedness and relativity of relativism, we will cease to see in the relativity of a position a reason for its rejection. Furthermore within the position we may find an explanation of how relativism is transcended that seems to account both for relativism and its transcendence more satisfactorily than can be done while one remains, or tries to remain, at the merely relativistic level. Just this is the achievement of Whitehead's thought.

For Whitehead there is no reality that is not relational. For example, one cannot talk first of what occurred at a given time and then separately of what was experienced or perceived. What occurred was just these experiences and perceptions. If we ask "what really happened," we should always be asking "what was really experienced." And all such experience was that of one subject or another. The question of what happened in general is ultimately meaningless. In this sense, the relativity of truth is absolute.

However, this relativity is limited in two ways. First, it is objectively true that such-and-such experiences occurred. Whether they occurred is not relative to *our* opinion, available evidence, or taste. The experiences of the past are objectively immortal. Also, what occurred was not limited to the human experiences. There were electronic, atomic, and cellular experience as well, and the reality of their occurrence does not depend on human knowledge of them.

Hence there is a reality to which our opinions and experiences as a whole correspond more or less well. Truth is an important relation in experience, although certainly not the only important one. Reality as known to us is a function of our interests and our instruments, but reality as it experiences itself is relative only to its own interests. We live in a very real and determinate world, a world in which all things are relative, but determinately relative.

From this perspective we may indeed understand how human experience and belief are functions of the everchanging situation. Certainly the genesis of ideas helps us to understand them, and appropriately so. The complexity of the reality which confronts us is so vast that our ideas can never have a one-to-one relation with it. Yet our ideas do emerge out of reality in a positive relation with it. The most diverse and even apparently contradictory ideas can have some correspondence to that reality, and the ideal of a greater, more inclusive truth-relation is by no means illusory.

Furthermore, when we combine the Whiteheadian doctrine of God with his triumph over nihilistic relativism, we can see that the truth we seek is already real. There is a perspective which shares all perspectives and relates them all truthfully to each other. And that perspective is already effective for us despite the exceedingly distorted and fragmentary character of our own participation in truth.

One may well object that the effort to explore a new world of thought beyond the dominant modern world is not "theology" but "philosophy." How then can one whose passion drives him in this direction characterize himself as a theologian? The answer to this returns us yet again to the problem of relativism. I know that when I most totally reject the word of the past as authority for my thinking or respond most affirmatively to ideas suggested to me by Whitehead, I am expressing the vision that has become mine as my very selfhood has been formed by my past. When I realize and acknowledge to myself the conditionedness of my being and my stance, there does emerge some degree of transcendence over that conditioning. I can affirm it or I can reject it. Even if I reject it, it still continues to operate in me, but its power over me is nevertheless broken in principle and incipiently in fact as well. If I accept it, what has operated as a blind force becomes now my own will.

I know that the selfhood I experience is formed in the church, in Christian history. What I see in others and in the world, I see through eyes given vision by a Christian past. Knowing this, I am free also to reject it. I might reject it because there are anguish and estrangement given with the Christian vision, a burden of responsibility for a world that denies Christian truth. I might reject it because I see that it is indeed an historical accident that I am grasped by this vision, that I can show no ultimate rational justification for retaining it. Or I might reject it because so much of the reality I perceive through that vision enters into me as destructive of it and as denying its authenticity.

But I do not reject it; I affirm it. It may seem that in this act I contradict all I have said about refusing the authority of the past. This would be true except that the grounds of affirmation can only be that the Christian vision forecloses nothing, conceals nothing, refuses all self-defense. It is particular, but not exclusive. The belief that this is so is itself, of course, a function of the vision. This circularity cannot be avoided. One can only seek in complete openness to expand the circle indefinitely.

Because I know that my quest for a new world is motivated by my Christian selfhood and that the new world I see is seen through Christian eyes, I must acknowledge that all my thinking is Christian thinking, whether or not it is acceptable to other Christians. I cannot claim, as philosophy seems often to want to claim, that any intelligent person should be able to see the truth of my premises and the validity of my arguments.

But why "theology"? If Christian philosophy is the open quest for truth of a self who affirms the Christianness of the vision which is his, then theology is thinking that reflects upon the given of that selfhood. Christian selfhood experiences itself as a gift in two modes. Historically, it is a gift of a community of faith grounded in Jesus Christ. Existentially, it experiences itself as a gift of God. Theological reflection must seek to understand how these two modes of giving are connected with each other, and in the process it must reflect on such traditional topics as Jesus Christ, the Holy Spirit, the church, the Bible, as well as God. Furthermore, even if such reflection in our day is prompted by our concern for our selfhood, the reflection itself must turn away from that selfhood toward its source in such a way as to bring that selfhood also under most radical judgment.

But this specific theological reflection upon the gift of Christian selfhood is never separable from the Christian philosophical reflection upon reality as a whole and in its parts. The theological must both illustrate and illuminate the categories of philosophical reflection. Each must act as criterion for the other, and each criterion in turn is modified and reshaped by the total reflection. At every point the decision to affirm rather than to reject the starting point in Christian selfhood and vision is open for reconsideration as reflection modifies its self-understanding or casts doubt upon its adequacy.

In this approach, theology is a part of the total reflective process and is *totally vulnerable*. There is no built-in safeguard to insure that in the end there will be any place in one's world for God, or Jesus Christ, or Christian selfhood. Because I believe God *is,* and that in Jesus Christ we find what it means to know God as he is, I also believe that reflection must ultimately lead us toward rather than away from these truths. But I know also that my belief may be shattered in the process, and I cannot appeal to some protected ground of confidence when all else fails.

HARVEY COX (1929–   )

The Death of God and the Future of Theology

In one sense there is no future for theology in an age of the "death of God," but in another sense we cannot be certain of this until we know what the phrase means and what the function of theology is. For "death of God" is sometimes used to mean different things, even by the same writer in a single paragraph. My own investigation has isolated three distinct meanings.

The first is nontheistic or atheistic. As Paul Van Buren has said, "Christianity is about man and not about God." For Van Buren it is futile to say anything at all about "God," since the word has no viable empirical referent. We must therefore construct some form of theology in which we stop talking about God. Religious devotion and even religious language may remain, but the referents are entirely changed.

Van Buren's methodology is borrowed from the rigorous techniques of British and American philosophical analysis. A very different viewpoint is that of Thomas Altizer, who seems to be informed by certain Buddhist and Hegelian themes that have led him to assert that there once was a transcendent, real God, but that this God became immanent in Jesus and finally died in his crucifixion. In contrast to Van Buren, Altizer insists that we must not only use the word "God," but we must make the announcement of his death central to our proclamation today. He is not puzzled by the word; he not only knows what it means but is willing to say more about the history of God than most Christian theologies have said in the past. Furthermore, Altizer insists that "only the Christian can experience the death of God." Experiencing the death of God is, for Altizer, close to what has traditionally been associated with conversion.

The second sense in which the phrase "death of God" is used occurs in the context of cultural analysis. For Gabriel Vahanian and sometimes William Hamilton, it simply means that the culturally conditioned ways in which people have experienced the holy have become eroded. Religious experience is learned in any culture just as other experience is learned, in the unspoken assumptions and attitudes which children absorb from their parents and from their closest environment. Our forebears learned from their forebears to expect the experience of the holy in socially defined ways, whether in the sunset, in a camp-meeting conversion or in holy communion. This experience was structured by a culture of residual Christendom, still bearing traces of what Paul Tillich calls "theonomy." But the coming of modern technology and massive urbanization shook the structures of traditional society and thereby dissipated the cultural ethos within which the holy had been experienced. Hence the "God" of Christendom is "dead." For most modern writers the phrase is metaphorical, but in a culture strongly influenced by pietism, where the reality of God is identified with the experience of God, the phrase may be taken literally as a somber and threatening event.

The third sense in which "God" is "dead" is one that I discussed in the last chapter of my book *The Secular City,* and it is in some respects similar both to Vahanian's and Van Buren's viewpoints. For me, the idea of the "death of God" represents a crisis in our religious language and symbol structure, which makes the word "God" ambiguous. It is not that the word means nothing to "modern man" as Van Buren contends, but that it means so many things to different people that it blurs communication rather than facilitating it.

For years the doctrine of God has been in trouble. Paul Tillich, who assailed the very idea that God "is" (in his *Systematic Theology*), would never have settled for an undialectical non-theism, although his attempt to move "beyond theism" (in *The Courage to Be*) probably contributed to the present situation in theology. Karl Barth's christological positivism may also have prepared the way. The "death of God" movement is an inheritance from them, dramatizing the bankruptcy of the categories we have been trying to use. It is more the symptom of a serious failure in theology than a contribution to the next phase.

Modes of religious experience are, as we have noted, shaped by cultural patterns. When social change jars the patterns, conventional ways of experiencing the holy disappear. When the thickly clotted symbol system of a pre-urban society is replaced by a highly differentiated and individuated urban culture, modalities of religious experience shift. When this happens gradually, over a long span of time, the religious symbols have a chance to become adapted to the new cultural patterns. The experience of the death of the gods, or of God, is a consequence of an abrupt transition which causes the traditional symbols to collapse, since they no longer illuminate the shifting social reality.

The "death of God" syndrome can only occur where the controlling symbols of the culture have been more or less uncritically fused with the transcendent God. When a civilization collapses and its gods topple, theological speculation can move either toward a God whose being lies beyond culture (Augustine, Barth), toward some form of millenarianism or toward a religious crisis that takes the form of the "death of God."

In our own period, which is marked by man's historical consciousness reaching out and encompassing everything in sight, the nooks and crannies formerly reserved for the transcendent have all been exposed. Pluralism and radical historicism have become our permanent companions. We know that all doctrines, ideals, institutions and formulations, whether religious or secular, arise within history and must be understood in terms of their historical milieu. How then do we speak of a God who is somehow present in history, yet whose being is not exhausted by the limits of history? How, in short, do we maintain an affirmation of transcendence within the context of a culture whose mood is relentlessly immanentist? Perhaps a rediscovery of the millenarian tradition, a reappropriation of eschatology tradition, is the way we must go.

The crisis in our doctrine of God is a serious one. This cannot be denied. Nevertheless, our continued and correct insistence on the need to encounter God in *all* of life and not just in a "religious" or cultic precinct fails to express anything that really transcends "history," the source of our experiential reference for what we usually talk about. Some theologians, like Schubert M. Ogden, have responded to the present impasse by going back to the only significant constructive work that has been done in recent decades in American theology—the thought of Charles Hartshorne and Henry Nelson Wieman—and to the philosophy of Alfred North Whitehead. This tactic may eventually produce results, but so far it has not really resolved any of the radical criticisms raised by the "death-of-God" writers.

My own response to the dead-end signaled by the "death of God" mood is to continue to move away from any spatial symbolization of God and from all forms of metaphysical dualism. I am trying to edge cautiously toward a secular theology, a mode of thinking whose horizon is human history and whose idiom is "political" in the widest Aristotelian sense of that term, i.e. the context in which man becomes fully man.

As I move in this direction, there are certain traps I want to try to avoid. First, though it may be satisfactory for some, I want to steer clear of the mystical-atheistic monism of Thomas Altizer. From the perspective of the science of religion, mysticism and atheism have always been similar. Both lack the elements of encounter with an "Other," a confrontation that is characteristic of most forms of theism. In Altizer this structural similarity has come to explicit expression. Second, I want to avoid the uncritical empiricism of Paul van Buren. I think his methodological starting point, derived from contemporary British and American linguistic analysis, is too constrictive. It does not take sufficient account of the nonempirical functions of many modes of human speech, the open and changing character of all languages, and the place of any language within a larger universe of symbolic, metaphorical, and poetic modes of expression. Kenneth Burke, in *The Rhetoric of Religion,* has laid out a type of religious-language analysis which does embrace these larger cultural dimensions, thus offering a corrective to the analysts' presuppositions.

Finally, I want to steer clear of the inverse pietism of William Hamilton, whose perceptive analysis of the cultural mood is sometimes confused with the theological task itself. Since he often deduces the mood of the culture from a description of his own moods and beliefs, the basis of his theology is extremely experiential. This may be good, especially in view of the unjustly severe disparaging of "experience" which was so characteristic of the followers of Karl Barth, but theology cannot become experiential in this sense without courting the danger of becoming subjective. Thus, while I can accept his diagnosis of the cultural *élan,* which is often correct, I decline to enlarge it into a properly theological claim.

Let me make it clear that I do not condemn the men I have just named. I do not wish to belittle their contribution. As Gordon Kaufman has suggested, many of us are engaged in different "experiments in thought," pushing ahead to think through the implications of this or that set of premises. This theological diversity is a mark of strength, not of weakness. Let me make it clear too, that if I regard undialectical religious atheism as too easy a way out, I also find most available "theistic" options equally unattractive. The road ahead often seems narrow, dark and perilous, yet we can neither retreat nor stand still. The best I can do now is to try to indicate where I hope a breakthrough might be found to point in the direction I want to go, not to a spot where I have arrived.

For me, the way out of the "death of God" miasma which leads forward rather than backward is lighted, however flickeringly, by two of the seminal minds of our era, Pierre Teilhard de Chardin and Ernst Bloch. Both of these men are intellectual vagabonds; neither belongs to the theological club. But if our present decrepitude teaches us anything, it is that the club needs massive transfusions of new blood if it is to survive at all. I believe it is only by listening to such outsiders as these that any new health will come to the faltering enterprise of theology.

Teilhard's theology is only accidentally scientific, in the narrow sense. It is really a Christian cosmology, the first that has really engaged the imagination of modern man. Teilhard correctly saw that for modern man the question of God would focus on the question of man. It would appear in, with and under the issue of man's place in the enormously expanded world of modern science. Teilhard's complex theories about the role of centrifugal and centripetal forces in evolution, the new kind of heredity seen in man as a culture-bearing animal, and the crucial role man's consciousness of evolution will play in that evolution—these cannot be discussed here. The point which they suggest, however, is that any thinking about God from now on must begin with the recognition that man now sees himself as the one who can and must carry through many of the responsibilities which men of earlier millennia have assigned to their gods.

Between Teilhard, the maverick Catholic, and Bloch, the renegade Marxist, there are many differences; but one cannot help noticing the similarities. Both of them discuss transcendence in terms of the pressure exerted by the future on the present. Both see the future as that pressure on the present which is only possible where there is a creature who can orient himself toward the future and relate himself to reality by this orientation, in short a "creature who can hope." They both regard reality as a radically open-ended process. Teilhard detected in the logic of evolution an ever deepening humanization of man and "hominization" of the universe. Bloch concerned himself with "man-as-promise" and mapped out what he called "the ontology of the not-yet."

Teilhard's world of discourse was the breathtakingly massive universe and the appearance within it of the phenomenon of man, that point where the cosmos begins to think and to steer itself. Bloch's place of philosophizing is human history, exhumed from its burial in timelessness and launched on a journey into the future by the "birth of hope," an orientation introduced into the world by the biblical faith but now lost sight of by Christians. Both Bloch and Teilhard affirmed the centrality of what the Germans now call the *Impuls der Erwartung,* or impulse of expectancy. The one examined the way cosmic space and geological time seem to dwarf man, the other how history seems to buffet him. But neither became discouraged; both saw hope in man's growing capacity to apply science and critical reflection to the shaping of his own destiny.

We need a no-nonsense "leveling" in theological discourse. I think that if we can affirm anything real which also transcends history, it will be the future as it lives in man's imagination, nurtured by his memory and actualized by his responsibility. Some theologians have already begun to explore the implications this would have for traditional ideas of eschatology and incarnation. Although I think Teilhard's legacy will increasingly help us in working out this new direction, it is Bloch who I believe will be more influential.

Bloch's massive book, *Das Prinzip der Hoffnung* (*The Principle of*

Hope), first published in 1954, though difficult and often unclear, supplies the only serious alternative to Martin Heidegger's even more opaque *Sein und Zeit* (*Being and Time*) of 1927 as a philosophical partner for theology. Heidegger senses life to be hemmed in and radically finite, but he still fiercely presses the desperate question of the *Sein des Seienden,* the meaning of the being of that which is. Heidegger's influence on modern theology has been enormous, but as I argued in *The Secular City,* it seems to me almost wholly deleterious. Bloch presses the same difficult questions that Heidegger raises, but he does so within an ontology that seeks to question and subvert the tight finitude of Heidegger's constricted human world.

Thus while Heidegger plumbs the caliginous depths of anxiety, care and *Sein zum Tode* (being toward death), Bloch deals with that "infatuation with the possible" without which human existence is unthinkable. "The basic theme of philosophy," argues Bloch, "is that which is still not culminated, the still unpossessed homeland," and instead of anxiety and death "philosophy's basic categories should be 'frontier,' 'future,' 'the new' and the '*Traum nach vorwärts*'." Like Heidegger, Bloch considers himself to be an atheist. But just as many theologians, such as Rudolf Bultmann, Herbert Braun and Heinrich Ott, have found ideas of worth and interest in Heidegger, so a new group has already begun to find promising hints in the work of Ernst Bloch. Thus Jürgen Moltmann's recent book, *Theology of Hope,* obviously owes much to Bloch, as does Gerhard Sauter's *Zukunft und Verheissung.*

One point of continuing interest for the theologians is that Bloch not only engages in a brilliant analysis of man as "the creature who hopes," he also postulates a correspondence between man as the being who hopes and dreams and the historical world itself. He sees this correspondence (*Entsprechung*) between the "subjective of hope" and the "objectively possible," and he even tries (often unsuccessfully) to describe and elucidate it. The relationship between "subjective" and "objective" hope raises in Bloch's mind the question of an "identity" between man-who-hopes and a structure of reality which supports and nourishes such hope.

Here the Christian naturally thinks of qualities sometimes attributed to God. Bloch is not unaware of the similarity; indeed he describes the identity between subjective spontaneity and historical possibility as the "demythologized content of that which Christians have revered as God." He therefore insists that atheism is the only acceptable stance today because the Christian God has been imprisoned in the categories of a static ontology.

There are many questions to be asked about Bloch's work from a biblical perspective. He does not provide us with a clearcut way out of the "death of God" morass. At many points in his argument Bloch's commitment to radical historicism, along with residual traces of his Marxist materialism, seems to collide with his passionate desire to picture a radically open world in which at least the possibility of something "wholly other" is not excluded in principle. There are several places where, for example, he insists that all possibility is already incipiently present in what is, thus betraying an Aristotelian bias. But his main thesis cannot be easily dismissed.

I agree with Wolf-Dieter Marsch's remark that so long as Christians cling to the static "is" as the normative predicate for God, such thinkers as Bloch must rightly continue to regard themselves as atheists. But if theology can leave behind the God who "is" and begin its work with the God who "will be" (or in biblical parlance "He who comes"), an exciting new epoch in theology could begin, one in which Ernst Bloch's work would be extraordinarily important.

If the present wake is for the God who *is* (and now *was*), this may clear the decks for the God who *will be*. I cannot say for sure that the opening of such a path will lead anywhere, but the task of opening it would first require a thorough reworking of our major theological categories. We would see Jesus, for example, not as a visitor to earth from some supraterrestrial heaven, but as the one in whom precisely this two-story dualism is abolished for good, and who becomes the pioneer and first sign of the coming New Age. We would see the community of faith as those "on the way" to this promised reality, "forgetting what is behind and reaching out for that which is ahead" (Phil. 3:14). Radical theology would have more radical social consequences than the so-called radical theology of the death of God has produced so far.

The doctrine of God would become theology's answer to the seemingly irrefutable fact that history can only be kept open by "anchoring" that openness somewhere outside history itself, in this case not "above" but *ahead*. Faith in God would be recognized, for our time, in that hope for the future Kingdom of Peace that frees men to suffer and sacrifice meaningfully in the present. Still, I would be the worst of imposters if I pretended that in the God of Hope we can immediately affirm the one who will appear when the corpse of the dead God of metaphysical theism is finally interred. He may not appear at all, and our efforts to work out a new and viable doctrine of God for our time may be fated to fail from the beginning. But before any of us throws in the towel, I hope we will exercise the freedom given us by the present Götterdämmerung of the divinities of Christendom, and use this freedom to think as candidly and as rigorously as possible about where we go from here.

The only future that theology has, one might say, is to become the theology of the future. Its attention must turn to that future which God makes possible but for which man is inescapably responsible. Traditionally, it is prophecy that has dealt with the future. Hence the fate of theology will be determined by its capacity to regain its prophetic role. It must resist the temptation of becoming an esoteric specialty and resume its role as critic and helper of the faithful community as that community grapples with the vexing issues of our day.

The "death-of-God" syndrome signals the collapse of the static orders and fixed categories by which men have understood themselves in the past. It opens the future in a new and radical way. Prophecy calls men to move into this future with a confidence informed by the tradition but transformed by the present. Theology helps prophecy guide the community of faith in its proper role as the avant-garde of humanity. This community must clarify the life-and-death options open to *homo sapiens,* devote itself unsparingly to the humanization of city and cosmos, and keep alive the hope of a kingdom of racial equality, peace among the nations and bread for all. One should never weep for a dead god. A god who can die deserves no tears. Rather we should rejoice that, freed of another incubus, we now take up the task of fashioning a future made possible not by anything that "is" but by "he who comes."

INDEX

387